D0419571

A
Pebble
On The
Beach

Tony Diamond

A Pebble On The Beach

First Published in 2006 by Queens Park Books
Revised Edition 2013

Copyright © Tony Diamond

ISBN

Cover Design and Layout by:
Trudy Ford

Edited by:
Linda Dobrozyski

PREFACE

Having been told by Tony that he was more of a doer than a reader, in fact that he seldom if ever read a book, I read his manuscript more in the spirit of friendship than in the expectation that I would find it an interesting read. I revised my opinion after the first few pages.

Tony has a natural talent and a feel for words. The book is very well written. Tony sees it as an adventure story - I see it as something more important. It seems to me to be a human document revealing an aspect of social history of our times, all the more valuable for being written with total frankness and sincerity. It is sad and funny but above all it gives the most vivid of pictures of what it is like for someone with Toy's difficult background to fight constant rejection and survive. The intense effort that went into the book's writing, the sacrifices made, the way in which the facts were assembled, are all part of the story.

We see Tony as a boy rejected by family and country and sent overseas to 'start a new life'/ A free spirit, lonely and homesick, but determined to be a master of his own fate, he plots his return to England, sustained by his desire to come back to an idealised vision of the family home. There is an immediacy and directness about this fascinating account of the journey home which commands attention.

Having read many, many letters and accounts written by children sent overseas, I consider this book to be an outstanding account of a triumph over adversity.

Dame Gillian Wagner
Chair, Barnardos 1978-1984

DEDICATION

I dedicate this book to all the people, past and present who over the last 63yrs have put a stamp on my life. Hopefully, I too in some way have made some sort of imprint on theirs, sometimes good sometimes bad, but then that's life. Sadly some are no longer with us, but never forgotten and always in our thoughts.

When I first started write to this story, It was more to exercise my demons than anything else, which have haunted me most of my life. Unfortunately during my months of research I was to find out a lot more than I bargained for. As one by one the skeletons came out of the cupboard, also the years in and out of care with my brothers had left its mark, with the mental, physical, and the sexual abuse we had to suffer, that came hand in hand with living in institutions.

At the age of sixteen, I met and later married my wife Linda, without her, I was destined for a path of self destruction, so for her, our life together has not always been a bed or roses. Living with some of the issues, that society had dished out not only to me, but to thousands of others who were unfortunate enough to be put into the care system during the 1950s and 60s.

So this special dedication go's to Linda, who over the last 45yrs of marriage has put up with me and my antics, plus my ever constant search for that pot of gold, as I took her, along with our beautiful daughter Pauline, to the far flung corners of the world, To you both I award the (Medal of True Love).

Finally I would like to thank my daughter Pauline and her husband Jim for bringing my search for that pot of gold to an end and placed her in my arms-my granddaughter. Danielle. She's solid 24 carat, my little ray of sunshine that make's it all so worthwhile. After years of searching for that missing something, it was right under my nose all the time. So the three special girls in my life

I SAY...THANK YOU

CHAPTER 1

It was cold, back on that 28th day of February 1961. It was a Saturday afternoon and Ricky – that's my best mate – and I were messing about in the local school ground, which luckily for me, was just a stone's throw away from the bottom of our garden.

We lived on a large council estate in Hove, Sussex on the south coast on England in a three-up, two-down semi and, at that time there was just the three of us. Mum, my sister Judith and myself. Although come the holidays it was filled to capacity with the return of my three older brothers who were at that time, under the care of Dr Barnardo's Children's Homes. Like most council housing estates everybody knew the ins and outs of everybody's business. You only had to fart to become a victim to the local gossips for the next day or so.

I was eleven years of age and had only just moved up to my senior school along with Ricky and the rest of the boys, to serve a four year sentence at the Knoll School for Boys. The very same that greeted me every morning as I looked out from my bedroom window. The school was built back in the mid 1930s along with the estate, to help with Hove's ever increasing population boom, the grounds covered more than half a square mile with its large red brick buildings, three playgrounds and prefabricated classrooms to cope with the constant influx of children. Being comprehensive, as private was a word only used by the rich, the school had an intake of over 1,000 plus. The boys and girls separated off course, by a large blue door, guarded daily by the 'witch of the west' their Head Mistress, Miss Shields, who had the body of a matchstick and the bite of a rattler. With up to thirty to forty pupils per class, sometimes it was impossible to even hear the teacher let alone see him, which came in handy sometimes especially for weirdos like Higgins and Jepson, who spent most of their time jerking each other off at the back of the Science class. It was a little wonder they both ended up wearing glasses, well, they do say it sends you blind.

Friday's being the best day of the week, as come 4 o'clock and home time, we would somehow get around the teachers along with a few other boys, each in different classes, to get the job of shutting the window's, as being the middle of winter our teachers thought the cold air would keep us awake and more alert. So while they sat there with their backs to the radiators, we froze our balls off. The purpose of our little quest was that by slamming the window shut, sometimes, but not always, they would refuse to lock, making it easy for us to break in over the weekend and help ourselves to such luxuries as ink, fountain pens, rulers and other necessary items needed to do our everyday school work then selling them back to unsuspecting victims come Monday morning. All was going well that day until someone shouted, "Caretaker," with that everybody split, including Ricky, leaving me half hanging out of a window with my shorts caught up on a window latch, so by giving an almighty lurch, I forced myself clear, leaving half of the seat of my pants behind me. Thinking of nothing but my escape I made my exit with pens flying in all directions from my pocket as I climbed the drainpipe like a mad man, even a rat would have been hard pushed to catch me, up on to the flat roof then up and over the main building and down onto the bike sheds which overlooked my back garden. Quickly jumping down to the ground, I headed towards the six foot high garden fence which stood between me and home, but by now I was out of breath as the sweat poured from my brow, I struggled to overcome my last objective – that 6ft garden fence. I had just managed to pull myself up and was halfway over when a voice from behind echoed as I fell to a bundle on the other side.

"I know who you are, Tony Bates."

Oh shit, I thought to myself, he's seen me – or had he? For a while I lay there without moving a muscle, trying to hold my breath, leaving only the sound of my heart thumping in my ears as his footsteps came towards the fence, standing there for what seemed like an age, then heard his footsteps as he slowly walked away until finally all sound of him was gone.

For me, it was only the first term at school and I knew I'd be for it come Monday. Lifting myself from the ground, I brushed myself down taking a quick look around me, as God alone knows what I'd landed in. Ours was not your average garden, covering an area of twenty by forty, looking more like an army assault course with its large holes in the ground, old bikes frames, pram wheels, and an old garden shed that had long since lost its windows and door, and scattered all around were the graves of our many pets that had died over the years. You name it; we buried it, dogs, cats, rabbits, mice, goldfish, etc. At the top of the garden just under the kitchen window there was a small vegetable patch which had been badly trodden down where I'd constantly had to climb in the window after being locked out, all this was lined down one side with overgrown privet bushes and down the other, apple trees from next doors garden which come summer hung conveniently over into ours, so we could help ourselves whenever our taste buds fancied. But it was February freezing cold and the evenings draw in early, making everything look dry and dismal giving the whole place the appearance of the day after the bomb.

Slowly, I made my way up the dirt track we called a path, which led up the side of our house and the back door. 'Mum's going to bloody kill me,' I thought to myself as I looked down at the muddy knees and arms, not to mention the large tear in my shorts exposing my arse to anyone in view. Although eleven, I was unusually small for my age with my spindly legs and a rib cage you could use for a xylophone – that's how I got my nickname Bony Tate's – but somehow, being the smallest of the crowd always seemed to get me into more trouble than anyone else especially as my voice towered way above my height, still, I wouldn't have had it any other way, for I was one of the boys' – the Black Hand Gang we called ourselves, my home was the streets. I knew every shortcut, alleyway, cul-de-sac on the estate and could out run, and out fox any copper on my tail. That isn't to say that they weren't waiting for me when eventually I did return home to No. 36, and not having a father, would get a right-hander from the local bobby saying "next time my boy, it'll be the cells for you."

Arriving at the back door, opened and closed it as quietly as I could so not to cause any disturbance, luckily there was no sign of life, still for me that was nothing unusual. My first though was to get cleaned up. So I headed straight for the bathroom which was conveniently situation alongside the kitchen, which to my surprise, was clean and tidy aside from the lunch time plates still on the table and the sink full of dirty dishes. Unfortunately ours was a kitchen of bare essentials, with an old butler sink in one corner and in the other an old electric stove, piled high with dirty saucepans. Our furniture consisted of an old table and four worn out chairs. There were no work tops or built-in kitchen units, just a couple of old shelves and a cabinet painted in blue, the very same as the surrounding walls.

With three strides I was in the bathroom, which looked very much like a builders after thought, with its partition wall dividing it from the kitchen leaving an eight by four closet sheltering an old

3

cast iron bath. Hot water for us was still a thing of the future and had to be heated up, which was done by means of an old copper tub conveniently situated at the head of the bath on a raised concrete platform which, along with the kitchen and bathroom floors, was painted red, as lino for us was still an expensive commodity.

Dropping my shorts to the floor, I kicked them under the bath and out of harms way, then taking a towel, I began to wipe off the dirt from my arms and legs – soap and water for me was still a dirty word. Wrapping the towel around my waist so as to hide my all, well what there was of it, I went in search for life. Moving through the kitchen into the front room, where I was greeted by a roaring coal fire, blazing halfway up the chimney, its shadows dancing on the living room walls. By now the evening was drawing in quickly, I switched on the light bringing life into the room.

Housework was never one of mum's favourite chores and it showed. She had often said the only time she couldn't find anything was when somebody had tidied up behind her, but like they say, when you live in it you don't notice, with the dishes still on the dining table, magazines and newspapers piled high on the chair and our three cats lounging all over the furniture, which was well worn and had seen better days. Our one luxury was tucked away in the corner – a television – black and white of course, affixed to the back was a slot meter which ate half crowns like they were going out of fashion, quite often we'd be watching a program only to be cut off in mid-stream because the money had run out and if there was none in the kitty, well that was the end of it, no more T.V. It was perched on an old tea trolley that grandma had given us which on the shelf directly below in mums old knitting box, were brandy one of our cats had not long since given birth to seven kittens which left a slight aroma in the air. The mother, exhausted from her ordeal, lay flat out in front of the fire trying to turn a blind eye at their ever constant cries.

Moving towards the window was our main attraction, as situated directly beneath was our sideboard, a regular antique, with its ornaments all set out for all the world to see – milk bottles, an open tin of cat food, cups, a teapot, yes, it was a real Aladdin's Cave, the public came from miles just to stare in disbelief. As I leaned forward to draw the curtains the street lighting came to life, one lamp being directly outside our house, so pulling the curtains to a close, I slowly shut out the dismal looking outside world.

The next thing on the agenda was to find something to wear as, apart from the towel covering up my essentials, I was naked from the waist down, except for my socks and shoes which were still covered in mud from the garden, but fortunately it easy to cover up any of my tracks and if they were noticeable, I'd just blame the cats. Making for the door in the far corner of the lounge which took you upstairs, also to our front door, I opened it, turning on the light in the hallway and called out, "Anybody up there?" I somehow knew there wouldn't be, but I called just the same. No answer came.

That house always gave me the willies, especially upstairs which was probably down to the fact that not long after the houses were built, the tenant before, who had found himself in a depressed state, hung himself by climbing up into the loft and putting one end of the rope around the roof support and the other around his neck, then jumped. Apparently, he wasn't missed for nearly two weeks, they say that when he was found, apart from the usual smells, his eyes looked life golf balls, protruding from his head, must have been a pretty sight. Then of course there was Grandad; he died in the lounge of some horrible chest disease. Mum often said how she'd be sitting in the quiet and seen him lying there, returning in his ghostly form and promptly telling us of her experiences the following day. That's enough to give anyone the creeps.

Looking up, I made a mad dash for the bedroom, my towel dropping somewhere between my flight, soon at the bedroom door I pushed it hard only to be stopped dead. For as long as I can remember that door never opened with ease due to the frame dropping, which apparently had something to do with the man who had hung himself, forcing the door to stick heavily on one corner and with its constant rubbing, the lino had long since been worn away and was now eating slowly into the floorboards beneath. With an almighty push the door swung open making a horrible scraping noise in the process, switching on the light, I entered the room which was situated directly above the kitchen. Ours was the largest of the three bedrooms. I say 'ours' because during the holidays I shared it with my three brothers, Terry – 13, Patrick – 14, and Michael – 15. The two youngest were away at navel training school in Dorset and Michael, well he was the brains of the outfit and was, at present, at Grammar School, although

5

it was fun when they were all home, I never really missed them when they returned, in fact I was often glad to see the back of them with their money and flashy clothes. Ours was not a close family relationship as spending so little time together we were almost strangers. Still, they made for company at nights in that cold, but spacious room with its two sets of bunk beds down either side of the room, which apart from mine; lay empty for the best part of nine months a year. Between them stood an old wardrobe and dresser which was cluttered up with model ships and aeroplanes made during my brothers vacations. In the far corner was a large cupboard set back over the stairs and on cold windy nights the wind would whistle down the chimney and out through the fireplace, and often as not would make the door rattle and sometimes force it open with a loud creek, then bang against the wall, putting my heart in my mouth as I lay terrified beneath the covers trying to get to sleep.

Quickly, I went in search of something to wear. My clothes or what there was of them were in short supply, not to mention seen better days. Being the youngest of four boys, hand-me-downs were a part of life and if they didn't fit me now there was always room to grow into and every time my brothers came home there would be a new supply. Spotting an old pair of jeans, I took a hold of them, first shaking off the dust then quickly slipping them on. Pulling the zip up faster than I should have, suddenly coming to a quick half with a gasp of pain, "Fucking hell," I said, with tears in my eyes, looking down at my predicament, and there caught between the zip fastener was my foreskin. Not daring to move as I didn't want to cause any unnecessary anguish, I took hold of the fastener and with a quick jerk releasing my red but hopefully undamaged tool. Rubbing it gently back and forth to see if it was still in working order taking particular care not to let it happen again I positioned it carefully, completing the operation successfully then letting out a sigh of relief. 'That was close,' I thought to myself as I came round to my surroundings, then heading for the door was soon on the landing, then descended the stairs three at a time, leaving all the lights on as I reached the bottom and opened the front door and stepped outside, funny that as there was particular reason for my fear, as there were no hands coming out of the floor boards or blood running down the walls, it was just a feeling I had that made me want to get out of the house, the very same feeling I have today when I know there's something unearthly about a place – like a medium who drums up the spirits. I know there was something there. My feeling was broken as I hit the cold night air and walked up to the gate to see if Mum was about, amidst the neighbours leaning on their gates gossiping while local kids caused riots in the streets. There was no sign of her although I did notice my little sister playing with some of her friends at the top of the street, "Judith," I called out, but she never stirred just carried on skipping. Oh well, Mum can't be far off if she's about I told myself, feeling the cold a little I turned back towards the house and looked across our front garden which was not unlike the back.

"You been in my greenhouse again?" a voice said from over next doors fence, I turned slowly, it was old man Collins.

"What was that?"I asked

"You heard me boy, you've been in my bloody greenhouse again, at my tomatoes," he said, his face going all red.

"Who, me and why would I wanner go in your stupid greenhouse? Don't even like fucking tomatoes, you silly old sod."

"Don't you talk to me like that or I'll give you a right-hander my boy."

"Oh yea, you and who's army?"

"You little" Near to the boil he headed towards our gate so I shot indoors slamming the front door behind me, once inside peered through the curtains and started pulling faces. By now old Collins was at the gate shaking his finger, "You wait my boy, your mother's going to hear about this, you'll see." Letting the curtain drop, I laughed to myself although I knew that wasn't the last I'd hear of it. "Rotten old tomatoes anyway they were only fit for frying and Mum can't talk, she ate half of them even if she didn't know where they'd come from." I said to my self

Looking across the mantelpiece I noticed it was 4.30, so I decided to settle down and watch some T.V., being Saturday and a day or sport, I might just be in time for a bout of wrestling, so I switched it on. Slowly the set came to life and I settled back in my favourite chair alongside the fire, resting my feet upon the mantle to give perfect comfort. The silence was broken by the one, two, of the referee as Mike Mac-Manas tried for a winning fall on Jacky TV Palo with jeers from the crowds as he was unsuccessful.

My total concentration was broken by a rat, tat, tat, at the front door. 'Oh shit, who's that? Not old Collins again,'

I thought, making for the window and peering from the side of the curtain, but couldn't see anyone; just a large black car (a London taxi) parked directly outside under the lamppost and could see the driver sat in his seat smoking a cigarette. 'Can't be for us, we don't know anyone with a car,' and I returned back to my seat when again came the knock, only this time louder, thinking to myself it was Judith as she'd only just found out the knocker was within her reach, I just shouted out, "go round the back." It just had to be her as aside from the Police and the rent and the tally man no one else ever came to the front door, and being Saturday it definitely wasn't the rent man, so thinking it could be the Police, I turned down the T.V. so to pretend that no one was home and peered once again through the curtains. The black car was still there, again the knocking came and this time even louder making me almost jump out of my skin as whoever it was, they were obviously getting very impatient, so thought it best to answer. Moving across the hallway to the front door I called out, "Who is it?" It was then a voice echoed back through the letterbox in a strange but sort of English dialect, "Is your mother no there?" Curiously I slowly opened the door, as I did the visitor stumbled back off the step. A strange little man, not much taller than me, about five foot nothing wearing this huge green sheepskin coat, "Hello Son is your mother there?" I looked at him for what seemed like an age. Mum had many friends, but this one I didn't know, yet somehow he looked familiar with his broad clean shaven chin and dark inset eyes with a tan that was so dark he could almost have been coloured, and his long dark hair brushed back off his forehead almost matching his complexion. Perhaps he's a new tally man come to collect some money so I answered him with the immortal words Mum always sent me to the door with, "I'm afraid she's not in can you call back next week for your money." He just stood there not moving, and then cracked a smile with his eyes glazing over like a man about to cry, "Do you not know when she'll be back lad? I'm an old friend and I've come a long ways." Looking at him then at the waiting car outside, somehow I knew they were connected so leaving the door wide open I walked around him and then rushed off out the gate in search of Mum leaving him standing there, being watched by over-interested neighbours while I went in search of Mum, which would not be one of my hardest quests, just follow the smell of brewing tea. After the normal rounds I ended up at Elsie's house, who lived just five doors up from us. I suppose you could say she was Mum's best friend and they shared everything from recipes to boyfriends, living in each others pockets daily. To me, she was a two faced old bag who would stab you in the back as soon as look at you. Her one ambition in life was to try and embarrass you, which, at that age of 11 wasn't funny one time she caught me jerking off and made it so I couldn't face her for weeks, and when I did; she just smiled and said pinching my cheek, "You know you'll have to wear glasses."

Knocking on her back door, I got the usual answer, "Come in if you're rich." I opened the back door and popped my head round the corner, "Is Mum…," before I could finish my sentence, I saw Mum sitting at the table alongside Elsie, "Come in Son, what's up?" She asked, "I suppose you want your tea." Looking at her then at Elsie, as I didn't want the world to know our business, I tried to be discreet, "We've got a visitor Mum, say's he's a friend of yours."

"Oh Mavis, a man, send him up here after you've finished with him." They both fell about laughing, "Until then I'll keep hold of this one" Grabbing hold of me and pulling me close, 'Get off me, you silly old cow', I thought, but never said it, as I tried to free myself from her grip. She had one of those piercing voices which went right through you. Mum on the other hand, spoke softly and along with her looks and figure, it was easy to see why men fell for her. Standing at 5'4, with long auburn hair that flowed on her shoulders, always immaculately dressed and made up,

"Put him down Elsie, you're making the poor boy blush," she then asked, "Who did you say this man was, Son?"

"I didn't, he just said he's come a long way."

Elsie opened the door giving me a pinch on the cheek as we left; my only thought was of her last sentence, "Fill me in later." With pleasure and a large crowbar, I smiled back as my thought amused me.

"Right Mavis, I'll pop down as soon as I've done John's tea."

John, that was her husband was a much older and a quiet sort of man who sold flowers out of a pram; he was also a man with no sense of humour, probably due to the fact of living with her for so long.

Closing the door behind her, Mum followed me up the path,

"Did he say what his name was, Son?" she asked.

"Na, just that he'd come a long way, funny looking bloke got a big chin."

Then, for some reason her face lit up and she nearly knocked me over as she rushed out the gate heading for No 36, Following close behind not realising I was about to get the shock of my life as she got to the gate, turned sharply – excited, like a kid with a new toy – saying "That's no stranger Son, that's your father," as she then ran into his open arms. Although I was only eleven, I was street wise for my age and even I knew men don't come back from the dead, I guessed she must have meant uncle. I'd had a lot of them, some stayed longer than others, but eventually they all left. My dad died when I was six months old in Korea or so I'd been told, still mine was not to reason, anyway why should I argue at least when there was a man about I never went short of a bob or two, especially if I hung around long enough, I'd always get a few bob if only to get myself lost for the day.

Like two lovers hand in hand, I followed them into the lounge and could see by the look on his face as he glanced around the room, he was used to better than this. Still holding onto his hand, Mum pulled me closer, "Tony, I'd like you to meet your father." Looking down at me, he held out his hand, "Hello Son, I see you've grown into a fine looking boy," he replied in his strong accent.

At first, I was a bit wary as I didn't know what the hell was going on. I shook his hand noticing his firm grip and short stubby fingers, all bitten down to the quick just as mine were, but still his face confused me. I'd seen it somewhere before but couldn't place where, then like a flash of light it came to me, "Mum," I cried out, "He looks like our Pat." In fact he was the spitting image, "Don't he Mum." All this must have been too much for him, either that or I'd squeezed his hand to tight, as it was then he turned to Mum and burst into tears, "Forgive me Mavis, I'm sorry, so sorry." Sorry for what? I asked myself, I was still a little confused and now to watch a grown man cry put me just a little, on edge. "Son, you go and fetch your sister while I make your father a nice cup of tea." That was typical; a cuppa seemed to be her answer to everything. Without a word I slid out the back door and went in search of Judith. The cogs in my brain turned frantically and I could almost hear them in my head. Was he really my father? Had he, by some miracle, been spared the gift

10

of life to return home to his family? Why had it taken so long? It was 11 years since he supposedly got lost or maybe he was put in a prison camp, yeah that was it, a Chinese prison camp that makes sense. It was all beginning to sound like a romantic novel, but this was for real and was happening to us. Rushing out the gate, I nearly collided with the still awaiting black car, with its driver also waiting, patiently, for the return of his passenger, while I went in search of Sis.

By now, the neighbours had gathered with curiosity, trying to assess what was going on inside No.36, but for once I knew something they didn't.

"Hello Tony, see you got a visitor, anyone we know?" A neighbour called out.

"It's my dad, he's come home my dad's come home." I shouted out for the entire world to hear. The looks on their faces were a picture as they turned to one another, their tongues all going ten to a dozen.

After a short search, I found Judith playing on the church green with some of her friends, running towards her I called out, "Sis, Mum wants you."

Looking up, she spotted me and ran off in the opposite direction. Sis could be a right cow at time as not only was I her brother I'd partly brought her up since the day she was born. Having fed and changed her, babysat her, also taking her out for long walks in her pram when it was necessary for the two of us to get lost.

Now, at the age of six she was cunning and sly, knowing the way to a man's pocket was by pulling at his heart strings, and it never failed. Although she was pretty, with her long auburn hair, Judith was a tomboy in every sense of the word. Never doing anything she was told and somehow managing to get away with it.

Eventually catching up with her I grabbed hold of her hand, "Come on, Mum wants you now."

"No she don't, liar, she's up Aunty Elsie's," she said, frantically trying to escape my grip, she started to pinch and kick me so I grabbed her by the hair in order to get her attention. Covered in head to foot by what looked like half the playing field, she looked up at me.

"I'm telling Mum on you and then she'll hit you over the head with the frying pan again, so there."

"Listen, you little cow," I shouted, "We've got a visitor and

Mum wants you home to meet him."

Her tears ceased and in its place a broad smile came across her little face, "Is daddy home?"

I smiled knowing that she didn't have a sixth sense, but she was taking it as yes. Pulling away from me, escaping from my clutches she ran across the green towards home, shouting out loud, "My daddy's home, my daddy's home," like a little song she'd just made up. Although Mum had lots of men friends who I got to call uncle, Judith always called them dad. I suppose never knowing any different, it came naturally and the boyfriends never seemed to mind.

Following her close behind I suddenly thought to myself, if he really is my dad and has been away eleven years that was feasible because of my age, but Judith was only six and even I know that two and two don't make five. The thought went as quickly as it came.

Increasing my speed so as to catch her up I arrived at the house, by which time Sis was out of sight and on entering the lounge found her sitting up on the strangers' knee, arms around his neck and smothering him with kisses. You'd have though he really was her father and not a total stranger. Her real father fresh home from a days work with Mum sitting alongside him holding his hand looking all starry eyed. His face by now was beginning to show signs of permanent damage. So lifting himself up with Judith still hanging on tightly, he put her down and almost at once put his hands in his pockets. Here we go again I thought, as Sis jumped up and down crying "Sweeties, sweeties, it's a couple of bob for us to do our disappearing act for a while." Then from his pocket he pulled out a wad of notes I'd never seen this much money before and he peeled of a £1 note and handed it to me "Thanks mister, thanks a lot." Judith's face was a picture and for one tiny moment thought she was going to miss out then in went the hand again and this time pulled out a half a crown. Sis, not knowing the value of money, just looked up and jeered, "I've got a silver one so there I've got more than you." They both laughed as I looked at her with contempt thinking little do you know stupid. I edged backwards to try and get out without being noticed only to be stopped by mums voice, "Hold up Son, take your sister with you. "Oh Mum, do I have to? You know what a cow she is."

"Yes you do," she replied, "and you my young lady hold

tight to your brother's hand, you hear me?"

Replying back with a coy butter wouldn't melt in my mouth voice, "Yes mummy yes daddy." Then looked up at me and poked out her tongue.

"Oh and Son, while you're out you may as well bring in some tea fish and chips suit you okay Fred?"

"Fine, luv," he replied, pulling out another pound note from his pocket.

"Right then, that's cod and chips for your father and I and whatever you two want."

We then left the house closing the door behind us. So that's his name is it Fred, he must be rich to keep pulling out all these pound notes. This might not be half so bad after all I thought to myself, as we headed out the gate the black car was still waiting patiently for its passenger.

We'd been gone roughly an hour when finally we arrived back at No. 36 only to see that the large black car had disappeared. We both rushed in to find out whether or not it had taken the stranger with it, only to find Mum laying the table while Fred for the want of a better name, was sat in my favourite chair alongside the fire looking a lot more at ease with his new surroundings. Making himself quite at home with his cup of tea in one hand and a tobacco tin perched on the arm of the chair, smiling as we walked in.

"You two get yourselves washed up and get sat up to the table," Mum called out from the kitchen.

"Washed up?" I said loudly, looking first at Judith and then back at Mum.

"Yes, your hands stupid."

This was new, I thought there for one horrific moment she meant the washing up in the kitchen, because if that was the case I'd have been out of there for the night.

"What've you got your dressing gown on for Mum?" I asked on our way to the bathroom.

"Oh, I spilt something down my dress, now stop asking stupid questions and do as you're told."

"Yes Mum," I said, knowing all along the real reason.

All washed up we took our seats at the table which made a nice change from eating off our laps, and while we ate Fred told us of his job which took him all around the world to exotic places like Australia, Africa and South America. Places that for me were just names on a map and seemed a lifetime away. As Fred was a merchant seaman and had only hours since left his ship to come and visit us. There was no talk of prison camps in far off countries or where he'd been for the last eleven years, somehow that didn't enter the conversation.

Mesmerised with his stories, I sat with gaping mouth at the excitement and thrill of sailing into those far off ports with their blue skies and the sun that always shined. For me, all of a sudden he was no longer a stranger more my own personal hero, he'd been and seen more places than anyone I knew and in my eyes that made him special which seemed to make everything alright.

"You two had enough to eat?" a voice broke into my thoughts

"Ere thanks Mum."

"Right, you two clear the table while I make your father a cup of tea."

Clear the table, what for? I thought it's usually still there come breakfast, still who was I to argue anything to keep the peace, as I didn't want her going off into one of her funny turns.

"Come on Sis, you can help."

Fred, by now, had made himself comfortable once again in my chair and while we cleared away, Mum fussed around him like a bee around honey.

"Right, I'm off out see you later," I said pulling on my jacket and making for the door, only to be stopped by mums' familiar voice.

"In by nine, now you hear me"

"But Mum."

"No buts, nine o'clock and don't be late."

A time limit that was new, usually I came in when I was tired or when everyone else had gone home and not before. Fred's only been here ten minutes and already the laws being laid down, besides how could I tell the boys what time I had to be home, they'd only laugh. Without saying another word, I shut the door behind me and headed off to call for my mates.

My first stop was Ricky's house. Just a short walk across the road, first to tell him of my news, then to make plans for the evenings events. Ricky was a couple of years older than me and although we'd known each other most of our lives we'd only been hanging out together for the last year or so, during which time we found ourselves in all sorts of trouble. It was with Ricky that I had my first smoke and he also introduced me to the 'Demon'

14

alcohol a whole new dimension for the both of us. Our favourite tipple was Merry Down Cider, and although after a bottle it made you feel good and capable of doing anything, come morning you felt and looked like shit and many a time I would be taken to the doctors by Mum, her thinking there was something terribly wrong with me. Each time the doctor in all his wisdom put it down to a new virus of some sort then issued penicillin tablets like candy. Still, it was always good for a few days off from school that was until we finally got caught and Mum took a stair rod to me, which didn't deter us only made us a little more cautious. Along too, came my introduction to the opposite sex. Most boys of our age wanted to play football and cricket, go fishing or bike riding, but for us physical sport was not our thing, so Ricky and I settled for girls and found it to be a lot more fun. Most nights we'd hang around the crescent, which was a short distance away from the estate. At that time we were going out with a couple of sisters, so after meeting up with them we'd head off down the park or beach, all according to the weather. Ricky being the oldest and the same size as me always got first pick that was to say that if a girl was tall or ugly I got her. Still it didn't always turn out the best for him as some girls tick faster than others as I found out early puberty. You know, that's the time when a young boy finds out that his pecker is not just for pissing out of, as I soon found when not just one, but the two of you were curious, which led to hours of stimulating enjoyment, not to mention wet pants without actually having gone the whole way, which I never got around to until a much later date..

Ricky's family, being quite well off and he, being the last of four boys, was totally spoilt and had a wardrobe filled to capacity with new clothes bought for him by his Mum, who had a heart of gold and never said a cross word about anyone. Most nights I'd borrow a shirt or jacket and if he had new shoes bought that day, he'd let me wear them, just to break them in. I didn't have many clothes of my own so was grateful at the time. I suppose you could say I was Rick's own personal model and if the girls like something I wore, Ricky would make a point of saying it was his and promptly wear it himself on the following night, still, it was better than wearing hand-me-downs.

Our evenings would fly by and it was shortly after ten when I got home that night only to find the house in total darkness. Shit, I'm in for it now I thought; they've gone out to look for me.

Nah, can't have done, she's never bothered before about what time I've got in, why should she start now. With nothing but the street lights to guide me, I ran down the path to the back door. Once inside, slammed it shut, relieved that nothing sinister had got me in the dark, then quickly switched on the kitchen light, thought for a moment I was in the wrong house. As I looked around me I saw that the table and sink were clear of dirty dishes and the room all bright and shiny like a new penny, then moving into the lounge, I could smell the distinct aroma of tobacco which made a nice change from cats and boiled cabbage. Switching on the light, I was once again taken aback, there were no magazines piled high or clothes scattered about, the sideboard was clear with little doyleys under the few ornaments we had. That Fred's got a lot to answer for, I thought to myself, either that or Mum's had another breakdown. Not knowing where either of them were I thought it best to go to my bed, as out of sight was out of mind. Opening the door that led into the hallway, switching on the landing light and leaving the rest of the house lights on, I quickly climbed the stairs, first checking in on Judith to find her fast asleep. Well, at least that was something I thought, at least I wasn't alone in the house even if she was only a little girl. As I pushed my bedroom door open, it scraped on the floor echoing right through the house making a ghastly noise, then, switching on the light I undressed as quickly as I could, just taking off my shoes and jeans as I'd need the rest of my clothes on to keep me warm on those cold winter night's as for pyjamas they were only for hospitals, anyway old habits die hard, then switching off the light and made a running jump for my bed and snuggled down deep beneath the covers. I had two choices in that room, one was to hide beneath the bed clothes and the other was to expose myself to the dark and the strange face like shadows that the outside light would cast upon the curtains.

As I lay there with my head under the covers trying to think of nice thoughts to help me get to sleep, I heard the front door go, followed by the familiar sound of laughter. At last, I said to myself, I could relax now as there wasn't anything to be frightened of. Mum was home. The distinct chink of glasses could be heard amidst the persisting laughing. Mum's laugh I knew, also the ever constant cackle of Elsie, but the others I didn't. That night as I lay there, I thought to myself who is this man who walks back into our lives after being away for eleven years? Was I going to

16

have to call him Dad? My brothers – how would they react to the unforeseen member of the family arriving out of the blue? Was I happy or did I resent him after all my life, and my brothers come to that, had been no bed of roses. I thought of the times I spent away from home in care or with foster parents, and my friends, how they would talk about trips out with their fathers, fishing, football matches – all the things you would expect to do with your dad, but all this had passed me by. The years of ridicule because I had come from a one parent family, the humiliation, and now to go to school on Monday and say, "Guess what lads – my Dad came home Saturday!" I would be a laughing stock – after all, he had only been gone eleven years. Had he got lost trying to find his way home? The thoughts came and went leaving me totally confused until finally I fell asleep.

Sunday morning came round and I was woken early by Sis pulling at my ear, "Wake up Tony, Daddy's still home."

At first, still half asleep, I took no notice, then realising what she'd said and remembering the stranger, I sat up straight then jumped out of bed. Fortunately I only had to put on my jeans, then ran straight to Mum's bedroom where, sitting up in her bed was this small, well-tanned wiry man, sipping his cup of tea. Judith, once again, was well ahead of me, this time sitting by his side, holding on tight, just to make sure this one didn't get away. Very rarely did anyone get to stay the night even if they did; they usually left by first light. This was serious, I thought, as he looked up at me.

"Morning Son, sleep well?"

I nodded, then just left the room and went downstairs to find Mum cheerfully singing away in the kitchen as the smell of cooking bacon filled the air.

"Morning Mum, that smells good," I said, pinching a piece of bacon from the frying pan.

"Leave that alone, that's your father's," she said, slapping me on the hand with a fork, "there's cereal in the larder if you're hungry."

That was rich, he gets eggs and bacon, and I get bloody cereal. Something wrong there somewhere, maybe I'd have to leave home for a few years then maybe I'd get some of this attention. In total disgust I went back to my bed, after all this was a day of rest, so I stayed there the best part of the morning, eventually getting up around eleven and going downstairs. Sunday

we were to find Gran sitting there with her feet up watching television. Gran was in her early sixties and only stood about 4'8", very petite with long white permed hair.

"Hello Mum, don't get up, you remember Fred don't you?"

"Yes of course I do," she answered, bringing a smile to her face, "Hello Fred, it's nice to see you."

Then Fred leaned over to give her a little hug. Well, you could have knocked me down with a feather. This was too much to take in one day.

"Hello Gran," I said, giving her a kiss on the cheek, to which she replied, with a stern look on her face, "Perhaps now your father's home you'll settle down, and some discipline wouldn't go amiss my boy."

Well, that was rich he's been gone for years and I'm the one who gets the lecture. Judith, by this time was perched on Ken's knee giving him the treatment which normally ended up with a financial reward. Ken's favourite word was "Shh" as his one love in life was his television, so the more noise you made the quicker he would give us some money, if only just to get rid of us, but not today, I still had most of the money left from Fred's generosity.

Ken was a mummy's boy in every sense of the word and never left home until he was well into his forties and he always called her, Mother, which I thought so pompous. At the time his favourite nephew was my brother Michael – he was the eldest and they always looked on him as from their side of the family as he was born well before Fred came on the scene the first time around, and had taken Mums maiden name – Woodcock. At the time Michael was at Grammar school in Eastbourne run by Dr Barnardo's homes and sooner or later we would have to go and visit him which for me, the later the better as we didn't get on at all.

Fred took a seat alongside Ken and discussed old times, Mum and Gran went to prepare tea while I nosed around looking at different things. Our gran loved ornaments and also liked to play the piano occasionally, which stood in the corner taking up a large proportion of her lounge. As I lifted the lid to play a few notes, Ken came down on me like a ton of bricks.

"Don't play that, can't you see we're talking."

"Sorry."

"Can't you sit still for just five minutes?" Fred butted in, "You're not at home now."

I told myself it was going to be a long evening, while Judith played merrily with her toys, I sat in the corner biting my nails then the door opened and Mum threw the table cloth at me.

"Here, make yourself useful lay the table, the cutlery's in the sideboard drawer."

Well, at least it was something to do and was no sooner done than Mum started bringing in the food from the kitchen. One thing you could say about Gran, she certainly knew how to lay on a spread, with all her fancy sandwiches and fairy cakes, and for Judith and me, homemade lemonade to wash it all down.

Tea was over and for me, time to go home, but no, we had to sit there for what seemed like hours until finally Mum suggested we make amove, so after we all said our farewells, we made our way back to No. 36. We were just in sight of the house when Mum, who was walking with me, as Fred was too busy playing with Judith, spotted a man going into our gate and looked at me as though she'd seen a ghost.

"There's Ray quick run and tell him your Father's come home."

I raced on ahead to give Ray the message, well, he just smiled and went on his merry way. Ray was one of Mum's boyfriends and would just turn up out of the blue when it suited him, which also suited me. He never told us what to do and would give us money whenever the occasion arose. He'd been on and of the scene now for nearly two year, he'd even proposed to mum a couple of times, but she always turned him down. Not surprisingly, after that his visits became fewer, and would only pop in just to say 'Hello', while Fred was away at sea. Unfortunately, Fred was to see Ray walk out of the gate, followed by me and head off down the road and on asking who he was, I just said, "Wrong house, he was looking for the Elm's and just left it at that. You could see the sigh of relief on Mum's face as Fred sort of accepted my story.

Sunday evening was to be like most, call for Richard and we'd go out somewhere or other. I was to get home about ten o'clock that night and go straight up to bed as tomorrow was school and remembering the Caretaker, and the threats he'd made, knew I was in for it! The normal procedure was to have your name called out in morning assembly and to be sent to stand outside the Head's Study. I think it was meant to humiliate you, but at the time, we all thought it was funny, that is until the cane

21

came out. Our Head was particularly keen on putting his cane across your backside and we were later to find out that was not all he was keen on and was dismissed for assaulting one of the first year boys. I went to sleep that night with the thought of my punishment to come. The next morning coming far too quickly for me, but then school always did. I dressed quickly in my uniform and headed downstairs for breakfast as time was getting on, most days I'd be late anyway. Still, not to worry, I knew I wouldn't get caught as I only had to jump over the garden fence and straight into school. It worked a treat – a lot better than being caught at the front gate by Prefects (the School Gestapo) and having to stay after school for detention. It was then my reprieve came by way of Mum.

"You can forget about school today, we're going to London to your father's ship and maybe we'll spend the rest of the day in London, if there's time."

Well, you can imagine, I was so disappointed, to say the least.

"So take off that uniform and get changed," Mum continued, "Oh, and there's a clean shirt in the airing cupboard, but get washed first."

"Yes Mum, thanks Mum."

Nothing more had to be said as no school and a day in London suited me fine and sounded great, as the only time I had travelled any distance at all was when I'd been taken to one foster home or another by the Social Worker. Mum was prancing around like she'd just won the pools, making it obvious that she was pleased with her present situation. Still, not to look a gift horse in the mouth, and it seemed like a nice change for both of us. Fred descended from his bed and had no sooner sat down than he was presented with a cup of tea. Shortly after, we were all ready and headed off to start what was a most memorable day. Arriving at Brighton Station just in time to catch the 10.05, which in those days was the non-stop Pullman train to Victoria. The train alone was an experience. As I walked down the platform alongside, what seemed like a never ending, brown and cream train with "PULLMAN' in big letters from one end to the other, we were soon to be met by a porter who showed us onto the train, which for me, was unlike anything I had ever seen before. Down each side of the brightly decorated carriages designed in a 1920 style, there were tables; all set out for four people with plush upright seats to sit in with small lamps perched on each table, finishing off with little brown curtains framing your own private windows. Eventually we were shown to our seats and almost immediately asked if we would like to eat or drink, by the waiter, passing us a Menu. Well, what can I say? I felt ten feet tall. Fred ordered for all of us and you could tell this style of living was not new to him, and thought at last maybe our lives are going to change and perhaps it would always be like this. As the train pulled slowly out of the station, the waiters all smart in their uniforms, rushed up and down taking orders and serving almost at the same time. Fred was all smiles, and could see from the look on our faces that we were all bursting with excitement at our new experience. Breakfast arrived, egg, bacon and tomatoes, toast and tea; a feast fit for kings which suited me fine because that's how I felt, tucking straight in and not leaving a scrap. As the train thundered through the countryside I tried to read the names of many stations as we passed by, but with little success, as we were going much too fast. We finished our breakfasts and our table was cleared almost immediately. To think that the waiters only had fifty five minutes from start to finish to serve, clear up and be in time to reach Victoria Station, but somehow they managed it. While we sat there awaiting our journey's end, Fred told of what was in store for us and how first we would go to London Docks to his ship and pick up his things and then back into the City, there we were to spend the rest of the day and had no sooner finished telling us than the train pulled into Victoria Station.

Never having been out of Brighton much, I thought, like most youngsters, that London was the centre of the world and at the time it seemed it. As we stepped from the train, the loudspeaker was hailing destinations of all sorts, some of which I'd never heard of before. Holding on tightly to Judith's hand, I followed Mum and Fred close behind, not wanting to get lost in the crowd. As I did, I tried to look at six different things all at once, but everything and everybody looked so big, it was almost frightening. The collector took our tickets and we all headed in the direction of the main entrance, soon to arrive outside the station. It was quite obvious that Fred knew his way around as he hailed a taxi, a big black one, the very same as the one that had brought him to our house only two days before. At first, I was under the impression that the driver must have been a personal friend being the same car and all that was until I noticed there were more of the same during our trip through London, in fact, hundreds more.

We climbed in and Judith, Mum and I took a seat while Fred, still outside, spoke to the driver and then got in himself. There was only one long seat in the back making only room for three so I got up to make room for him to sit down. He just laughed saying, "here lad sit yourself down," then pulled a seat down from behind the drivers' seat. Well how was I to know? This was my first trip in a real London taxi, Slowly the driver pulled away into the Cities busy streets, a trip which if you have never done before you will experience as I did, with amazement, the size and height of the buildings and the many people – thousands of them all hurrying to get to one place or another. Our journey was to first take us along the Embankment, by which time the driver realising this was our first time in London, pointed out all the places of interest. During the journey we were to go by way of the Tower of London, passing Tower Bridge then down onto Commercial Road and a journey which was to last about 30 minutes in all. It was after midday by the time we arrived at the Dock Gates and on approaching we were to be stopped by Dock Police, asking us who we were. Fred produced his Seaman's Identity card and gave the name of his ship to which the guard smiled and waved us on. Our destination was the Royal Docks, Victoria in particular. There was also the Albert, George and so on. The driver, knowing his way around, took us straight to Victoria Docks and from there onto the quay and as close to Fred's ship as possible. There she laid – the 'Afric', sitting high out of the water waiting to be loaded for her next voyage. While Fred paid off the taxi, we walked towards the ship which as we got closer, seemed to get even bigger. Then after telling us to wait on the quay, he went on board and started to ascend the gangway which to me seemed a mile high, eventually reaching the top and disappeared from view while we stood there and looked around in total amazement. Then, on hearing a loud cry, looked up to where Fred was beckoning us on board. Well, you didn't have to tell me twice – I was there. I remember thinking how high it was and what a mess it would make if I fell, so I held on tightly until I reached the top and went on board. I stood by the rail alongside Fred and looked down at Mum and Judith who were still on the quay hesitating to climb so in the end Fred went down and got them, during which time one of Fred's mates introduced himself to me.

"Hello, young man, I'm your Dad's workmate, the name's Kelly, you fancy a look round?"

"Yea great" I said, to which he called out to Fred.

"I'm going to show the lad around," and without waiting for a reply we went on our way. By first taking me from bow to stern, then up into the wheelhouse and from there back down into the crew's accommodation to find mum and sis making their selves comfortable in Fred's cabin which included one bunk, a chair and a wardrobe-cum-dresser. Fred finished packing then suggested, "While we're here we may as well stay for lunch, okay with you love?"

She nodded and we all agreed.

"Right then, let's see what's on the menu."

Following Fred from his cabin we made our way to the Mess Room, a meeting point for all the crew where they would eat their meals and generally pass the time of day.

"Mavis, you and Judith take a seat, the lad and I will go and see what's to eat."

The crew by now were already seated and enjoying their lunch. While mum and Sis took a seat, Fred and I went off to the ships Galley.

"Hello Jock what brings you back so early?" said a tall, stout man, all in white, complete with chef's hat.

"Just come to pay off and get my gear, going to have me a spot of shore leave, this here is my youngest, Tony. I've also brought the wife and the wee girl up with me."

"Well hello master Tony, pleased to meet you lad, are you hungry?"

I was always hungry and just nodded.

"Well fine, I'm known as Cookie I've known your Dad for years."

As he spoke, the sweat rolled down his face, the heat from inside being almost unbearable.

"Well Jock, I'm afraid there's not much of a choice, pork chops or fish and chips."

So we chose the chops. Cookie made up four plates, each held enough to feed two men.

"There you go, get stuck into that my boy – put hairs on your chest," and handed me two plates and gave Fred the others.

"Come and see us before you go Jock, don't forget."

"Aye, I will, Cookie," and with that we returned to the Mess. By which time Mum had made herself at home and was enjoying the surrounding company of the other men. We took our seats alongside and ate what was to be a very nourishing meal, at the same time holding a conversation, with Fred across the table.

"When you've finished your lunch Tony, would you like to go below and see where I work?"

I nodded furiously, choking on my food at the same time. Anxiously I started to shovel the rest in.

"Slow down lad, there's plenty of time."
Despite his advice, I was still finished long before the rest of them.

"You don't mind if I show the lad around do you Mavis?"

"No, not at all Fred, I'm sure I'll be safe enough here."

So off the two of us went, leaving the women to be spoilt by the rest of the crew. From the Mess we went back past Fred's cabin which was on the Starboard side, along with the Officers and the rest of Engine Room crew. Our first stop was a small room with bars on the doors and ports.

"This room here is the hospital," and opened the door, "It's only small, with two beds, but it's enough."

"So why are the bars on the windows" I asked curiously,

"Well, that's so it can also be used as a cell if the occasion was ever to arise, for stowaways and such like," little did I know then that one day it was to my home, continuing down the alley way we arrived at our destination.

"Well, here we are, Son," said Fred opening a door which led onto an iron grid platform, "Now mind your step, it's sometimes slippery, so take a firm hold. Now Son, if you take a look down there and nearly to the bottom, that's where we're off to," and without warning Fred started to descend the iron stairs with me following close behind, leading onto one platform and then another, more stairs and so on, until finally we could go no further.

"Here we are, and these here are my babies," Fred said pointing to a row of huge engines, then following Fred along the platform and down a few more steps only to be met by Kelly, Fred's friend and workmate.

"Hello Jock, you just can't keep away can you?"

Fred smiled and put his arm around my shoulder, "I thought I'd show the lad around."

"Alright lad, well what do you think of our little kingdom?"

Obviously not dressed for the occasion the sweat began to drip, I asked, "Is it always this hot?"

Kelly, dressed in jeans, T-shirt and what looked like a hanky with knots upon his head, answered with a smile on his face, "Hot, this isn't hot is it Fred? Wait until she's steaming." It was then that Fred explained what Kelly meant.

"At the moment Son, only the Boilers are burning to keep the generators running for such things as lights, hot water and the galley, but once we leave the quay those large pistons over there, just in the way as a car engine works, are put into motion, moving up and down which in turn turns the propeller shaft so the faster they rotate the more knots she does, the faster the ship go's."

"Well done, Fred, I couldn't have said it better myself."

By now the heat was getting too much for me and on Fred noticing it was time to make a move

"I think I'd better take the lad topside before he melts away, I'll see you later Kelly."

"Yeah, right you are Fred."

We left Kelly to his work. It seemed to take longer on the return journey but soon reached the top and fresh air.

"Well Son, what do you think – would you like to work down there along with all the machinery?"

My first thought was to breathe in some fresh cool air, then replying, "Na, it's not for me, too 'hot! But I wouldn't mind working up here on deck."

Fred smiled, "Come on, let's go and find the girls, it's time we were thinking of making a move," returning back to the Mess to find Mum and Sis all alone.

Lunch break was over and the crew had all turned to (returned to work).

"Sorry Mavis, forgot all about the time down below, didn't we Son?"

I just nodded as Mum returned a smile, "That's alright; we've had a fine old time haven't we Judith?"

Sis just held out her hand which was filled with small silver coins, slyly sticking out her tongue when no one was looking. By now time was getting on and after saying our farewells we left the ship and made our way to the main gate. There to catch a taxi back into the City. By now I felt like a veteran traveller. This time our destination was Trafalgar Square and were to return much the same way we had come only with one alteration, turning off into the Strand, as we did we passed Australia House and Charing Cross Station, finally stopping on the corner of the Strand and Whitehall, Fred paid off the taxi and we walked down Whitehall, passing the stall-holders selling their flags and souvenirs, rubbing shoulders with tourists of different nationalities, from all over the world, packing the streets, we passed Downing Street, the home of the Prime Minister, who at the time was McMillan, then down onto Cenotaph and back up the other side until finally we reached Trafalgar Square where Nelson stood high above the streets of London. Crossing the road into the Square where the tourists nearly outnumbered the pigeons and it wasn't hard to see why Nelson had a patch on his eye, as it was plain to see they weren't fussy where they dropped their messages. Luckily, I was fortunate as they missed my eye, but instead redesigned the front of my jacket, I was not impressed. Soon after leaving the Square, we walked up to Piccadilly Circus going into the many souvenir shops, then we strolled up Regent Street to window shop, so you can imagine the next two hours were for me, were boring to say the least. The girls, on the other hand, were having the time of their lives, spending Fred's hard-earned money, but he didn't seem to mind and after all, I did get a new outfit that day.

The time was by now getting on, as someone suggested tea. Food at last! The choice was Lyons Corner House, a huge restaurant , and there we were to have our fill of tea, sandwiches and cream cakes, after which, we all made our way back to the Piccadilly Circus, which was all lit up and looking even more spectacular with neon lights flashing on and off, advertising all sorts. By now, everyone was tired and it was time to make our way home, so Fred hailed a taxi to take us back to Victoria.

By the time we got home it was late and I was ready for my bed, so after saying goodnight I went up. As I lay there in my bed thinking about the things I had seen and done that day on our little family outing. And that's what it had been, for the first in my life a family, mum Fred Judith and me. If this was what it was like to have a dad, then I was up for more (but still couldn't bring myself to calling him dad).

The View from 36 Bellingham Crescent -
The Family Home

school at bottom of garden

SEAMAN'S CARD
PARTICULARS

Serial No. **95800** **A**

National Insurance No. _KR/075.04 C_

Union or Society No. ....

Photograph of Holder

M.M.O.
Embossing
Stamp

R 591731

Signature of Holder
(or, if Holder is unable to sign, his left Thumbprint and the signature of a witness)

Frederick G. Bates

R 5012

17 CERTIFICATES

Compiled from Lists of Crew and Official
and Copy of Report of Character

No.	*Name of ship and official number, and tonnage.†	Date and place of		*Rating
		Engagement*	Discharge	
31	**S.T.S. VENASSA** PORT REG. 300092 GROSTON LONDON 21391 NETTON 12644 S.H.P. TON 12500		—7 MAR 1960	
32	M. NEWCASTLE STAR LONDON O.N. 187465 G.T. 8397.07 N.T. 4933.82 N.H.P. 1250	14.3.60 v.c. DOCKS	—8 APR 1960— LIVERPOOL	
33	M.V. NEWCASTLE STAR LONDON O.N. 187465 G.T. 8397.97 N.T. 4933.82 N.H.P. 1250	11 APR 1960 LIVERPOOL	AUG 1960 DOCK STREET	
34	S.S. BEAVERFORD 166218 LONDON H.P. 7000.	30/8/60 LONDON	13 OCT 1960 LONDON B.A.	
35	M.V. "AFRIC" OFF NO. 300093 SOUTHAMPTON GROSS 6552·67 NET 337249	16.10.60 Hull	DEC Dov	
36	B.H.P. 10100 OFF NO. 300093 SOUTHAMPTON GROSS 6552·67 NET 337249 B.H.P. 10100	5 MARCH 1961 VICTORIA ENGLAND	—4 JUN 1961 VERP	

*These Columns are to be filled in at time of engagement.

CHAPTER 2

Normal family life was something I wasn't used to, maybe you could argue that it was part of the reason why I was always getting into trouble, as having no father figure to keep me on the straight and narrow, plus my life with mum had always been a bit up and down. So with Fred just walking back into our lives there were a lot of questions to be answered.

Apparently it started back in early 1948. Michael was 2 ½, Pat was just a year and Terry had just been born, and me, well, I wasn't even a twinkle in anyone's eye! They all lived at my Grandparents house, it was over crowded but somehow they seemed to manage. Governement housing was scarce back then so there was a long waiting list. Fred spent long periods at sea in the Royal Navy which did not help their marriage much, so while Nan looked after my brothers to give Mum a break she was to meeting up with an old boyfriend from her school days Fred being the last to know came and went back from leave not having a clue what was going on and no one told him so the affair continued behind his back,. Then in early 1949 she became pregnant, fortunately Fred being home earlier that year naturally assumed he was the father, so life continued much the same way as it had always done, the only difference being with me in side, mum got larger. Due to her situation, fourth child on the way and constant complaint of over crowding the Council offered Mum a place, and on June 27th, 1949 they moved into a three bedroom house on the very same estate as Gran. The choice of neighbours was to be of sheer coincidence and also made Mum's secret romance even more convenient as Charles her lover was only to live two doors away, still totally unaware Fred being happy with his new surroundings, came and went and was now based down in Portsmouth, shore side, which gave him more opportunity to come home most weekends.

The family settled into the three up, two down and awaited my arrival, and eventually came into the world taking my first breath at 4.06 a.m. on Friday 2nd September, 1949 and given the name Anthony Roy. Apparently I had a good set of lungs and liked to air them far more than I should, which drove everyone around the bend. Christmas of 1949 was on the horizon with Mum looking well after my birth, and was nearly back to her trim figure and apparently still seeing our friendly neighbour Charles. Unfortunately, Fred was to come home on leave unexpectedly catching them together. Naturally he was not pleased and evicted him very quickly. His suspicions were always there, even on looking at me, knowing deep down I was not a Bates and to this day the Bates' features are so prominent, I of course looked different more on my mother's side, and on finding out how long the affair had been going on knew for a fact I was not of his blood, packed his bags and left that very day. Too young to understand I grew up without a Father, not knowing that he only lived next door. We were to stay in that house until July 21st, 1952. Charles, at this time, was doing his National Service up in Worcester. So with bags packed and without a word to anyone we followed him north to try and start a new life with Mum's new fiancée. But it was not to last as the responsibility of four children was too great for him, so he left us to fend for ourselves. So after spending the next few days sleeping rough in a local park she somehow managed to get the fare together and we returned home to Sussex, going straight to Gran's house where my brothers and I were dumped, before making a hasty retreat trying once again to sort out her life. A week went by without any contact from her so Gran finally called in the N.S.P.C.C.; subsequently Terry and I were taken into care and placed at Horsgate Nursery Sussex, on August 8th, 1952. The family had been split up, the romance had ended, and mum along my two older brothers admitted to Furze House Flimwell the Workhouse. Mine and Terry's stay was to be short-lived, soon to move on to new pastures green by means of foster parents, Mr and Mrs Simms, Wardowns Bungalow, just a short walk from Furze House, so Mum's visits could be more frequent which was emphasised as very important as being only two, this was a traumatic time in mine and my brothers lives and to lose family contact now would be damaging, but it was not to be so.

We were taken to our new home by car and on arrival at our destination, turned off the road and started off down a dirt track and, after some hundred yards or so we came to a large iron gate, with trees all around us towering high above, then taking a sharp left we were to see our new home. There deep in the English country side stood this old a bungalow, Wardowns Bungalow, and there waiting to greet us was our new family. Mr Simms, (Ernie) a tall, broad shouldered man, towering over six feet and, from where I was standing looked more like a giant. He had a moustache and wore round rimmed glasses and on being introduced, picked me up as you would a feather.

"Hello boy," he said, holding me at arms length.

Mrs Simms (Edie) was much shorter, plump and always had untidy look about her but she more than made up for it in a thousand ways. Then taking us both by the hand, she introduced us to their newly adopted son Colin who was about the same age as Terry. At first although very strange it became a place I grew to love and Ernie and Edie became my mum and dad. That place stays in my thoughts to this day, it was like a small farm, with its chickens, ducks, geese, two sheep, a cow and a pig, and all this was surrounded by thick woods.

Soon after our arrival in Flimwell, Mum and the boys returned back to Hove making her visits less frequent. For Terry it was hard as being older, he understood more of what was going on, but I soon settled down. Mum was like Father Christmas, didn't come often, but when she did it was a time for presents. Our stay was to last nearly two years. For me it was home and this was my family until finally the day was to come when we were to leave all I had grown to love and return to the family fold in June of 1954.

We were to be met by Mum at the end of the journey. Although nearly five, my big brother led me by the hand everywhere we went. After arriving at our destination Hove Town Hall, and climbing the winding staircase of the old Victorian building, we were sat down outside an office and left to wait for her arrival. As I sat there, Terry went to look over the stairs to see if there was any sign of her. On her arrival Terry recognised her straight away and started to run downstairs towards her. I remember leaving my seat and going over to the top of the stairs to see a young woman coming up towards me. Terry, who by now was half way down, cried out to her as she opened her arms and took him in. It was then I felt a warm hand clasping mine and a woman standing beside me knelt down and told me gently this was my mother. By now, a little mixed up, started to cry as I'd been calling someone else Mum for two years and now I'm told I've got a new one. Terry and Mum reached me and taking me by the hand, she spoke to the lady and soon after we left. Once outside we were met by an older lady who approached us pushing a pram. It was my Grandmother and she introduced us to our new brother James Allen. I didn't really understand, well I suppose at four you wouldn't, I only know that his stay was short-lived and he was later put up for adoption. Our James was born on September 2nd, 1953 which made him four years to the day younger than me – a million to one chance. Another mistake, who knows? There we were being pushed from pillow to post not knowing what day it was and then to be told we'd got a new brother, but still no father and supposed to understand. James's father was just one more of those affairs, a local man, Roy Howle, but once again on mum hearing the sound of wedding bells she dumped him, We all returned to our new home which was only a short walk away and to a ground-floor flat in a large house, very close to the seafront which made for long walks and picnics on the beach during that summer holiday.

Unfortunately, for my brother and me Mum went out to work and left us with a babysitter, a man who lived in the adjoining flat alone with his wife, who also went out to work, he had strange ideas on child care and on his wife coming home early one day, found all three of us naked and playing this game he invented to keep us amused, or was it him. In shock with seeing her husband in this compromising position she immediately called the Police, along with Mum. The Social Services were called in and all hell broke lose, but although it all went down on record no charges were ever pressed; as after we were examined they said no real harm had been done to us. Well what did we know, we thought it was just another game and after all, he'd only been looking after us a few months, and there was the fact that Mum didn't want to cause a fuss, What's more his wife had thrown him out so where was the harm, so life carried on much the same. With the arrival fifth birthday, on the 2nd September, I started my first school, the Knoll Infants, which was a bus ride away. .

Terry and I would take the journey to school together, my first day being a tearful one, but I soon got used to the surroundings yet never the discipline.

In early 1955 we moved to our new address, 36 Bellingham Crescent, my Grandmother's old house which was also only a short walk away from the school. Terry was soon to leave and go up to Junior School along with Pat and Michael, which meant finally I was on my own and gradually adjusted to my new surroundings, that was until late in September when I was collected from school and from there taken to my brothers school to collect Terry and off we went again. This time it was to Southdown House which like Flimwell, was also in the country, but this time it was a children's home, no fun at all, and we were to stay there three months, returning just in time for Christmas. On our return we were to find another unexpected guest, this time my new baby sister, Judith. All got back to normal and I especially remember looking forward to Saturday evenings, as that was the night the baker would come – a special friend of Mum's. He would bring all types of cakes, fruit loaves, biscuits, etc., and we would have a feast. My sister's nickname was Judy Blue Seal and the bread the baker delivered had a blue seal around it. Our friendly baker was Judith's father, his name was Somme Tanner, but he was soon to disappear off the scene and went to Australia shortly after with his wife and family. Well, I suppose it must have been a little difficult for him living on the very same estate as us, not to mention the gossip. At that time I was only six so it didn't seem at all strange and at least I had someone younger than me around. I would push her up and down outside in her pram and play for hours with her. Things were looking really good that was until Chris Butler our friendly neighbour moved in, and in the summer of 1956 the car came once again in June 1957, this time Terry, Pat and I were put together. Returning once again to Southdown House, but this time I was older and not the best of children my Social Report read, "Tony, a dirty little ragamuffin, a cheeky little adolescent who lacks control." Terry and Pat's reports were not much better either, so to me, just coming up for seven, the name of the game was to survive and that's exactly what I didn't. The worst times I remember about that place were after lights were out, especially if you were young. The older boys from other dorms would get satisfaction out of abusing us younger ones and if you screamed they would hold a pillow tight across the back of your neck as sexual abuse was ripe in those days, There was even a special room a few of the carers took you to if they took a shine to you promising all sorts just to keep there dirty little secret, even your own brothers turned against you in those institutions. Finally our sentence was over and off home we went again, but for how long? On our arrival back, our lodger had gone and Mum had lost immense weight by the way of the twins, Valerie and Bridget who were put straight up for adoption.

This time on my return I was to start my new school, Portland Road Juniors, although it was only to be a short stay, as by now I was categorised as uncontrollable in the classroom. The other kids, on hearing tales from their parents about my mother and her wrong doings, they intern shouted their opinions, but what did I know? I just thought every kid went through what my brothers and I had, so didn't believe a word, and in one particular case in an art class, threw a jar full of water across the classroom at my oncoming abuser but he ducked, unfortunately the teacher didn't, hitting her straight in the head putting a cut above her eye. So it was, at the ripe old age of 8yr, Mum was called and I was escorted off the premises and expelled from school.

So it was now on too my next school, by now under the keen eye of the N.S.P.C.C. (National Society of the Prevention of Cruelty to Children) and with Mum being told to get her act together or we'd be taken back into permanent care, but for me it was just a little too late with my constant disrupting in the classrooms, swearing at teachers supposably telling lies about my time in care and just walking out of the school whenever I felt like it. This was to carry on for nearly two years until finally enough was enough and my elders the Headmaster of my school, Social Services, not to mention Mum, all agreed that I needed psychiatric help. So it was agreed and arrangements were made. By now, at the age of 10, thought I knew everything, but boy was I in for a shock, as finally my appointment was made for me to see my saviour.

This time taken along to the Child Guidance Clinic, 33 Clarendon Villas, Hove Sussex, and can remember that place as if it was just yesterday, with the tall white three storey building standing right in front of us. At first, Mum thought we had come to the wrong place, as above the door it read 'Sussex Chest Clinic'. We were then to be guided to the side entrance, that took us along a path and down into the basement, soon to be at the reception. On taking our seat was soon to find out this was, for me, going to be a trip closer to hell than heaven. My name was called and I followed Mum into this large dingy room with only the outside light peering through. As we entered, sat behind a desk was this large stocky elderly gentleman in a white coat and he looked up over his glasses at me. As I sat there with Mum alongside me, he started to ask me all sorts of stupid questions, showing me pictures, asking what did I see, and asking did I love my mother, stupid question I thought, 'course I did – she was my Mum, and on and on he went. This was to last for about an hour, at one stage he asked me if I had any problems and would I like to tell him about them. What problems? – I thought, I was 10 years old,

I had no problems, I was just here to please you lot, I thought but never said. By the end I'd come to the conclusion that he needed help more than I did, but who was I to argue, it was over and I was the one to get the day off school.

As we left the clinic a further appointment was made for the following week and Mum signed a number of forms. I thought to myself, 'that's handy – another day off school', but the week went too quick for me as I arrived back at the clinic, this time things were to be different as I was to receive something called E.C.T. Treatment (Electro Convulsive Therapy), but what did I know. So like a lamb to the slaughter, I went along with the man in the white coat and was soon shown into this room to be greeted by a nurse.

"Hello Tony and how are you today?"

"Great," I said, not knowing where she got my name from or what was in store for me.

"Well, I want you slip into the cubicle and put on this gown?" she asked handing me this hard crusty white gown, which only did up down the back.

Shortly back after doing what she asked, she laughed, telling me "first you have to take your clothes off" So back into the cubicle I went, stripped down to my undies, putting on that horrible gown.

Once back in the room, confronted by the long black bench "Up you jump Tony, and just relax." Then they proceeded to start strapping me down, first my legs and then my arms, which by now I was getting a little worried. The nurse smiled, a smile of reassurance, which was supposed to tell me everything was okay and proceeded to stick these strange rubber things on my temples, then attached the wires to them. By now this was no longer just a day off school, me I felt like the condemned man awaiting the electric chair, only I was lying down. I was finally asked to open my mouth by the man in the long white coat, who inserted a large piece of black rubber into my mouth, and was told it would stop me biting off my tongue.

By this time my heart was going ten to the dozen, as the old man said "All clear." And slowly turned the dial on the machine, sending the electric shock waves rushing through my brain, making my eyes roll and my whole body shake, but there was no escape as I lay there strapped to that long black couch.

This treatment was to continue for a number of visits,

although very reluctant to go, I had no choice, after all – this was supposed to be good for me, or so they told Mum, as back in the 1950's what the man in the white coat said, 'stood', and was not to be argued with, not realising that I was just another guinea pig doing my bit for science. Unfortunately for me, it was to do me more harm than good and was sharply stopped after I started to experience serious mood swings and bouts of violence. After years of trying to control it, having brain scans and so forth, I was finally put on a permanent drug to control the damage that they had done to my brain and informed I would be on them for the rest of my life.

So I'd been through quite a lot for your average eleven year old, but with Fred coming back maybe things would be different from now on. Well that's what I hoped. And it certainly looked that way after our trip to London, and tomorrow we were of on another. Morning came swiftly and I was ready once again for another day of adventure. Our destination was parkstone sea training school in Poole Dorset, which was also run by Barnard's to see my older brothers Terry and Pat. Mum had made a number of visits, but this was to be my first. Terry had just turned thirteen and had been there for the past two years while Pat on the other hand was fourteen and only been there a year. Although I looking forward to seeing then both, I was looking forward to seeing Terry more 1 as before he went away there was always a bond between us, (probably due to our younger years in care together) I quickly washed and dressed and we were once again off to the station, With Mum and Fred arm in arm, while Judith would as usual – get tired and want to ride on my shoulders, so up she'd go. The train ride was a lot less exciting than the previous day. This time we were to ride an old rattler. Also having to change trains twice didn't help, then after a short journey by taxi, we arrived at the school entrance. Where we were met by an elderly gentleman who introduced himself as the Commanding Chief, then taking us directly to his office, the boys were sent for, all very formal. Judith and I were asked to sit outside while they had a chat. Obviously they too wanted to know where Fred had come from after all this time. At this time, Terry and Patrick were in the sole care of Dr Barnardo's until they were eighteen and for Fred to turn up out of the blue made them more than a bit curious. At last Terry and Pat arrived; "Left, RIGHT, left, RIGHT, attention. Stand easy boys." Their escort knocked firmly on the office door, while the boys stood there all smart in their uniforms, awaiting their surprise, The office door opened and they were marched in, so Judith and I followed in close behind, Then mum introduced Fred to the boys. Terry at first was a bit weary, Pat on the other hand was in his element and you could see why – as the two stood there together there was no doubt, he was definitely his fathers son. It was then the boys were given permission to have the rest of the day off, but first we were to be given the two bob tour. It was typical Navy – spotless. You could have eaten off the floors. As we passed the parade ground, cadets marched up and down and alongside the band playing in full tune. We did the full tour, classes, dining area, dormitory, kitchen, the lot and by the looks on their faces, you could see they were proud of their school and all it stood for. Fred, on the other hand, was not so impressed. He seemed to think that the place was some sort of approved school for misfits, saying they should be home with their family, strange attitude for someone who's only been around a few days. The boys changed into their civvies while we waited for the taxi to take us into town. Poole is a very popular with the tourist in the summer, but like most English seaside resorts, bloody cold in winter. Fortunately for us the day was dry with the sun trying to break through over the sea. On arriving in town we were all like one big happy family, laughing and joking. Our first stop was of course the shops, naturally with the amount of money Fred was spending on the boys, they too thought he was well off, with the smile on Mum's face beaming for all the world to see, as if to say, well it was worth waiting for, wasn't it boys. Pat and Terry were loaded up with gifts and it was soon time for my favourite pastime – eating. After lunch we went down on the front by now the sun had broken through and it was quite warm and while they all talked, I kept a lead on Sis, as, at her age, you needed eyes in the back of your head. Eventually we arrived back at the school and the time came for us to depart and after saying our goodbyes you could see the boys couldn't wait to get back to their friends to tell them all their news. The train journey home was to be a long one and eventually we arrived home about nine o'clock, so after quickly changing, there would still be time for me to go out. I rushed downstairs and was about to go out the front door when Fred asked where I was off to. I replied "Out." It was then, for the first time, he looked at me in a stern way and told me it was too late. Anyway, he didn't want me playing with those hooligans anymore. Is this what Gran meant when she said discipline? It was like trying to eat an apple whole, hard to swallow. Anyway, who was he to call my mates hooligans, He then finished his speech by reminding me that I also had school tomorrow, (I needed to know that like a hole in the head, especially when you knew what was going to happen), and that it was time for bed. Well, he was bigger than me so I didn't argue just said my goodnights and went up to my room, and sat there until it was all quiet, it was then I made my move. One thing I could guarantee was that once in my bedroom, I would not see anyone until the following morning, as nobody ever bothered to check on me. Just outside my bedroom window was a drainpipe and my means of escape, I opened the window quietly and looked down. It was about a 10 foot drop, but I had done it several times before. The hardest part was coming up! As I climbed out of the window I grabbed onto the pipe and began to slide down soon to reach the ground below, Mum was in the kitchen so I waited patiently until the lights went out then made my way out into the street to find the boys.

I arrived home late that night, so I sneaked quietly around to the back of the house and was just about to climb the drainpipe when the bedroom light came on, with the window bursting open and Mum looking down to see me standing there.

"Why don't you use the bloody door like normal people?" she shouted, then slammed the window hard and I could hear her shouting as she left the room. Well that was it, I was for it now. Typical, I thought to myself, most people get caught breaking out; me I get caught breaking in. I didn't even get the chance to reach the back door before Fred came out, grabbed hold of me by the scruff of the neck and marched me in saying a few words in his broad Scottish tongue then gave me a swift clout around the back of the head. Discipline and pain, I thought, and from someone I had only known for three days, this was just not on. Somehow this man had to go. I then scurried to my bed like a wounded dog nursing the back of my head. Next morning I got up and left the house early without saying a word to anyone and for once was on time for school. The bell went, so as usual, we made our way to the main hall for assembly which to my surprise, ran smoothly. Nothing was even said about my exploits in the school grounds during the weekend. Maybe the Caretaker hadn't recognised me after all, I thought. By now the news of Fred's return was throughout the school. Some made snide remarks, others just laughed as I expected and I was particularly glad when that day was over. On arriving home from school, Fred handed me a peace offering by way of a model of the HMS Victorious Aircraft Carrier, but never having the patience for that sort of thing, I never did finish it, but I did like presents and at least it broke the ice between us. And on Saturday 4th March, 1961, after only being back for seven days, Fred and Mum were to be remarried by Special Licence, on Sunday the 5th. The News of the World read, "Couple Re-United and remarried Again after Eleven Years. Good Luck and Congratulations." So now at last, after all this time, we were to have a father. Better late than never – or was it?

At first everything seemed to be okay. Nice clothes, good food and pocket money. Well who was going to complain at that, but sooner or later Fred would have to go back to work which he did, on the 15th March, 1961, returning to his ship, the 'Afric' and was gone for a period of three months. Before he left, Fred bought me a world map which he put up on my bedroom wall, also some coloured pins so to follow his ship halfway round the world, to Australia, New Zealand and back. Life for us went back to normal while Fred was gone and I did more or less as I pleased. Mum would occasionally threaten me that, on Fred's return, I would be for it, but who was to say that he'd be back. No one could be certain, least of all her, so I had much the run of the house as I had for years, well, at least since the last of my older brothers had gone into care. Also being the only man left in the house, so I made the most of it, but it was to be a short reign.

Time was to go swiftly as I followed Fred around the world, pin-pointing his every move on my map. The weeks came and went, as did the months. Spring was behind us bringing summer with all its colour and beauty and the nights grew longer as the day's got warmer which meant I could stay out longer and later, always to have the voice of Mum hanging over my head, "You just wait until your Father comes home." Summer was soon upon us as we went into early June which meant the return of Fred and also, the long awaited school holidays and six weeks of Heaven. Fred arrived home in mid June, and returned home from school one day to find him sitting in his fire-side chair looking well, with his golden tan from all those months in the sun. On seeing me Fred stood up and greeted me with a hug which for me, was a whole new experience and made me feel a little uneasy at the time.

"Hello Son, your mother tells me you've been a good lad while I've been gone."

Well that was a relief anyway, I thought to myself, as he drove his hand deep into his pocket and pulling out a crisp one pound note, said "There you go lad, now don't spend it all at once."

That night, we all sat around while Fred told us all about the places he had been, especially Australia and how some day we would all go out there to live.

Fred, by now, had decided not to return to sea and take a shore-side job and would start looking in the next few days. Eventually he was to get a start at the local gas works as a boiler man and so after years at sea, Fred started his new employment on land.

The school term was coming to a close and with this came the school reports, every school boy's nightmare. Fortunately, my report was to be a good one and was put down to the change of circumstances at home as my Form Master wrote, "I am pleased to notice such an improvement in this boy's attitude. I am quite sure he could do even better if only he would concentrate more, although he is still rather emotionally unstable." signed A. Dewhurst. At the time, I was pleased with the result and so too were Mum and Fred, but unfortunately it was to be the only good report I was ever to get during my school days.

The summer holidays went quickly that year, as they did most years and in September, shortly after my 12th birthday on the 2nd, a new term would start. I was twelve and raring to go. Fred, by this time, was becoming very disgruntled with the whole situation – his money was a lot less, Mum was pregnant and for some reason I could not seem to do anything right. Fred was like a fish out of water and I had the bruises to prove it. Things were to lighten up a little in November with the arrival of my brother Tom. Fred was proud as punch and seemed to settle down for a while after that, but it was not to last. Christmas was soon to be on us and soon once again my brothers would all be home and it was to be our first Christmas as a family, complete with new arrival. Our small three bedroom house was to be packed to the rafters. My brothers and I would all share one room. It was bedlam, but a good time was had by all that Christmas and Fred being a true Scotsman, insisted we all celebrated the New Year his way which included a midnight feast, first footing and then a party which took us well into the Year of 1962. The old year had gone and with it so many events that had changed all our lives one way or another, but somehow something was always missing. As we entered into the New Year, life went on much the same. I went back to school, my brothers went back into care and Fred returned to work, only to once again get more and more disheartened with his present position in life so in February he said his farewells and returned to the sea. This time he was only to be gone a short period, six weeks, and returned home a different man. For me, it was six weeks of freedom, but for Fred it was life itself. Then once again, he decided not to go away again and said how the next time he went away it would be altogether as he was taking us to Australia and in March that year we all went to London together to visit Australia House in the Strand Of course as you do, I went and told everybody in sight that we were going to Australia, not knowing how long the process took.

Australia House itself was a huge building right on the corner of the Strand and on entering was just as impressive, with its walls covered with pictures of blue seas, warm sunshine, complete with the houses of your dreams and it seemed just the place for me. We made enquiries and spent hours waiting around while Fred and Mum filled in all the appropriate forms which after, we returned home to await their reply. During this time, Fred got himself a job at a local Engineering Factory and for a time was quite content, and for nearly a year things went smoothly. The months came and went, but still no reply and our hopes of emigrating faded, still, at last things were beginning to look good, that was until early in 1963 on the home front.

Mum was like a time bomb and would very often blow up, leaving a trail of disaster behind her. That was some temper! We were later to find out why, as once again, she was pregnant. Tom, by this time, was about 18 months old, the interesting age, but the thought of another baby just did not appeal to me. You had to be in my shoes to be able to understand the situation as it was then, and another body would only make things worse. As the months flew by summer was soon to be with us once again the difference being that this time when the boys came home only Terry would return, as Pat and Michael were now old enough to find work. Michael who was nearly 17 had just finished all his examinations and went straight into the Insurance Business. Pat, on the other

41

hand, only being 15, didn't find it so easy. Summer passed and Terry returned to school by which time Fred, had once again, had enough of shore work and returned to sea in August of 1963, but this time he was only to be away a couple of days a week working on the Cross Channel Ferries. Pat unfortunately, had still not been able to get a job which was causing friction at home because he was unable to pay his way. The holidays ended and I, of course, returned to school to find on entering my third year we were to have a new Form Master by the name of George Harman.

George's last position before coming to us was Government Approved (Borstal) so we were all on tender hooks not knowing what to expect. The first day of term was always started the same way, a mass assembly in the Gymnasium. Usual thing – couple of songs, prayers and so on. All the Form Masters sat either side of the Head and when all was done, Mr Turner would stand up and say his piece. Our turn came with the introduction of Mr Harman, a tall stocky man, not the sort to argue with, with short blond curly hair and staring eyes, giving you the impression they were only on you, completed by a distinct grin which covered his face. Stating to each other our opinions, we returned to our class to await his arrival. By now our class was full of the so called 'misfits' of society, so he was to have his hands full and on his entering the room, he smiled, saying "Good Morning, boys," then went straight to the blackboard, chalk in hand, and wrote HARMAN, and looked what seemed to be straight at me and said, "My name is Harman – Mr Harman to you – now is that clear?" We all returned with a quiet "Yes Sir." His smile slowly left his face as he came back with, "Pardon, I didn't quite hear that, shall we try again boys?" Everyone having the same thought, dug to the bottom of their lungs and came back with a loud, 'YES SIR!" which was probably heard at the other end of the school and returned our reply with a slight grin as if to say 'like that is it?' Thinking it was funny, I smiled to myself, seemingly looking at everyone at the same time, he shouted, "Name, boy?" Not thinking for an instant he was talking to me, "Yes, you boy with the stupid grin on your face – did I say something funny?"

"No," I said casually.

"No," he scowled angrily, "What do you mean no? What's your name boy?"

"Bates," I answered, not thinking anything of it. It was then he walked over to my desk and looked down at me saying,

"Bates, what?"

"Just Bates," I replied. Slowly his face grew redder and a bead of sweat hung upon his forehead as if something I'd said made him angry, "Bates, Sir," he shouted, "Now shall we start again? Your name boy

By now the other boys in the class were pulling faces trying to make me laugh as I came back with a loud, "Bates, Sir."

"That's better, now we shall continue with the Register Master Bates," he continued, "I will call your names and as I do so you will stand and give me your Christian name."

Well mine just had to be at the top of the list. "Bates" I stood, "Not a very good start is it master Bates?"

"No Sir."

"Well, what is it, boy?" he shouted.

"Tony, Sir."

"Thank you Tony, now sit down. I've got an eye on you and anyone else who thinks I'm a soft touch."

I suppose you could have said I had blotted my copy book and was not going to forget my name in a hurry, as he was to be with us for the next two years. My only reprieve was to emigrate so I anxiously awaited the reply from Australia House.

The weeks rolled on and in October 1963, my youngest brother Ian was born. At first, just like terry and me put up for adoption, then later changed their minds and brought him home. The house was now full up to capacity – leaving no room to swing a cat. Pat, by now, had tried to get into the Army, Navy and the Air force without any success and ended up in a local Paper Factory. Unfortunately, for him, even though he was the image of his father, their only interest in him was his wage packet at the end of the week and because of their lack of enthusiasm for him, he became very insecure and very within himself and I only hoped it would be better for me when my turn came.

Time went on. Christmas came and went, as did the New Year of 1964. Home life was becoming unbearable for me. I had to become a cheat and a liar to survive as on Fred's bad days he would use me as a punch bag and on his good ones, Mum would wind him up to such a pitch as to tell him something I had done previously, so that as I entered to door he would lay straight into me, not so bad if you know what it's for, but half the time I didn't, and no sooner had he started on me than Mum would tell him to leave me alone, trying to make him look like the bad guy.

By now, at nearly 14 years old, I was not about to stand and take it any longer so I fought back when I could, making it a lot worse for me. Summer came and Terry arrived home to stay for good. Things would be different now, or so I thought and for a short while they were. Fred got Terry a job alongside him on the car ferries which naturally made him the blue eyed boy, following in his fathers footsteps. Pat, was naturally quite put out about this, but his opinion was not of any interest to anyone – especially Fred. The summer of 1964 was hot that year and little did I know, but for me, it was to be the last I would spend at home. Unfortunately I wasn't 15 until September and where my classmates were leaving school to go into the world in July, I alone, because of my age would have to stay on until Easter of 1965. Still, I had the whole summer holidays in front of me before returning to school. At that time, I was courting my real first love – Beverley Saunders – and to me she was beauty itself. Standing at 5'4" in her bare feet with long auburn hair, a slim figure and a body to die for, I was in love – or so I thought – and we spent all of that summer together.

Summer was over and at first they were to put me in a higher class, but the work was more advanced than I had been used to so I just walked out the class room and went home. A week later I was summoned back to the school. By now, no one was going to make me do anything I didn't want to. Arriving at school early on the Monday morning with Mum, had to wait outside the Heads Study, eventually to be asked in, but first Mums presence was requested. So there I sat for what seemed an age until at last to be summoned in. As I entered the office I was to find Mum sat in an easy chair, all smiles, and from behind his desk sat the Headmaster, Mr Turner. He was a short, slim man, in his mid forties, with a hairstyle that only went down the sides and back of his head – the rest being all highly polished.

"Well, Tony, what seems to be the problem?" He asked, looking down his nose at me. This is new, I thought, as I didn't even know he knew my first name, it was normally 'Bates' or 'Master Bates'.

"No problem Sir," I answered smugly, "I just don't like school so I'm not going to come." With that Mum burst out to give six penny worth.

"I told you Sir, it's no good, we just can't do a thing with him, and he's out of control."

Taking a quick glance to the corner, I noticed his cane which had been across my hand, back of knees and at one time a dozen times across my arse.

"Now listen Tony," he started, "you've only got a few months left to do – that's not so long and it'll soon pass. It's unfortunate that due to your age and the law that I'm afraid you must come to school."

Looking back at him in disbelief as I was 15 the same as my friends and they were out working, so why couldn't I?

"Now what's your favourite subject?" He continued, "Maybe we can help you there."I thought for a moment then came back with woodwork

"Just suppose we could arrange for you to do woodwork until the end of term, how would that suit you?" Turner waited for me to jump up and down with excitement.

"It might make a difference." I replied, shrugging my shoulders.

"Right then let's see if it can be arranged. Perhaps we could also find you other jobs around the school which will excuse you from all other class duties, how would you like that?"

It seemed fair, but highly improbable. I was then told to leave, but wait outside while he and Mum had a final word. Eventually, Mum came out.

"Thankyou Sir, you've been a great help, it's a huge weight off my mind."

She'd done everything apart from kiss his arse and you could see he was almost relieved to get rid of her. No sooner had she gone than he called me back into the office.

"Sit down Bates and let's see what we can do for you."

'Bates', well I thought, that didn't take him long to forget my first name. Then with a sharp knock at the door came the entering of Mr Lumsden, the Woodwork Teacher. A tall, slim man with black wavy hair (it always amazed me how he got those waves to stay up that high – everyone put it down to wood glue!). Closing the door behind him, he approached the Head. Teachers must have been poorly paid back then as most of them always wore the same clothes week in, week out, like some form of uniform. Brown leather beetle crushers shoes which, as he walked, left sparks behind, grey trousers, varied sports jacket, all in disgusting colours and brightly coloured ties to go with their checked shirts. After a short but brief discussion it was decided for the next term I was to be relieved of all school duties and spend the rest of the term helping around the school and I was to report daily to Lumsden in his workshop. This, to me, seemed a fair arrangement and I agreed. During my time with Mr Lumsden, I was to see the other side of him and would often let his guard down as a teacher and prove to be a good friend. As the time went on I was to become quite a craftsman and at one time it was suggested that I should even take an 'A' level but my maths were poor and always to let me down. The practical side being easy, but the theory was never one of my strong points. So the next few months my time was spent finishing items left behind from the older boys who had gone out into the world, and found that on completion that I could make easy money selling them on, which came to be quite a profitable exercise. Then shortly before Christmas I was approached by the Head and told it was time to start looking for a job as time was moving quickly and it would be soon my turn to face the world.

My choice, was obvious as by now, considering myself quite the craftsman, I decided to become a carpenter joiner, so filled with enthusiasm I started my search, but without success. Always my school report and past was to let me down and was considered a bad risk. At that time, I could not understand what that had to do with it as I had the experience and was also very keen. Finally, Lumsden used some of his resources to get me an interview with a boat building firm and even wrote me a personal reference. The interview was a success and I rushed home to boast of my news, only to be cut down in my tracks as my wage as an apprentice was only to be £3.00 a week and on leaving school, would have to pay at least £2 for my keep, which only left me with a pound for fares, clothing tools and entertainment. So on making my regrets to the company turned the job down. Lumsden was quite disappointed after that and lost interest in me, shortly after I was assessed at school by their so called experts and it was suggested I should go into catering so once again, I started to apply for jobs eventually getting an interview with the Grand Metropolitan Group as an apprentice Chef. The interview was to last a long time which afterwards I was shown the kitchens to see other apprentices at work, then finally the job was offered to me. This time at £6.00 a week, the only problem was that I had to supply my own uniforms at a cost of £18.00, which to me was a fortune, but even so I accepted the job and once again rushed home to tell of my good news, all the time thinking of myself all in white, wearing a tall chefs hat. On my arrival home I told my good news to Fred and Mum, and at first they showed delight and seemed pleased for me that was until I showed them all the literature that I had received during the interview, eventually coming to the sections on uniforms.

Well, that was the end of that. I was beginning to think I had been born in the wrong era. Nevertheless I once again took it on the chin. Christmas of 1964 arrived and the last Christmas we were ever to spend together as a family, not that we were close. The three oldest brothers were all working so all had their own interests. Judith by now was nine and quite the hand full. Then there was Tommy 3 and Ian 1, which left me standing in the middle of a minefield. The younger ones never did anything wrong and the older boys with their money and new possessions weren't interested in their younger brother. It was then I made a promise to myself that if I ever had any children of my own, we would always be a family and they would never want for anything – be it love, money or possessions.

Christmas of 1964 passed quickly and a New Year was here – 1965 – and only fate knew what was in store for me with good fortune coming my way by a stranger, one Friday evening late in January, by the name of Mr Wright. He had been sent to us from Dr Barnardo's Homes and had come to see my brothers Patrick and Terry, to ask them if they would like to go to Australia with their next group leaving in April as there had been a cancellation and arrangements had been made for two other boys, who had dropped out, and how this was an opportunity of a lifetime. Pat smiled and almost immediately said, "Yes," what had he to lose, things weren't going that great for him anyway, but Terry on the other hand was to decline this excellent opportunity as he, at that time, was working on the Cross Channel Ferries with Fred and felt he was going places.

"Unfortunately, this placing is for two" Wright said, "and I would prefer two brothers to go together or not at all."

That's when Fred came up with the bright idea, suggesting I should go, as this was too good an opportunity for me to miss. No more being the underdog a new life and new friends. Mum also seemed very keen on the idea, and they both signed my life away, as if to be sending me off to a penal colony for some terrible deed I had done wrong, but I didn't care, I was off to the sun and sand. The place where fortunes were to be made with me to fly halfway around the world was just too good to be true. The agreement was made that my older brother Pat and I were to go together. Mr Wright said his goodbyes saying he would be in touch in the next few days and would also send us an itinerary of our departure. The excitement was just too much and I had to tell someone. My first thought was my long standing friend Richard, who immediately looked at me with disbelief as he had heard the same story so many times before. The days passed, but still no letter with the event of the day being to wait for our Postman, Les Hindle.

Les had lived on the estate all his life and saw the coming and goings of everybody, back into the late forties when he and Fred were in the Navy together. The strange coincidence was that Les also lived in the same street back in 1949-1950 and used to come home on leave together and returned to Portsmouth to their ship the H.M.S. Abercrombie after their weekends at home. A week passed and still no sign. I was beginning to think Richard was right and once again it was just another dream, and then out of the blue it arrived. Les knocked personally, as he to had been patiently waiting to find out the contents of this long awaited letter. On answering, he handed the letter to Mum.

"I think this is what you've been waiting for Mavis."

Mum looked at the letter all official with Dr Barnardo's stamped across it. "Come in Les, fancy a cup of tea?" Following Mum, he came in shutting the door behind him.

"Don't mind if I do, Mavis." He entered the front room with Mum close in front. Fred and Terry had already gone to work as they were on shifts. Pat was just about to leave for work and me; well I'd only just got out of my bed. Mum opened the letter and proceeded to read it to herself.

"Well, what does it say?" I asked impatiently.

Jokingly, she looked up, saying, "Well, it looks like we've got rid of you two at last," and then just threw the letter on the table. Pat got there first and already his face had lit up.

"Great, that's just great," and then looking up at me, he handed me the letter saying, "Well, kid, looks like we're off," and proceeded to read the letter.

We were to leave home on Tuesday 20th April. The day after Easter and from there, travel to the village homes in Barkingside Essex the largest of all Barnardo's Homes, where we were to meet the rest of the party travelling with us. There to stay until Wednesday 28th April, then to be taken to Heathrow to start our journey to Australia. I looked up and around me and it was as if everybody was talking at once, but I couldn't hear only see their mouths move. Was this really happening? I asked myself. Was I really going all that way?   After all I was only fifteen. Had I been so bad that my family were looking forward to my departure? I was excited but also frightened. A voice brought me back to reality with a start as if I had just come out of a terrible dream, as Les put his hand on my shoulder, "Good luck Son," and with the look in his eyes I could see he meant it, "Thanks for the tea, Mavis," Les said closing the door behind him.

Pat was still walking around like the cat that had just caught the mouse, "Well, I'm off now," and with that he went off to work, proudly, the first time I'd ever seen him go willingly and happy – an unusual sight for him. All the excitement seemed to put Mum on edge a bit for some reason and on trying to talk to her she spoke back very abruptly as if I 'd done something wrong. She would often go off into her funny moods and learnt to just leave her as she would come around sooner or later, so getting myself ready went off to school. Not that I went much during those last few weeks as by now, I could not see any point.

Those last few weeks of waiting were to be long ones but Easter was soon upon us and the end of my schooling. My final school report was not a good one, unfortunately this was to be the one that I would take with me to Australia and thought just maybe I could lose it, but no, it was to be sent straight to Barnardo's'. Funny when I think back, this was to be my last Easter at home and on Tuesday, Pat and I would be off, but things went on just the same as they had always done. My last night was memorable as there was a dance at the local Church Hall so all dressed to kill, I met Richard and Mike, who lived across the way and decided that I should go out in style and when Mike told us his parents had gone out we immediately thought of the booze cabinet his Dad had. Well I can tell you now that was some cocktail we made up. We put in everything we could think of and it tasted horrible, but it was alcohol. I don't know what proof it was but we had it in one of those old lemonade bottles with the screw top and know sooner had we left Mike's, the top blew off and was never to be seen again, but fortunately the bottle was still in tact. That night everybody said their farewells and I was beginning to have regrets, but I was going and I wasn't the sort to back out at the last minute. That night I was to get drunk, so drunk that if I had gone home after, I'd have been in for it so after the dance we decided to try and walk it off and so the three of us along with Bev, Eileen and Carole decided to go down the beach. The next thing I remember was waking up in a beach hut freezing cold at 4.30 in the morning. Mike and his girl had already gone which left the four of us all huddled up like a litter of pups on the floor.

"Do you know what time it is?" I said, trying to wake Richard up. He stirred, as when Richard slept, he really slept. The girls, by now were up and ready to go. Funny how they never looked so good first thing in the morning, mind you I felt like shit and probably looked it. Eventually, he got up and after taking the girls home and saying my final goodbye to Bev promising her all sorts, it was then back home to face the music. Before parting Richard and I said goodbye and he promised that he would see me off later, but knowing him knew he'd still be in bed when we were half way to London. Crossing the road, I was to find the house all in darkness and dreaded knocking on the door, but for some reason hesitated and went around to the back door to find it open, and after quietly creeping in, went straight up to my bed. Luckily no one stirred. As I entered the room, Michael lay there in his bunk, snoring like a pig. Terry used to mumble like he was having a conversation with someone and Pat was well hidden beneath the covers. For a while I stood and stared at them all, thinking this time tomorrow there would be two empty bunks and Pat and I were of to start our new lives as brothers. We had never been close, but maybe this would bring us together. The house would now be less crowded and the two younger boys could move into our room and take our places. Still in a bad way after a good night out on the tiles, I lay there wondering what the next day would bring and must have dozed off as the next think I knew was that I was being woken by Pat.

"Come on mate, time to get up."

As I more or less fell out of bed, I hoped that I didn't look how I felt, staggering slowly downstairs to be greeted by Fred, "Morning Son, sleep well?"

"Err, yes thanks," I replied in disbelief.

Mum, at this time, was doing a fry up, "Sit yourself down Son, your breakfast is nearly ready."

Well, this was too good to be true. They must have gone

to bed early and not known what time I'd come in. So I sat at the table and awaited my breakfast which was almost immediately put in front of me. Then Mum, Fred and Pat all sat around the table. Mum was all smiles, "Well," she said, "Your Father and I have decided that we too are coming out to Australia and should be out there in six months, and when the time comes, you and Pat can look for somewhere for us all to live, that is apart from Michael and Terry who want to stay here."

Then Fred assured us this was so and would have no sooner settled down and they would be there. My face lit up and thought at last it would give us both something to work for. I was going to miss my family more than I knew, even though we weren't close, blood is blood and you can never alter that fact.

"We're also coming on the train journey with you today and going to stop off at Australia House on the way home." Mum said, as she started to clear the table, "Well, if we're going you all better start getting ready."

I finished my breakfast almost choking it down, frightened that Mum was going to take the plate from in front of me, then one after the other we took our turns in the bathroom. Our cases were packed and it was soon time for the off. By now most of the street knew of our departure and turned out in full force to see us off. The taxi pulled up and I said goodbye to my friends then got into the cab. I took a last look at the house, No. 36, where I had spent a good deal of my life on and off, wondering if I would ever see it again, but I was too excited to be sad and felt like royalty, as everybody waved us of except for my old mate Rick. As we pulled away I took a last look around at everything as this would probably be the last time I would ever see it.

<u>ANTHONY BATES, born 2.9.49.</u>

Mother :   Mrs. Mavis Bates, 36, Bellingham Crescent, HOVE.

Father :   Ex-stoker in the Navy; divorced 19/.11.51.

   Siblings : Michael Woodcock, 23.9.45.   Illegitimate child born before
Mrs. Bates marriage.

            Patrick 4.2.47.

            Terence 9.2.48.

06.08.52   Mrs Bates and the two older children were admitted to Furze House,
            Flimwell. Tony and Terry received into care and placed at Horsgate
            Nursery.

            Mrs Bates stated that on 21st July, 1952, she vacated her Council
            house owing to arrears of rent of about £8. She and the 4 children
            went to Derby and stayed with a Mrs. Hunt who was stated to be the
            mother of the alleged putative father of Michael woodcock. She
            remained a week at this address and then went to Worcester where her
            finance Charles Sole was undergoing 15 days military training. His
            home address is 22. Stapley Road, Hove. Mrs Bates stated she could
            not find accommodation and she and the children slept under the
            trees in the Park until 1.8.52 when she returned to Hove with the
            children, and her mother was persuaded to keep the children over the
            weekend.

            On 5.8.52 Inspector Odey called on the grandmother. She informed
            him that her daughter was staying at Mr Sole's home and the children
            had been with her but that she herself had to go out to work and
            could not continue to look after them. Inspector Odey saw Mrs.
            Bates and told her she must go round to her mother's house and look
            after the children. He then contacted the Welfare Department but
            they could only offer accommodation for the mother and two of the
            children.

25.10.52   Mrs. Bates interviewed. She has made application for the 2 children
            remaining with her to be accepted by the Church of England's
            Children's Society. The application had failed and Mrs. Bates
            wishes the Council to take these 2 children into care so that she
            might go out to work. She was told that this was not possible as
            she had accommodation for herself and the children and must be
            responsible for them. Mrs. Bates stated she and the 2 children
            intended spending the weekend with her parents in Hove and she will
            try and get accommodation there and also a job so that she does not
            have to return to Flimwell.

24.06.53   Letter received from Almoner, southlands Hospital regarding Mrs.
            Bates. Mrs Bates is to be confined about 13.9.53; the baby is
            illegitimate and she wishes the child to be adopted.

14.07.53   Mrs Bates interviewed. She was quite certain that she wished the new baby to be adopted. She stated that the father was a local man who lived at home with his parents. He had not spoken to her since she had told him she was pregnant and there was no possibility of the two of them making a home for this child. In any case, Mrs. Bates stated he was a most unreliable man who was out of work for about 9 months during the year. Both Mrs. Bates and her mother Mrs. Woodcock stated that the baby could not return to the grandmother's house. Mrs. Bates was told very little could be done until the child was actually born, and she would be informed later whether the Children's Officer would be prepared to take the child into care until it could be placed with prospective adopters. Mrs. Bates then asked that the two children Michael and Patrick might be received into care.

22.07.53   <u>Visit.</u> Mrs. Bates again seen. She was told that under the circumstances her two sons, Michael and Patrick would be received into care when she goes into hospital for her confinement. It was emphasised, however, that as soon as she came out of hospital the children would be returned to her care.

Mrs. Bates stated that she was sure when the new baby was born she would wish it to be adopted although she might change her mind if it was a boy. She stated that the father was Roy Howell of 54, Lincoln Road, Portslade. He lived at home with his parents; he had two sisters, one of whom was married and had two children. As far as Mrs. Bates knew the other members of his family were normal healthy people.

Mrs Sims said that she hoped to have all her children in the not too distant future. Mrs Sims felt that this was all extremely vague and probably without any foundation.

02.09.53   Mrs. Bates admitted to Southlands Hospital, James born.

17.11.53   <u>Visit.</u> Tony was having his afternoon rest when I visited but he woke up later and came down to see me. He was very weepy at first but very soon became cheerful and talkative. Tony seems to present very few problems and the family are devoted to him. Mr. and Mrs. Sim's have an excellent understanding of the children's needs and difficulties and do their best to cope with this. Mrs. Bates has not visited the children since my previous visit. She has written to them on two occasions abd each time said she hoped to have a house for them soon. Mrs. Sims does not feel it is wise, as it makes the children extremely excited and their hopes are dashed when they have no definite news of returning to their mother. The home and sleeping conditions are perfectly satisfactory.

15.12.53   Mrs. Bates called at the office and I interviewed her. She apparently came to enquire whether Tony and Terry could be moved to The Haven Nursery at Lancing, as this would enable her to visit more frequently. I told her I thought it extremely unwise to uproot the children now as they were extremely happy and well cared for in their foster home. She complained that the journey to Flimwell was an impossible one and that she was unable to visit the children for financial reasons. In view of this arrangements were made for her fare to be paid to visit both boys before Christmas. Mrs. Bates said that she had now decided not to have James adopted, she hoped in the very near future to marry the child's father and the family would then be completely reunited. This appears to be a very Vague sort of arrangement.

21.01.54   I saw Mrs. Sims and the children on their way to the village shopping, the family appear to have had a very good Christmas and the boy's thoroughly enjoyed themselves. Mrs. Bates visited the foster home for a few days before Christmas. She did not as I suggested send adequate notice of her intended visit and in consequence arrived on a day when Mrs. Sims had taken all the children to the pantomime. She was most annoyed about this and went to see Mr. Sims at the garage where he works to voice her complaint. She was assured that the children were quite fit and well and it was explained to her that her letter had not arrived before Mrs. Sims left. Mrs. Sims told me that Terry continues to talk a great deal about his mother, his constant topic of conversation is the imminence of his return home. Both foster parents feel Terry will never really be happy until he is reunited with his mother. Tony, on the other hand, appears quite disinterested and is a fairly stable and settled child. The foster home is entirely satisfactory at present although I suspect that Mrs. Sims is becoming a little tired of the perpetual uncertainty, she is extremely fond of both boys and the thought of their departure obviously distresses her.

24.02.54   I visited during the afternoon and did not see Terry as he was at school. Mrs. Sims reported that both boys were very well and presenting few problems. Terry was recently seen by the school doctor who suggested that he should be referred to an orthopaedic specialist regarding the probability of flat feet. Both boys seemed quite happy in their foster home and I have no doubt the foster parents are extremely fond of them. Home conditions are satisfactory.

12.04.54   Visited: both boys were playing in the garden with Colin Sims; they looked fit and well and seemed to be quiet happy and settled in their foster home. Their mother visited recently and Terry particularly was delighted to see her. Mrs. Sims has not yet received Terry's special built up shoes from the clinic but hopes to have those within a week or two. Material conditions in the home remain quite satisfactory.

03.06.54   Telephone message received from Mrs Bates. She has been allocated a council flat and hopes to move at Whitsun. She plans to have Terry and Tony home on the 14th June.

04.06.54   Letter to Mrs. Sims informing her that Mrs. Bates has been granted a flat and suggesting that the children should be returned to their mother on the 14th June.

14.06.54   Terry and Tony returned to their mother. No longer in care.

In 1954 the mother associated with a man called Smith, by whom she gave birth to the half-sister Judith in 1955.

According to the mother, Smith never assisted her in any way. The mother has been at her present address since 1955. It was originally the home of the grandparents, but the grandmother, who is now a widow, now lives in a small council flat on a council estate. The family has been known to the NSPCC for some time, and the local Inspector has a very poor opinion of the mother, whom he considers to be a thoroughly immoral woman.

Complaints were made about the mother leaving her children in the house unattended, and there were also complaints about the mother enticing a married man called Butler, away from his wife. The mother is said to be in a pregnant condition by Butler.

The mother gave birth to twins, Bridget and Valerie, on 25.07.57 and they were placed for adoption on 08.08.57 directly from Southlands Hospital, Shoreham.

Foster Home in the middle of the countryside

CHAPTER 3

Arriving at the station, we were just in time to catch the 10 a.m. train to Victoria. A journey which by now I had done many times, but this was to be a one way trip, as usual it took about an hour, and from there we had to travel by underground to Barkingside in Essex. We arrived at the station to find the village home was no more than several hundred yards away, so within minutes we were standing outside the main entrance. It was unlike anything I had ever seen before, as there in the heart of Essex was a small village surrounded by walls on all four sides. As we entered, it was like walking into a fairytale, in front of us was the village green edged by cottages on all sides with each one having its own name. We were met at the Gate House and taken directly to the office where we were then introduced to the Rev. Collins and his wife, the Governor of the village, at that time. After a short introduction we were then to be taken on a tour of the grounds, leaving the office, we walked off to the right where, at the end of a slip road stood a small church which was used not only by the villagers, but also people who lived in the surrounding area. The church itself looked as though it had fallen out of the sky into a perfect setting and was just as magnificent inside, shortly after we left and returned to the main road which ran up and around the village green. I say 'road' but it was more of a dirt track made by the passage of time. As we walked, passing the cottages all with different names, we came to a stop outside 'Ivy Cottage' and were then told that for the next week or so this was to be home, along with the rest of our companions, before making the long trip to Australia. We continued our tour which took us up and around the top of the green and then down the other side until we came to a large house on the corner, complete with tower and clock that chimed on every half hour, just like any other village.

"This is where my lady wife and myself live – if there are any problems during your stay, don't hesitate to call on us."

I looked at Pat and smiled, 'problems' I thought, why would there be? This looked perfect to me. Across the way from the Governor's House stood a monument to the man himself, Dr Barnardo, sitting in his seat looking down on all that passed him by. As we headed back towards the main entrance we passed the village shops from where the whole village was supplied.

"There's a lot more to see," said the Rev. Collins, looking

at Mum and Dad "but the time is getting on and we have to settle the boys in," and with that we all returned to the office.

"I do hope you'll stay and have lunch with us, Mr and Mrs Bates?"

"Thankyou Sir," replied Fred putting on a posh accent, "that would be nice."

Once inside the office, we were to be met by our House Parents.

"Oh jolly good," Collins piped up, "You're here already, Patrick Tony I'd like you to meet Mr and Mrs Taylor these are your House Parents for the next week or so. If you would like to go with them now, perhaps you could meet some of the rest of your group."

With that Mr Taylor picked up our cases and Pat and I followed him like lambs to the slaughter, leaving Mum and Dad to discuss our future.

Mr Taylor was a tall, slim man, very smartly dressed. His wife, on the other hand, was short and a very petite woman but it was obvious that Mr Taylor was in full control of the situation.

"Well boys, this is it. Welcome to Barnardo's," his voice was strong but kind and I took an instant liking to him.

"I bet you boys are hungry," said a soft voice from behind.

"Yes Miss, we sure are," once again thinking only of my stomach.

"Well you're just in time for lunch and it will also give you a chance to meet the rest of the group, Tony. It is Tony isn't it?"

"Yes Miss."

"And that's Patrick, yes off course, with so many names it takes a little getting used to."

Within minutes we had reached our destination 'Ivy Cottage'.

"Well this is it boys, home for the next eight days," Mr Taylor said as he ushered us through the front door. 'I take there bags straight up Mary so you can get the boys settled in."

"Okay John."

"I'll put them in the front room with the other boys," and he disappeared up the stairs.

We followed Mary into what was the Dining Room where all nicely laid out was a large table surrounded by chairs.

"Well boys, take a seat, the dinner bell is just about to go."

No sooner said than the sound of a dinner gong went and all

hell was let lose, bodies came from everywhere, all taking their places at the table.

"Hush now, you know Uncle John doesn't like noise at meal times."

The door opened and in he walked, taking his seat at the head of the table, "Afternoon gang, as you can see we've two new additions to our family which now makes it complete. This is Patrick and his younger brother Tony."

One by one they all introduced themselves.

"Hi, I'm Archibald Hill, this is my brother James and these are my two sisters Kathryn and Irene," and one after another they all said their hellos then a voice came from the side of me.

"I'm Peter Lewis."

We shook hands and made instant friends.

"I'm Kenneth Hutton and this is my sister Anita," she smiled and I just knew we were going to be friends.

"Right, that's enough of that for the time being, let's have some lunch."

The cook by now had finished putting the dishes of food on the table and took her seat alongside us altogether there were twelve of us. Then the loud voice of John broke up all the chattering.

"Now can I have your attention for Grace?"

A deadly silence fell.

"Would you do the honours please Peter?"

Saying no more, my newly found companion said clearly, but quietly, Grace.

"For what we are about to receive, may the Lord make us truly thankful."

With Peter trying not to laugh, as from under the table a foot from the other side was trying to distract him.

"Thankyou Peter, you may start."

One by one the dishes were handed around so that you could help yourself. While we ate, no one was short of conversation. It seemed that instead of just a short while, we had known each other for a lifetime. We finished our lunch and it was the boy's job to clear the table and girls to wash and dry up. A reasonable request I thought.

"Right then Peter, since you and Tony seem to be getting on so well, perhaps you would show him and his brother to their room and, yes James, you go too."

Pat's face lit up at John's suggestion. Peter was younger than me by about two years, James on the other hand was much the same age as Pat, so they probably had a lot more in common. We made our way upstairs and into the front bedroom.

"That's your bed there Tony, Peter pointed out while Pat took the bed between Archie and Jim."

Putting our cases on our beds, we started to unpack when Peter called out, "Leave that Tony, there's plenty of time for that later. Come on let's go out and meet some of the others."

So following Peter out the door and onto the landing and we were no sooner halfway down the stairs when we were met by John.

"And where do you think you're off to?"

"Yea, well, I thought I'd show Tony around and meet some of the others."

"Good idea Peter, but first his parents are waiting to say goodbye, so if you would be so good as to take Tony and his brother over to the Governor's House, they can say their goodbyes."

Pat by this time, was already behind me, followed close by James. So leaving the cottage together we headed across the village green. Peter was a little shorter than me standing about 5'2"; James on the other hand, towered way above all of us to the height of 6'1". In a very short time Peter and I had become instant friends, both finding out we had a lot in common.

As we approached the house, Mum and Fred were already outside waiting for us, accompanied by Collins and his wife.

"Well boys, settling in alright?" Collins asked

"Yes thank you Sir." we both said more or less together.

"Well your mother and father have to go now as they have got business in the City, so perhaps you boys would like to walk them to the station, it might be just as well if Peter and James went with you, as we wouldn't want you to get lost on the way back now would we?" He smiled and then turned to Mum and Fred to say his farewells, "Very nice to meet you Mr and Mrs Bates. Do come again – you're welcome here at the village anytime."

Fred shook Collins hand, then leaving the village we all headed off towards the station.

"What a nice man, Fred, and what a beautiful place."

You could tell by Mum's voice she was getting a bit tearful. Fred too, could also see this and immediately butted in.

"Well boys, this is it, you're going to have to make way for us and with a bit of luck we'll be with you in the next few months or so."

Then mum did a strange thing. She took my hand and squeezed it as if she wanted to say something but somehow couldn't find the words. Fred, for the one and only time, put his arm around Pat and was given his 'Father – Son talk. All this time, followed closely behind by Peter and James. We arrived at the station shortly after and went with them onto the platform, their train was to be about 10 minutes or so and I shall never forget the long period of silence that was then to follow. None of us knowing what to say to each other, it was as if we were all total strangers on that long lonely platform, all going our own separate ways, only the sound of the train coming down the track broke the silence, as it eventually rolled into the station. Mum hugged us both and told us to be good and with tears in her eyes, got onto the train. Fred followed with the exact same sentiments. Pat, by this time was also a bit tearful but for some reason I was more embarrassed with all the affection, as for me, this was all new. Did I really have to go halfway around the world just to receive a little love from my own mother? Something I had been begging for all my life. My thoughts were broken by the sound of the guard, "Mind the doors," and as they closed between us, the train slowly pulled away and we stood there waving until they were out of sight.

"Come on Tony, let's go and have some fun," said Peter pulling at my jacket bringing me back to reality, then Pat piped up.

"Well Son, we're on our own now."

He was doing his big brother bit, but taking no notice, Peter and I made off leaving them to do their own thing and within minutes we were back at the Home.

"Come on Tony, we'll go over the back by the swimming pool its empty this time of the year. No one goes there except us oldies there you can have a fag and not get caught."

Following Peter closely behind, we crossed the green, then passing the Governor's House, up and around the back of the cottages where in front of us stood their very own private school.

"Blimey, you've even got a school here."

"Yeah, but don't worry, we won't have to go."

Beyond the school and over some waste ground and we were to soon come across the swimming pool and just as Peter said it was empty, beyond the pool there were more open grounds – playing fields all around.

"Is all this part of the village Peter?" I asked, thinking it was more like a huge park.

"You ain't seen nothing yet."

We then walked over to what looked like old games huts where we were to find a mixture of girls and young fellas just passing the time of day.

"Hi ya Peter, who's your friend?" asked a young coloured boy.

"This 'ere is Tony, he's coming with us to Australia."

"Hi Tony, so how is it? I'm Mick, want a fag?"

"Yes, thanks," and saying no more he pulled from his pocket a squashed up packet of 10 Park Drive.

"You'll have to share it though, as I've only got four left."

That was fine by me and stoked up, and Pete and I puffed away like a pair of old chimneys.

"Hi, my name's Linda," came a voice from the crowd, "I'm in the cottage just across from you." She said nearly knocked Peter clear over as she confronted me.

Linda was about the same age as me and was attractive with it.

"Give us a puff of your fag," and without saying another word I handed the cigarette over to her.

"Have a look will ya, he's only been here five minutes and already he's pulling the birds."

I nudged Peter to shut up as I wasn't complaining anyway it would make things more interesting during my stay here. She handed back my cigarette, all the time looking directly into my eyes.

"Thanks," I said as our sparks must have met in mid air – as for me once again, it was love at first sight. Taking thoughts of my folks not to mention Bev clear out of my mind. Well I was having fun and so might as well make the most of it, and for the rest of the afternoon we laughed and joked about until it was time for tea and the village clock struck 4.30.

"Come on Tony, time to make a move. Tea's at 5 o'clock and we've got to get back and."

"Yeah, it's time we all made a move;" replied Mick, "make sure you leave no fag butts lying about."

We all looked around to remove any evidence that could

incriminate us then set off back towards the cottages.

"Mind if I walk back with you Tony?" Linda asked looking at me with those big dark brown eyes.

"Course not" and taking my arm we made our way back to her cottage.

"See you later," I said hoping to get an answer back.

"Alright, I'll meet you under that big Oak tree outside your place say 6.30."

"Yeah, sure, see you then Lin." Then ran across to Peter standing outside the cottage waiting for me.

"You don't waste time do you? Meeting her later?"

"Yea under some old oak tree"

"Oh she must mean that one there," said Peter pointing to a tree and being the largest of all the trees in the village was hard to miss. Heading off around the back of the cottage and in the back way to the kitchen, we were to find Mary cutting sandwiches for our tea.

"Hello boys, and what have you two been up to? I hope you haven't been leading Tony astray, Peter?'

"Who me Miss"

"Yes you, Peter Lewis," and looking at each other we both laughed, "You'd better get along and washed up for tea."

We did as we were told and left Mary to finish her chores. By this time it was 4.50 and everybody was trying to get into the bathroom all at once. Peter and I had what was commonly known as a lick and a promise. You know, a quick look at the soap and flannel and a promise to use them later. The gong went and we rushed downstairs to the Dining Room to take our places at the table and as we all sat waiting to start the door opened and in walked John, closely followed by a female companion.

"Good Evening all, we have a guest for tea. Would you all say hello to Mrs Granowski."

We all looked on, wondering what was so special about her, as she took her seat at the head of the table, then looking up she smiled.

"Good Evening, my name is Margaret Granowski, and for the next week or until you arrive in Australia I will be your Guardian Angel."

She then opened a small attaché case which she had resting on her lap and pulled out a large file, placing it on the table.

"In here, I have a run down on all your past histories, but

I would like you all, one by one, to introduce yourselves and tell me a little of what you think is in store for you on arriving in Australia."

I suppose you could say we were being psycho-analysed as she sat there waiting for our responses. Miss Granowski was a big woman who stood about 6 feet and had shoulders to match, making her look like an all-in wrestler, but apart from all that she had her good points. John broke the silence.

"Right then, first things first, let's have Grace, Patrick would you do the honours."

No sooner had he finished than a voice from beside me rang out.

"I'm Peter Lewis, Mrs Cranowski," trying very hard to pronounce her second name.

"If it makes it easier you call all me Margaret."

"I'm Archie Hill and this is my brother and these are my sisters." and so on until it came to my turn.

"I'm Tony Bates, Miss."

"Oh yes, you have taken your brother Terry's place and of course, you must be Patrick."

"And what do you want to do when you arrive in Australia Tony?"

"Join the Australian Navy, Miss, they say it's the best paid in the world."

"Do they, and have you a second choice?"

"No Miss, just the one."

Patrick, I see you want to join the Air Force?"

"I sure do Margaret," he replied in that sometime silly American accent he would use, but nobody took any notice.

"Well we will have to see what we can do about that then."

We all talked amongst ourselves and finished our Tea. All full of the excitement of the weeks to come. John's voice then broke into our chatter.

"Right then, I presume we've all finished so we'll clear away, but before we do I've just a couple of points to make. First Patrick and Tony, Margaret would like to see you afterwards. Also, now the whole group is together, you will all meet with Margaret at 7 p.m. in the lounge and that includes you Peter Lewis, so no disappearing acts."

Peter looked up as if to say, who me? We all laughed.

With that all hell let lose. What with the sound of chairs

scraping on the floors and the constant sound of crockery, we could hardly hear Margaret as she spoke to us.

"Right boys, shall we go up to your room where it's quieter"

I led the way, all the time thinking of my 6.30 date with Linda, with Pat on my heels and Margaret close behind, opening the bedroom door, and put on the light as by now it was getting dark outside. Margaret then broke the silence.

"Well don't look so worried boys, all I want to see is what extra clothes you will need for the trip. You first Pat, are you short on any clothing?"

He opened the wardrobe, by now all our clothes had been neatly put away.

"Well, that seems to be okay," she went through everything one at a time and then made some notes, "well, you seem to be alright for most things, maybe a few new items wouldn't come amiss."

Pat had been working for the past two years and most of his clothes he had bought himself. Then it was my turn, "Well, that's you sorted out, now how about you Tony?"

I opened my side of the wardrobe which you could nearly see right to the back that was apart from a few lonely items. I then opened my drawer which was also just as bare. Margaret quickly took notes, then looking up she smiled.

"Well Tony, I can see we shall have to go and do some major shopping for you tomorrow," then walked towards the door, "I'll see you boys downstairs at seven," and closed it behind her. This was the first time Pat and I had been alone since we arrived and once again he was doing his big brother bit.

"Well kid, all systems are go now – any problems don't bottle them up you come and talk to me."

Talk I though about what, problems what problems? everything was just great as far as I was concerned, but offcourse, deep down I knew there was just one thing that I was terrified of, the unknown and to me that was where we were going. My thoughts were broken with the entry of Peter.

"Come on Tony, its 6.30, Linda's outside."

I rushed to the window and there she stood with one of her friends, under the big Oak tree, immediately outside. From the window you could see nearly all the village with its cottages all lit up and neatly placed around the village green and over in the far corner stood the village clock, just striking 6.30 – it was a sight you had to see for yourself to appreciate.

"Come on Tony, we've got to be back in at 7 o'clock."

I rushed to the door and headed for the stairs and was to hear a final few words from Big Brother as we started to go down the stairs.

"Behave yourself now, don't get into any mischief."

We arrived outside to find the girls still standing there and on meeting told them we had to be back for seven for a group meeting, so could obviously not go far, so we decided to take a short walk around the village grounds which, unknown to me was further than I thought. Peter, who was laughing and joking all the time, was eventually to stop on the sound of the clock striking seven, we both realised we were late, the meeting was about to start and we weren't there, so taking Linda by the hand we started to run back to the cottage. Peter on the other hand, thought it was funny but I was new here and was already in trouble. We saw the girls to their cottage and rushed across the green to find John standing at the door.

"You're late, I said seven not ten past."

"Sorry John, I forgot my watch," looking at Peter and on hearing his terrible excuse, just grinned, saying, "Don't let it happen again."

Sliding past him, we made our way to the lounge to find everybody all sitting around Margaret and as we entered, all the faces turned to the door.

"Ah, there you are, I though we'd lost you two, come in and take a seat with the others."

Margaret's voice was soft and she smiled as she spoke. I somehow think she could see, we were going to be a handful!

As we took our place along with the others, looking directly at Peter and me, Margaret spoke.

"Right now, for the sake of the late comers, I'll start again. For the next week a full itinerary has been worked out for you starting tomorrow, with your photographs to be taken, medicals and for some, a shopping spree to kit you out."

Straight away I thought of the sorry look Margaret had given me on seeing my wardrobe.

"And to follow we will be going on a few sight seeing tours, Tower of London, Regent's Park, Buckingham Palace and perhaps even a West End Show. Your departure date, as most of you know, will be next Wednesday, 28th April, a week tomorrow. So we all have a lot to see and do so let's make the most of it, and just to let you see what's in store for you I have here a short film to show."

John was then to take over.

"Right, now, if you'd all move around and face the screen and make yourselves comfortable, we'll begin."

One of the girls just happened to sit between Peter and me, Anita, and was like putting a rose between two thorns. Mary then entered the room with a tray of cold drinks, placed them on the table and took a seat. All this time, Margaret had been setting up the projector.

"Right, I'm ready now – lights."

John turned down the lights and the film began to roll, starting with a picture of Sydney Harbour Bridge and then on to the sandy beaches of Manly and Bondi crowded with people swimming and surfing. It all looked great, just the place you would dream of going – your own paradise island. Continuing with more shots of the outback, sheep stations, everything looked perfect. The film was to run for about 20 minutes with the call of 'lights' at the end from Margaret. The lights went up and everybody showed that look of excitement on their faces. Peter and I talked of what we would do together once we arrived. At that time, not knowing it would be impossible. Then John took the floor.

"Right now, Mary has kindly made us a cold drink and some sandwiches so help yourselves."

After a short mad rush to the table, the rest of the evening was spent asking questions and each in turn everyone stating their future plans. By now we were all at ease with one another, just one big happy family. It was 10 o'clock already and time for bed. Early for some and late for others, but I was ready. For me it had been a long day and each and every moment had been full. I needed a good nights sleep as tomorrow was to be just as exciting. We said our goodnight's and made our way upstairs, each in turn made our trip to the bathroom, soon after to undress and get into bed and lights out. For an hour or so we all talked and joked about. Peter by this time, with sheet over his head, had made his way to the girls room to give them a fright which started all sorts of larking about including pillow fights, but on hearing all the rumpus it was all put to a stop by the entry of John.

"Settle down you lot, and you girls, get back to your room now. You've got a long day tomorrow so how about you all get some sleep," and with that he left the room.

Shortly after all was to go quiet and everyone was to settle down. I think for me it must have been the worst time as here I was once again in a strange bed far away from home and soon to be on the other side of the world. Would I ever see my Mum again? Come to that, my brothers and sister? We were not close but they were all I had. Scared and uncertain the tears began to run from the corner of my eyes. Trying not to cry, I swallowed the huge lump which had gathered in the back of my throat, I had to be strong. I was fifteen and soon to be an adult. After all this had only been the first day of my new life and already I had made friends. How many boys get the opportunity that I had just been given. I was the lucky one, drying my eyes and began to think of the future and the film we had just seen. Sun, Sea, and surf blue skies the huge parks, Sydney Harbour Bridge, Bondi Beach and so much more. Anyway, it would not be long before Mum and Fred and the boys would be with us. Yes, I thought, today had been the first day of my new life and for me the first day of the rest of my life.

That night was to be a restless one. When I did eventually drop off into a deep sleep, I was woken by the sound of a voice.

"Morning boys, it's 7.30, breakfast is at 8 o'clock."

I pulled the covers over my head hoping that they would forget I was there.

"Come on Tony, time to get up," yelled Peter, pulling the covers from my bed. "You'll be late for breakfast."

I was not amused as I crawled from my bed and made my way to the bathroom. A cold water splash was just the thing to take the sleep from my eyes. I dressed and was just in time for the breakfast gong. By the time I arrived downstairs, everyone was at their place.

"Morning Tony, sleep well?"

"Yes thanks John," I said taking my seat alongside Peter.

That first breakfast of cereal, toast and scrambled eggs was to go down a treat. I felt recharged and began to feel almost human again when the door opened.

"Morning everybody" said Margaret as she came through the door

"Oh we do look happy, still half asleep are we? We'll soon change that," she said, taking her seat at the end of the table.

"Coffee Margaret"

"Yes Please John," then opening her little attaché case which never seemed to leave her side, she pulled out a small folder, placed it on the table and opened it.

"Now let me see," she said studying her paperwork, "Tony and Patrick Bates, Peter Lewis, Kenneth and Anita Hutton, this morning you will be coming with me. Archie, James, Kathryn and Irene, you will be going with John to have your photos taken and we'll meet back here around lunchtime, but first you must do your chores."

Saying no more, the table was cleared in a flash. That only left the girls to wash up and by the sound of the crockery crashing into the sink, it wouldn't take long before they finished or broke it all in the proceeded. The minibus was due to arrive at 9 o'clock sharp so there wasn't long to get ready and by 8.55 we were all washed, changed and ready to go. While all this time, Margaret waited patiently in the lounge.

"Ah, good, you're all ready and in good time too."

The sound of a motor could be heard pulling up outside, "Ah, that sounds like the bus is here," said Margaret as she peered out of the window.

"So we'd better not keep him waiting."

Outside, we all boarded the bus while Margaret got in the front with the driver, who seemed a funny chap, never said a word at first just got back in the drivers seat and drove off down the dirt road leaving the village behind. We were only to drive a short distance and out of the gates when the bus pulled up in a busy main street and we all climbed out. Then the driver shut the door behind us looking at Margaret, "I'll be back at 11.30, Miss Cranowski," and with that he drove off and was obviously a man of very few words.

"Right now, keep together," Margaret said heading us all together, "it's only a short walk, I know you're nearly all adults but you're in a strange town and it's easy to get lost."

Soon after, we were to arrive at our destination a large clothes store. Once inside, we made our way straight to the men's department where Margaret spoke to the assistant as if she knew him personally.

"Now you boys, Mr Jones here known's exactly what you need, so it's just up to you to help him pick it out, meanwhile I shall take Anita into the girls department, so behave yourselves while I'm gone," then she disappeared through an open door.

"Right then boys, who's first?"

One by one, Mr Jones read out the names off a list. Patrick came first, then Peter.

"Now which one of you is Kenneth Hutton?"

"I am Sir," so it was then his turn.

Well I was the only one left, so I had to be next. Anita and Margaret were soon to arrive back on the scene, I say soon, they had been gone for over an hour and in this time our man had already fitted out three of us.

"Well now, how are you boys doing?"

Pat and Peter were all smiles, loaded down with their bags.

"Look Miss, do ya like my new suit?" Peter said pulling it from one of the bags.

"Yes, it's nice."

"And I've got some new shirts and trousers, and look at these shoes."

"Yes Peter, they're all very nice, now put them away you can all have a fashion parade when we get back to the village."

By now Ken was fitted out and the shop assistant finished writing the last of his items on his list.

"Right then, you must be Tony – last but not least. Your list seems to be the longest, so I've left you until the very last."

We started on the bottom drawer, socks, pants, vests, and worked up to pyjamas, shirts, trousers, shoes and then came the piece de resistance, my new suit. Slowly I worked my way down the rack until I finally came to the one I liked, black with a white fleck.

"Like this one Miss"

"Yes, very smart – try it on. Let's see if it fits."

My first suit, I tried it on and found to my surprise it fitted perfectly, made to measure you could say. I pulled back the curtain of the changing room and boldly walked out for all to see, complete with grin of shear contentment on my face.

"Oh yes, that is smart Tony," said Margaret, "is that the one you want?" I nodded furiously as Margaret turned to the assistant and winked.

"Well, Sir had better take it off and we'll get it wrapped for him."

I couldn't believe my luck. Margaret could see I was pleased and commented, "Just you wait till the girls at the village see you all dressed up, there'll be no stopping them." Everyone laughed. "Right, that's all of you fitted out."

The assistant presented Margaret with the bill which she just signed.

"Now then, what's the time? Oh, good it's only 11 o'clock, anybody fancy a drink?"

A reply was not needed. The look on our faces said it all, gave our thanks to the assistant and left the store, and went for a snack, after to head back to the bus and there waiting patiently by the bus was the driver looking up and down the road for us. Finally spotted us he waved and on reaching the bus, was this time to be greeted by the same but much more cheerful driver.

"Had a good time have we?"

"Yes thanks," we all answered, noticing the difference. Still it was nearly midday and we're all entitled to our bad moments.

"It certainly looks like it. What did we do? – buy the shop up."

He opened the door and started to load up the bags as one by one we started to get in.

"Can we ride up front Miss?" Peter asked.

"You'll have to ask the driver."

He looked down on Peter and me, just smiled, "Go on mind you, no sky larking around."

No more words were necessary. We were there and so after closing the back doors, the driver started the engine and pulled away heading back in the direction of the village. On the way we chatted to the driver who told us for the next few days he was to be our chauffeur.

"Oh good," cried Pete, "Does that mean we always get to ride up front?"

"We'll see shall we, the others might also want a turn too."

All the time Peter asked questions, "So what do we call you then Mr Driver?"

"The name's Bill, but once we're back in the village grounds it's Mr Edwards, now don't forget, or you'll get me into trouble."

"Right Bill, Mum's the word."

Shortly after, arriving back at the village, Bill parked right outside the cottage.

"Here we are."

Peter and I jumped from the front seat and opened the back door and while everyone climbed out, Bill handed out all the bags.

I could hardly wait to get mine inside just to have another look.

"Thanks Mr Edwards, see you later."

"Okay boys mind what you get up to now."

Peter and I rushed on ahead, only to be met by Mary at the front door.

"Hey, slow down boys, where's the fire?"

"No fire, Miss, just got to unpack our new clothes," I said going straight up and into our room.

This many new clothes I had never seen before coming from a family with three older brothers and not a lot of money. Clothes had to last, so you can imagine by the time they reached me they'd had their fair share of wear. So for me this was like Christmas. Peter and I unpacked and had our own fashion show, then tidied up and had just finished in time for lunch. That afternoon we were to go and have our photographs taken, after which, the rest of the day was to be free. So Peter and I headed off to meet Linda and the rest of the gang out back at the swimming pool. We all met up and spent the afternoon together. That day was to go quickly and was soon over. Tomorrow was Thursday and the start of our day trips out. During which, for the next two days we were to see half of London. Regent's Park, The Tower of London, Westminster Abbey. You name it, we went there. We even went to matinee show, Oliver and got meet the cast and even got to shack hands with Jack wilder (OLIVER) afterwards it was then onto the Lyons corned house, and as we entered the band stuck up with waltzing matildas, Margaret had left nothing out. By the time we got back to the village in the evening we were all bushed and ready for our beds.

Saturday arrived and for us a day of rest which we were to spend in the village. By now we were counting the days. Not that we weren't having a good time. The weekend passed and Monday came around once again we were off out for the day, but this time to the East End of London to be exact, the Head Office of Barnardo's in Stepney causeway, to check our papers, have a full medical and to generally chat with the Heads of Staff – a day which we were all glad when over. We said our farewells and made our way back to the village. The days had flown by, tomorrow was Tuesday, our last day at the village before our long journey. Now it was nearly here, I found it quite frightening, but I'd come this far and I wasn't going to turn back. Anyway, so far it had been great new friends, new clothes. I pushed the bad thoughts to the back of my mind. We arrived back at the village just in time for tea. John was his normal jovial self and as for Mary, a better house Mum you couldn't have asked for. She would flutter and fuss over you as if you were her own and to each and every one of us showed a little favouritism.

"Would you say Grace, Tony?" The moment I dreaded.

"Err yes John," I mumbled away completing with a loud 'Amen' and was glad it was over.

"Thankyou Tony, now have you all had a good day?" John asked curiously.

Everyone started to talk at once.

"Hey slow down, one at a time now."

Peter and I, not having time for talk, gulped our food down as we wanted to get out, not that it made any difference as we still had to wait for the others. No sooner had we all finished than John stood up.

"Now then, before we all leave the table, I would like to have a word. Tomorrow is going to be your last day with us and it will be a full one, so I want you to listen carefully to what Margaret has to say, also for those of you who have made friends in the village, it would probably be better if you said your goodbyes tonight as tomorrow night you will be busy packing and sorting out last minute problems."

His eyes looked in our direction as he knew we couldn't wait to get out. "Now I think Margaret has a few words to say before you leave."

"Thankyou John," said Margaret still holding on firmly to her folder, "Now tomorrow is going to be hectic for all of us. In the morning the press will be here to take more pictures and to interview you all. Then last minutes check to make sure you all have everything you need. Which reminds me – you will all be getting a new suitcase and a small hold-all for on the plane and tomorrow night, after your tea which I believe Mary has something special in mind. You will all get packed, after which I've got another movie you can watch, also some cartoons, for those of you who are interested. Well that's all for now, I'll see you all in the morning."

Great, I thought she was never going to stop. That night I think the table was cleared in record time.

"Now you boys, not be too late now."

We nodded and made our exit and were soon to meet up

with the rest of the gang.

Linda and me, by this time, had become very good friends so I was going to find it hard to say goodbye, as the evening flew past. Well it always does when you don't want it to. As I walked Linda back to her cottage we made all sorts of promises to each other, also making arrangements to meet the following night. Somehow I would have to sneak out, as I knew with Peter's help anything was possible. We kissed goodnight, holding each other close, neither one of us wanting to let the other go. Young love or puppy love as it is known, to me always seemed to be the most painful. Eventually, we parted and I returned back to the cottage. Once inside, I made my way to the lounge where everyone but me seemed to be full of excitement.

"What's up son, you look a little down?"

"Oh nothing," not wanting brother to see I was unsure of the situation, "I'm alright, probably a bit tired." Saying no more he returned to the others.

"Anyone for a drink?" asked Mary, making her way towards the door. Answers came from all directions.

"Game of cards Tony?" asked Peter looking up at me. It was then I realised I had to snap out of it and quick.

"Yea okay then"

I was soon back to my old self and we played for about an hour or so.

"Right, you lot I think we should call it a night – finish what you are doing and we'll make a move shall we?"

John's voice was law and everyone apart from Pat and James said goodnight, as they were older and allowed to stay up. Bed times were always good for a laugh. All trying to get into the bathroom first, sneaking into the girls' room after lights out, but that night I was to go straight to sleep. The next thing I knew was the sound of a John's voice waking me from my sleep.

"Morning boys"

And like the clock on the wall, you could always rely on him to be punctual and like the village life itself everything was run to perfection. It was a family life and those who lived here loved every minute of it, but for us it was our last day.

The day started as normal. First breakfast cleared up and washed and changed for the day. Only this time we were to get dressed in our best clothes for the Press. Apparently there was some sort of human interest in us as we were to be the first large group from Barnardo's to fly to Australia. We quickly washed and changed the girls in their best dresses and us all in our new suits. As I stood there looking in the mirror, I was no longer a boy, for there I stood a young man with my whole life ahead of me and somehow I was going to make an impression on the world.

Standing admiring myself, I looked good and now felt the same.

"Come on Tony – you'll wear that bloody mirror out."

Peter was all anxious to show the world his new suit.

"Slow down will ya there's plenty of time, Press don't arrive until 10.30."

Finally we then descended to the lounge, in our new outfits.

"My, you do all look smart." Mary made a point of letting each and everyone of us feel we were receiving the same attention.

"Come here, Peter, let me straighten up your tie."

"It's alright Miss, I can do it."

Somehow it didn't matter what Peter put on, it could have been a handmade suit and paten shoes, but he would still look as if he'd just got dressed in the dark, then John walked into the room.

"Well, are we all ready then? If so we'll make our way to the Governor's House."

Leaving the cottage behind, we made our way to the large red brick house on the far side of the village just as the clock struck 10.30. That day had been made to order. The sun was shining, it seemed just on us, and with the singing of the birds high in the trees it was a perfect April day. We arrived to find Margaret and the Rev. Collins waiting outside for us.

"Good morning all, are you all ready for you big debut?"

We all laughed not knowing what to expect.

"The Press haven't arrived yet, so we'll all wait inside shall we."

Margaret was in once again in full control as usual as the Rev. followed her inside only to be met by his wife.

"Come in and take a seat – I'm sure they'll be here shortly."

No sooner had she spoken these words when a car pulled up outside.

"Oh good, here they are."

Rev. Collins went out to meet them and during which, the next hour or so we were to have our photographs taken and be asked all sorts of questions. Where had we come from? What were we going to do in Australia and so on? At last the time had come for the Press to leave and for us to return to the cottage for lunch. The clock had just struck twelve and we were late. So made our way back quickly, but before we could sit down for lunch we had to change out of our good clothes. That afternoon had been set aside for visitors and also to make any calls to close friends or relatives. So for us it was to be a long and quiet afternoon although the arrival of our new suitcases broke the monotony for a while. A couple of visitors had shown up but none for us, trying not to show the disappointment, went for a walk. Thinking at least someone would come and say goodbye, but I suppose out of sight, means out of mind. Feeling a bit sorry for myself, I headed to the playing fields behind the village.

"Hi Tony," a voice called out.

I turned and running towards me was Mick and a few of the boys." Had a good day Tony?"

"Oh yea, not bad, you?"

"You're joking, we've just finished school and there's nothing good about that," slowly we walked back into the village. "So where's Peter then?"

"Ah, he's got a visitor."

"How about you, anyone come to see you off?"

"Na not yet"

Then all the boys split up and went in their different directions while I carried on walking with Mick to his cottage which just happened to be next to Lin's and there she was talking to some of her friends. They all giggled as we got closer.

"Hi Lin. Mick called, "I brought Tony to see you."

I hung around for a minuet then Mick went in, so slowly walked across the green towards 'Ivy Cottage'.

"Tony wait for me," a voice called. I turned to see Linda running towards me.

"Are you coming out tonight?"

"I'll try, but it won't be until late, say about 8.30. I'll meet you outside your place."

"Okay, see you later," then she ran off back to her friends.

It was nearly 5 o'clock and soon be time for tea. Peter came running up the path and met me at the front door.

"Can't wait for tea, Mary's laid on a real spread."

In my mood, I'd forgotten all about it, but once inside the atmosphere hit you. Music was playing everybody full of excitement.

"Just in time you two," said John, "wash up and make it quick."

The gong went and everybody rushed to the dining room as this was not the time to feel glum; it was a Bon Voyage party time. This was to be out last night here in England, so we were to make the most of it. We took our places and were joined by Margaret, John and Mary who had gone to great lengths to make this a night to remember. Nothing had been left out, right down to a box of Christmas crackers and a good time was had by all and at the finish I could hardly move having eaten so much.

"Well then" John stood up "if we've all finished, shall we clear all this mess away? Tonight even I'll give you a hand, just to get it out of the way," and John started to gather up the plates, and on noticing the time it was already 7.30 so as we cleared and the girls washed up.

"Right now that's a good job well done. Now you boys can go upstairs and start on your packing. The sooner you've got that done we can all sit down."

John led the way to our room. Me, I was bushed, still suffering the after effects of that huge tea. I collapsed on the bed.

"You won't get your packing done laying there Tony."

"Oh just five minutes, John, I can't move."

"Alright, I'll leave you to pack yourselves, but I'll be back to check it later," and leaving the room he shut the door behind him.

One by one they all collapsed on their beds and for a while we talked of what was to come tomorrow. Eventually lifted our bodies from our beds, we started to pack our bags. All that was to be left out were our travelling clothes. Everything else was to go in, that was apart from what we were wearing. Peter finished first and I was close behind.

"Oh great, you've finished – come on then Tony let's go downstairs."

It was then, the door opened.

"And where are you two off to?" It was John come back to do his spot check.

"We've finished packing and thought we'd go out for a little while."

"Sounds fair, but first we check your cases."

Peter opened his and it looked like he was going to the

72

Laundrette.

"You've obviously done this before Peter, no? Well I'd never have guessed. Now let's have a look at yours.

I opened my case and he just began to laugh, "Yours is not much better either is it?"

I shrugged my shoulders.

"Well, I think we had better start again."

By now, the others had finished and could see the funny side of it as they left the room.

"See boys, less haste, more speed."

We emptied both cases and started again only this time under John's supervision until at last we had finished.

"Well, that wasn't so bad was it?"

"Alright, can we go now" Peter asked already halfway out the door.

"And were do you think you two are going at this time of night it's a bit late."

"We just want to say goodbye to some friends."

"Okay, but in by 9.30 at the latest."

We headed downstairs and out of the front door and across the green to Lin's cottage. I was late and she was nowhere to be seen and it was far too late to knock. We hung around for a while to see if anyone came out but without success.

"She might be over the field, Tony."

So we made our way to the usual meeting point, running all the way as the village clock struck 9 o'clock.

"Blimey, is that the time, we'd better hurry up" but still no one was to be found.

"We've missed them – we might as well go back to the cottage."

Peter agreed, and slowly we made our way back, not seeing a soul all the way. I was sorry I'd missed Linda, but maybe it was for the best. Soon to arrive back at the cottage, went straight in and could hear the sound of laughter coming from the lounge, on entering, letting the light fill the room.

"Hurry up, you two, you're distorting the film," so quickly shut the door, "anyway what's up with you two. I said 9.30 and you're early." John commented.

"Oh we thought it would make a change."

We made our way through disturbing everyone at the same time to get the best seats. After watching the films for about an hour or so, we after settled down to have a hot drink before bed, while John got up to make a little speech.

"Now, before you go to your beds, Mary and I would like to say what a pleasure it has been having you here. We will still be seeing you at breakfast but tomorrow morning will be a little bit hectic as Margaret will now tell you."

"Thank you John. Right, instead of 7.30 you will be called at 7.00 which will give you plenty of time until 8.00 to get bathed and ready, then breakfast followed by a last minute check to make sure we've got everything. The driver doesn't arrive until 9.30 so that should give us plenty of time, so it might be a good idea if we all get off to bed early as tomorrow is going to be a long day for all of us."

No more had to be said as we made our way to beds. It had been a long day and a good night's sleep wouldn't go amiss, but that was easier said than done. The excitement had built up so much that when you shut your eyes none of us could get to sleep. We talked for what seemed ages and one by one the conversations dropped off until all was silent. As I lay there my thoughts were to drift back to thinking of all the good times and none of the bad and how no one had come to see us off. There must have been a good reason why, but why didn't they telephone? I felt all alone in the world and for the first time since I had left home my shield dropped and I began to cry. Burying my face in my pillow so as not to let anyone hear, eventually falling of to sleep, but that night was too be a restless one and was glad of the appearance of John early the next morning.

"Right lads, 7 o'clock, no time to lay there so let's have you straight up and into the bathroom. Today's the big day and I want you all washed and dressed and packed by 8 o'clock in time for breakfast." Thinking I was the only one that had had a bad night, was wide awake, jumped out of bed to make my way to the bathroom, only to be stampeded by the others. They too had the same idea.

I managed to get there first and locked the door behind me, only to hear a tap at the door "Come on Tony, let me in – I'm busting for a piss." Peter's voice sounded desperate, so I let him in, "Thanks, mate you're a pal."

We were soon all washed and changed, and togged up in our best Sundays. All that was left to do now was to finish packing our bags, making sure everything we needed for our journey went into our hand luggage. All was done and we were ready for breakfast with still 20 minutes to go.

"You two finished already?"

"Yes John."

"So where are you bags" he asked. We both shrugged and said "upstairs

"Well, they're no good up there are they? You'd better go and get them, oh and before you go, take these labels with you, one for your case and the other on your hand luggage. Peter, you take these up to the boys. Tony you give these to the girls and mind you knock on the door first!" By this time the girls were all dressed and packed and their door was open.

"Here you go girls, one on your case the other for your hand luggage," then returned to my room to do mine.

Everybody was ready and one by one took our bags downstairs.

"Where shall we put these John?" I called out.

"Just stack them neatly by the front door."

The last case was placed in position and I returned to the room to see if anything had been left behind. First looking around the room, then went over to the window, and looked out onto the village which was slowly waking up to the day. We had only been here a week or so but it seemed longer. I had made new friends and of course, Linda, but like ships in the night it was time to move on. I would miss her, and always remember this place. As I turned and took a last look around, I said goodbye to the room, silly I know, but at that time it seemed the right thing to do. I then returned downstairs just in time for breakfast and for the last time we took our usual places. John entered the room, followed closely by the Rev. Collins.

"Good Morning, are we all ready then? This morning we have another guest at our table and I don't think an introduction is needed."

"Morning girls and boys," said the Reverend then took his seat alongside Margaret.

"Would you do the honours Sir" "Certainly it would be my pleasure"

We all bowed our heads: "God protect and keep these your children, O Lord, on their long journey and I pray that their new lives be long and happy ones, AMEN".

Breakfast was soon to be over, and today we were to get

away with the chores. Peter and I dismissed ourselves and went outside. It was not yet 9 o'clock so still had some time to wait. The sun, by now, was through and we had picked a fine day.

"Tony!" A voice cried out, it was Linda running towards me closely followed by a friend, reaching me all out of breath.

"Sorry I missed you last night, but we had to stay in."

She took me by the hand, "You will write to me won't you?"

"Yeah, course I will."

"And I'll try to find out if I can come to Australia with the next group OK?"

"Come on Lin," her friend called, "We'll be late for school."

"So what, I don't care."

Her friend walked ahead as Lin and I walked slowly together across the village green towards the school, still talking of our plans we had made a couple of nights before.

"I'd better go now – we're late already."

She said before Kissing me on the cheek, then just ran off, so returned to cottage to find Bill had already arrived.

"Hello boys, going to give me a hand with the bags then?"

"Yeah sure," and soon, the three of us had the bus all loaded.

"Well boys, I bet you're excited?"

"Yeah, I suppose so," I answered, but it was a hard question to answer.

We had waited so long for this moment and now just wanted to get going. At last, the time eventually came for us to board the bus. Mary gave us all a little hug and I shook John's hand.

"Thanks John, it's been great."

I always hated goodbyes and even after a week, this one was not easy as we climbed aboard, Peter and I naturally sat up front.

"All aboard for the skylark, airport here we come," said Bill as we slowly pulled away.

As we drove past the cottages and towards the main gate I looked around to take a last look, thinking what a clever man Barnardo had been to build a village here in the heart of Essex and the children in care had come from all over England to live out their childhood here. How lucky they had been to be given the opportunity and then to go from here with the largest family anyone could ever want before going out into the world - or so I thought.

Knoll Secondary Modern School

COPY

COPY   SCHOOL REPORT.

Name: BATES, Anthony Roy   Form: 4 L.

        SUMMER TERM, 1964.   No. in Form: 20.

Age: 14. 9.   Average age of Form: 15. 2.

Subject	Term	Exam	Pos'n	Comment of Subject - Master.	
Scripture	D+	28	13	Lacks concentration.	W. Jones
English	C-	60	10	He should take his work more seriously.	G.A.H.
Mathematics	D+	36	11	A fair effort has been made.	J.A.H.
General Science { Physics/Chemistry }	D	30	18	Fairly good on the whole.	R.B.
General Science Biology	D+	23%	16	Inattentive and untidy.	D.L.M.
Commerce	D	52	6	A satisfactory exam result.	R.J.
Geography	C	23	17	Could do better.	A.R.
History	C-	56	7	No real interest displayed.	W.J.M.D.
Music	D	18	16	Little work done.	B.W.
Art	C-	49	14	Can work quite well, but too easily distracted.	E.W.
Metalwork	C-	43	11	He shows little interest	D.V.
Woodwork	C	44	9	Satisfactory	P.L.
Technical Drawing	D+	44	11	Work has been of an erratic nature.	O.M.

Final Mark: 40.1.   Position in Form: 13th.

Comment of Master i/c Physical Education: Poor attitude - reflected in poor
                                             ability.   J.S.

Comment of Form Master: Progress has been marred by a poor attitude towards work.
If he were to take himself in hand I am sure his work
would show a distinct improvement.   G.A.Harman.

Comment of Head Master: He has not done too badly this year, but next year he must
remember that he will be one of the senior boys and I shall
expect him to be quite grown-up.
                               J.K.T.

Last School Report

Dr Barnardos Village Homes
Barkingside
Essex, England

CHAPTER 4

Our journey to the airport was to last about an hour with Bill taking us across London to Heathrow. We'd spent the last week walking back down through the path of time. The Tower of London, Big Ben, the Houses of Parliament, Piccadilly Circus, Leicester Square and so on. Nothing was left out, but that too was now all history and we were on our way. There was a certain silence in the bus which was hard to explain. I suppose this was a little like saying goodbye to an old and close friend, never to see him again and knowing that there was no turning back, so we were all paying our last respects in our own way, as this was where we'd spent our youth and remembering the good times as well as the bad, but there was also that terrible feeling of not knowing if any of us would ever come back.

We were soon to be on the outskirts of Heathrow and everyone started to liven up and could see in the distance planes taking off and landing simultaneously.

"Well, here we are you lot, Heathrow airport. Not long now, said Bill. Turning off the main road, shortly after coming to a tunnel where overhead in bold letters the words, 'WELCOME TO HEATHROW – GATEWAY TO THE WORLD'.

"Well this is it you lucky devils, wish I was coming with you too."

I somehow got the impression that Bill was more excited than the rest of us all put together. Coming out of the other side of the tunnel we made straight for the international terminal.

"Now listen carefully you lot," said the stern voice of Margaret, "this is a very busy place and we don't want to lose any of you – well, not just yet anyway, so first things first, when we come to a halt, only take your hand luggage. Bill will sort out the rest of your things. The next time you all see your cases will be in Australia. So if there's anything inside that you want it's too late now. We're to be met by the Press and other Barnardo's officials so stay together and behave yourselves that goes especially for you two."

Once again looking directly at me and Peter, making the others laugh. Arriving in the terminal, we slowly came to a halt, as Margaret had predicted a reception committee was there to greet us. No sooner were we out of the bus than the cameras started flashing, followed by pressmen asking all sorts of questions.

"Right now, keep altogether and no wandering of, Patrick

you follow up last and keep them all in order."

Trust her that was like giving Hitler the H bomb.

"Come on lads, get a move on," Pat said, giving us a gentle push. "Take no notice, Pete, it's gone to his head," and we carried on walking.

The Press, at this time, were still following, taking photographs and still asking questions like 'Were we excited, what were our names, ages and what we were going to do once we got to Australia'. We were soon to arrive at our destination and Qantas Airways check-in desk, only to find that our cases and Bill were already there. While Margaret and the others sorted out all the official papers, Bill put our cases on the scales to be weighed, tagged and gone from sight, it was now Bill's turn to say goodbye leaving us until last.

"Okay boys, this is it, look after yourselves and don't forget send us a postcard will ya?"

"Sure thing Bill and thanks for everything."

I shook his hand, followed by Peter.

"Yeah, be lucky mate, see ya around," and away he went taking one more glance and waving as he disappeared from sight.

Our flight was to be Q.F. 531 departing 12 noon, so with all tickets checked and all baggage gone, we made our way through to passport control.

"Right, stay together and follow me," called out Margaret, checking that Pat was still bringing up the rear.

This was as far as the officials went. Margaret quickly said her goodbyes to them as they inturn all wished us luck. One by one we went through passport control, Margaret was now on her own but then so were we, for this was no mans land and it was too late to turn back now. Once at the other side, she counted us all making sure none were left behind then we followed her to the departure lounge where you could eat, drink and buy numerous items of duty free – whatever took your fancy, if you could afford them that is.

"Now listen," Margaret said, as she took a seat, "you can all tell the time, so if you want to look around the shops you may, but I want you back here at 11.00 sharp or else."

Another word was not necessary as Peter and I were off like a shot, while all the time the loud speaker called flight numbers of destinations for all over the world. After a while we returned to the meeting place, more through lack of money than anything else, not that there was anything we wanted to buy apart from cigarettes and then they wouldn't serve us anyway.

"Ah, good, you're all back now" Margaret then took a final count " Wont be long now" no sooner said and it was time to hear what we'd all been waiting for.

"Would the passengers on flight Q.F. 531 to New York, San Francisco, Honolulu, and Sydney Australia, please go to Gate No. 7."

"That's us, are we all ready? – Well then let's go."

Our faces lit up as we followed Margaret down a long corridor, passing by all the different rooms giving their gate numbers finally to reach ours.

"Here we are, Gate No. 7."

We all followed her inside where some of the other passengers were already waiting. Margaret quickly showed our boarding cards to the man on the desk.

"Ah, you must be with the Barnardo group, we've been waiting for you. Theirs ten of you, I believe," looking up at the rest of us.

"That's right, Sir."

"Well, if you'd like to go through that doorway you can go straight on board, they're waiting for you."

This was good, the V.I.P. treatment. We followed a stewardess through the door and down a few steps which led down on the tarmac, there to be taken across to our plane. This was the moment we'd all been waiting for; at along last it was now time to board the aircraft. A Boeing 707 with a red line going from one end to the other and written above was 'Australian Overseas Airline QUANTAS' and high up on the red tail was a white kangaroo and written underneath were the words, 'Qantas V-Jet'. Reaching the plane, we climbed the stairs; I turned to take a last look.

"Come one Tony, let's get inside," said Peter pushing me on.

At the top we were met by an Air Hostess, "Welcome aboard boys, just follow, the Stewardess who will show you to your seats."

My eyes were all a goog as I took in the surroundings it was not unlike a large coach inside with seats either side of the aisle, but more compact and a lot larger. Following the others, we came upon our seats right at the rear of the plane in the rows of three. We piled in with Ken going first sat next to the window as he wanted to take photographs; Peter was in the middle leaving me on the aisle.

"We'll take it in turns at the window shall we" Peter said looking first at Ken and then at me, not that once you were up there was much to see.

"You boys alright?" enquired the Stewardess.

"Err, yes thanks Miss. She's a bit of alright, what do ya reckon Tony, nice arse?"

I was sure Peter was a twenty year old midget in disguise as his thoughts didn't do his age justice.

"Not bad, not bad at all," I replied watching her small round bum wiggle as she walked back up the aisle.

"Here Tony, look at all this lot," said Peter taking the magazine also examining the rest of the contents from the pocket in front of us. Ken and I quickly followed suit, apart from the magazine there was a menu of all the meals we were to receive between London and New York, a few novelties which included a kangaroo badge which I promptly pinned onto my jacket, and a book telling us all about the aircraft. Meanwhile, slowly but gradually the plane filled up until not a seat was left untaken and I wondered how on earth the plane would ever take off with all this weight. Finally the cabin crew were ordered to shut the doors and with the sound of them closing, I felt certain discomfort. 'It's too late to change your mind now Tony,' Pete muttered 'we're on our way'. Looking around, I tried to see Pat, but could only hear his voice. I needed to be reassured that everything was alright but it was too late, the steps had been moved and slowly we were being pushed backwards.

"We're moving Tony, we're moving."

"Yeah I know Pete, I can see."

Just then, the Stewardess came up, "Sweet boys?"

"Yes please," I said as she leant forward.

"Take a couple, have one just before we take off as sometimes the pressure as we get higher can hurt your ears."

"Thanks Miss."

We started to move forward and proceeded to the main runway.

"Good afternoon Ladies and Gentlemen, this is your Captain speaking. I would like to take the opportunity to welcome you aboard this Qantas Airways Boeing 707 bound for Sydney

Australia, stopping at New York, San Francisco, Honolulu, so sit back and enjoy your flight and if there's anything you require do not hesitate to ask one of the Stewardesses. Meanwhile, would you please fasten your seat belts and refrain from smoking. Cabin Crew safety drill please."

Then a couple of the Stewardesses stood in the aisle and pointed out the emergency exits, followed by life jacket instruction, including how to use the oxygen mask – very reassuring but I suppose necessary. Soon we came to a halt.

"Cabin Crew, stations please," came a voice over the loud speaker.

The engines started to get louder and louder, then like a shot from a gun, we tore down the runway, moving faster and faster, a slight bump, the nose was up and gradually we started to climb, all the time sucking my sweet furiously remembering what the Stewardess had said. Higher and higher we went, leaving what I could see of land, way behind, up into the clouds and the clear blue skies above. Finally we began to level off and the Cabin Crew left their seats making straight for the Galley and shortly after came around with the drinks trolley.

"Good afternoon Ladies and Gentlemen, for those of you who are interested, we shall be passing over the cliffs of Dover any minute ,our flight time to New York will be 8 hrs and we shall be climbing to an altitude of 35,000 feet with a cruising of speed of 600 mph, thankyou."

The seat belt sign went out so I leaned across to the window and looked down just as we passed over the cliffs and headed out to sea.

"Drinks boys" a voice came from behind.

"Oh yes please," noting the selection on the trolley, "three beers please."

The Stewardess laughed, "Don't you mean three cokes?"

We decided to settle for second best when a familiar voice came from the back, "You boys behaving your selves up there?"

"Yes Miss, Miss is it all right to leave our seats"?

"No, she almost shouted back "you'll be getting something to eat soon. Leaning across Pete, I took a last glance out of the window and could just see the coast line of England in the distance. It was a strange feeling, everything had happened so fast. Only a few weeks before I'd have jumped at the opportunity to be here, leaving everything behind I knew and loved. My mates – would I ever see them again? Bev, my girlfriend, who I swore to be faith full to, and a family that were glad to get rid of me

"Get off Tony, food's coming," Pete cried, waking me out of my day dream.

"Sorry mate, what's to eat?"

"Err lets see salad steak and potatoes, trifle for afters

One by one we all got served. Each course had its own little compartment, all neatly set out

Settling down to the serious business of eating, we cleared our trays.

And sat back and enjoyed being waited on.

"You know what we need now don't you, Pete?"

"Na, what's that?"

"A fag – I wonder if droopy drawers will notice"

Leaning forward I lit up, trying to disperse the smoke from going back in Margaret's direction.

"Quick Tony, give us a drag," I passed it over to

Unfortunately the smoke wasn't dispersing as quickly as we'd liked and soon the girls behind noticed.

"Quick, give it back here, you get caught and we'll all get a bollocking. Me, I'm 15 so it make's no difference."

After a few puffs each I put it out not wanting the girls to drop us in it, also couple of passengers opposite were giving us funny looks so decided put it out and get rid of the evidence in the toilet.

Getting up, I looked around and noticed it was at the back, probably why we'd been conveniently seated here, out of harms way, close to the amenities also not to upset the rest of the passengers. The toilets inside were no bigger than a cupboard and once inside couldn't help noticing all the perfumes not to mention the aftershave which couldn't resist trying, splashing on some Old Spice before returning to my seat.

"Phew, what's that horrible smell?" peter asked

"Old Spice aftershave you like it?"

"You smell like a fucking chemist shop – so where'd you get it from?"

"In the bog there's loads of it in there"

Pete couldn't resist the temptation and had to try some for himself but on his return had gone overboard a little, trying on a bit of everything in sight.

"Good in there ain't it, Tony?"

He only had to move and it left an aroma you couldn't help but notice, everybody looking around wondering where this strange but nice smell was coming from eventually getting back to Margaret.

"What's that awful smell?"

"It's Peter, Miss, he's got perfume on."

Trust the girls to let the cat out of the bag, dropping us both in it.

"What are you boys up to now?"

"Nothing Miss, just trying out some aftershave."

By now, the back end of the plane smelt like a beauty parlour and as Peter made for the toilet to wash it of everyone in sight was in hysterics, and still laughing when he returned five minutes later, he smelt a lot better but the aroma was still very noticeable.

"I can't leave you three for five minutes and you're up to something, now settle down or else," Margaret threatened before returning to her seat

Pat, James and Archie played cards. The girls had befriended a couple with a baby so were in their element. Peter, Ken and me decided to become apprentice stewards and were allowed to hand out magazines and answer the call buttons. It all helped to pass the time away plus it kept us out of trouble. Although at first, the time went quickly, soon it started to drag and apart from getting the three meals they dished up you soon ran out of things to do, finally to hear what we'd all been waiting for.

"Good Afternoon, Ladies and Gentlemen, this is your Captain speaking, we have just started to descend and we will be arriving at Kennedy Airport in approximately 30 minutes. On our approach, we shall be coming over New York and if you look to your left you will see the statue of Liberty. The visibility is clear and the temperature on the ground is 61 degrees, and the local time is now 2.10 pm, and on behalf of myself and my crew, I hope you had a pleasant flight for those of you travelling on Qantas airways, have a safe journey Thankyou."

Descending through the clouds, we could only see water. The seat belt sign was on and the Stewardess came around to check that they were all fastened properly as we went in flying straight over the top of New York, looking down I could see the Statue of Liberty out in the middle of the harbour, the huge tower blocks were truly a magnificent sight, and after circling round, started to descend into Kennedy airport.

"Cabin Crew your stations please," and so we landed on the first leg of our long journey.

Our stopover in New York was short lived and apart from the American accent on the loud speakers, it was not unlike Heathrow. We'd no sooner had a drink and a quick look around than we were being called back on board in our seats. The plane doors were shut, sweets came round, safety demonstration, also to be welcomed on board by our new Captain Carlyle Richardson and crew. Soon after to all take their positions and were off once again. By now we were all feeling a bit tired. It had been a long day although here in New York it was mid afternoon, but back in London it was nearly 10 p.m., unfortunately sleeping was easier said than done.

Our flying time to San Francisco was about 7 hours so after eating and drinking whatever was put in front of us, generally making pigs of ourselves, we tried to get some sleep with little or no success. So Pete and I made a general nuisance of ourselves again helping the Stewardess. Time went much slower this time around. Finally, after more drink, another meal and what must have been only an hour's sleep, we made a final approach to L.A. International Airport, arriving at 6.50pm local time. By now we had been travelling nearly 17 hours and this was only halfway. We were all tired and getting a bit niggled and after landing were glad to get off the plane. Our stopover was short lived, 1 hour, 10 minutes, during which time we were given a little V.I.P. treatment by way of cold drinks and souvenirs which none of us really wanted but had anyway. The only one bit of excitement was when Ken, on helping himself to a drink from the waiter, sent the whole lot flying and apart from one very red faced waiter, there was coke everywhere which struck us as funny at the time. The hour went quickly and was soon summoned back to the plane. What at first was a novelty we now dreaded and knew the procedure inside out? Another new Captain, this time it was Bunny Lee. He and his crew would only be with us as far as Honolulu. Our flying time was to be only 5 hours, 20 minutes. This time, apart from pointing out the Golden Gate Bridge, soon after take off which I only just managed to get a quick glimpse at, it was your average flight, managing also to get a little more sleep. The best part of the flight was the Captain telling us we were soon to land arriving at 10.00 p.m. local time, still having to put our watches back. Funny when you thought about it, we'd been travelling for over 24hrs yet it was still Wednesday. Landing at night made us unfortunately miss out on what was to have been a picturesque view but by this time only interested in one view, the final one. We were no sooner off the plane than it was refuelled and we were back on board, all within an hour at the most.

Next stop Sydney, the longest haul on the journey 10hrs plus a new Captain and crew. This time it was Jack Bale, an Australian. Our estimated time of arrival was 8, 30 am local time but this flight it was to be different. We'd be flying over the International Date Line losing a day so instead of Thursday, we arrived on Friday. The flight was to be much the same we had the meals, played cards, noughts and crosses, eye spy, anything to pass the time. The girls occupied themselves playing with a couple of the younger children Pat and the brothers slept most of the time. The worst of the journey was over or so I thought, suddenly we hit turbulence which bounced us around like a cork in a bath, giving everybody the frights. Apparently, according to the Captain we'd hit an electrical storm, the seat belt sign came on and he told us it was nothing to worry about. On lifting the shades I wasn't so sure. It was bad enough when there's a storm on the ground, but up in the air it was horrifying. Closing the blind, I said a quiet prayer. I wasn't religious, but every little bit of help counts.

It was like a living hell and at one stage that's where I thought we were to go. Peter held on tight to my jacket and froze to the seat. It had been the first time I'd seen him show any sort of feeling even if it was fear. I too, like the others, was frightened shitless but tried to hide my fear so to give my newly found friend, a little reassurance. The next hour for all of us was hell not knowing what was to the final outcome. Finally we left the storm behind us, all sighing with relief and laughing it off, but underneath knew it wasn't an experience we'd want to go through again. The moment of truth arrived with the sound of the captain.

"Good Morning Ladies and Gentlemen, I do hope you didn't find the last hour too uncomfortable. Unfortunately due to technical difficulties we will shortly be landing in Fiji for minor repairs and are presently on our descent, so would you please keep your seat belt is fastened and kindly refrain from smoking Thankyou?"

"What do you think he means by technical difficulties

Tony?"

"Don't know, probably got something to do with the storm."

Slowly we started to descend, as Ken tried to answer the question.

"They wouldn't tell you if it was serious anyway."

That didn't help much it only put Peter and myself a little on edge. Slowly still descending, "Cabin Crew your stations please," looking out I could see the lights of the city of Suva and with baited breath waited for the wheels to touch down. First the rear ones, then the nose wheel speeding along the runway, gradually slowing down and finally to a halt. It was quite a moment for all of us as the passengers began to clap and cheer and it was good to know we weren't alone. Seemed like everyone had the same thoughts for the Captain and crew it was probably an everyday occurrence, but for us a once in a lifetime event as slowly we made our way to the terminal.

"Would all passengers stay in their seats and wait until the aircraft has come to a stand still. Stow all hand luggage in the overhead lockers, taking all valuables with you when you disembark, thankyou."

By now, after travelling for more than 30 hours, I felt how I looked. My nice new suit was all crumpled up, not only looked like, but had been to sleep in. I was tired and also hungry, fed up with the taste of pre-packed food and longed for something decent like a bacon sandwich. We soon came to a halt and the doors opened. Margaret was up keeping her usual watchful eye on us.

"Sit still you lot, wait until the other passengers are off first."

As usual we would be the last off, following the others; we reached the door and stepped outside. The warm night air just hit me.

"Keep together now."

Following the crowd, we made for the transit terminal. At first the heat made it almost hard to breathe, but were soon inside where the temperature was completely reversed by the air conditioning. Like the mother hen, Margaret counted her chicks once again. By now, she too, was looking a little harassed.

"Right this way, Pat you follow last. Let's try and get you all something to eat."

We followed her to a snack bar of sorts, where after a short discussion with the counter staff, resulted in nine of the largest scrambled egg sandwiches you ever did see. They must have been two inches thick with ice cold milk to wash it down with. Not that there wasn't plenty to eat on the plane, but after a while it all seemed to taste the same. This, for us, was a real treat. Apart from us all being asleep that was probably the quietest time Margaret had the pleasure of, but not for long. Soon we'd finished and were re-energised and raring to go.

"Attention, Qantas Airways, would like to announce the further delay of Q.F. 531 to Sydney Australia which will now be departing at 07.30 hours. We are sorry for the delay and for any inconvenience caused. If there is any change we will notify you accordingly, thankyou."

"Well, that means us, so if you want to go and have a look around you may but stay together. Now you might go and have a look at the tropical gardens, they're well worth seeing but I want you all back here by 6.30, understood?"

"Yes Miss."

At first, altogether, Peter, Ken and I managed to lose the rest of the group and went on our own tour. There wasn't much to see inside, so we made straight for the tropical garden. The heat nearly knocked us over as soon as we went outside. The gardens were a rare sight for us, our first view of tropical life with its tall palms and plants of all shapes and sizes. In the centre a pond with tropical birds, pink flamingos and the whole place was floodlit to give a special effect. Looking through the fence which surrounded it, I could see our plane being loaded, accidentally finding a gate that was not locked.

"Ere, Pete, Ken, have a look at this," both of them coming straight over I pointed it out, "Come on there's no one about, how's about we go for a walk."

"What about the plane how are we going to hear if there's a flight change?"Ken asked

"Na, we'll keep it in sight all the time, it's only over there look. Anyway we've got plenty of time it's not leaving until 7.30."

"Okay then, I'll come, but no messing about."

Making sure the coast was clear we made our way through, closing it gently behind us.

"Come on quick," I called, "before anyone sees us."

Making a hasty exit, we started our tour of Nandi Airport,

all the time keeping our plane in view, all the time getting further and further away not realising the distance we had covered

"Hey, look over there."Pete pointed across to some aircraft hangers.

So we went to investigate, on finding one of the huge sliding door was open ajar, we went in. It was a workshop of some sort and inside was a plane, not unlike ours, being repaired?

"Here Ken, Tony, have a look at these will ya."Pete shouted

He had found some pictures stuck up on the wall of oriental nude women, posing showing off the different assets of their bodies. It was worth the risk – just to find the workmen's art gallery and Pete jumped up on the bench to get a closer look

"Look at the fucking knockers on her, mate."He shouted pointing to one

Too busy admiring our lucky find, we didn't hear anyone approach us from behind and were all stunned to hear a voice. Turning quickly at the strange language, to find two men who were obviously very curious to where we'd come from. Then the second man spoke in broken English.

"What you doing here in?"

"Err, yeah, sorry mate we sort of got lost," I said.

Peter at this time was still standing high up on the bench and the two guys looking up at him could see the funny side and started to laugh, talking in their own language. Pete quickly jumped down.

"We're for it now Tony, let's make a run for it."

"Don't be daft you two, that'll only make it worse."

Ken was right, still laughing; one of them walked over to the phone and after a short conversation, turned.

"One of you named Tony Bates?"

"Yeah, that's me."

"You all in big trouble – look for you everywhere, Plane waiting for you."

"I said we should have turned back, now we're in for it," moaned Ken. . The stranger returned from the phone.

"Car come and takes you to plane so you wait hear, yes?"

We had no choice; we'd been caught red handed and were in for a tongue lashing when we got back.

"Don't worry," I said trying to find a good side, "it's not as if we've done anything wrong. It'll all be forgotten by the time we reach Australia."

"Yeah, you're right Tony, don't worry Ken."

We waited patiently for our lift with our two escorts and on its arrival were whisked quickly back to the plane. Briskly we jumped from the jeep.

"Thanks for the ride boys," we shouted and boarded the plane, only to be greeted at the top of the steps by Margaret on arrival.

"I'll see you three later; now get back to your seats."

The passengers could see the funny side of it, but Margaret was red with embarrassment and almost foaming at the mouth. The door shut and we were all strapped in ready for take off.

"Good Morning Ladies and Gentlemen, this is your Captain speaking, we're sorry for the delay, aren't we boys, we should be taking off in the next five minutes or so, our flying time to Sydney is 3.45 and we hope to make some of the lost time up. Fasten your seat belts and extinguish all cigarettes, cabin crew, stations please."

With that we were off again. Next stop Australia and the end of our journey. Soon after take off as usual, first drinks then a meal came round and after that was cleared away everything was back to normal apart from being ordered not to leave our seats. Then we were struck by a bit of luck. The Captain had sent a Stewardess to ask if we'd all like to go up into the cockpit two at a time. Hesitatingly, Peter and I were allowed to go first which the others felt was a bit unfair, but we were sitting up front. Following the Stewardess closely up into the cockpit, into an opened doorway we marched in to find the Captain the Co Pilot and three others.

"Oh, not you two again," the captain said, "Come to highjack the plane have we" his crew all started laughing.

"Here ya go Jack; I'll grab a coffee so to give the lads a little room. Here you go son, sit here."

Peter sat down on what was the Radio Officers seat, "And don't touch anything Peter."

We then got the third degree from the Captain.

"So what happened? Where did you all get to after all that?"So I told him,

"Oh we got bored and went for a walk, just forgot about the time," I said while Peter looked around in total disbelief.

"I should think you did – your Governess was nearly going out of her mind, poor old cow. Bet she gave you a right bulling off."

"Na not really."

"Well let me tell you a bit about the plane, and then you can ask questions okay? As you've probably gathered, I'm Captain Jack and including me there are five flight crew members, and the plane you're flying in is a Boeing 707 138B. There are only 13 in service. This one was built in 1961 and has a cruising speed of 600 mph at a maximum altitude of 42,000 ft in Pilot's talk, that is at mark 888 speed 511 knots and has a range of 4,4000 nautical miles, carries 6 cabin crew and 104 passengers, 84 economy and 20 first class. It has a wing span of 130 feet 10 inches with a 35 degree Cantilever sweep. Her length is 135 feet, height 41 feet 8 inches and her four engines are Pratt and Whitney JT 30-1 turbo fans each giving a 17, 5000 thrust. Well I think that just about covers it. Any questions"

He went through the list like the manual was right in front of him, Peter still sat in his seat looking all round, "What's all these switches for? He asked.

"Well that's a hard one, it'll take me all day to go through them, let's just say every one serves a purpose, okay? Well so how you do like flying, I expect you've had enough by now?"

Peter pulled a face, "It's boring, there's nothing to do, just eat and sleep."

"Well, it won't be long now, only a couple of hours so you'd better go now so as to give the others a chance to come up."

Peter made for the door, "Thanks mate, thanks a lot."

"That's alright boys, ow and good luck," we then made our exit and returned to my seats.

"Took your time didn't you?" Big brother was on the offensive.

"Sorry Pat got carried away with the time."

"You're always sorry – no consideration for anyone but yourself."

"Ahh, take no notice Tony, he's only jealous coz he's not a star like us. He'll get over it," and like a bear with a sore head he followed Archie to take his turn in the cockpit

"Don't wind him up for fuck sake Pete; he's bad enough without your help, come on, let's go and see if there's any help we can give," and did so by answering the call buttons for the Stewardess.

"Yes Sir."

"Any chance of a cold beer Son" asked this elderly block

"Yes Sir, coming up straight away," returning within minutes.

"Thank you Son, you're doing a fine job son so where you from then"

"England."

"I can tell that, but what part?"

"Place called Brighton down on the South Coast."

"Oh yes, know it well," and what started as a question turned into a conversation.

"The name's Tom Skillman and yours?"

"I'm Tony Bates."

"Pleased to meet you Tony and we shook hands, "will you join me for a drink

"No thanks, any more and it'll be coming out of my ears."

Compared to me, Tom was a giant of a man, broad – must have been over 6 ft, in his late forties, slightly receding in the front but distinguished looking and also noticed he had hands the size of dinner plates.

"So what are you going to do in Australia Tony?"

"Well I hope to be going to the Merchant Navy soon after I arrive."

"Sounds like a good life," he answered showing a great deal of interest and we talked for about half an hour about this and that. All the time he listened with care to my every word and made me feel totally at ease.

"Well Tony, it's been very interesting talking to you, perhaps when you settle in you might give me a call, perhaps we, that is you, your brother and myself could have dinner one day – my treat. Here's my card, just give me a call. You'd better write your guardian's name and address down so as to check with them first."

Doing so, I just wrote my name and Dr Barnardo's, Sydney.

"Thankyou Tony, I do hope we meet again," leaving my seat, I shook his hand.

"Thanks Tom, nice to meet you."

"Likewise I'm sure," Then I rushed back to my seat.

"Where you been?" enquired Peter, "I've been looking for you everywhere."

"Well, you didn't look far; I was only sitting up there in the First Class." Then told Peter about the stranger and his invitation, showing him his card.

"Not a brown hatter is he?"What'd mean "you know queer?"

"No, he seems genuine enough, even said he'd get in touch with Barnardo's in Sydney."

"Says here he's a building engineer of some sort you never know might be a chance of a, job don't hurt to have more than one iron in the fire do it". Our conversation was then interrupted by the news we'd all been waiting for.

"Good Morning Ladies and Gentlemen, we shall shortly be descending into Mascot, Sydney's International Airport. Our estimated time of arrival is 9.30 a.m., with an outside ground temperature of 74degs. We hope you had a pleasant flight and on behalf of myself and my crew look forward to travelling with you in the near future. Thank you for travailing with Qantas airways"

The seat belt sign came on for the last time, as slowly the plane descending through the clouds and could see land in the distance, bringing us closer until I could see Sydney Harbour Bridge. We'd made it at last, we were finally here.

"Cabin crew your stations please."

Dr. Barnardo's in Australia

Annual Report for 1965=1966

Heathrow Airport 1965

PASSENGER STRAYED IN FIJI

Losing three children in the exciting airport gardens at Fiji was the only untoward moment for Australian social worker Miss Margaret Granowski during a 32 - hour flight from London with nine children emigrating through Dr Barnardo's Homes.

Miss Granowski arrived with her charges by Quantas on Friday.

She said the flight was an experiment but had proved so successful she felt it would be repeated. The children enjoyed themselves, and apart from the three older ones who were captivated by the beautiful flare-lit gardens at Nandi Airport and wandered away from the main party, there were no incidents.

The Group arriving at Mascot Airport Sydney

CHAPTER 5

After nearly two days travelling, feeling tired and slightly uncomfortable having to wear the same clothes the whole period, we finally touched down for the last time. We were here at last – Sydney International airport (Mascot). All buzzing with excitement and enthusiasm, we couldn't wait to; once and for all leave this plane for good as slowly we taxied to the disembarkation area, finally to come to a halt. We could see from the window a crowd of onlookers waving in our direction, probably relatives of the other passengers, also photographers presumably awaiting our arrival. Finally the steps were brought to the plane and the doors opened.

"Right now you lot, stay in your seats and let all the other passengers get off first."

Margaret was up and once again in full control as we watched out of the window at the cameras flashing. It was obvious we were not the only celebrities on board, as a large man descended the stairs complete with bushy beard and a skull cap, obviously a religious man of some sort. I didn't take much notice. Finally it was our turn.

"Right, without too much fuss, take your bags from the overhead lockers and slowly make your way to the exit."

Pat and Archie led the way, followed closely by Peter, me, Ken and Anita and so on, with Margaret checking we'd left nothing behind and bringing up the rear. We reached the exit and there waiting to say goodbye was our hostess.

"Well boys, here you are good luck. Don't go and get lost again will you?"

By now it must have been a standing joke with all the crew. I pecked one of the hostesses on the cheek as I said, "Thanks a lot it's been a pleasure having us."

They laughed and in turn, wished us luck. I followed Peter out on to the stairwell, when almost immediately the cameras began to flash. There was no time to think of anything else. Just savour the moment and enjoy all the attention.

"Right lads, that's far enough, stay where you are, we'd like to take a shot of you all coming down the stairs, smile... give a little wave... ready?... That's it... hold it... one more. Right now, let's have you all down here with the plane in the background. Yes, that's great... hold it... one more... this time again with a wave."

Then the questions began to come. Margaret, by this time, had met up with some of our welcoming committee who were obviously Dr Barnardo's' Officials, and soon after one of them took control and was later to find out that he was Mr Price, the Manager of Dr Barnardo's, Australia.

He herded us off in the direction of the main arrival terminal, followed closely by the press and the rest of our welcoming committee. Margaret had by now been relieved of her command and after saying her goodbyes to us, she officially handed us over to Mr Price.

"Right, stay together you lot while we make our way to passport control. Okay, nine faces and nine names, so let's see who's who. Now the Hill family, Archie, James, Kathryn and Irene, make your way to the front. Good now the Hutton family, Ken and Anita, Peter Lewis and last but not least the Bates boys. Now stay in that order while we go through passport control and customs. We finally arrived in the main lounge to be met by the rest of the welcoming committee where we exchanged introductions and then were asked to make our way to the Press lounge, where once again we were to be interviewed, we following Tom Price into a large room where more Press were waiting to ask more questions. We were no sooner inside and had shut the door when a head popped around the door – "Mr Price." He walked over and exchanged a few words, then turned, "Kenneth and Anita Hutton." We all turned and looked.

"Yes Sir." Ken spoke out

"Will you go with this gentleman; I believe your foster parents are here to meet you."

There were no chances of goodbyes, Ken just turned and smiled, taking Anita by the hand and led her through the door and closed it behind them. The sound of that door closing, awoke the reality that our little family was slowly breaking up. What was my destiny to be? Where were Pat and I to go? Were we to stay together? My line of thought was broken by the Press Officer.

"Ah, good, you're here. I presume you've all met our other celebrity," looking towards the corner surrounded by cameras and reporters. We all looked bewildered. There he was again, the tall stout man with the beard skull cap.

"No? Well, we must remedy that," and on approaching the tall, but weird looking man, introduced us.

"Ladies and Gentlemen, this is Shlomo Carlebach the

singing Rabbi."

He smiled and one by one shook our hands, speaking in a somewhat broken form of English.

"I think this call's for a group picture," and we were placed strategically around him while he strummed his guitar.

"That's It lovely"... click... "One more for luck"

None of us had ever heard of him before, but if our photograph was going to make him famous who were we to mind!

After the picture was taken, he placed his hand upon each of our heads and mumbled something in Hebrew, then left. Now it was our turn again. First of all they wanted to know which 3 of us had gone astray in Honolulu. Peter and I stepped forward.

"And where's the third one?"

I answered quietly, "Him and his sister have already gone. His name was Ken Hutton and it was Fiji mate"

"Sorry my mistake, and what's your name Son?"

"Oh I'm Tony Bates and this here is Peter Lewis."

"So you're the three – what made you do it?"

"Do what?"

"Go off like that – weren't you scared?"

"I suppose we got carried away with the sights."

"You're lucky; the plane apparently nearly left without you." he commented

We just laughed, with Peter saying, "Seemed like a nice enough place to spend a few days," which brought large grins to a number of reporters faces. It was then he started to ask the same old question with us giving same old answers.

Finally the press conference was over and we followed Mr Price back out into the arrival lounge there to find our cases all ready for the off, also some new faces. Mr Price took from a folder from his briefcase.

"Right, now who's going where? The Hill family, you'll be going to Normanhurst, the boys to Ladd House, the girls to Fairfax House, don't worry they're both in the same grounds so you won't be split up, this gentleman here is Mr Elms. You will be in his care."

The introductions were made and soon it was time to say our goodbyes which again were short and to the point, soon to depart leaving just the three of us. At least Peter and I would be together or so I thought. We had grown to become good mates and it would be silly to split us up now that we made some sort of bond. Something my brother Pat and I had never had. Mr Price's voice brought our plans tumbling down.

"Peter, you'll be going to Karinlal House Lindfield, this is Miss Bickmore, and you will be in her care."

The shock hit me like a brick as it did Peter. Why were they doing this to us? Couldn't they see we had been inseparable and that for the past week or so we had grown to lean on each other, both sharing our most inner thoughts like Siamese twins, we were meant to be. Not to look upset over my friends' departure, I put on a brave face, as did Peter. Couldn't they see the lump in my throat and the tears in the corner of my eyes as we shook hands, or didn't they really care? Were we to them just cattle to be herded from one paddock to another? Only to be counted daily to see if we were still there. Who knows? Only they, in their wisdom could answer that. As I watched him slowly walk away he turned, as if to take one last look, raising his hand holding up his thumb. My insides crumbled and built up like the lava in a volcano. Not wanting anyone to see my feelings I fought back the increasing rock at the back of my throat. After all, we were both men and it wasn't natural for one man to feel this way about another. Maybe it was just the fear of having to start all over again. Somehow it seemed that all my life, the things that I had grown most fond of were taken away from me and on starting a new life, I thought that was all in the past, but now to travel half way round the world and it was here again. Eventually Peter and his escort turned the corner and disappeared form sight and off he went to his new destiny. What was mine to be? I thought, and looked at Pat for that older brother security. It had never been there before so why did I look now.

"Tony and Patrick, I'd like you to meet Nat Smith and his wife. For the next few days you will be staying with them at Rickard House, West Ryde. Final arrangements have to be made as to where you will be going."

I shook Nat's hand.

"Good'day Tony, welcome to Australia, you'll like it with us, proper home from home."

That was all I needed! Nat was a tall, slim built man with a large round face, well tanned with short but smart black hair swept back. Hilda put out her hand to greet me. She could see I was a little unsure and tried to comfort me with her words.

"Hello Tony, things will look a lot better once you've

changed your cloths and got some hot food into you."

Like Nat she was tall, with a fine figure to match her complexion which was fair, as was her long flowing hair. Nat took our cases and we said our goodbyes to Mr Price and Co and left following Nat and Hilda out of the Airport across the road and into the car park.

"Well, here we are boys," he said standing alongside what seemed to me to be the longest car I had ever seen in my life a Ford Falcon Station Wagon.

"Let's get these bags in the back and make tracks," Nat said unlocking the car and loading the bags in the back.

"Would you like to sit up front with me Pat?"

"Oh yeah"

That was typical of him, only been here five minutes and already he's talking like an Australian. I got in the back with Hilda and was amazed by the amount of room; you could have sat two more with comfort in the back with us. No sooner were we in than we were off.

"Well boys, sit back and enjoy the scenery takes about 45 minutes to get to Ryde, that's on a good day, so why not take in the view. It's definitely like nothing you've ever seen before. Here you can see the sky above the rooftops, and smell that fresh air?"

I looked out of the window anxiously, my face nearly pressed to the window trying to hide my disappointment.

"Did ya have a good trip?"

Pat replied almost immediately, going into every little detail. He and Nat were getting on like a house on fire. Then a soft voice spoke, "and how was your trip Tony?" I turned to face her. Her voice was one of kindness and just wanted her to hold out her arms and take me in. I needed something or someone to reassure me, to tell me everything was okay, but deep down I knew that it was not possible. We talked of the trip and some of the things Peter, Ken and I had got up to during our stay together in Barkingside and on the flight across. They were good times and I was never to forget them and some day I made a promise to myself we would all meet again to find out where life's highways had led us all to and to what avail.

"Well, here we are folks – West Ryde your home for the next few days."

It was not unlike the rest of the journey with clean streets, lined with old and new bungalows on unusually large plots of land. It all looked so perfect, what more could a man want, but somehow something was missing.

"This is our local shopping centre Nat pointed out, "then it's on Marlow Avenue, No. 21 and home."

No sooner said, than we pulled up a steep driveway with two garages.

"Right boys, we'll leave the bags till later, let's get in and have a cup of tea and meet some of the others."

Rickard House was an unusually large bungalow on a corner plot. In the front, a well kept garden of flowers and shrubs, and around the back it was all lawn apart from a rockery in the far corner and the whole place was surrounded by a white picket fence. We were no sooner up the steps when the front door opened.

"Hi Uncle Nat"

"Hello John, these are the Bates' boys, Pat and Tony."

John was about 14 at that time the oldest at Rickard. He was one of about eight children that lived here, all of school age ranging down to the age of about 9.

"Ah, that's good, now you're here you can help the boys with their bags, put them in your room for the time being, we'll sort them out later. When you've done that, give them a quick tour then back to the kitchen for lunch."

Following John closely, we took the cases from the car and returned to the house. All the time John asked questions. How old? where you from, all the usual things. He was nice enough, about the same height as me, but a lot thinner in his features. He, like us, had come from England, a few years previously, only he came by boat.

"Here we are this is our room. Just put your bags anywhere, you can sort them out later," and proceeded to give us the tour, bathrooms, toilets, etc., lounge, dining room, T.V. room, and on to the kitchen. Nat rose from his chair.

"Ah, good, just in time – this is Judy, our cook."

She was a short, plump woman who obviously tried out her delicacies before passing them on.

"Hi, I'm Pat and this is my younger brother Tony."

"Nice to meet you boys, anything you don't like, tell me, waste not want not is my motto."

"Oh you don't have to worry about us two, we'll eat

anything."

Pat made the most of it. He was much older which gave him an edge and was used to living away for long periods at a time.

"Come and meet some of the others."

Hilda took us out into the back garden, she clapped her hands.

"Children, I'd like you to say hello to Tony and Pat. They will be staying with us for a couple of days."

Being so young they were not of much interest to me, but returned with a polite "Hello". All the time nagging at the back of my mind was the phrase "staying for just a couple of days." Returning back to the kitchen for the first time since I'd arrived, I spoke a full sentence.

"Nat Do you mind if I ask a question?"

"No, not at all, that's what I'm here for Son."

Looking at Pat then staring Nat straight in the eyes I said, "all I keep hearing is a couple of days' so what then? What is to become of us?"

Not taking my eyes off Nat, he turned to Hilda, then back to me. The silence could have been cut with a knife. His answer was not immediate, and knew then that something wrong.

"Well, err, you being the age you are, they're not too sure whether to send you back to school or to the training farm, whichever suits you best." and then came the final crunch.

"And Pat, what's he to do?"

Pat looked on in surprise wondering how I could ask these questions.

"Well, being 18, he will be found accommodation until it's time for him to join the Air Force, maybe at the same time you can make your application for the Royal Navy. No time like the present. How about I'll take you into the city on Monday to apply" He said trying to change the subject

I'd put him in a spot and was making him answer questions he did not want to.

"So what you're saying is after a few days we'll be split up."

Pat wasn't much but he was all I had and a half brother was better than none at all. Nat was stuck for words, uneasy to say the least. I got the feeling of 'now we've got you here, what the hell are we going to do with you.' Pat broke the ice.

"Don't worry kid, they won't split us up, we'll be okay."
Good words, but they lacked confidence.

"Come on boys, tomorrow's another day, is that lunch ready Judy? Hilda was trying to change the subject.

"We're having a barbecue tommorrow. Have you ever been to one Tony?"

I looked into Hilda's eyes and all of a sudden the lump in my throat burst and the tears ran slowly down my face, as much as I wanted to control it, it was no good. Because of the enthusiasm of a 15yr old boy, thinking he knows what's best, Fred and Mavis given the opportunity to pass on their burden of a lifetime, signed me away like you'd strike a match, sending me half way around the world, and now be separated from my only relative in the southern hemisphere, was just too much to bear. Had I really done something so dreadful to get such a punishment? I turned and made my way back to our room, throwing myself onto a bed and broke down, finally crying myself to sleep and so it was my first day in Australia was one of disillusion to say the least. A few efforts were made to bring me round, but without success. I was stubborn and wanted to get my point across. My cries for help were not heard and in the end I was only hurting myself. What was done was done. So I would have to make the most of it and try to accept my fate.

Staying in bed until the following morning, I eventually got up, moping around for the whole day like a bear with a sore head. They left me alone to get over my problem staying in my room most of the time, only getting up for meals, the rest of the time I slept as the jetlag had caught up with me so there I stayed. I was woken by the sound of birds singing and the sun shining in through the gap in the curtains. It was Sunday; already things didn't look so grim. They couldn't get worse, only better so it was time to stop feeling sorry for myself. If the game was to survive, I would learn to play and play it well. I got out of my bed, slipping on my dressing gown and made my way to the door, passing Pat on one side, John on the other, still deep in the land of nod, and made my way quietly to the kitchen.

"Morning Tony, how are you feeling?"

Judy's face was a friendly one and a delight to meet first thing in the morning.

"Cup of tea"

"Yes thanks, love one."

"You sit down and I'll get us both a cup."

It was early and the rest of the house was still asleep as we sat there listening to the dawn chorus together, drinking our tea. We talked not about anything significant, just general chit chat. It was good; she made me feel at ease.

"Morning Tony, sleep well?"

"Yes thanks," Nat was the first to rise, followed closely by Hilda.

"You're up early, are you feeling better today?"

Feeling a bit silly at making a fool of myself I smiled, "Sorry about yesterday."

"No explanation needed Son, being in your place, I think I'd have felt the same."

Nat's answer made me feel a lot better. They were good people at the end of a long line of pen pushers. Their job was to try and put right everyone else's mistakes. Here the numbers stopped and you once again became a person. One by one the rest of the household emerged on the scene. John followed by Pat the last to arise.

"Morning all, sleep well brov?"

Pat took his seat alongside me, showing his concern."

"You missed a great feed last night Son."

"Not to worry Tony, we'll have another barbecue tomorrow."

The young ones' faces lit up at Nat's suggestion. He was trying very hard to please. The young ones, just like in Barkingside all had their separate jobs. Breakfast that day consisted of Skippy's, the Australian answer to corn flakes, boiled eggs and toast Tea or coffee for the older ones. An average daily breakfast, but somehow it all tasted different to what I was used to. Still a lot of things would be different now. Breakfast was over and the table cleared away.

"Right, now you young ones, get ready for Church."

I looked on in surprise.

"It's alright don't panic," Nat said smiling, "it's optional in this house. Since it's a nice day how would you like to see some of the sights? We'll take a drive into the city and if there's time, we'll take a look at Bondi."

The little ones pulled faces, not wanting to miss out on anything.

"You've seen it all before, now off you go and get yourselves ready for church".

Hilda went off with the youngsters, me and Pat; John went of in the car to see the sights. This time I was the one in the front, so had a scenic view.

"Right, we'll head off much the same way as we came on Friday."

Nat and John pointed out places of interest as I looked on – the budding tourist. We'd been driving about 30 minutes when I got a full view of the bridge.

"Well, there she is, won't be long now. This will interest you Tony. Down there is where all the Merchant ships come in. With a bit of luck it won't be long before you're coming in and out of there yourself."

I looked in detail with great interest. A seaman was what I wanted to be and it felt good, Nat talking as if it was only a matter of time.

"Well, here you go, Sydney Harbour Bridge, a spectacular sight even if I do say so myself."

He was right, like nothing I'd ever seen before. Unlike our Tower Bridge but spectacular just the same. Once on the bridge we could see for miles around.

"That's circular quay down there, from where you can go by ferry to a number of destinations. I think we've got time, fancy a ride."

No words were necessary; the look on our faces was enough.

"Right, that's settled; soon as we get across we'll go around and come back."

"So what's down there then?" I asked

Nearing the end of the bridge on the North shore I could see an amusement park with a large clowns head towering overhead.

"Oh, that's Luna Park, and over there to the left a little, they're building our very own Opera House. Well, that's the plan anyway."

We soon came to the end of the bridge. Nat paid the toll and we were soon moving off into some back streets which branched out under the end of the bridge.

"Here we go, we'll get out here so you can have a look across the harbour. This is Milson's Point."

We left the car and walked across the lawn which went down to the shore. Everything was so clean like a new penny.

"There you go, there's Luna Park again, a good day out if you've got plenty of money."

Looking across I could see the other side of the Harbour and the city tower blocks which dominated the skyline a view that could not be missed.

"Right, you lot back to the car."

We were soon in and off again and after a few turns were back onto the approach to the bridge, once again slowing down to pay the return toll.

"That's a bit of a cheek," Pat gave his opinion on having to pay twice.

"Well, that's the way it is, built by the British and we're still paying for it."

Back over the bride the view being just as good as the first time.

"There's a bit of luck Tony, the Canberra is in, see down there. We'll get a better view going out on the ferry."

Nat was no fool, he was making me feel good, more at ease and he knew it. They definitely gave the right man the right job. Soon across the bridge, pulled off and made our way to Circular Quay and found a parking space.

"Well this is the oldest part of Sydney; here most of the buildings were built back in convict days. It's a pity they don't do something with them to restore some of our heritage."

Through my eyes, they just looked old and out of place, but I suppose to the historian this was Australia (and is now known as the rocks). Soon we reached Circular Quay and the ferries going to all different destinations, Manly, Tooronga Park Zoo, Milson's Point, harbour cruises etc.

"I think we'll go on the return trip to Tooronga Park Zoo."

Nat paid the fare and we boarded the ferry. For us it was a novelty, but for the locals, a way of commuting daily, bringing them into the heart of the city. A bell went off and the all clear was given so we pulled away from the quay out into the harbour, passing first of all the ocean going liner the Canberra that had just arrived, probably bringing more immigrants searching for a new life in the sun. Compared to us, we were like a cork in a bath tub. Ours was to be a short trip and no more than ten minuets each way. Just across to the far side of the harbour, but this time to see it all in a different context, as the view for the ferry made it all look even more spectacular. The private yachts tied up in their moorings, local residents spending the day on their boats taking in the morning sun and idyllic setting for a postcard, complete with the bridge in the background. Our journey's end came quickly. We stayed on board and waited for the passengers to disembark then to reload for the return journey. The whole trip no more than 30 minutes but was well worth it.

"Right lads, let's get straight back to the car and off to the beach. Well what did you think boys? Glad you came? Sorry it's all a bit rushed but if we don't get home for dinner, I'll get shot."

We arrived back at the car and set off for the beach. The sun was high and by now getting quite warm, well compared to what we were used to, about 70 degrees. I opened the window, letting the breeze hit me in the face. It felt good and by now I didn't have a care in the world. Pat too was happy, asking all sorts of questions and Nat only too pleased to answer.

"Well here ya go, Bondi Beach."

For us, our first sight of the sea and not unlike the films we had seen only this was for real. We drove slowly down the front trying to take it all in. Even though it was April there were still people on the beach, grabbing that last bit of sun.

"So what are those towers on the beach Nat.?"

"Oh, they're for the life guards. See down there, the surf rescue teams practising."

He stopped the car. There were 5 or 6 groups all running in line out over their heads down to the shore attached to the lead life saver who rushed out into the water and swan out and back and could see they were racing against each other. Further down the surf boats were coming in from a make believe rescue all looking very impressive.

"In Bondi most of this is all put on the tourist, we prefer to go somewhere a little quieter, don't we John."

I remarked on the surfers and how they stayed on there boards.

"Wouldn't mind having a go at that myself"

"Give it time Tony all good things come to those who wait. You never know, we could have another budding surfer on our hands, John."

"What about the sharks ain't it dangerous?" I asked

"No, we don't get many attacks these days, what with shark nets, spotter planes and the surf patrol. Occasionally one gets through."

"Oh great, that's reassuring, just my luck it'll be the one that gets me." They laughed.

"Don't worry Brov, there's not enough meat on you, you've got nothing to worry about

"Now, now boys I think its time to make tracks

Soon we came to the end, following the road round to the right, leaving the coast behind and heading inland back to Ryde and Sunday dinner. I had built up an appetite and was ready to eat a horse. The journey back seemed to take no time at all, finally pulling up, once again, in the driveway of Rickard House.

"Here we are, so what do you reckon lad's?"

Pat and I expressed out thanks at Nat going to all that trouble.

"No trouble boys, it was my pleasure."

Once inside we met Hilda – not so much met as nearly knocked her down as we rushed in the front door.

"Slow down you boys, where's the fire?"

"Sorry Miss."

"Well, you're just in time for lunch so go and wash and tidy yourselves up"

Rickard House was only to be a short stop over for us and apart from my first day, a good one. Nat and Hilda Smith went out of their way to make us feel at home. Monday soon came around and with it came the summoning of Pat and myself to Head Office in the city, obviously to discuss our futures.

"Well boys, your fate awaits, are you ready"

Ready or not, we made our move Nat informing us that we would have to make the return trip home by train and pointing out the station.

"There's the station, just a short walk up to the house it's an easy run straight through from the city you can't get lost. I'll show you where to catch the train. You'll also be given maps etc."

Looking at Pat, thinking we might turn up in China, he smiled, "No problem, we'll find it."

At least he was a lot more confident than me.

"I'm sure you will, it'll give you a chance to get your bearings."

The trip in, took longer than the day before, due to the weekday traffic. Finally we reached our destination.

"Well, here ya go boys; this is Jamieson Street, the home of Dr Barnardo's Australia."

We luckily parked right outside the large old red building

and leaving the car, we followed Nat closely inside where high above the door read, 'Assembly Buildings.' It was as old inside as it was out and after getting in the lift, wasn't sure if we'd ever make it. Luckily we were only going to the second floor and soon back on safe ground, straight in front the glass panel in the old wooden door read, 'Dr Barnardo's.' We entered a large waiting area and to both Pat and my surprise, found some familiar faces, the Hill family, Archie, James and the two girls, all pleased to see one another, forgot about everything around us, all taking 18 to the dozen. It's hard to explain what it was like. You had to be in our situation to begin to understand, all I know is that it was like coming home and this was our family, all talking about our weekend events, wondering if that any moment now Peter would walk through that door. Finally our chatter was broken up by the introduction of the after care officer and just like an old school Ma'am, she clapped her hands together to get our attention, introduced herself as Miss Stevenson. Little did she know then that I was to become a large thorn in her side? After a short speech, she asked for the Bates boys Tony and Patrick.

"Will you come with me?"

Doing as she asked, not even saying goodbye to the others, as we naturally assuming that they would still be there on our return. She led us to an office and sat behind her desk peering over the top of her glasses.

"Sit down, boys, I won't bite."

At first, not having much of an opinion became quite fond of her. She was in her late 50's, tall with white hair, a spinster and as I said a typical old school Ma'am. She opened a file on her desk, all the time looking up, peering over her glasses, "You must be Pat."

"Yes Miss."

"I see that you want to join the Air Force. Well, we shall have to see what we can do about that."

The smile on Pat's face looked like the cat that had just eaten the mouse.

"Meanwhile, what else did you have in mind?"

"Engineering or electronics, Miss."

"Yes well, we shall have to see."

Then she looked over in my direction, breaking her face into a small grin, "and you're Anthony, or do you prefer Tony?"

"Tony, Miss."

"Well, I see by your latest school assessment your grades aren't the best so I don't think there's any point in prolonging the agony, so there's no point in enrolling you in a school here. What line of work were you thinking of Tony?"

"The Merchant Navy or Royal Navy, Miss."

"Is there anything else?"

"No Miss, just the Navy."

She made a few notes on our files, "but your first preference is definitely the Merchant Marines, is that right?"

"Yes Miss."

The conversation was to last about an hour. With her asking all sorts of questions some that were totally irrelevant to our situation until finally it was over.

"Well, I think it's time for coffee don't you, are you hungry?"

She didn't have to say another word,

"Just a little" I said knowing that I'd always find room for food

Taking some money from a tin, replacing it with a petty cash slip, she said, "There's a delicatessen down the road on the corner, go and buy yourselves some lunch."

My estimate of her got high on my who's who scale after that. Without another word I made a hurried retreat back to the front office hoping Archie and family would still be there, but unfortunately we'd missed them and that was the last I was ever to see of them. A little disappointedly, we made our way out to the lift

We left the building for the first time like two uncaged animals, we were let lose in the big city, going straight to the local delicatessen and then back to the office

We had our coffee and ate our lunch just in time for Miss Stevenson's return.

"Right, there's no point letting the grass grow under your feet, so I've made a few appointments for you. Here's a map of the city each. First call is for you Pat, R.A.A.F. Recruiting Centre, then on the R.A.N. It would be better if for a couple of days you stay together so as to learn your way around. Afterwards, you can go to this address Tony. It's the Merchant Marine Office. They will be expecting you there, so to get your application in. As for engineering Pat, I suggest you keep a careful eye on the newspapers. Sydney Morning Herald is usually the best. After that you can either look around or make your way back to Ryde. I've marked the station out clearly on the map, but if you're not sure, make your way back here. Now here's some money for additional expenses, off you go and good luck."

So with maps under our arms we went out into the city. Hard at first, but once you got your bearings it was easy.

"I think it's this way Pat."

"No, it's this way."

Neither of us too sure of which way to go first ended up at the R.A.A.F and after Pat sorted himself out it was then on to the R.A.N. The joining age was 15 years, 6 months, which just made me old enough. I filled in some forms with Pat's help and was afterwards told they would be in touch, just as they told Pat. Then on to the Merchant Navy Office, which took us back the way we come and more or less under the bridge

"This is it, Sussex Street what number did you say" asked Pat

"289, but I don't suppose it's the sort of building you could miss."

This time I was wrong. The road led under the bridge on the left hand side of the wharf and on the right, a lot of old buildings, some pulled down and replaced by prefabs.

"There it is, Seaman's Union of Australia, painted along the top of a large hut."

Once inside, I gave my name.

"Oh yes, Harry, it's that lad you're expecting."

He came over to the counter, "so you want to join the Merchants do you?"

"Yes Sir."

"Well, for the time being all you can do is fill in these forms and we'll go from there, but I'll tell you now, there's a long waiting list in front of you so be patient."

Doing what he asked, I completed the forms and handed them to the Superintendent.

"Right, the next thing is, you must join the Union, without that you can't get a ship, so through that door there and just tell the chap behind the counter you want to join."

"Thankyou Sir," and shook his hand.

"Good luck, mate."

We made our way next door to the Union Office. It was busy so I waited my turn in the queue along with the others.

Somehow the surroundings made you feel as if you were already one of them. My turn eventually came again being asked to fill in a form and return it.

Returning to Pat, who'd been patiently waiting, I filled in the form and returned to the queue eventually reaching the front, where once again I was told "We'll be in touch," an anti climax if ever I'd had one. Leaving the office we returned to tell Miss Stevenson the results of our meetings while she made notes, we were about to leave when Nat walked into the office, which gave us a reprieve from the train which after all the walking we were grateful. It had been a long day and we would be glad to get back to Rickard. For Pat and me, it had been a new experience and we were getting on together maybe because of the situation. I don't know, but that day we were closer as brothers than we had ever been before.

"Good day boys, I wondered if you would still be here, Listen Pat, I might have some good news for you, I've been in touch with a friend and there's a good chance of a stores job – if you're interested?"

"Yeah great let me at it" Pat was full of it.

"That's good, because you've got an interview at 10 o'clock sharp tomorrow."

His eyes it up – as all he had to do now was get the job.

"Oh, that's good Nat; do let me know how he gets on." She asked taking down more notes "then wished Pat good luck.

We started our journey home. Naturally Pat was all questions. Where was it? What sort of firm and so on. I just sat in the back and took in the view, finally reaching the home. That evening went quickly, tea, a night of telly then bed, the worst time of the day for me just laying thinking, until I'd finally drop off. The following morning we were called after the others, so they could be got off to school. Pat was rushing around, sprucing himself – for more like a date than a job interview. Breakfast was over

"Well, time's getting on Pat, shall we make a move?"

"Ready when you are Nat. See you later kid, wish me luck."

That morning I decided to write a couple of letters home, Mum's letter came hard so I gave up. Bev's on the other hand was easy, so I sat there, pen in hand, telling her of the trip and the many events that had happened since arriving, naturally telling her of how much I missed her. After finishing the letter I wished I hadn't, it only made me feel homesick, putting me back where I started. Sealing the letter, I decided to walk down to the Post Office.

"Just off down the shops Judy, anything you want?"

"No thanks, Tony don't go and get yourself lost now will you."

"Na, I won't be long," and took the short walk, not hurrying as I had plenty of time. I posted the letter and strolled back to the house, only to be met by Nat pulling into the driveway. Pat jumped out all smiles.

"Only bloody gone and got the job didn't I" and he rushed off to tell the others.

"We're going straight into the office, coming for the ride Tony?" Nat asked "Yeah why not, hang on a sec I'll just change."

We arrived at the office around about lunchtime. I amused myself talking to some of the office girls while Pat and Miss Stevenson held a conference, all the time wondering if I'm not going to school and they don't seem too bothered about finding me a job, what did they have in mind? I was about to find out.

"Tony, can you come in for a moment?"

Going into her office, I closed the door behind me. Pat was all smiles.

"Sit down Tony. First of all I've been in touch with the Seaman's Union and they tell me you've been accepted so it's only a matter of time. It could be a week or six months. There's no telling, so we're going to have to find you something to do meanwhile. Pat's luckily got himself a job so will be moving out of Rickard House into private boarding tomorrow; ready to start work on Thursday. How do you feel about that?"

How did I feel? What difference would it make? It looked like it was all arranged. I shrugged my shoulders.

"Also Rickard House being for the younger child, we have decided to move you on. We have a farm up country in Scone where we send our older boys on a training course, but for you it will be only until your call comes up."

Her voice was shaky, that I shall never forget. I was at the age when no one could decide what was best for me so just agreed; knowing that anything I said would make no difference.

"Good, well that's settled then. Andrew Crawford, the Manager of the farm, is coming down Thursday so you can return with him Friday morning. I'll leave that with you Nat, to get him here about 8.30 Friday morning."

"You'll like it up there Tony; they're all about your age and seem to have a great time."

I sat there in amazement. What was going on? Had I come 13,000 miles to become a farmer? I was speechless but then what choice did I have,-none- I thought to myself, well I suppose it could be worse. I could only give it a go you never know I might even like it.

"Well, I wish all my boys were as easy as you two to sort out, so good luck Pat, you know where I am if you need any help, after all, that's what we're here for and I'll see you on Friday Tony," and with that we left her office followed by Nat.

"Give me a couple of weeks and I'll get a car and come and see you, kid."

"Yeah, right," knowing he was living in cloud cuckoo land.

Couldn't he see what was happening? This was no different from being in England, only this time he was on his own. Come to that, finally, so was I.

We made the return journey to Rickard with Pat still full of the moment, new job, prospects and tomorrow to move on to new accommodation. I was a little envious but somehow could not help feeling pleased for him. For the last two weeks he'd been with children, no one of his own age to communicate with and now a chance for him to return to the real world. He was a lot older, so needed more. We would be separated, but he wasn't my keeper, finally to go our separate ways but somehow we'd survive. No sooner back at the home than Pat was packing away his things.

"Well kid, we'll show 'em and when Mum and Dad come out we'll be ready for 'em."

I agreed, wondering how long it would take them. Pat thought and mentioned nothing else. They say that absence makes the heart grow fonder and it did. You forget the bad times and only think of the few good ones. Pat only lived for their arrival and only hoped they wouldn't let us down.

"Your tea's ready boys"

"Thanks Hilda, just coming."

"Ready kid, let's go."

The conversation that night was concentrated on us. Pat, on what he was going to do, get a house and car ready for the family and on Nat telling me all about the farm and I must admit he made it sound a good place to live. That evening went quickly, finally all going to our beds.

"Lights out boys"

It had been a lot to take in for one day, but I suppose it was all for the best. I lay there for a while thinking and must have dozed off. The morning came swiftly and must have overslept as apart from me the room was empty. Looking around, I also noticed Pat's case was gone. Surely he hadn't left already, without saying goodbye. I leapt from my bed, putting on my dressing gown and rushed into the kitchen to find him sitting there large as life.

"I thought you'd gone already."

"Without saying 'bye' to my kid brother, you know me better than that. Mind you, I would like to get an early start so I can check the place out. Here, I've written down the address so you can drop me a line."

Taking the slip of paper, I sat down to the table. I knew Pat was going, but somehow I wished it would be soon. It was like saying goodbye at a railway station; the words just weren't there and couldn't think of a thing to say. Anyway, I hated goodbyes. Finishing my breakfast, I got showered and changed, wondering what was in store for me today.

"Hey, Tony where are you, I'm off now kid." Pat shouted

By the time I got outside his case was already in the car and Pat was thanking Hilda and Judy for their hospitality.

"Well kid, this is it, now you've got the address, so keep in touch. I'll try and get up to see you in a few weeks."

He was excited and like the Matador in the ring. Just couldn't wait to grab the bull by the horns. I was frozen for words as he climbed in the car and opened the window. Nat started the car and pulled out the driveway.

"Good luck," I shouted, as the car drove off down the road and out of sight.

It was hard to say how I felt. We were brothers I know, but our ages and the fact that apart from the last couple of years we had only met during the holidays, I spose was sorry to see him go but that was about it, this was just another good bye and I'd had loads of them, so just turned and went back into the house.

"Coffee Tony" Judy was being diplomatic but I was alright.

"Yea that'll be good, any of that chocolate cake left

"Hello, you two what's going on here?"Asked Hilda as she

walked into the room

"Tony and me are going to gorge ourselves silly, like to join us?"

"Why not" And so there we sat the three of us eating large hunks of chocolate cake washed down with coffee.

What more can a man want? I was in good company. The sun was shining. The birds were singing. It was good to be alive. What more indeed. Tomorrow it was my turn, off to God knows where or how far.

Friday came around quickly. My cases were packed and time to say goodbye. It had been a week to the day since I arrived and such a lot had happened. I had no sooner got to know Pat than he was off again. Our trips to Sydney were a whole new experience for a young man. Then there was Hilda and Nat, not forgetting Judy – and how we'd been dumped in their care to cope with us the very best they could, and they did.

Anthony & Patrick Bates 1965

Home in Ryde on arrival

CHAPTER 6

The traffic wasn't so good to us this time, as Nat and I arriving in Jamieson Street and the head office just before nine o'clock.

"You jump out Tony, while I park the car. "Ah don't forget your bags."

Bags in tow I made my way to the main door. And instead of struggling decided to chance the lift and was soon after to be on the second floor, making my way to the office I could hear voices so I dumped my cases in the corner and called out.

"Anyone home" there was no answer so I called again,

"There's no need to shout we're not deaf," came a voice from behind as Miss Stevenson came walking towards me followed closely by a tall thick set man with wavy black hair, wearing a rather badly fitting blue suit, and in his hand he carried a flat rimmed cowboy hat.

"Hello Tony and how are you today?"

"Fine thanks Miss."

"I'd like you to meet Mr Crawford, he runs the farm up at Scone, you'll be driving back up with him today."

"Hello lad," his voice was deep with a slight Scottish accent, "are you ready to make tracks then boy"

"Yes Sir."

"You can dispense with the formalities lad, the boys call me Andy or Andrew, whichever you prefer, probably more names besides, fortunately I don't get to hear all of them."

I took an instant liking to Andy as he was straight to the point. The door opened.

"Oh good, you found someone, sorry we're late Miss Stevenson," said Nat, making our apologies.

"Well you're here now and that's what counts."

"Well Tony, we've got a long drive ahead of us, so we may as well get going, these bags your?" he said, taking hold of one then the other.

"Right then, Nat, Miss Stevenson, we'll be making tracks, see you when I'm next in town."

"Okay Andy, safe drive."

Andy was in a hurry and just wanted to get on the open road and away from the hustle and bustle of city life.

"Good luck Tony, I'll be in touch as soon as I hear from the recruiting office."

"Thanks Miss Stevenson, and thanks for everything Nat."

"My pleasure Son, keep in touch."

I almost had to run to keep up with Andy, soon in the car and on the road out of town. Well, I was off again, I thought to myself, and turned to my companion.

"So where is Scone Andy?"

"Oh it's about 200 miles north of here in the Hunter Valley, it'll take us about 5 hours to get there so settle back and make yourself comfy. We'll stop about halfway to grab some lunch alright?"

It suited me fine, and we were soon well on our way. At first we headed inland and watched as the town's grew smaller and smaller.

"This is the Pacific Highway," said Andy, breaking up the silence, "it takes you all the way to Brisbane and as far up North to Cairns, a thousand miles or more. Won't be long now and we'll be in National Park Country and the fresh air, then on to Gosford where we hug the coast line as far up as Newcastle then head inland to Maitland, Singleton and finally Scone. It's a long way. At Gosford we'll grab a bit to eat, then we'll head on into bush country, leaving civilisation, as you know it, behind."

All I could see for miles on either side were the tall trees bush and scrub land for as far as the eye could see and was getting bored.

"Not long now," said Andy, "and we'll be heading into Gosford."

During the trip we talked of my past and how I had come to be here in the first place and in return, Andy told me of the farm – 1200 acres of lush green pastures, well sometimes anyway. They had beef cattle, pigs, chickens, sheep, a couple of bulls and a small dairy herd and there was also a large creek to swim in and on Saturday nights Andy would take the boys to town to let their hair down. He made it sound like something from an old western. We soon came to the halfway mark and could see the ocean in the distance.

"There she is Tony, Gosford, playground for the idle rich and the Pacific Ocean."

As we came closer the view was breathtaking, all inlets, coves and small islands.

"There's Plats Bridge. See the islands over on my right? That's Long Island there and beyond that is Danger Island."

Then leaving the bush behind, we made our way across one of many Bridge's.

It was like a geography lesson without the books and pictures only this was more fun. We were soon to come to the end of the bridge as Andy continued to point out different landmarks. Like the place, the names had character and we'd no sooner left the bridge behind than we dropped down into Gosford. On one side its big plush houses, and on the other, the blue waters of the Pacific washed up gently on the golden sands.

"This is where all your well-to-do people buy their holiday homes, so to get away from Sydney and city life at weekends and holidays."

"You mean to say, they own a house here as well as in Sydney?"

"Aye, that's right, if ya put your mind to it, it's there for the taking if you got the brains and know how. This is a rich country and it's here for the taking."

Taking in the view, needing eyes in the back of my head to get it all in, I compared these homes to ones back home and they made No. 36 look like an outhouse and you'd be lucky to fit just one in our whole street back home, and thinking, if I set my mind to it, one of these could be mine one day. Slowing the car down and gradually pulling off the road alongside a beach kiosk and there I was to taste the fine Australian cuisine, of two meat pies with sauce and a can of coke. At first a little uncertain of Andy's choice of food, thoroughly enjoyed it and was to make sure they weren't to be my last during my stay. Shortly after we were back on the road again, continuing up the coast to Newcastle. As I just sat there with the sun shining through the windscreen, my stomach which had just been replenished, I was soon to do the inevitable and fall asleep. Thinking I'd only had a nap, eventually I woke up in a start, then realised where I was.

"How long before we reach Newcastle, Andy?"

"Oh you're awake are you? I thought you'd died on me. We've passed Newcastle ages ago, heading inland now to Scone."

"Is it much further?"

"About an hour I'd say."

During my nap, the landscape had completely changed and was more flat and open as this was farm country. The last hour went swiftly, passing Singleton with the next stop being Scone.

"You're in the Hunter Valley now Tony, we'll soon be

home."

Home for him maybe, but what about me, I thought a new place with new people and I had to start all over again to make new friends. Besides what did I know about cows and pigs I was no farmhand, but little did I know, I was about to learn.

"Well here we are Tony, what do you think?" Andy said as we all of a sudden came off the open road to a few buildings on either side and eventually arrived on Main Street, which was exactly what Scone was. A town built either side of the highway, looking as if they'd been put there by some magnetic force, hugging them to the road's edge, I suppose the whole town covered no more than a quarter of a mile with the main road running right through the middle, with well graded dirt roads, leading off at either side. Apart from the unusual amount of Hotel's, three in all, there was one of everything, including a cinema. Although if you were driving through at more than thirty miles an hour and you blinked, you would probably have missed the whole splendour of it all. Pulling up, we stopped outside what looked like the General Store.

"Is this it? It looks like an old western town, you'd see on the T.V. back home."

"Well what did you expect, a city?"

"I don't know really give."

"Anyway, I don't normally come this way it's just that we've got a few supplies to pick up for the farm. Come on, you may as well help me now we're here."

Leaving the car, I followed him into the store. Being a small town, everybody knew him and it was obvious Andy was quite a celebrity. The atmosphere was more relaxed as everyone wandered around at their own pace unlike the city were I had just come from.

"Well, let's get this lot loaded into the car and get back to the farm. Not far now, only about ten miles."

"That far," I said, thinking it would only be just up the road, "So how often did you say the boys get to come into town then Andy?"

"Every Saturday night, I bring them in myself."

A little shocked, decided to keep my thoughts to myself. Thinking, so what did they do every night for the rest of the week? I was used to doing my own thing and not used to being tied to one place. Soon we'd left the main road behind and on to a dirt track kicking up a trail of dust behind as we went. It was getting more like a movie set than I first thought a town with one main street, the open range and now the dirt roads. What had I let myself in for, although uncertain, I was about to find out.

"Well there she is, Tooloogan Vale, all 1200 acres. It's not much, but its home."

Andy was a farmer at heart and the sight of the Vale brought back a smile to his face and could see he was glad to be back. I don't quite know what I expected, just the mention of training farm alone, made it sound like a big place, but that was to be my first shock.

"Here we are Tony," Andy said as we pulled off the road down an old track, "that's the main house there."

The car came to a sudden halt and scattered all around were buildings which looked more like old sheds to me. Andy got out of the car.

"Come on Tony, let's get you settled in first, then we'll get you shown around the place. You'll find this a little dry at the moment, that's because we've had a hot summer, but soon the rains will come, then it looks a lot different, all fresh and green."

We walked towards the old looking homestead; it was large, built of timber and painted in a light green colour with a red corrugated iron roof. No sooner were we halfway to the door when it opened and we were greeted by our welcoming committee.

"Welcome back Mr Crawford, how was the City?"

"Ow you know the same, crowded and stuffy; it's sure good to be back."

"And who might I ask have we got here?"

"Tony, meet ma, this is Tony Bates, the new hand."

"Hello Tony, so what do you think of the country so far?"

"Well it's different I'll give you that; is it always this quiet?"

"Most of the time, but that's the best part of it anyhow let's get you inside and we'll have a cold drink."

"Is Mrs Crawford about Ma?" asked Andy

"I'm afraid not, she left a few minutes ago, went up to the house she did mention that she might have to pick the girls up from school though."

"Oh right. Tony give me a hand with the supplies, then I'd better go and tell her I'm back."

Leaving my case just inside the door, I returned to the car

and helped unload and had no sooner finished than Andy was off.

"Well, I'll leave you in the capable hands of 'Ma' I'll be back shortly?"

"Okay Mr Crawford, he'll be quite safe with me," then he left without saying another word.

"Where shall I put these boxes Mrs Lee?"

"Oh call me Ma, everyone else does. Just through there on the kitchen table. In case Mr Crawford never told you, I'm the Chief cook and bottle washer around here and I also live in the house with you boys. Mr Crawford and his wife, Jan, live in the house across the way. But Andrew likes to keep to himself. Jan, on the other hand, spends the best part of the day down here. She has two little girls, both at school, you'll meet them later."

Ma was short and slim with a very soft spoken voice. She would have been in her late 30's, but you could see the sun and also the years had taken their toll, leaving their lines and the grey streaks in her hair, but she was to make our problems hers just like a real mum.

"Now Tony, let's find somewhere for you to put your bags, then I'll show you around the place."

Going from what was a very large kitchen into a lounge, then from one side of the house to the other and around to where I'd left my case, I followed Ma to a room at the front of the house.

"Now that's your bed there and you take the bottom two drawers of the dresser and share the wardrobe."

There was nothing special about the room, three beds, a couple of dressers and a wardrobe, and apart from the rest of the house, it was lacking in sunlight.

"Why's it so dark in here, Ma?"

"Well if you notice it's also cool in here, that's because the roof overhangs further so to keep the sun out, also the surrounding trees and the corrugated roof helps to keep it cool. You'll appreciate it on a hot day. Now leave your bags there, and I'll show you where everything is."

Just outside our room was the front door which nobody used, but Ma opening it, it led out onto an open veranda and on the far side was a small flower garden and a vegetable patch. Ma pointed in the direction of a house, "See up there on the hill, that's the Crawford's place." Theirs was a more modern place, smaller in size and conveniently overlooked the farm.

"Well, come on, I'll show you where the little boys room

is, then I'd better get the boys afternoon smoko or I'll have them all after me."

I looked at her in bewilderment and smiling, she informed me that smoko was their afternoon tea break.

"Right, here's the bathroom, three showers and of course the essentials, W.C., and wash basins." I looked at her still a little bewildered, "Don't worry, you'll soon find your way around. Right, come on, I'd better get a move on."

I was just about to follow her when the door opened, "Ma looking after you okay?" It was Andy, "Sorry about leaving you like that. So what have you seen so far? Have you met any of the boys?"

"No not yet."

"Well let's do that first."

I was beginning to feel a bit silly walking around in a white shirt, suit trousers, complete with pointed toe boots but no one commented. Leaving the house, my tour started with the chicken house, stables, where only a couple of horses were kept, Hopper Hall, a recreation building for the boys, then we worked our way round to the back of the house, there to find what was to be the rest of the hands, all sitting around.

"Good day, Mr Crawford," muttered one of the boys.

"Alright boys, this is Tony Bates, he'll be working with you from now on, treat him gently he's only just arrived out from England."

The boys all nodded as if to say hello, then got back to the serious habit of eating and looked like they were also enjoying whatever it was.

"Come on Tony, you'll have a chance to meet them all later," and we left them to their smoko, "We'll take a walk over to the milking sheds, that's in easy walking distance. Like I said to you before, it doesn't always look this dry. We've had no rain for nine months which makes water around here the most important commodity. Most of ours is pumped up from Dartsworth Creek for irrigation, drinking troughs and so on. It also makes a good swimming hole for the boys as you will no doubt find out. Apart from what you'll see today, we've also got a heard of Marino sheep, some beef cattle, pigs, two bulls, a Black Angus called Fernando, also Denby who's an Ayrshire. Just remember to keep well out of their way when they're mating – they're only interested in one thing and God help anyone who gets in their way. We also grow cereal crops so there's plenty here to keep you busy and after a few days we'll see how you fair. The boys work in pairs – so you'll soon get the hang of it."

We were soon at the dairy and entered the holding pen where the cows were put waiting to be milked, and could hear someone working inside.

"Hello Jim, you still at it? Tony, I'd like you to meet Jim Chambers our Foreman."

He was also English but had a slight Aussie accent, "Good day Tony, getting the two bob tour then, well as you can see this is the dairy. Each morning about 4.30 the cows are brought in, washed, milked, fed and put out there to graze in time for breakfast, after which all the equipment has to be washed and sterilised and that's done out here in those big troughs."

"So how many can you do at a time?"   I asked more out of something to say

"Just the eight, it's only a small herd, about 150 head. Well, do you think you'll make a dairyman?"

I held back from answering as I wasn't even sure if I wanted to stay, let alone milk cows.

"Have you met our prize bulls yet?" he said breaking into my thoughts

"No we haven't got around to that one yet Jim," said Andy, with a grin on his face.

"Well there's no time like the present let's go."

Leaving the dairy, we cut across the paddock, "Can you drive a tractor Tony or maybe ride a horse?" asked Jim.

"Who me, I have enough trouble staying on a bike." Wondering what they had in store for me.

"Don't worry, we'll teach or kill you in the process, won't we Andy?" They both laughed, "Well, here we are, what do you think?" Jim asked as I looked at the angry looking beasts.

"I think if they stay that side, I'll be safe on this."

"Don't be daft boy they're more bloody scared of you. Here I'll show you come on."

Opening the gate, Jim went up to them, bringing one over on a rope attached to the large ring in its nose.

"Remember, all animals sense fear, so you must be in control at all times, but beware of these two bastards."

"Don't worry I will," and felt better after he'd returned it. We then started walking back to the house while Andy pointed out anything of interest.

"That new building over there is the slaughter house it's not long been finished. You'll see more of that later."

I got the impression that somehow they were enjoying this young man, fresh from the city, as apart from today, the only farm animals I'd ever seen were the geese back at Flimwell and I was terrified of them. Still I reminded myself this was only temporary and it was only a matter of time before I'd be called up for the Navy so I'd just make the most of a bad situation.

We continued our walk towards the house, all the time Jim and Andy talked about nothing but work.

"Well Tony, we'll leave you here now as we've got work to do, so I'll see you later. You might as well go and settle in. Tea won't be long, then you'll get a chance to meet the rest of the boys." With that they both walked off leaving me alone at the back of the house. Feeling a little bewildered I went inside to be met by a dog jumping up on me.

"Get down Perdy, get down."

"Whose dog is it Ma?"

"She's ours, but she won't hurt you, she's harmless."

Perdy was a bit like a Corgi in shape with a long black shaggy coat, a bitsa of some sort but I couldn't tell you what.

"Here ya go Tony this'll keep ya going through 'til tea, sit yourself down," and placed in front of me what looked like stodgy bread pudding which Ma called 'plonk' probably because of the way it stuck to the plate, and a glass of ice cold milk.

"When you've eaten that, you may as well beat the rush and get shower and change before the others."

Finishing my little feast, I did as she suggested and after unpacked, putting my clothes in my two nominated drawers. Afterwards, I returned to the kitchen to meet the rest of the boys as one by one gradually they all came in.

"Hi Ma, what's for tea?" getting a cold drink from the fridge and sitting down.

"Good day mate, names Trevor Lindley, we're in the same room. This 'ere is Roger, Colin, Paul and his brother Stanley, Michael, David and last in as usual that's Frank Sumpton. He also shares with us."

The next half hour or so was spent asking what part of England I'd come from and so on – all but one of the boys was originally English.

"Now you boys, out of my kitchen and get washed up before I set the dog on you."

Gradually they did as they were told Trevor being the last to leave. I'd made a friend and fortunately we also shared the same room. Soon all had washed up and it was time for tea. Ma sat at the head of the table making sure all our manners were in tact. She was fair, but strict at meal times. After tea, they all went their different ways.

"Had your guided tour yet Tony?" Trevor asked as he made for the door.

"Yea, had it earlier on with Andy Crawford"

"Well, come on let's find something to do."

So following him outside I asked, "So how long have you been here?"

"Oh about four months now seems longer though"

So what's it like 'ere" I asked

"Alright I suppose if you like farming, not much to do in the evenings though unless you're like Frank and Colin and read all the time, gets a bit boring sometimes. The highlight of the week is Saturday."

"So why's that then?" I asked

"Didn't Crawford tell ya? We get paid."

"Yeah how much" I asked as things were starting to look up.

"All depends on how long you've been here, not that there's much in town to spend it on, still, roll on tomorrow night. Although the choice is limited unless you like the pictures, or you could go to the milk bar, couple of nice girls in there. Sometimes if you're lucky you may get asked to go into town with either Crawford or Chambers during the week for supplies."

"Don't you call them by their Christian names?" I asked curiously

"Well, they say you can, but no one does. I suppose it's what comes of living in these institutions, all your life it's either Mr and Mrs, Uncle, Auntie, but I don't have to tell you that do I, it's what you get used to. Ma makes a nice change, she's alright. Crawford's wife ain't bad either, her name's Jane, also Chamber's wife, Elaine, she comes down 'ere a fair bit, they've got two daughters, Barbara and Pauline, about the same age as us but we very rarely get to see them. They probably don't trust us anywhere near them; instead he brings his young son Steven down here Saturdays"

"Do they all live near here as well?"

"Yeah, not far, see that building on top of that hill, that's their place. Anyway, half day tomorrow, then we get Sunday off that's apart from the dairy hands. We all get a turn up there; it's worked on a rota system. I start Monday and move into the bunk house on Sunday night so not to disturb the others. Try and get on it if you can, it's a good laugh, plus we get to finish early. Maybe tomorrow afternoon we'll take the tractor for a tour around the property. Can you drive one?"

"Who me you must be joking."

"It's easy, just forward and reverse you can't go wrong, you'll soon pick it up, no worries. Come on let's head back and see what the others are doing. Have you been in Hopper Hall?"

"Not yet, whys that?"I asked thinking there I was in for a treat.

"Oh nothing, I just wondered. The story go's that it's named after a handyman that worked around the place. Rumour has it that he was an eccentric millionaire, bumming his way round Aus, looking for his lost youth or something like that. Crawford gave him some work and he ended up staying about six months. Hopper Hall was the last thing he built before leaving so it was named after him. Most nights we go in there, play table tennis, darts, a few of the lads have started up a band called – of all things – The Red Backs. Frank, our room mate's in it. You interested in mechanics? We've got a new workshop full of old engines to strip down and rebuild if you're that way inclined."

"Na, it's not for me."

"Me neither."

The eyes all turned to the door as Trevor and I entered the hall. The brothers Paul and Stan were playing darts.

"You two fancy playing doubles" Stan asked

"Yeah go on then, I spose its better than doing nothing come on Tony, let's give them a fucking hiding."

"That'll be the day, we're unbeatable," and so the rest of the evening was spent playing one game or another and a lot different from back home where I'd be out with my mates and having a good laugh. What a way to spend a Friday night, I thought, still tomorrow was the highlight of the week for these boys, a night on the town. This was going to take some getting used to. By nine o'clock we'd had enough so we ended up going to bed. My first night there was somewhat hectic. Little did I know that as a new boy, came the initiation test but unlike the others, I didn't find it quite so funny? Lights were out and all you could hear were the crickets singing their way through the heat of the night. So just lay on top of the bed wearing only my shorts, when out of nowhere came this great furry thing and landed on my chest. In shock I must have lifted my whole body about two feet in the air, eventually landing on my feet. I was terrified. As I turned on the light I saw the largest spider I've ever seen running down over the pillow and down the side of the bed. I went berserk like a mad man, then Frank started laughing, "He won't hurt you, that's George, our house spider, he keeps the flies down."

I wasn't convinced and could not see the funny side at all. By now the rest of the boys rushed in wondering what the fuss was about. I'd seen money spiders and daddy long legs, they gave me the willies, but this one, well he had boots on. Ma rushed into the room.

"What's all the noise about?"

"It's only George Ma he fell on Tony and gave him a bit of a fright."

"Fright Nye took ten years off my bloody life."

"So where is he now Frank?" ma asked trying not laugh

"Under his bed somewhere I think, waiting to pounce."

"Right boys fun over back to your room and you three back to your beds."

"There's no way I'm sleeping in that bed."

"Here, take mine, I'm not frightened of a little spider."

I quickly changed over with Frank. That night I hardly slept a wink, wondering whether my furry friend was coming back.

The early morning call came with the word of Perdy, Ma would send her to rouse us out which she did cleverly by pulling off your covers, and to my displeasure they started early, up at six. Early morning chores – feed the stock, everyone had their own job. Breakfast at 7am until 8 then apart from the dairy boys up with chambers; meet Andy to get your work for the day.

"Morning boys all rearing to go are we."

"Morning Mr Crawford."

"You boys can all work together this morning it's a nice easy one for you – irrigation. Frank, I want you and the others to continue down the south pasture where you left off yesterday.

It's going to be a hot one so has anyone got a spare hat for Tony?"

"Here ya go mate, you wear this, it'll give me a chance to break in my new one."

"Thanks Trev, you're a mate."

"I hear you don't like spiders Tony."Crawford said with a smirk on his face

"News travels fast around here," I said while the others laughed, "No I bloody don't."

"Well remember, it's the small ones you've got to worry about around here and if you're not sure, ask the others, they'll put you right."

Trevor returned shortly after with his new hat, "Well, so what do you think?" No one commented.

"Right then boys let's have you, and Trevor, no messing about out there, you hear."

With that the four of us went about our business, Trev me Frank and Colin. After hitching up the tractor, Colin took the wheel and off we went.

"So what do we have to do then Trev?"

"Oh it's easy, just move the irrigation pipes from one paddock to another, join up and turn on the water, give it a soaking and move on."

It sounded straight forward enough, all in good spirits because it was Saturday and half day. My episode the night before was forgotten and wasn't mentioned. It was still early when we set out and there was not a cloud in the sky as the sun beat down on us.

"She's going to be a hot one today alright" Frank said "Looks like we landed the right job guys."

"What's he mean by that" I asked.

"Well, if she to gets too hot, we can just strip off and jump under the sprinklers."

Soon the homestead was out of sight as we continued our journey.

"Not far now, just over the ridge. Tony, you and Trev work one end, Frank and I will do the other." Collin said taking charge

The tractor stopped and I was shown what to do. Like Trevor had said, it was easy, just uncouple the pipes, move down a section and recouple. As the morning wore on, it got hotter and hotter with the eventual arrival of Jim Chambers with our smoko and cold drinks which was much appreciated.

"How's it going boys? Any problems"

"Na, she's right, no worries here Mr Chambers."

"Right then, I'll leave you all to it."

With that, he left us to continue in our own sweet time. We finished our smoko and returned to work. My skin, at that time, was still quite fair, unlike the others, so I had to watch the sun a little, leaving my shirt on while the others were all stripped down to their shorts.

"We'll just finish the paddock then we'll call it a day." Frank called out.

The ground was hard and the tubes by now, which had been lying in the sun unused, were getting a little to hot to handle.

"Not far now Tony, one more row."

I carried on. This wasn't so bad, in fact we were having quite a laugh when all of a sudden, I picked up this pipe and from underneath, disturbed this bloody great big snake. "Shit, what the fuck..." I didn't even hang around to finish my sentence, just let loose and ran like crazy, looking behind, trying to put as much distance between me and the snake and couldn't believe my eyes as I turned quickly, only to see the thing coming towards me at no slow pace. 'Jesus', I thought, 'the fucking thing's coming after me'. All I could hear was my heart pounding and the distant sound of the boys laughing. This was no laughing matter – my life was at stake. Eventually running in a wide circle and to lose the snake, I made my way back to the tractor where all three of them were in hysterics.

"So what you bastards fucking laughing at thanks a lot for your help."

"Help, what for? It was only a bloody carpet snake," said Frank, "They're harmless and he was probably just keeping out of the sun."

Oh great. If this was farm life, I though! You can shove it as twice in less than 24 hours I'd been frightened half out of my wits, both times by creatures that were completely harmless.

"Don't tell me it's only the small ones that bite. Well, that's it; I don't think this farming life is going to suit me at all."

"Listen mate you're like the rest of us mate, haven't got a choice."

"Is that right Frank, well, we'll see about that."

"Look you stay here, while we finish off the last section."

I did just that by sitting on the trailer and keeping my feet clear, waiting for them to return, which they did soon after, still laughing. By now, I too could see the funny side and joined in. Frank and Trevor jumped on the trailer while Colin started up the tractor.

"Hold on tight, Tony, we don't want you falling off, the ants might get you."

"Ha fucking ha."

"Don't laugh mate, you haven't seen the ants we've got here. Now, they do fucking bite"

"Shut up Colin, I think he's been wound up enough for one day, don't you."

We slowly made our way back to the farm in time for lunch, knowing I was going to be the joke for the afternoon, was not looking forward to it one bit. After lunch, I hid myself away in my room to keep out of the way, out of sight and out of mind. They'd soon find something else to laugh at. By now I was feeling tired from my loss of sleep so I had a couple of hours after which, I wrote a letter home trying not to make it sound to depressing, eventually finished it. As I did, the door opened and in walked Trevor.

"It's time to get ready Tony we're going into town early tonight."

I washed and dressed and was well in time along with the others and ready for our night out on the town. As yet, not one of the boys had received their allowance which was normally given out early so we all waited patiently for Crawford. His arrival came with a fist full of envelopes and on calling our names, gave us one each. Although I didn't really expect one, only being there the one day, but was glad – not to mention surprised – when I did, and on opening mine, found the sum of one pound.

"Right then lads, are we ready? Then let's go."

It was just like in the movies. The men, after a long cattle drive were off into town to kick their heels and wash the dust from there throats, as we all rushed out the bunk house to get into our transport, an old opened back ute. Two up front and the rest sat in the back and were off on our ten mile drive to town arriving about 30 minutes later. The long dusty ride had put a dry patch in our throats, so naturally our first stop on arrival was offcourse, the bar and there we'd sit for a spell, in our case it would be the Milk Bar, as unfortunately our age didn't permit us to indulge in the delights of alcohol.

"Right boys, I'll meet you all back at the Niagara at 10-30'clock sharp so don't be late any of you."

As I looked around, the town was almost deserted apart from the cars parked outside all three pubs, as Crawford made it one more and parked outside the Royal and then went inside. He'd have to be quick as it was nearly six and last orders, what they called back then the 6 o'clock swill.

"I could just go a cold beer myself, what do ya reckon Trev?"

Frank laughed, "You'll be bloody lucky, can't even shit in town without Crawford or Chambers hearing about it. If it wasn't for the girls in the milk bar we'd never even get a packet of fags."

We all split up, just leaving Trevor, myself and the two brothers, making our way straight to the milk bar.

"I see what you mean about the choice mate, there ain't much here is there?"

"Told you didn't I"

The music could be heard clearly from the jukebox and as we entered, recognised the tune straight away it was the Beatles and 'She's got a ticket to ride'. The Niagara was the only spot in town for the youngsters to go and was not unlike the cafes' back home, but a lot more modern. A voice came from the other side of the counter.

"Hi Trev, what'll you have",

"Good day Helen, give us a couple of cokes will ya."

"So who's your friend?"

"This 'ere is Tony, new bloke he's just come out from England."

"Hi I'm Helen and this is Linda." she said pulling her close as to give her a hug

"How do you like it here so far?"

"Well, it's a lot different from where I come from I'll give ya that."

"I'll bet."

Helen finished serving us and we grabbed a table near the jukebox.

"So what do ya recon Tony? Not bad a"

Looking over, I could see them both giving me the once over and the 'new boy in town' look of approval.

"Helen's 16 and Linda, I think, is 17. They finish at 7 o'clock, what do ya reckon, shall I ask them to join us?"

"Why not, but I don't fancy our chances much."

Saying no more, Trev went back to the counter, calling Helen over. She was obviously his choice and returned with a big smile all over his face.

"No worries, we're in mate, they're going to join us after work."

Looking once again across, I noticed Linda staring and on catching my eye, smiled. It must be something about the name, as it seemed to follow me wherever I sent. Still who was I to complain? Only my second day here and already I'd got myself a date. Things were looking up. The rest of the fellers turned up after a while. Half of them decided to go to the cinema, the Civic, which was just across the road. We, of course, had already made arrangements, so stayed behind with the others. It was just coming up to 7 o'clock, so eagerly we waited for our company and after fixing their hair and faces, after a days work they joined us. Although at first, unlike Trev and Helen, Lin and I were total strangers to each other, but we seemed to hit it off straight away.

Linda was about 5'5", with long black hair, pretty with a fairly dark skin and could tell she was of Italian origin, having a nice body and personality to match. After a while it seemed we'd known each other ages as we sat around and drank coke, listening to the latest records from the jukebox. Later that evening, we decided to go for a walk and so it was, romance once again for me blossomed, my one true love Beverly was thousands of miles away and doubted if Id ever hear from her, let alone see her again, before leaving that night, we arranged to meet up with them both later in the week. Somehow we would make it into town. The evening had gone quickly but for me, a good one, although all good things must come to an end and did with the arrival of Crawford for our return to the farm.

"See ya Lin, I'll try and get in during the week say Wednesday"

With that, I climbed aboard and we made our way back for the farm. At least now I had something to look forward to and was going back in a different frame of mind. That night I slept like a baby. George could have fallen on my face and I wouldn't have noticed it. It was only the sound of Perdy barking that woke me from a deep sleep in time for breakfast. Sunday was a lazy day and to me, no matter where you lived, was always a bore, so like the rest I lazed around all day in the scorching sun. Crawford turned up early evening to dish out the weeks chores.

"Right, now the following are on dairy next week, Trevor, Stan, Frank and Tony, so move your stuff out into the bunk house now and get yourselves an early night. I'll sort the rest of you out in the morning."

"Err, Trev what's he mean by move your stuff out, all of it?"

"Na just you're work clothes and your bedding, dickhead. Come on, I'll show you."

Stripping our beds and taking our working gear, we made our way out to the bunk house and made up our beds.

"So who gets us up, Trev?" I asked.

"Chambers, he gives us a shout about 4 a.m. then we have to go out and round up the herd, but it's a good laugh, you'll see."

So after a hot drink and a couple of games of cards, we hit the sack. The morning came round, and was woken by Jim's voice.

"Okay boys, hands off cocks and on with your socks, come on let's have ya."

Then he turned on the light, blinding us all. It felt like we'd no sooner gone off than it was time to get up. Quickly getting dressed along with the others, I followed Trev closely as we left the bunk house.

"Here Tony, take this," Frank handed me a torch, "Here you'll need this."

Outside it was still pitch black and apart from the touch only had the stars to light our way.

"This way Tony, come on, keep up."

Following Trevor's every move, trying not to let him out of my sight, as gradually my eyes adjusted and it became easier to see. We didn't have to look far for the herd as they would only be in one or two places. Today we were lucky and came straight across them so started to round them up.

"Make sure you don't leave any of them beasts behind Tony," Trev shouted.

"Ya, ya, get up there!" All I needed was the horse to feel like Clint Eastwood in one of his spaghetti westerns.

At first a little afraid of the huge fat beast, I waved my arms, "Go on ya, bastards," lucky for me, the dumb beasts took notice and once you got them going they would make their own way. All you had to do was open and shut the gates after them walking close behind to avoid stragglers; we finally made our way to the dairy, closing the holding pen gate behind them, to be met by Chambers.

"Took your time you boys – where you been? Teas in the pot hurry so get a cuppa and let's get down to work."

"Is he always like that?" I asked.

"Na, only first thing, he comes round later – come on, let's get a brew."

Trev led the way out into the dairy washroom.

"Cut the chat you two and let's get moving – as you two girls have stuck together like a pair of lovers you might as well work together. You show Tony what to do Trevor and take the end four stalls."

"Fucking smart arse" I mumbled almost under my breath

"What was that?"

"Yeah, right you are Jim, anything you say."

I turned my face away so as not to see me laughing.

"Yeah, that's what I thought you said."

Jim was alright it was just that sometimes he thought we were still kids. Frank and Stan had already started, the gate was open and the first eight made their way into the stalls.

"Come on Tony, we'd better get a move on."

At close quarters the cows looked much bigger, and I was at first a little apprehensive, but it was quite safe, once in the pen they were interested in their food, plus a bar went down to keep them firmly locked in the stall.

"Now watch what I do Tony, then you can have a go. First you have to wash the cow tits," and taking a cloth from the bucket close by, washed her down, "then after taking the tit holder, place one cup on each of her tits like this," the holder looked like a spider with four legs dangling over his hand, and one by one connected them on, the suction pressure just pulling the tit in, "see, it's easy isn't it?" Straight away you could see the milk being taken, pumping its way through the system.

"So how long does it take to finish Trev?"

"Ah not long about five minutes or so"

Moving into the next pen it was my turn. I was still a bit unsure.

"Show us again will ya mate?"

So he went through the whole procedure one more time.

"Next one's yours."

I finally accepted the fact that I had to do it, taking the cloth I started to clean my first cow.

"Ere fuck it feels horrible."

"Just make believe its Linda and handle them with care. That's it now put on the teat holder"

Lifting the holder to the teat I could feel the suction pulling it on, that was one, then another till I'd done all four. Feeling pleased with myself I looked up to find Chambers there.

"Good job it's not a frigging race, it's a cow not you're fucking girlfriend, so pull your finger out."

Trust him to spoil the moment.

"Take no notice, he's only winding you up, should have seen me first time around."

"Now what do I do?"I asked nervously

"Just wait till they finish, see that glass bowl there, it's full of milk, when it goes down that means she's finished so take off the holders, open up the front of the stall and out she goes, close back up ready for the next one. There you go, that one's finished, let her out, oh and make sure you hang up the holders or you'll get shit all over 'em."

Following Trevor's every move I disconnected the holders, replaced them in the rack, opened the stall and out she went. No sooner gone than the next one was in.

We were a little behind the others as there was a certain knack to it but gradually I was getting the hang of it. No sooner and out than the next was in.

"You do those two stalls Tony – oh by the way, if you get one with a dried up tit, give us a shout."

Not asking why, I carried on, by this time getting much quicker.

"How's that – don't take long to get the hang of it. So what's the dried tit all about?"I finally asked

"Oh that's mastitis, a disease cows get so their milk dries up, just miss that one out, leave the holder hanging down but still connect up the other three."

So here I was, milking cows. If anybody had told me back home that in a month's time I'd be getting up at four in the morning doing this I'd have bet money against it, but there I was and up to my waist in cow shit and milk churns. By the time we'd finished the herd that day I was more confident and putting them through on my own.

"What a team, nice going Tony, now's the worst part mate, we've gotta strip down, wash and sterilise all the equipment then put it all back together."

It seemed to take longer than the milking, but eventually getting the job done, all that was needed now was to wash down the dairy and take the milk churns out for collection. We got to wash down while the others took the herd back to the paddock to graze, both getting soaked in the process. By the time we'd finished, the others returned along with Chambers.

"Nice job, now you can go and have your breakfast, see you later."

It was still early, 6.45, and apparently we'd made good time.

"Is that it for the day?" thinking 3 hours, that's what I call a day's work.

"You must be joking", cried out Frank "That's it until this arvo then we start all over again. Mind you after breakfast we still have to work until 10 o'clock then we get the rest of the morning off."

Washed up we all went for breakfast. By now the sun was well up and knew it was going to be another scorcher, and that's how it was all that week. Bed at nine, up at four, eat, drink, work, and sleep. We never did make it into town on the Wednesday and there was no way of getting in touch with the girls. Saturday came round quickly, had finished the afternoon milking and was washed and changed before anyone else. I knew how it felt, this time it was me who was eager to get away from this place and get into town. It had only been a week since I'd wondered what all the excitement was over, now I knew. Crawford arrived shortly before six, "Ready boys? Well, let's go." I didn't have to be told twice, in fact, I'm not sure who got to the Ute first, me or Trev, closely followed by the others. On our arrival in town, we headed straight for the Niagara. I'd only known Linda a few hours, but somehow it was the highlight of the week, wondering if after not turning up Wednesday, they'd still be talking to us. Why should they? After all, we'd stood them up. Not that we had much choice unless we'd done a runner with the tractor or kidnapped a couple of horses not that it hadn't crossed our minds. We were totally isolated, like trainee monks at a monastery. At last, arriving at the milk bar, I went in first and was to see Helen was serving.

"Hi Helen" I called out

"Hi Tony, Trev so what happened to you two then?"

"Tell y a later, where's Lin?"

"Out back – she'll be out in a minute. What'll you have?"

"Give us couple of cokes when you're ready."

Making my way to the table, I left Trevor to pay and explain. Linda then appeared on the scene, Helen pointing over in my direction and she smiled, that was a promising sign, I thought, at least I was still in with a chance, then walking over to my table, she sat down.

"Hi ya Lin Sorry about the other night." And tried to explain

"That's alright, I understand, look I'll be finished soon, we'll talk then okay?" then went back to her work.

"What'd she say Tony?"

"Nothing much but she seems okay, so how did you get on?"

"Bit mad at first, but I managed to bring her round with my irresistible charm. We're going to the cinema are, you two coming?"

"Don't know yet, I'll have to wait and see what Lin wants to do."

Arriving just after seven, Linda sat down while trev and Helen tried to persuade us to go with them

"We're of to the pictures you two coming?"

"What do you reckon Lin?"Fancy going

"Na, you two go on, we'll see you back here for coffee later."And with that Trevor and Helen went off.

"Are you sure you don't want to go with them Lin?"

"No, let's just go for a walk then we can talk."

"Okay, whatever you say."

Our walk was to be short, only as far as the small playing reserve next to the train station. There we sat in total privacy and shared each other's company. For me it was love, but then every girl or woman who ever showed me any affection I'd fallen in love with, but this was here and now and it seemed real enough at the time. Together we made plans for our next meeting knowing that it was near impossible, being stuck out on the farm from one week to the next.

"Why don't you move into town and get a job?"

The idea was good, but I knew Crawford wouldn't stand for it, if we were to last we'd just have to settle for Saturdays.

The evening went quickly already it was ten o'clock so slowly we made our way back to the milk bar. Trev and Helen were already there so too were the rest of the boys who on making our entrance started whistling and making snide remarks, taking no notice I ordered two cokes and we went and sat with the others.

"Alright Trev so what was the film like any good?"

"Don't know mate, didn't see much too busy snogging weren't we Hel," Helen's face went all red.

"Shut up tell him the truth, it was good."

"Okay so the film was good, whatever you say."

"So where have you two been?" Helen asked curiously

"Oh nowhere special just for a walk up the park"

"What for three hours must have been some walk"   She said laughing.

"Oh shit, here comes Crawford Trev, he's early," his car door slammed and in he walked, "Okay boys, ready? Let's go," and like little children we all followed him out.

"See ya Lin, I'll try and get in some time in the week."

I was embarrassed leaving her like that and you could see the look on the local boys faces, laughing at us as Crawford called us in from play, and we all went running. That night I couldn't get Linda out of my mind and thought of all sorts of ways to get into town, not knowing luck was going to be on my side. Sunday was for Trev and me our last day of work in the dairy which was soon over going to bed early that night as there was not much else to do apart from table tennis and dominoes. Monday arrived and after breakfast came Crawford with our work roster. I was to work with Frank in the yard, mucking out, feeding the livestock, tending the chickens and generally helping out to get me used to the different jobs. During my next three days I learnt how to shovel shit of all kinds, horse, pigs and chickens. The horses would kick, pigs would chase you and chickens, well Frank showed me how, by taking their head and shoving it under their wing, swing 'em round two or three times they would go to sleep so to give us no trouble during the cleaning out. Thursday I was put on the bailer which was simple enough. Just feed in the bales of hay, put sacks at the other end to collect the final result which was used for feed. Although you had to watch yourself, one wrong move and you'd lose your hand. This was where my luck came in. No I didn't lose my hand; I was bitten on the hand by a bull ant. At first, although it only irritated a bit, later it was to swell up like a balloon, losing all feeling in my right hand. Ma was so concerned she called Crawford.

"I think he'd better see a Doctor Jim, it doesn't look too good to me might be better to get it checked out."

Although at first he was a little reluctant he took Ma's advice, "Come on Tony let's go."

After a short ride to town and the doctor's, a couple of injections and a box of pills, Crawford dropped me in town, "While we're here there's a couple of things I'd like to do. I'll pick you up in an hour at the Niagara." So that was how I got to see Linda in the week, even if it was only for a short while. It made Saturday come that much quicker. Friday for me was a day of rest due to my hand, spending the morning lounging around. After lunch, all hands were required up at the slaughter house, as a Veterinary surgeon had come all the way up from Sydney just to show us the correct way to slaughter stock. Gathering us all together the demonstration started with Chambers taking hold and putting a sheep between his legs then with a knife held firmly in one hand, held its head up with the other. The Vet, in detail, explained his every movement then taking the knife, he cut its throat with the warm blood going everywhere. Although dead, the sheep started to twitch and made me feel quite sick, one guy even fainted. That was it for me, I knew I'd never be able to do that and to make things worse, Lamb was on the menu that night for tea but I couldn't bring myself to eat it as just the thought of it turned my stomach. By Saturday my hand was on the mend so I could return to work. My job was not pleasant, but one I had done before – cleaning out the pigs, also to be joined by Trevor and Frank. The sty was way over the other side of the creek so we had to take the tractor.

"Come on you two, haven't got all day," Frank called, returning with the tractor and getting a little impatient, "Come on Tony, we'd better go or Crawford will get a shit on."

"Hold your hair on, we're coming," and both jumped on the back of the tractor

"I hate this fucking job it makes the stink of pig shit get right into your clothes. Tell you what, why don't we go for a swim after, what do ya reckon Frank?"

"Sounds good to me I'm game for a laugh."

Arriving at the sty, got stuck into it literally, so to get it over and done, when Frank came up with what seemed a good idea.

"How about we barbeque one of the piglets this arvo we could get the rest of the lads over here and have a party no ones going to miss it, only the mother what do' ya recon."

"You're fucking joking," Trev replied, but with a smile on his face.

"I'm not, it's easy, all we've got to do is distract the mother away from her babies, get in bash one over the head, and we'll come back and barbecue it later."

We all agreed and put franks plan into motion and while he distracted the boar I got the sow away from her babies, then like a shot, Trev rushed in and grabbed one, it was then all hell let lose. The mother went crazy and the boar chased Trev who let lose his catch slipping in the process, then whilst trying to straddle the fence and caught himself on the barbed wire, cutting himself badly in a very uncomfortable place.

"Oh shit, I'm fucking bleeding I think I've cut my fucking bollocks open."

At first thinking he was joking, we fell about laughing, then realised the seriousness as he moved his hands covered in blood.

"Quick Tony, get him on the trailer, better get him back to the house."

It had all gone pear shaped, but there was still a funny side to it and through his pain, Trevor could also see it. On reaching the house, we called for Ma who came running out to see what all the commotion was about.

"It's Trev he's had an accident up at the sty."

"Where is he hurt?"

"Err, well it's a bit delicate," Frank said laughing.

"Bring him in here and let's have a look."

"You're fucking joking she's not looking at my tackle."

Frank and I fell about laughing. Ma called up the house telling Andy to get down here and fast.

"Carry him into the kitchen boys, put him on the table and take off his trousers," doing as she asked, "now let's have a look."

The smile left Trevor's face.

"Don't worry mate, just make out its Helen doing the examination."

"Ha, ha, very funny smart arse," trying to get up off the table saying, "I'll be right Ma, it's only a scratch."

"Don't be silly, now open your legs."

Luckily Crawford arrived at the crucial moment and after a short discussion, decided it best to take him straight to hospital, doing just that.

"You two return to work, and I'll want to see you both later."

It was early afternoon when Crawford returned, but to our surprise, on his own.

"Where's Trev, Mr Crawford?" I asked

"They want keep him in for a couple of days just for observation."

"So he's alright then?"

"Well, he's got a few stiches, but the positioning makes it a little hard for him to get about. Where's Frank?"

"Don't know some were about?"

"Well, I want to see you two in ten minutes so you'd better go and tell him," he said with a not too pleasing look, "I'll be in the games room."

Returning to the house, I looked for Frank, as usual he was in our room reading.

"Frank, Crawford wants to see us."

"Oh shit, what sort of mood is he in?"

"It's hard to tell, always looks the fucking same to me."

"Come on then, let's get it over with, we'll be alright if we stick to our story."

"What about Trev? You don't think? No he wouldn't."

"Lets just hope and pray he never said what we were really up to."

We both made our way to Hopper Hall, were inside were sat chambers and Crawford, like judge and jury, were waiting to hear our plea. Chambers took the floor putting me first on the stand.

"Right, what so happened?"He said throwing the first question at me

"Nothing really, there we were minding our own business and that pig just went berserk."

"So what did you do to upset him?"

"Nothing, like I said, we were just cleaning them out."

Then it was Frank's turn to take the stand.

"And what's your explanation Frank?"

"Well, it was like Tony said, the boar just went for us, I

couldn't understand it, never happened before."

"Well neither can I," Chambers piped up, "I've just come back from the sty and they are alright with me which only makes me think that the three of you were playing around upsetting the stock." Crawford nodded. "This is a farm not a bloody playground put here to teach you boys a trade and now someone's been hurt through what I believe to be stupidity."

We'd been tried and found guilty without witnesses. Crawford then passed sentence.

"Like Mr Chambers, I agree that there's more to this than meets the eye and I think you both know what I'm talking about so you're both grounded until next Saturday."

"That sound okay with you Frank?"

"Yes, Mr Crawford, whatever you say."

"Tony?"

"Don't know, what's grounded mean?"

"It means no town tonight."

I could feel my face getting redder and redder until it eventually made me explode.

"That's what you bloody think. I'll get there if I have to fucking walk there myself."

I then stormed out slamming the door behind me leaving them all with a look of disbelief on there face's, making straight for my room, waiting for one of them to run after me to give me a clout – it didn't happen. Now I knew their limitations. Sitting in the dark, I thought of all that had happened over the last three weeks. Do this, do that, everything had been decided for me. I'd had enough of it. It was time to go it alone, so packing my bags; I sneaked out the front door so not to be seen and started my long walk into town.

Tooloogan Vale Homestead and Farm

CHAPTER 7

The road was hard and long as, step by step, I drew further away from the farm until eventually the 'red tin roofs' were just a speck on the horizon, but still I carried on, I was young, had nice clothes and had even managed to save a few quid and had the world at my feet, or so I thought. I'd been walking for two hours or more with my case getting heavier and heavier as the heat of the sun beat down on the back of my neck. Looking behind could see in the distance a car coming towards me, travelling at a good speed, kicking up a trail of dust behind it. Hoping there would be a good chance of a lift, I stood in the road waving my arms only to recognise it as Crawford's pick-up. As it drew closer until it was finally in front of me, he then got out.

"So where do you think you're going?" he said with an angry look in his eyes.

"Don't know yet, haven't quite decided."

"Well you can't just leave without saying a word; I'm responsible for you, so tell me, what's your problem?"

"No problem, I'm just fed up of being treated like a bloody kid – besides it's not my idea of living, being stuck out here in the middle of nowhere from one week to the next. I'm no farmer and never will be and wouldn't have come if I'd known it was going to be like this." I'd had enough of being pushed around and somehow I'll make it on my own."

"Now come on Tony, let's just go back to the farm and talk this over like two adults."

There's nothing more for me to say so picked up my bag and started to walk, there was no turning back. I was headstrong and my mind was made up.

"Look, I've got an idea, jump in the car." Crawford called out in a much softer tone

"I'm not going back to the farm, IL be of as soon as your back's turned. I mean it."

"Just get in we're not going to sort anything out standing here in the blazing sun."

So, throwing my bags in the back, I got in and nothing more was said. We just headed off in the direction of town, stopping almost opposite the milk bar where Lin worked.

"You wait here, I'll be back in a minute," and he headed off in the direction of a large house, the sign outside read 'Rialto Boarding House', not thinking any more about it, I just waited for his return.

"Here you go Tony, I've booked you in to stay here for the time being and on Monday we'll think about getting you a job in town. Does that suit you better?"

At least it was the land of the living and was no longer completely isolated in the back of beyond I thought to myself

"Yeah, whatever, I'll see how it goes."

"Well come on then, get your bags, I can't stand around here all day."

It couldn't be better, right in the heart of town, although it seemed a funny place to have a boarding house, right on the main street. Things were starting to look up – independence at last. I followed Crawford inside and he introduced me to the landlady.

"Mona, this is Tony."

"Hello Tony, welcome to Rialto."

"Mona and her husband Malcolm own the place, so don't go upsetting him or he'll clip your ear."

"He'll do no such thing, come on Tony, I'll show you to your room."

"I'll be back later Mona, and Tony don't let me down, mind what I say"

As Crawford left, I followed Mona to my room. Mona had a broad Scots accent, short and dumpy with a heart of gold, you know the real motherly type.

"Here you go Tony a room all to yourself. Now you settle yourself in then come to the kitchen and I'll give you your keys," then left, closing the door behind her.

The room was small, clean with a wardrobe, chest of drawers and two single beds. Room for one more, but for the time being it was to be all mine. I could come and go as I pleased. No more rules and regulations. Feeling like a kid with a new toy, I unpacked my case. For me this was a first. Not to have to share with anyone and a choice of two beds this was more like it. Quickly unpacking, I made my way to the kitchen where Mona was sitting watching television.

"Settled yourself in have you? Now here's your key. Breakfast is between 6 and 8 a.m., evening meal between 5 and 7 p.m. If you want an early morning call, just ask. The bathroom is down the hall, there are showers inside and out, but we like you to use the outside ones if your work is dirty, okay?"

"Yeah, all I've got to do now is get a job."

"I'm sure you'll find something. Well I must get on, you make yourself at home."

"Yeah, right thanks, I think I'll just go for a walk and get my bearings."

My first stop of course was the Niagara, which came as a bit of a shock for Lin as I walked through the door.

"Tony, what you doing here, you're early tonight? Take over Helen, I'm going to take my break now," and during the short time we had together, I told her the whole story and how I'd left the farm and now lived at McPhee's across the road.

"Is Trev hurt badly?" she asked

"Na, he's alright, be out in a couple of days, just a few stitches."

"Hear that Helen, Trev's in hospital."

"Why? What for"

So then I had to go through the whole story all over again.

"That's alright Tony, when we've finished, we can all go up the hospital and see him."

"Okay, sure, I'll meet you back here at around seven. See you later Lin," and I made my way to the door.

"Yeah, bye Tony and don't be late will ya?" Then I headed back to the boarding house.

"That was quick. Tea's ready, if you're hungry" said Mona greeting me as soon as I walked in the kitchen, "You might as well eat now as most of the others eat at the pub and roll in hear well after closing. I think there's a couple of others watching TV, be a luv and tell them tea's ready for those who want it. Just through there."

I could hear the TV and just followed the sound into a large room full of armchairs. Over in the far corner stood the TV and as usual on a Saturday afternoon, it was sport.

"Been told to tell you lad's your tea's ready."

Yeah no worries kid, tell Mona we're coming." and returned to the kitchen

At first it felt a bit strange being around no one of my own age. I was just a kid and didn't know a thing about sport or racing results so the conversation didn't include me. After tea I went to my room and sat there until it was time to meet Lin and Helen. That evening we went to visit Trev, who was a little embarrassed to say the least at the whole situation, thinking that it was his fault that I'd left the farm, and I reassured him it was for the best.

After we returned to the milk bar, and met up with the rest of the boys from the farm who by now had wondered what had happened to me, and it seemed strange when Crawford arrived at 10-30 sharp that evening, and they all left leaving me still sitting there. The day ended with me walking Linda home and after saying goodnight I returned to my new digs. The room was dark, unlike back home there were no street lights outside to comfort me, so slept with the bedside light on all night.

Sunday was a little different than previously, at least there was somewhere to go even if it was only the milk bar. It was Lin's day off so we made arrangements to meet that afternoon, but after waiting an hour she never showed. So it turned into a long day with only me for company so ended up watched TV the rest of the day and then had an early night. By the time I'd got up Monday, all the lodgers had gone out to work leaving only a couple of travelling reps behind for breakfast.

"Morning Tony" Mona was full of the joys of spring, "Ow and by the way Andrews been on the phone, he'll be here around nine, Sounded like good news."

"Yeah why what did he say?"

"He said something about a job."

"Great, did he say where or what it was doing?"

"No, but you'll find out soon enough, he'll be here shortly so you can ask him yourself."

So far this only being my second day, and had hardly spoken two words to anyone apart from Mona and Linda. Mona's husband had gone to Sydney on business for the weekend and wasn't due back until later that day and as for the others, well they more or less only ate and slept here. Crawford arrived shortly after nine with a big smile on his face.

"Good day Mona, any chance of a cuppa."

"Coming right up Andy"

"Alright Tony, you settled in okay?"

"Yeah fine, thanks."

"That's good, all you need now is a job and I think I've found just the one."

"Yeah great, so what is it?"

"Plumber's mate, the guys a friend of mine so don't let me down, in actual fact you may have already met him. He lives here, name of Ray, Ray Walters."

"Na Can't say I have."

Mona butted in, "He's not been here all weekend, only to sleep you know what he's like."

"Aye, I know. I managed to catch him early in the bar Saturday night

So I hope he still remembers." they both laughed

"Well come to think of it, he did mention something at breakfast."

"That's something I suppose we'll take a run out and see him Tony. You change into your working clothes lad, while I give him a ring."

Quickly changed, I returned.

"Okay it's all settled, he's waiting for us down at his yard. I'll speak to you later Mona."

"Okay Andy, good luck Tony. I hope you get the job."

The journey was short and only around the corner, pulling up outside an old tin shack. On hearing the car, the door opened, and out walked my future boss a true Aussie in every sense of the word.

"Good day Andy, so how's it going mate?"

"Good Ray, good. Ray this is the lad I was telling you about wants' to be a plumber – Tony meet Ray."

"Good day Tony so you want to be a plumber do ya." I just agreed with Crawford after all it was better than being stuck out on that farm.

Ray was everybody's impression of a true Aussie, short but stocky, in his early forties and by looking at his stomach he liked a lot of the amber nectar (beer) a lot more than most. Underneath his hat, a round weathered beaten face that was still a little red from where he'd had one too many, standing there in his large baggy shorts, T-shirt and beetle crushers, he looked a real picture. I'd have recognised him if I'd seen him before.

"Andy tells me you're staying at Mac's. Good one, at least you won't be late for work. The pay's nine pounds a week and I don't stand for no slacking. Treat me right and we'll get on."He said short and to the point

"Yea sounds fair to me." I said not really having a choice but it would do for the time being

"Okay then Ray, I'll leave the boy with you."

"No worries Andy, he'll be right mate," and without another word he got into his car and drove off, while I followed Ray into the tin shack.

"Can ya make tea?"

"Yeah course I can," I said confidently.

"We'll see, over there, mine's with milk and three sugars, go for it."

Ray was a man of few words, well with me anyway, and at first finding it a bit hard to understand him, soon I could not only understand, but started picking up the slang myself. He wasn't a bad bloke to work for and for the first few days he just eased me into it. He shouted and I ran, and if something went wrong with the jobs, God help you. First few days, we drove all over the place doing all sorts from new taps, stand pipes and putting up a rain water tank and at the end of each day I'd go home, shower, and have tea, and wouldn't see Ray until the following morning. Things were more at ease by now. I'd meet Mac and the rest of the crowd over meal times, and Mac treated me a bit more like an adult than the others, occasionally giving me a beer or two. My evenings were much the same. Milk bar by seven then off out with Lin, except for a couple of nights when she had to stay at home. Then I just stayed in and watched TV. Finally Friday came round and my first ever, real pay day. Going to work as usual with Ray, first stopping of at the yard to load up and drove off to where a new house was being built.

"Right mate, we've got all the silly jobs out of the way, now we can get on with some serious work. I've got a nice little job for you today."

I didn't like the look of the silly grin that came across his face.

"Follow me, and bring that bar and shovel with ya." Then, walking about 30 yards or so from the house, he stopped. "Right, I want you to dig a hole here," marking out a square for a septic tank, "six foot by six foot, there ya go lad, call me when you've finished," and he walked away laughing, just leaving me standing there. Well, at least I'd had some experience. My brother Terry and I had dug enough holes in the garden back home and this one wasn't going to beat me. Taking up the bar, I started to dig it into the ground, it barely made a mark as after nine months of no rain it was like trying to break up concrete and I knew I was in for a hard day. After a couple of hours I was still only down a couple of feet. Now, down to just my shorts and boots, all the time the sweat dripping off me.

"So how ya doing boy, are you getting there?" Ray shouted

over

"Yea no worries"

My back by now was stiff from the bending and the blisters on my hands were split and getting worse with every shovel full, but I was determined to finish. It took me nearly all day but felt a certain sort of achievement on completing it and staggered off to tell Ray Id finished.

"About fucking time, come on then let's have a look," spending the next half an hour or so straightening up the walls, "Now it's finished, think we'll call it a day," he said, patting me hard on the back, "Load up will ya, I don't know about you, but I need a drink."

So did I. Covered from head to foot in dust, I looked and felt like I'd just been hit by a truck. After loading, I tried washing my hands carefully, they weren't used to hard work and today they'd had more than their share. "Piss on them" Ray said "that'll take the sting out and harden them up" strangely enough he was right, Ray changed a little towards me after that. It must have been the thought of the weekend ahead driving straight into town, parking outside the pub.

"Right let's go, if you can do a man size job, you deserve a man size drink."

I didn't believe what I was hearing. Was this the same man I worked with? Still not to argue, I just followed him inside and up to the bar."

"Good day Ray, what'll you have"

"Two schooners Dick one with a top on, don't drown it the boy deserves it, he's worked hard today."

"No worries, two schooners coming up."

Putting money on the bar, so Dick could help himself, we took up the glasses, "Good health," neither one of the drinks touching the sides.

"Same again Dick"

"Here ya go Tony, your wages, oh and here's an extra quid for a good day's graft. Get that down ya and be off or you'll get me in the shit. Early breakfast in the morning, we've got a few hours work so tell Mona will ya?"

"Yea no worries and thanks for the beer Ray."

Then leaving him drinking with his mates I walked the short distance to McPhee's. After tea all washed and dressed up, I made my usual visit to the Niagara to meet Lin from work, but that particular night I'd missed her as she had already gone home ill earlier in the day, so I ended up going to the Cinema on my own, followed by an early night.

Saturday, Ray and I were up and away early so as to get as much done as we could while it was cool, arriving home about eleven. Ray dropped me off first and then headed straight for the pub to get the dust from his throat. Me, I'd settle for a coke across the road and also to see how Lin was. First I'd wash and change, make myself more presentable.

"Hi Mona, what's to eat?"

"Hello Tony, there's two guys in town looking for you; one of them said he was your brother, Patrick, I think he said his name was."

"Yeah, that's him, where are they now?"

"They just said they were going for a drink, be back at around twelve."

"Did they say which hotel they were going to?"

"Na, I don't suppose they know themselves"

"So how did they get here? Did they come by car?"

One after the other, I threw the questions at her. We weren't close, but we were brothers nevertheless, and I was glad he was here.

"You go get showered and changed and by that time they'll be back."

Mona was right so I did as she suggested, soon to be back under her feet.

"Why don't you go and sit on the veranda and wait, you're driving me round the bend!"

I was excited, it had only been a few weeks, but it seemed longer. Maybe he had some news from home, and already found us a place to live and just come to collect me in his new car. The suspense was too much and I had to go outside and wait. It was just after twelve, but still no sign of them. They couldn't have gone far, I thought to myself, there was nowhere really to go and there was only a choice of three hotels and they were all within walking distance. Patiently waiting I watched all the cars go past until finally in the distance I could see a bright red F.J. Holden and as it got closer I noticed a large white spot on the bonnet, as slowly it came to a standstill outside McPhee's and there was Pat sitting up front in the passenger's seat with his arm out the window.

"Good day kid so how ya going"

His accent was terrible and a complete put on, but I didn't care. He was here.

"Hi ya Pat, where ya been? I've been waiting ages."

He got out of the car followed by the driver, "This is a friend of mine, Rick Manson."

"Hello mate, nice to meet ya."

"Good day."

"So what do ya think of the wheels bro?"Pat asked in his new lingo

"Yea great, must have cost a few bob."

"All Rick's own handy work should have seen her on the way up, she nearly flies. Left Sydney at 6 o'clock and was up here by 10."

Pat had found himself a new hero by way of Rick. He was about the same age blonde hair, well built and good looking to match and, what they called at the time, a surfer.

"Well come on then let's go and grab a coffee Tony, you know the layout, so where's the best place."

"The Niagara, just across the road there, it's the only place."

"Real one horse town this bro, so what do ya do for entertainment?"

"There's not much to do, just make the most of it."

"Wouldn't suit us would it Pat, that's for sure." Rick said as we entered the Niagara.

"Sit down fellas I'll get 'em in." And approached the counter

"Alright Lin, so how ya feeling"

"Ow much better thanks, so who are your friends?"

"Oh that's me Brother Pat and his mate just up from Sydney. Give us three coffees will ya?"

"No worry's so who's the nice looking one blond hair sitting in the corner?" she asked curiously

"That's Rick, see that car outside McPhee's that's his, smart ain't it?" "Yea very nice" she said handing me the coffees

"Well I'll see ya later, come over when you get a break." and returned to the others. Almost pouncing on Pat

"Well come on then, so tell me all the news. Have you heard from home yet?"

"No first you, so what happened out at the farm, old Ma

Stevenson got in touch and asked me to come up and sort you out."

"Nothing to tell, just didn't like it, too much do this, do that. Anyway, it's all worked out for the best. Nice digs, good job that's about it so what about you then?"

"Well I've got a bit of bad news, but first here's a couple of letters for you, one from Bev and the other from Mum and Dad to both of us saying they're not coming."

"What do ya mean, there not fucking coming?"

"Well that's what the letter says, you read it for yourself"

"But it's only been a few weeks, they made that decision a bit quick what about us, they can't just fucking leave us here and forget we ever existed, can they?"

"Sorry kid but it looks that way. Don't worry, we'll make out somehow."

It was all a bit of a shock to the system, something I'd not given much thought to and just out of the blue to be told like that was hard to swallow. So while they carried on talking I read my letter from Bev, which only made things worse, telling me all the news of our friends, and of how much she missed me and would always wait no matter how long also enclosing a photo of herself reminding me of what I'd left behind. That was it for me. Somehow I would get back to England, no matter how or what the cost.

"Oh yeah" pat said braking into my thoughts "there is a bit of good news, you're Royal Navy test papers have come through, I think Crawford's got all the details, it's on Monday week, apparently you'll be travelling down on the Saturday and staying at Ryde and coming back up here on Tuesday."

That's what they think, I thought to myself, once back in Sydney there was no way I was going to come back here, girlfriend or not, number one came first and that was me. So I would keep quiet making sure not to let anybody know of my intentions.

"So why can't I stay with you Pat?"

"Well, it's a little difficult see I live with Rick and his family. Besides, I think they'll want to keep their eye on you. They're not sure what you're going to do next."

The arrival of Linda broke up the conversation. .

"Oh hi Lin, this is my brother Pat and his mate Rick."

"Hello Pat, Rick. So how long are you up here fore?"

"Just tonight, we'll be heading back first thing in the

morning."

"Nice car." her eyes were all a gog with his long blond hair and he knew it

"She's not a bad old car if I do say so myself I'll take you for a spin in her later, if you like."

"Yeah great, what time?"

You'd think I didn't exist as she sprawled all over him like a rash and to make things worse, Rick pointed out the picture of Bev which was lying on the table. Even if I was only going to be here one more week, with friends like him I didn't need enemies. It wasn't long before Lin returned to work and apart from going for a short ride in the car, spent the rest of the afternoon in there until Pat suggested they returned back to the pub for tea.

"Listen Tony, we'll meet you back at your place say around six."

"Yeah, I might as well leave my car there Pat, if you like Tony we'll take a ride down to the coast later tonight."

"How about Lin, can she come?"

"Yea no worries, it's okay by me."

"Terrific, I'll ask her later."

Going our separate ways, I returned to McPhee's first to my room where once again I read my letters, then to the kitchen for my tea. Pat returned early while Rick headed straight for the Niagara. As we talked, I got the impression that he was settled and talked of Sydney like there was no other place on earth. Being older, it must have made all the difference going to discos, pubs, etc. While most boys of my age were still at school spending their nights at home doing school work, and found it was hard being a fifteen year old in a man's world, even worse in a strange one. Time was getting on so we made our way to meet the others. By the time we got there Rick had already asked Lin if she wanted to come with us, moving in on my territory, but I didn't care, in a week or so I'd be off and she'd be just water under a bridge. No sooner had I ordered my drink than the door opened and in walked Trev and the others from the farm.

"Hello Tony you old scumbag, fancy doing a runner" he said laughing "So how's life in the big city then?"

"Great, beats being stuck out on that farm."

"You seeing Lin tonight"

"Yeah, we're going for a drive down to the coast with my brother over there and his mate, there up from Sydney." And pointed in his direction, "That's my brother Pat, the other one all over Lin, is his mate Rick."

"I think the feelings mutual mate" Kev voiced his opinion "either that or it's his car she wants."

"So what about you and Helen"

"Na, that's all history, not doing too well are we mate," I said trying to reassure him, "still plenty of more fish in the sea."

"Easy for you to say, you're not stuck on that fucking farm."

"No one says you've got to stay there look at me, I got away."

He was envious, but for what? It wasn't so different. We both still worked. Yea true I got to go out seven nights a week, but now it was just to find someone to talk to. His board was guaranteed. I had to pay for mine every Friday or I was out. The situation gave me no choice but to grow up and do it fast. He, on the other hand, had room to breath.

"It's not the same without you Tony, No more laughs. That's the only thing that keeps you going out here."

"So what happened to you and Frank over the pigs?"

"Nothing, after you left everybody was so shocked it was all forgotten. So, tell me mate, how's the job?"

"Yea its okay, at least I get to travel and Ray's not a bad bloke bought me a pint Friday night

"Can't be bad, aye up here comes Lin, time for you to trot off like a good little boy."

"Ha, ha, like you said it's not me she wants it's my brother's mate and his bloody car."

"Are you coming Tony?"

"Yeah okay, see you later Trev, be lucky mate

Following Linda and the other two, we made our way across to the car.

"Lin, you ride in the back with Pat so Tony can sit up front."

Reluctantly she did just that.

"Okay then, let's go, Newcastle here we come." Rick said, slipping into first and pulling away.

"How far is it?" I asked curiously.

"Oh about an hour or so, why you don't have to worry about getting back do ya mate?"

"No I'm alright, I was just thinking about Lin."

"It's okay Tony I rang me Mum and told her I was staying

over at Helen's tonight, so there's no problem."

"Right then, let's go and have some fun." Putting his foot down on the accelerator, we roared away. Pat was right in one thing, this car certainly shifted and we were soon out of Scone in the open country. After about half an hour, Rick asked Lin if she'd like to sit in the front with him, giving him a big smile we pulled over and Lin and I changed places. By now totally in the dark, only had the headlights to guide our way, started off once again and Rick wanting to show the full potential of the car, put his foot down to the floor.

Luckily there wasn't a car in sight so had the road all to ourselves.

Suddenly we came on to a bridge crossing the Hunter River just outside Singleton. Rick, not knowing the roads, didn't realise there was a sharp left turn at the end until it was too late. Slamming his foot on the brakes at the same time following the road which he did successfully, but on the wrong side and coming straight towards us, was another car, but it was too late. All you could hear was the screaming of brakes and then the impact which fortunately was not that bad only the screaming from the other car made it worse. Rick and I were unhurt so he was quickly out seeing what he could do for the others. Pat had injured his ankle getting it wrenched under the front seat and Linda had smashed her head on the dashboard, leaving a large gash down the side of her forehead. All the time, the screaming carried on, taking off my jacket, then my shirt, I tore it up so Linda could hold it tight against her wounds. Then went to see if there was anything I could do to help in the other car. Luckily no one was hurt badly. It was a mother and her four children. All had been thrown around on impact. But there were no serious injuries from what I could see, just cuts and bruises and did what we could to make them comfortable until help arrived. The town was only up the road and already a passing motorist had gone for help which within minutes was racing towards us by way of two ambulances, and of course, the Police.

"Anyone hurt?" the ambulance driver shouted over.

"Yeah mate", I called out "the kids have been knocked about a little, but the mother seems alright."

"What about you Son, you got any injuries?"

"Na I'm okay, but my girl's hurt."

"You see to the kids Bruce and I'll check out the girl."

After doing all that could be done, they loaded up the ambulance.

"Whose shirt is this?" The ambulance men asked.

"That's mine mate."

"Well it's not much use now, but quick thinking on your part anyway."

Linda and Pat went off in the ambulance while Rick and I were left to try and sort it out with the police.

"Right lads, first, we'll try and get these cars off the road."

Fortunately Rick's car suffered little damage on impact, as the old F.J. Holden cars were built like tanks.

"Don't seem to be too much damage – she might even drive."

"I'll park her off the road." He said to one of the officers. Wait a minuet first things first came the reply, as the police thought we'd been drinking so came down a little hard on us making Rick walk along the white line in the middle of the road luckily proving them wrong. A natural assumption I suppose as we were the ones on the wrong side

"Right let's get some details. I presume it's your car?"

"Yes Sir."

"So what's your name mate?"

"Richard Manson 151 Pitt Street, Redfern, Sydney."

"You're a long way from home aren't you?"

"Yeah well I bought his brother up from the City to see him." pointing to me

"And you son, what's your name?"

"Me guv Tony Bates, McPhee's Guest House, Scone."

"You mean old Malcolm McPhee's place?"

"Yeah that's right mate."

"You're a bit young to be living in digs aren't you?"

"Yeah, tell me about it but it's a long story."

"So what's your age and date of birth then Tony?"

"I'm 15, born 2.9.49."

"So where do your parents live Tony?"

"England."

"This all seems a bit complicated. I think you'd better come with us Tony. Mr Manson do you think your car's okay to follow us?"

"Yeah no worries, she's alright."

So we made our way down town, during which I gave more

details. Once in the station they started to check out my story first by ringing McPhee's then Crawford out at the farm.

"Looks like you're telling the truth but seems a strange set up for a lad of your age."

I just laughed "How do you think I feel?"

With Rick's papers all checked out, it was only a matter of me getting back to Scone.

"Can you tell me how Lin and my brother are?"

"They're keeping her in for observation over night, but your brother's okay. He's waiting to be picked up."

"What about the others?"

"Nothing much just a few minor cuts and bruises. You were lucky you could have all been killed."

By now time was getting on it was way past eleven as during the excitement, the time had flown by.

"Okay if we go now?" Rick asked as his only interest now was to get back to Sydney.

"Yea okay mate, but contact your local Police Station as soon as you get back to Sydney. You sure you're alright to drive? What's more, is the car going to make it?"

"Yea, I checked her over, no major problems. She'll make it okay. So we'll be off then, can you point us in the direction of the hospital?"

"Yea sure," as Rick and I headed for the door, "Err, not you Tony, there's someone coming to pick you up, a Mr Crawford."

"Oh shit, that's great he's going to fucking love me."

"Well, I'll see you around then Tony, sorry about all this mate."

"Oh well can't be helped just one of those things, tell Pat I'll see him in Sydney next week

He left me waiting there for Andy, who arrived about 12 o'clock, not looking very happy, and after a short chat with the police we both headed off back to Scone. I don't think he said two words the whole way, just as well as I was in the mood to be nagged. What a day. First my brother arrives out of the blue then a letter from home tells me the family aren't coming out, and finally I nearly get killed in a car crash. If only Rick hadn't asked Lin to sit in the front. Still it was too late to turn back the clock now. We arrived at McPhee's and like a naughty boy, I was sent straight to my room. Mona and some of the others were still up and could hear Andy talking to them, and I got the impression they thought it was my fault. Poor Lin, she ended up worse of all, first by lying to her parents and then by ending up in hospital 50 miles away. The fact that we were together, making it look like my fault that she came along with us, that would make me really popular in town, but I was too tired to worry, and tomorrow was another day.

After a good nights sleep I woke about 10:30 Sunday morning. I got dressed and made my way to the kitchen. Although too late for breakfast, a coffee would go down a treat. As I entered the kitchen, it was as if I was a leper, as they were all staring at me through the deadly silence.

"Morning Mona, morning all, any chance of a coffee?"

"Help yourself, water's hot."

"Thanks." short and sweet but I expected nothing less.

The silence eventually broke and they continued their conversation. After making my coffee I went back to my room more a case of out of sight, out of mind. Not that I'd done anything to deserve the cold shoulder. The rest of the morning I spend writing home to Bev. Then reread the letter once again from home. I thought about replying to it, but what was the use? My future was clear, the past, well, that was history now. For the rest of that day I stayed clear of everyone, apart from going over the milk bar to find out how Lin was, also getting something to eat, stayed in my room. That was a long and lonely day and I felt the walls of my room closing in on me, and it was as much as I could do to keep them at bay.

At last Monday came around and back to work. Although quiet at breakfast, once out on the road Ray broke the silence.

"That was a stupid thing you did Saturday. Going off like that, you were lucky you weren't all killed."

"It was an accident, Ray, it could have happened to anyone."
"I don't think Lin's folks we'll see it that way" he was right but what could I do.

He then spent the next hour talking of responsibility. That was a joke. He hadn't been dumped half way round the world in the middle of nowhere getting a bollocking for something he hadn't done. Over the next few days I made myself scarce, just leaving my room for work and meals, occasionally I'd slip over to get any news of Lin, Helen telling me she was home, but not back at work yet. My only comfort was my letter from my Bev knowing that someone cared. Life wasn't totally pointless after all. Thursday evening arrived and so did Crawford with details of my trip to Sydney.

"Good' day Tony, So how you been?"

"Good thanks." What else could I say, what ever I did was wrong?

"I suppose your brother told you about Monday? This is your return railway ticket to Scone. You'll catch the 7:40a.m, Saturday morning arriving at Sydney at 12 noon and you'll be met by Nat Smith. You'll have to check your return on Tuesday which gets you back here just after midday. Make sure you pay your board before you leave then you won't be tempted to overspend. Got any questions?"

"No seems clear enough to me."

"Fine, you know where the station is so don't forget give yourself plenty of time, as we would'ent want you to miss it now would we." I sensed a note of sarcasm in his voice. As problems like me he could do without.

That I could guarantee. I'd sleep on the station bench if necessary and I definitely wasn't coming back here. No longer was I the green boy that arrived a month ago and like the card in the pack, dealt out to whoever would take me. I was now on my own. They'd made that clear enough, so now I'd do things my way. Crawford shook my hand, wishing me luck in the exams.

"See you next week then Tony, Good luck." I played the game to the very end.

"Yeah, no worries thanks Andy, thanks a lot."

The rest of that evening I packed my bags only leaving out the essentials.

Tomorrow I'd have to keep out of Mona's way to avoid paying my board and have to watch my every move so as not to slip up. I needed my wages for future expenses. After packing my bags, I slipped across the road for a while to check out any news of Lin and after being told she was still not back at work, just stayed for a coffee then went back to my room for an early night. Friday arrived and my last day in Scone.

"Morning Mona, what's for breakfast I'm starving?"

"You're in a good mood today."

"It's working here with my terrific boss it's a pleasure to go to work."

I was probably over doing it, but I didn't care.

"It's no good bull shitting me Son, you're not getting any

more money, you're over paid as it is." Ray mumbled from the other side of the table

"Ray, I wouldn't dream of upsetting you by asking." He laughed.

After a hearty breakfast or last supper, whichever you prefer, Ray and I went off to work. It was strange how on the last day we got on so well. Mind you at the end of the day there was no drink or extra quid, just straight wages then he dropped me outside McPhee's before making off to the pub.

"See you Wednesday Tony, have a good weekend and don't be late back."

"Yeah, alright, Ray see ya mate."

As I walked inside, I could hear Mona singing in the kitchen. It'll be safe for a while, I told myself, as she never accepted your board until after the evening meal, so tonight just to be make sure, I'd eat out.

"Hi Mona, have a good day?"

"Yes thanks, how about you?"

"Not bad, stomach's a bit dickie, but apart from that okay." At least now if I didn't show up for dinner, she wouldn't come looking. "Well I think I'll get cleaned up, see you later," and quickly showered and changed, going straight out after. First stop was the milk bar to see if there was any news of Lin. It had now been a week since and there was still no sign. Once inside I had a nice surprise as Linda was back and working behind the counter.

"Hi Lin, how are you" So how long did they keep you in?"

"Came home Sunday, but had to rest for a few days, but it's good to be back."

"What about you?"

"Oh me, I'm fine, off to Sydney tomorrow to do my naval exams."

"You are coming back aren't you?" She asked flashing her big blue eyes

"Yea sure be back on Tuesday arvo."

"Oh that's great, but I'm going to miss you! I'm really sorry about last Saturday."

"Sorry for what? It wasn't your fault."

"You know, for flirting with Rick. Should have let Pat sit in the front and stayed in the back with you."

"Oh well, its over and done with now and as long as you're alright, that's the main thing. Anyway, give us a coke and two hamburgers, I'm starving."

"Okay, I'll take my break in a minute and joint you."

At least she was okay, nothing serious, just a couple of stitches in her forehead. I sat there for what seemed hours then at seven Lin finished and joined me.

"So what do you want to do tonight?" I asked

"Don't mind you decide

Anything just to keep out of the way, so suggested that we go to the cinema and then to the Niagara for coffee. The evening passed quickly. Lin told me of how her Dad thought I was a bad influence on her and to keep well away from me, although she had other plans. I must admit I did think about returning to Scone a couple of times that night, but my better judgement told me not to, besides what would happen when another Hooray Henry arrived in town with a nice car, would she be off again? I wasn't going to take the risk. After walking her home, did the romantic scene bit, loves young dream and all that. Errol Flynn would have been proud of me.

"See you Tuesday then, meet me from work. I love you, bye."

Words came cheap and I wasn't buying, "Yeah bye, oh and say hello to your dad for me." She just laughed as she ran up the path to her front door. It was late when I got back to boarding house so I would have to be quiet so not to disturb anyone. Once I was in, I set my alarm for six and finished packing my bags then just lay on top of my bed, day dreaming. Where had the last month gone? My life was like a roller coaster, one minute up the next down. So far I had three moves and now again I was off to God knows where. Perhaps I'd get digs with Pat just until my call up for the Navy. At least I'd have more scope for a job. Maybe I'd get in touch with the guy on the plane who knows, he might be genuine, my prospects were unlimited.

The next thing I knew was when my alarm went off, so not to wake the household quickly throwing it under my pillow before switching it off, dressed a quick check around the room – all clear and off, locking the door behind me and taking the key. That way I'd be long gone before anyone knew. I arrived at the station with still had an hour to kill which seemed more like six then finally the train rolled into the station. Quickly I dashed into the ticket office.

"Here mate; do you know the McPhee's Boarding House on

Main Street?"

"Yeah coarse I do?" He asked with a look of surprise

"Well I've come away with my room key, any chance of dropping it back for me."

"Yeah, no worries, who shall I say sent it?"

"Just say Tony, Tony Bates, there no who you mean."

Boarding the train, I waited for it to pull out of the station as slowly we left Scone behind and headed for open country. The journey was to take just over 4 hours. Stopping at nearly every station, at first, taking in the view which was scorched from the sun after months of no rain, but it still had a certain beauty. The early morning sun started beating in on the windows and I knew we were in for another hot day. The old rattlers as the trains were called, had sliding doors which were left open so as to let the breeze in and it wasn't long before I'd settled down and started to doze off, just waking at each station, now and then looking out to see where we were, each time finding it more built up until finally on the outskirts of Sydney, It had been a long journey and I was glad it was nearly over as the stations were more frequent. Soon to have the city in full view and finally to pull into Sydney Central Station and journey's end.

Mcphees Boarding House
Scone

The Local Cinema

Main Street - Scone

CHAPTER 8

Waiting at the barrier as promised, stood Nat Smith and his wife Hilda.

"Good'day Tony welcome back to Sydney so how's it been mate?" said Nat, putting out his hand in friendship.

"Hi Nat, Hilda, thanks for meeting me you didn't have to, I could have made my own way to Ryde."

"Don't say that" Hilda butted in, "you'll put ideas in his head, anyway it gives me a change to drag Nat round the shops for a couple of hours."

"Devious creatures, these women, Tony, as no doubt you're finding out. Well let's get going, here I'll take one of those bags, better get back and see what sort of mischief the others have been up to."

Outside, the excitement of the city hit me with the noise, high buildings and the heavy traffic. Compared with Scone, this was heaven. The car was just a short walk away out front and was soon loaded up and on our way.

"Well come on Tony, tell us all about it, what's living in Scone like? We heard you didn't see eye to eye with farm life." Nat said smiling

What could I say? I wasn't going back anyway, so it didn't matter.

"All right, I suppose, if you like the quiet of the country, but it's not my idea of paradise."

"You just wait my boy, a couple of days down here and you'll be glad to see the back of it," he said, with a touch of sarcasm.

"Well I'm telling you now mate, I'm not going back there."A look of surprise fell over both there faces

"What do you mean not going back?" Nat's face was a picture

"That's right; I'm staying down here in the city."

"Come on now don't be silly Tony, what about your job and board? I heard you made a lot of new friends."

"I've quit, done a runner, shot through, call it what you like, but I'm not going back up there."

"Does Mr Crawford know about this?"

"No, not yet, you're the first. I'm going to stay and work down here until it's time for my call up, but I'm definitely not going back up to Scone."

"Well, there's not much we can say or do until Monday, Nat, so we may as well forget it and have a nice weekend."

"Yeah, I spose you're right luv."

"How say you Tony? Sound like a good idea to you?"

Our journey was quicker than I remembered and was soon to arrive at Rickard House, Ryde and once inside, was met by Judy.

"Hello darling how are you?" Then taking me in her arms, squeezing the life out of me, "Didn't think it would be long before we saw you again, you know, I just had a feeling. I bet you're hungry after that long trip. Now how about a nice cup of tea and some of my chocolate cake? A growing lad, like you needs to keep his strength up."

"You've filled out," she said, looking me up and down like a prize bull, "the country air must agree with you. Come and sit down next to me and tell me all about it."

Meanwhile, Nat headed off in the direction of his office, probably to ring around to find out what the hell was going on, while Hilda and I took up Judy's offer. He returned a short while after, with a smile on his face.

"You've got them running round like headless chickens looking for you young man. Mrs McPhee found your room empty so called Crawford, apparently you gave the Station Master the key to your room which got everyone wondering."

"Oh yes," said Judy breaking in, "there's been a couple of phone calls while you were out Nat, one from Miss Stevenson and the other from Mr Crawford."

"You've certainly put the snake amongst the chickens. Why?" Nat asked, "Why all the secrecy?"

"Well, I thought if I told anyone my plans they'd stop me coming."

"It's not funny Nat, but you've got to laugh," said Hilda giving me a smile, "you'd better ring Miss Stevenson and let her know he's here."

Later that day, I settled into my room and back into their family routine. The rest of the weekend went smoothly, just sitting around watching TV and enjoying the rest, after my days of hard labour in the outback. Monday arrived and the day of my navy exams. I was to report directly to the recruiting office in George Street, Sydney, promptly at 8:30. Nat drove me, setting off early, giving me plenty of time to find my way round.

"Here you go Tony, the Recruiting Office good luck mate. When you've finished, make your way back to Jamieson Street, I think Miss Stevenson wants to see you."

Getting out of the car, I watched him drive away and after hesitating for a short while, I made my way inside the building and was directed up on to the second floor then shown into a room, where already a number of other hopeful recruits were waiting. The room was clean and had a distinct clinical smell with its white walls and highly polished floors. A few pictures of ships were scattered about, just to let you know where you were and finished off with strategically placed desks not one being out of place, where sat neatly behind were the rest of the contenders, waiting patiently. So along with them, I took my seat right at the back of the class. No one said a word they just sat there in total silence like puppets waiting to be worked by hand. It was like being back at school and we were all waiting for the form master. Eventually, the Recruiting Officer entered and the rest of the recruits stood, coming to attention while I stayed sat behind my desk as I didn't know what the hell was going on.

"Good morning Gentlemen, you may sit, my name is Captain Hope, and I shall be with you for the next hour or so. As you have already noticed, in front of you there is a folder and inside are three test papers, each one lasting 20 minutes. When I give the word, you will open them and commence the first one. If, however, you finish one before the given time, you may carry on with the next. Every 20 minutes, for those who have not finished, will be given a time check so to commence with the next. Any questions Gentlemen?"

Looking around, I noticed everybody apart from me had come prepared, and I felt like crawling under the table as my hand was the only one to go up.

"Yes Mr?"

"Bates Sir, Have you got a pen I can borrow?"

"Yes Mr Bates, I do believe you were told to come prepared. Anyone else not come prepared?"

There must be someone else I thought, as I went to the front of the class to get a pen, but no, there was just me, looking a complete fool in front of everyone. And noticed some of them sniggering with there smug faces as I returned to my seat, asking myself, why did I have to stick out so?

"Right, any more questions? No?" then checking his

watch, he gave himself a little countdown, "3, 2, 1, right, you may begin."

So I opened the folder. the first paper was maths, well when it came to anything to do with money, I was great, but this wasn't to be the case, instead I was confronted by fractions, logs, algebra, square roots, oh and a couple of adding and long division. Well I might just as well have played noughts and crosses for 20 minutes as I didn't have a clue. Maths never was one of my strong subjects and half of these I'd never seen or done before anyway, but not losing heart, I quickly turned on to the next page. That was just as bad, problems, as if I didn't have enough, you know .....' Fred had 100 donkeys, Pat 10 Terry had 60 and so on by the time I'd finished reading it, I still wasn't sure who had what. Nevertheless, I gave it a go coming up with so many donkeys I could have started up a farm of my own.

"Time's up Gentlemen, turn to the next page please."

I was only half way through the first one. The next paper was English. Verbs and nouns, spelling –well that was just about it for me. There was no point in carrying on. I could just about read and write let alone spell and as for the other, well! The sweat just started pouring off me, more from embarrassment than anything and I just wanted to crawl out of there on all fours without being seen, but I could only do my best, doing what I could in the time allowed. Finally, the last test was to be a written essay in particular on why you wanted to join the Navy and of your ambitions. At least I'd come up against something to write about. Scribbling down a couple of pages in totally unreadable writing before the time was up and the papers were handed in for marking.

Meanwhile we were offered refreshments; next we were to be interviewed in a nearby room and awaited our ordeal. After a break of half an hour, one by one our names were called out, luckily for me in alphabetical order. My name was one of the first and that was as far as I got. After walking into a small room where three officers, including Captain Hope, sat behind a long table and on letting me down gently, told me my exam marks were poor at this particular time so I wouldn't be accepted, but if I'd like to try at the age of seventeen, they would reconsider my application. It was what I expected at least they had the decency to tell me in private and discreetly. I left the building with one of my dreams shattered and walked around for a couple of hours to kill time so as not to get back to Stevenson too early. Walking for what seemed like miles, I felt depressed and homesick, I just wanted to shut my eyes and open them as if from a terrible nightmare and wake up in my bed back at No. 36, but it was not to be. Trying to cheer myself up I thought of the Merchant Navy, at least that was a bit more promising. So I'd had one disappointment – big deal! It wasn't the end of the world. Bucking myself up, made my way back to Jamieson Street and my next ordeal, like the Christian going into the lion's den, I entered the Barnardo Office.

"Hello Darling, Miss Stevenson about? The name's Tony Bates."

The girl on switchboard was not much older than me and quite a dish. She rang through, giving me a smile as she waited for a reply.

"Miss Stevenson will be with you in a minute, if you'd like to take a seat."

"No thanks darling I'll stand," and just walked around the office reading the different notices on the walls until she arrived.

"Hello Tony, how did you get on?" She made me jump as she came up behind me.

"Yeah, great, they said they'd be in touch."

"Come on through to my office. Were the test papers hard?" She asked as I followed her.

"Not to bad."

"Well it all sounds very promising. Now sit down. Would you like a coffee?"

"No thanks, Miss, I must be going soon."

"Well now, what's this Nat tells me you're not going back to Scone."

"Just that, I want to stay in Sydney and get a job I don't like the country."

"You are naughty first from the farm and now Scone. What am I going to do with you?"

"Send me back to England Miss."

"Don't be silly Tony you've only just got here. Now let's be serious."

I was serious, but my opinion didn't count.

"Now why don't you go back to Scone just until your Navy call up? I've been in touch with Mrs McPhee and she'll have you back and Mr Walters said your job's still there if you want it."

Wasn't anybody listening to what I was saying? I tried

again.

"No Miss, I'm not going back. I'll get a job down here, I'll be okay, you'll see."

"Now you're being difficult, it's not as easy as that. Good jobs are hard to come by, especially at your age. What about accommodation? You can't stay at any of the homes, there's no room for you plus the fact you're too old"

If that was the case, I thought to myself, why bring me out here in the first place?

"Look Tony, you go and have some lunch and come back in an hour. I'll see what I can sort out."

My break was short lived soon to be back in the office to await my destiny all most bumping into Miss Stevenson in reception.

"You're back early, I haven't had much time to ring around, but as you seem so persistent on not returning to Scone, I've arranged for you to stay at Ryde for the time being or until you find work and suitable accommodation. So I want you to report here early each morning then we can go through the papers together."

So that's exactly what I did. Each day going by train to the city, applying for jobs and going to and from the office. I was becoming a permanent fixture, unfortunately without a lot of success. Also daily I would go to the Merchant Marine Office just to show my face, hoping they would give me a ship, if only to get rid of me. After a week of trudging all over Sydney, I finally got a job on the north shore at a plastic company as a labourer. My job as a guillotine operator started at £10 a week, which was good money for my age. Miss Stevenson was over the moon, so was I come to that, and she pulled out all the stops to find me some accommodation which fortunately for me was also on the north shore, just around the corner from my new place of employment, and on Saturday morning, 12th June, Nat moved me into 16 Glen Street, Milson's Point. The landlady was a Mrs Spinazzi she was short and fat and well in her forties and wore more make-up than Coco the clown. By now, most of my savings had gone so I was to have a quiet weekend only waiting for Monday and the start of my new job. I don't know which was worse, living in the country or the city but without any money either way was hard, spending the weekend either in my room or watching TV with my other lodgers. The digs were clean and comfortable but the other tenants were much older so I was to spend most of my time on my own.

Monday came around with the start of my new job, arriving promptly at eight, reporting to the foreman. My training took exactly five minutes then only had to do the same thing hour after hour just waiting for the lunch and dinner bells to go to break the boredom. After work I went back to the digs, showered, had dinner then either went to my room to write letters or took the short walk down to the river bank. There I'd sit and look across the harbour at the city and all its lights, wondering what everyone else was doing. One evening, I also took the desperate measure to call Tom Skillman, hoping in some way he might be able to change things just a little and on making the call, he invited Pat and myself to lunch on Sunday at a restaurant of our choice, and so for the first time since arriving back from Scone I contacted Pat to see if he would be available, which after a short chat about how great times were going for him, we agreed to meet on the Sunday. Giving me something to look forward to, Friday soon came and pay day, although only a short week of three days pay as they kept some in lieu, luckily my board was paid up so what I'd earned was mine. That evening I thought I'd spend with Pat so I made the long journey across the bridge to Redfern only to find on my arrival he had moved out of the Manson's

"We were sorry to see him go," said Mrs Manson politely, "but after Rick's trip up to Scone and the damage to the car they both seemed to fall out." So after saying my goodbyes I made my way back to the station. Arrangements had already been made for Sunday so I wasn't worried. I meet Pat at Circular Quay at 12 o'clock, and Tom would pick us up at 12:30, for once everything went like clockwork. Tom arrived shortly after 12:30 in a large flash car. After a short discussion on our astronomical delights we settled for Chinese during which Pat and I told him all about ourselves and our plans for the future. Never at anytime did he mention his family, not that we gave him much chance, he just listened. Instead of asking him for the help like I'd planned, I made out I was happy at my work and at home, finally just before we said our goodbyes Tom mentioned that if either of us ever needed anything be it help or money, not to hesitate to ring him, then he drove off, leaving us both standing there back where we started. It was then Pat and I decided it would make sense to move in together so we could share the rent, as he too was by now feeling a little homesick. On the Friday I went to work as usual and quit my job, then went back to get my digs to get gear, but first waited for Mrs Spinazzi to go out shopping then sneaked in the back way, all was left to do was to hang around all afternoon to pick up the rest of my wages. By the time I got to Pats it was getting dark and for the first time I saw the conditions in which he lived. It was pitiful; he was almost ashamed to let me in. His one room had two single beds and a wardrobe although you had to be careful not to shut the door to hard, as when you did the window frame actually moved. He also had the use of sharing a kitchen I wasn't sure who with, the tenants or the cockroaches, that roamed around freely, every so often hearing the loud crunch as you stood on one, some being the largest I'd ever seen. We decided we'd cook our home speciality. Onions, tomatoes and sausages, mopped up with a loaf of bread just like Mum used to do. So after a visit to the local shops Pat and I cooked up our slap up meal and washed it down with more than a couple of cold beers, both getting slightly drunk and after slamming the door once too often, sent the loose window frame crashing to the ground below which we both thought hilariously funny, at least until we realised what we'd done. That night you could say we slept under the stars, but it wasn't long before the funny side and the beer had worn off and we started to worry about the consequences from the landlord the next day.

The following morning we were both up and out early. As we had to find me a job and new digs, eventually taking us to a place called Marickville and to a boarding house at 10 Sebastipole Street. A large old bungalow surrounded by high walls, tucked away in a side street. It was owned by a Mr and Mrs Jose, Tony and Avril an English couple. Tony was tall and slim with short blonde hair, in his late twenties, and had obviously done well for himself since his arrival in Australia. During my stay there I never saw him much as his job at the airport was shift work, Avril on the other hand I did see a lot of, and would have most certainly liked to have seen a lot more. She was young, in her mid twenties and one hell of an attractive woman with her long black hair and a figure that was straight of a playboy magazine, making it almost impossible to miss her as she brushed past you in the corridor, at the back of the house was another door which led you into a large extended kitchen and dining room, where tables were laid for twenty or more boarders. From there Avril took us outside to the accommodation area which was in cabins surrounding the house like a miniature town each one housing two lodgers. It was spotless and most of all friendly.

"Well what do you think boys, will you take it?" Pat jumped at it.

"Yeah no worries, this'll do us fine."

"What do you recon kid" He said, Looking in my direction.

"Looks great we'll take it

"Good then, that's settled. Yours is number eight. Will you be moving in today? If so, dinner starts at 5 until 7, I presume you'll be wanting it."

"Sure thing, we'll just shoot off and get our gear."

"Okay fine boys, see you later."

Pat was full of it, come to that so was I. This was the nearest thing to home since we'd arrived in Australia. Returning to our new digs, first we settled in then made our way across the yard to the Dining Room where already most of the others had already started. It was a kind of self service. Just queue up at the kitchen hatch and wait your turn.

"Hello Tony, Pat, have you settled in okay?" Avril went out of her way to make us feel at home and just knew I was going to like it there.

"Yes thanks." Taking more notice of the food that was going on my plate.

"Ann, these are two new boys, not long out from England."

"Hello boys, any likes or dislikes."

"No, just as it comes." I said, noticing her over developed body.

Ann was a full-time student who also lived in, paying her way by helping in the kitchen morning and night. She was about nineteen. Pretty, but short and a little top heavy which made it a little hard to miss with the tops she wore, making it well worth turning up for your meals. Finding a space at a table, sat down, introducing Pat and myself to the others, although only got a grunt from some, two made instant friends with us, Wilf and Jerry.

Wilf was tall, north country and after many years still had a strong accent. In his early 30's, he wore a rather shabby beard his appearance was one of any old biker who'd somehow been left behind in time. His spare time would be spent washing, cleaning and polishing his Triumph 650 and promising some day that he would take me for a ride. Jerry, on the other hand, had an appropriate name. He was German also in his early 30's, very stocky with short, cropped hair, concealing his round and rather red face. His room was the next one up and sometimes entered his room without knocking and on one occasion found him giving Ann one, which was a bit of a shock for all of us as I didn't know it was possible to do it in more than one position and just stood there staring and thought to myself, he wasn't only getting big helpings at the dinner table, every time I saw her after that and she smiled, could see a mental picture of her in my mind. Next morning Pat was up and off early for work. I was one of the last for breakfast so I was joined by Avril and Ann which made a nice change from some I'd spent breakfast with. Afterwards, I headed off in search of work. I finally landed an interview in Sydney with a printing company, Express Plan Printers, only a small firm, two basement rooms in the heart of town, run by a Polish couple who, after a short interview offered me the job which consisted of learning the copying machine and delivering blue prints all over the city. My wage was £9 a week; take home pay after tax £7.10. Pleased with myself, I wanted to tell everyone, but thought better of it. I'd wait a while before I told Miss Stevenson. As at that particular time I wasn't her favourite subject so I went straight back to Marickville to tell Pat my good news and started my new job on Thursday, 24th June and settled in nicely to both my new home and employment.

At first everything was great, my job took me all over the city, meeting different people, occasionally popping into Barnardo's office for a laugh and a joke. Mr and Mrs Sabrinski treated me like the son they didn't have. Each day she would bring me all sorts of dishes so I'd put on more weight. At weekends Wilf would take me out and about on his bike to the beach or up the coast. A couple of times we even went up to the blue mountain to a place called Wentworth Falls. If it hadn't been for Wilf, I'd have never gone out at all, but he soon got tired and reverted back to his own age group which was only natural enough. After that I never went out much, Pat by now had his own friends so I only saw him at meal times. He also earned twice as much as me so could afford to go out more. My wages never went anywhere and after paying my board of £5, left me with £2.10 for fares, lunches, clothes, washing facilities, there was nothing left to go out and enjoying myself. So apart form an occasional bus ride to the cross and to spend the evenings walking around the flesh pots of

Sydney (Kings Cross) that was as far as my budget went. Finally I decided to look for something with more money. Although I was sad to leave the printer's as by now I was like one of the family, but my mind was made up. Unfortunately, although they wanted to, they couldn't afford to give me a rise. My final day being a sad one as although it was only short stay of ten weeks it made a mark on all our lives, leaving there on Friday 13th August of all days. That's the first and last time I'd ever seen an employer sad to see me go. I started my next job on the Monday. This time on nights at £12 a week, but like jumping out of the frying pan into the fire, I got fed up with being stuck at home during the daytime, which only made things worse and by now my homesickness was like a terminal disease and would go to any lengths to somehow try and get home.

I wrote home, but received no replies even when I approached Miss Stevenson her reply was always the same, "Pull yourself together man, you don't know how lucky you are."

I was just another homesick kid who'd soon get over it. During my spare time, I'd go round the travel agents trying to find the cheapest way home. When I did, the £150 they wanted was like reaching for the moon. At one stage I even wrote home for help not knowing, helping me was the furthermost thing from their minds. Only the letters from Bev gave me some hope and some nights I'd go down to the docks to watch the ships come and go, thinking some day I'd be out there, but when? How long? By now my only aim was living for the day I was homeward bound and I lost all interest in life around me. What was the point if I earned too much they'd take away my boarding allowance so I'd be back to square one. No matter how I tried there was never any left to save? Pat, by now, was sick of my whingeing and we started to row. Come to that everybody was getting tired of my moping around except Avril. Although she never said, I could see her concern for me in her eyes and it was her suggestion that it would be better for all if I moved into the house to share with someone more compatible to myself. At that time Pat was hanging around with one of the lodgers named Ray who recently just came out of Long Bay Jail. Nice guy, but a poor home life and a bad start had led him off the rails a bit, but now running back on the straight and narrow, so he moved in with Pat and in return I moved into his old room. My new room mate was John Barnes who'd only been with us a couple of weeks. He was from the Alice (Alice Springs) and had only come to Sydney to leave behind him the bad memories of losing both his parents, who'd been killed outright in a car crash. There were no brothers or sisters so in a way, like me, he was on his own. He was older, eighteen, but he didn't look his age. A bit taller than me, slim but with a good build. Dark hair with a fair complexion and we hit it off from the start, having one major thing in common, He too, wanted out of Australia. John worked at the Shelley drinks factory. No sooner had he got home than I was going out nights to the bakery so I decided to change my employment once again, that job lasted two weeks, leaving on the morning Saturday 28th August. That night all four of us, Ray, Pat, John and me went up the Cross. Although I didn't look eighteen, it was easy to get served at the bars. It was another world. Strip clubs, gay bars, and amusement arcades. This time I had money in my pocket so I made the most of it. That night was also my first glimpse of a real star. Mickey Rooney was in town, staying at the Cheveron Hotel, which was also in the Cross and on entering the bar which ran underneath the hotel, saw him, large as life, drinking with the every day punters. That was a good night and for once I didn't have a care in the world. Mind you the next morning was a different story and I swore I'd never drink again.

After a hectic weekend, on Monday I went to work with John in search of new employment and more or less getting a start straight away. I was put on the bottling plant loading the empties ready to be washed for re- use and with the sound of rattling glass, you couldn't hear yourself talk. After a couple of days John and I were put on a line together which made things more interesting, even managing to have a laugh now and then. Thursday came round and with it my sixteenth birthday, 2nd September, receiving only a few cards. There was only one from England, but unfortunately it wasn't from the old folks, it arrived early in the week so Avril kept it until breakfast on the day. That was one of the few birthdays that made their mark as along with cards from Pat, Avril and Ann, there was one from all the guys and there were presents, only little ones, a tie and shirt and a large card from Beverly with Across the miles I send my love inside, together with two records by the Dave Clark Five, As I write my letter, and Trains, Boats and Planes. Unfortunately, I didn't have a record payer so Wilf offered to lend me his. There was more surprise to come, after a good day at work I went home to what was an emotional time for me. I'd just finished my tea when Avril turned down the lights then Ann came in with the cake, complete with candles while twenty rowdy blokes all sang 'Happy Birthday' a sweeter sound I'd never heard and I fought back the tears as my eyes became all glossy. I was sixteen, a man and had been taught men just don't cry, well not in public anyway. That night after what was a great party, I went back to my room and for the first time had a chance to play my records. If you've ever heard those records you'll know just how I felt. They said it all, leaving a lump in my throat as large as a tennis ball. On my list of memorable days in my life this one would be high up on the chart.

Things got worse for me after that day. John and I got the sack the following Monday for messing about, although we did have a couple of other jobs during that week, one lasted a day and the other only an hour or so. On the Friday we both applied for a job as driver's assistants and were told to start on the Monday morning. By now my financial status was looking pretty grim so was glad to start. The job consisted of delivering dairy products to Hotels and Hostels, one of our calls was the Long Bay Jail. My first experience in such a place where the van was checked on the way in, then allowed to proceed through a number of gates until you finally we reached the kitchen where the unloading was done by prisoners. It was all so dull and dingy with the prisoners all dressed in their grey uniforms, but even under those circumstances they still had time for a laugh and a joke, but it wasn't the sort of place you'd want to spend an extended visit. After my second day at my new job, I arrived home to be handed a letter from the child welfare dept of Barnardo's, threatening me that if I didn't sort my self out, they would have no other option but to prosecute me.

What did it mean? Were they going to take me to court? Perhaps I'd even get put away. My recent visit to Long Bay Jail didn't make the thought all that appealing. What was I going to do? As for the rest of the letter, how different was Christmas going to be without money anyway? In my case being without it was a permanent situation. Could they do that, just prosecute me for being out of work? Perhaps come and take me away. The letter fare put the wind up me. Maybe that's what they wanted, but I couldn't be sure so I showed my room mate John.

"Hear John do us a favour and have a look at this will ya,

and tell us what you think?" He read it carefully

"Looks like they've got it in for you mate. Might be time you moved on."

"Moved on where?"I asked curiously

"Up North, Melbourne anywhere, even Perth, Western Australia, as long as it's far away from here as possible. Tell you what, I'll come with you. We'll stick this job out for a month or so just to get a few quid together and then just shoot through without telling anyone."

"Shoot thought? Who's shooting through?" Came a voice from the opening door.

"Oh hi Ray, Young Tony here has just had some bad news come. Looks like the Welfare are after him. Here show him Tony."

So passing over it over to Ray awaited his opinion "Ah they're just trying to put the frighteners on ya mate, your be right, don't worry about it."

It was easy for him to say, but I wasn't so sure. John's idea sounded the better of the two options. We'd just have to wait and see. The rest of that week John and I made plans staying in our room each night. We'd acquired an old electric radio, with it's age the casing had long since fell apart, but once we wired up it worked a treat and we'd listen to it in the evenings while playing cards, anything to keep us occupied during our spare time just to save money. All was going well at work. A week had gone by and even quite use to it, but only waited for the day we'd make our escape out of Sydney. Sounds dramatic I know, but we intended to go ahead with our plan. Pat, by now, was getting a little suspicious, but I couldn't tell him as he'd only contact the office, making things worse for me. Although we did think we'd have to bring our plans forward as he got more inquisitive. We were nearing the end of our third week, already September was nearly over. Friday came round and the 1st October, pay day, and another week was over. As usual, after tea, John and I went and sat in our room. Pat and Ray had already gone into town so after breaking into a couple of beers we were all ready for another night in. Glancing through the paper as I did most nights, turned to the shipping page from habit more than anything just to see what was coming in and going out and from where when Spotted a familiar name.

"Ere, have a look at this will ya John."

"What's that?"And handed over the paper

"The shipping news see there" and pointed it out "It's the S.S. Afric Piermont 7, she's from England."

"So how do you know that then?"

"It's a Shaw Saville boat, been on it with my old man a couple of years back. Wonder if there's anyone still on board who remembers him, this might be our chance mate, fancy going to England?"

John looked at me with a surprised look on his face, "You're joking they won't just take us on board like that."

"Course not stupid, we'll stow away, then once at sea we'll stay hid for a few days then turn ourselves in, easy there not going to turn the ship round just for us so its next stop England."

"You're fucking mad course they will."

"No not if we take food and drink, say enough for a week, we'd be miles away by then and they'd have to take us with them. Well, what do you say?"John tried to shrug the whole Idea of

"Let's sleep on it, maybe go down in the morning and have a look around."

"It'll be too late by then she sails on the early morning tide."

"So alright smart arse suppose we go down then what how we going to get on board? They're not just going to let us walk on. What about the security?"

John could think of a dozen obstacles not to go, I was the opposite, with or without him, I was going to give it a try. This could be my last chance so had nothing to lose. We sat for a while sinking a couple more beers, all the time our Dutch courage getting stronger and stronger.

"Well what do ya say John, shall we give it a go?"

"Ow go on then why not? What about your brother? You gon'na leave him a note?"

"Na he'll only dob us if we do get lucky, best to say nothing. Come on then let's do it."

Without any more hesitation at all we left our room and 10 Sebastopol Street behind us, not seeing or saying goodbye to anyone. All we had were the clothes on our backs a few quid and a photo of Bev which I carefully slipped into my back pocket. Making sure we didn't carry any form of identification on us at all, we set off for the station and our journey into town. The night was still young with the warm evening air making the conditions perfect. Summer was slowly coming, but we were going, going off on an adventure of mystery and danger.

Our journey across town was swift, soon to be in the heart of the city and central station then the short walk down to Darling Harbour and Piermont, at no time looking behind or having second thoughts. Our only thought was to get on that ship no matter what. On the way we stopped off to buy supplies at a nearby Deli in George Street, which ending on a pack of hamburger rolls and two cans of coke, just in case our mission was a complete failure, we didn't want to waste unnecessary money, although come later we wished we had. Soon we were down at the harbour and crossing Piermont Bridge where in the distance we could see the lights of ships waiting to be loaded and unloaded.

"So which one is ours" John asked

"I don't know, it just say's here Piermont 7 not sure where it is but it can't be far."

Soon across the other side of the bridge we came to a pub, The Montgomery.

"There ya go Tony ask that bloke coming out the pub, he might know where it is."

"Excuse me mate, can you tell us where Piermont 7 is?"

He looked at us as if we weren't quite right in the head, as if it was right under our noses, "That's Piermont 7, just down there, see all those lights?"

"Yea thanks a lot mate."

"So what ship you looking for boys?"

"The Afric" I said as if I was already part of her crew

"Yea that s her, can't miss her she's still being loaded" again pointed down to the right.

Following his instructions we were soon in sight of her. There she was and just as he'd said all lite up, still loading and looking smaller than I remembered, but it was her alright and written high across her stern "AFRIC'. At last we were here but now to overcome our first obstacle – the gatehouse. For a while we watched blokes coming and going, noticing they all showed some kind of pass.

"Well that's us out we're not going to get through there in a month of Sunday's. Come on Tony, it's a waste of time lets call it a day."

"Hang on mate I didn't say it would be easy. There's got to be another way in somewhere, once we get inside nobody will take any notice of us with all the commotion going on. Let's take a look around."

We followed the fence along the back of the gate house into the dark and noticed a blind spot and a small gap.

"Here ya go John we'll climb over here."

"Yeah right you go first while I'll keep a look out."

By now it was about 11 o'clock, we'd have to make a move now or it would be too late. I scaled the fence and stood in the dark and waited for John.

"Come on mate coast's clear your turn."

Over he came, "So now what?"

"I don't know we'll play it by ear."

We stood back in the shadows for ages just waiting to make our move, when we got our first lucky break, "Watch out Tony, here came's the fucking gate keeper."

Standing back to the fence as close as possible only the sound of beating hearts could be heard as he walked by, all the time flashing his torch soon to turn the corner and out of sight, then came the sound of running water.

"Hold up Tony, he's having a piss, come on quick let's make a run for it."

Making our quiet but very hasty exit, we were soon to be on the wharf mingling amongst the other workers.

"That was some stroke of luck, so now what?" John was full of negative questions

"We'll just walk on board, I suppose, we can't just stand around here sooner or later someone's gon'na notice us."

"So come on then, you go first."

"Why me" I said, trying to edge John in front of me.

"Why, because it was your fucking idea in the first place so move your arse."

"Okay mate, shit or bust, let's do it."

All correspondence should be addressed to:
THE DIRECTOR,
BOX 18, G.P.O., SYDNEY.
Telephone: 31 0244
Telegraphic Address: WONNAI, SYDNEY
Please ask for Mr. Pashkevich

CHILD WELFARE DEPARTMENT.,
CNR. WILLIAM AND YURONG STS.,
SYDNEY.

_____19

In your reply please quote OS4754/1/2

St. 1895

GP:BC

The Manager
Dr. Barnardo's Homes,
1 Jamison Street,
SYDNEY.

CS:BC

13th September, 1965.

Dear Tony,

Your work history is getting more and more ridiculous. Its no good you saying you are working at places unless it's true.

You ought to settle down and start learning a trade. You will have all the kids who are leaving school to compete with soon.

You do not want to be out of work over Christmas or not get paid for the holidays You will have to be on the pay roll and at regular work for a couple of months if you want paid holidays over Christmas. It's a dreary time when you have not got any money.

Get stuck into a job or else we shall have to get the Child Welfare to prosecute you.

Get a bit of sense man!

Cheers,

Yours sincerely,

N.S.W. CHILDREN'S OFFICER.

Mr. A. Bates,
10 Sebgstapool Street,
MARRICKVILLE.

Party N.S.W. 54/65.   <u>BATES Anthony Roy</u>   Born 2. 9. 49.

Arrived 1st Party By Air. 30. 4. 1965.

TONY BATES.

Placed		Wages
30. 4. 65.	To "Rickard House", 21 Marlow Avenue, WEST RYDE.	
13. 5. 65.	To "Tooloogan Vale", Scone.	
30. 5. 65.	Boarding at: Mrs. McPhee, Scone. Guest House.	
5. 5. 65.	Working for Ray Walters, Plumbers.	
17-6-65	*Returned from scone for R.M.N Test. Failed. Taken to hire Spurazzi 16 Glen St North Sydney's point board. (90-4046)*	
16.6.65	Working at Transparent Sheet Trading Co, 114 William Street, NTH SYDNEY 92.8245. *Redfern (nolell phone) one weeks advance hire own board Paid*	
26.6.65	*Moved to board at Mrs Marram 155 Pitt St*	
1.7.65	Commenced employment at Express Plan Printing Service 183 Liverpool Street, Sydney. 61-5849	
5.7. 65	Moved to share board with Patrick Bates, (brother) - 96 Pitt St. Redfern.	
26.7. 65	Moved to board at - 10 Sebastopol Street, MARRICKVILLE. Mr. Jose. Tel.-5608730.	
16. 8. 65	*Started Johnsons Bakery /week - left 26.8.65 (now award)*	
6. 9. 65	*Shelleeo stated he had left care. earned £10.4.1 in all.*	
14.9.65	Commenced working at Eta Products, 74 Edinburgh Rd, MArrickville	
5.10.65	Too commence working as copy boy with Sydney Morning Herald, Broadway	
5. 10.65	Arrested at Auckland. Stowed away on "Afric"	

CHAPTER 9

Heading off down the quay, neither of us knew what was in store for us.

"So what're you gon'na say if we get stopped Tony?"

"I don't know. I'll think of something, stop looking on the black side," as we walked along the quay, the loading continued. As far as anybody knew we could have been either crew or shore workers, nobody took any notice of us. Finally the moment arrived and I took my first step on the gangway, leaving Australian soil behind.

"Come on John there's no turning back now." Slowly we climbed the gangway, so far so good, at the top we were greeted by a young boy who couldn't have been much older than me, sitting back in a chair with his feet up, reading a book.

"Yes mate, can I help you?"

Thinking quickly, I said the first thing that came into my head.

"Err, yeah, good day mate, we're from the Sydney University and we're doing a survey on British shipping. The bloke on the gate said it would be okay to take a quick look around the docks, so we'd thought we'd take a chance on coming up." What was I thinking here it was nearly midnight and I was coming out with all this shit, Id blow it or so I thought

"Yeah sure, help yourselves."

"Thanks mate, you're a real gent." I couldn't believe our luck, we were on.

"Its unofficial mind, so don't be too long, or you'll get me in the shit."

"No worries, we'll be back before you know it, oh and thanks again." So leaving him there to make himself comfortable once again burying his nose back into his book, while we walked around the ship like we owned it. We first went aft (the back for non-sea goers) where it was all lit up like a Christmas tree, as the work continued, strange that now we were on board, the ship a lot seemed smaller than I remembered, and with all the commotion could see there was little or no place to hide.

"Come on Tony let's get out of here before someone starts asking stupid questions, like what the fuck are we doing here?" Up to now no one had taken any notice of us, but John was right, we were beginning to look a little bit on the suspicious side. So leaving them to their work, we made our way back along the Port side (left side) noticing on return, the disappearance of our young friend at the top of the gangway.

"That's handy, John, the geezer's gone off somewhere so when he comes back and don't see us he's naturally gon'na think we've gone ashore"

"Yea right let's see what's up here, before he does." We'd come this far, So John lead the way." He was older than me and a lot more logical, probably realising the consequences if we just happened to get caught. We passed the top of the gangway and headed up fored (the front) soon to come across a few steps that would take us down to the lower deck and where, apart from a few lights, there was no one to be seen.

"This looks a lot more like it mate, there must be somewhere to hide round here," said John, leading the way into the unknown.

"Yeah, great, I'm right behind you mate," I said with a slight tremor in my voice, "What about the life boats?"

Unlike when you see on T.V. unfortunately for us, they were way out of reach on the upper deck and far too risky to chance going up there, so we continued our search, moving slowly down the steps onto the lower deck, soon to notice a number of lights coming from the bridge face, also the sound of voices and it was obviously some sort of crew accommodation. Slowly, but quietly, cutting across the ship, all the time keeping close to the bridge face, we made our way to the starboard side (right hand side), when John noticed a potential hiding place.

"Err Tony, look at these hatches, they're still open and there's a light down there. What do ya reckon?"

Looking over the side, I could see way down to the bottom. "Bloody long way down ain't it mate?"

"You wait here, I'll see if I can find a door or something."

As I sat there crouched down in the shadows, John went in search for a way down, only to return a short while after.

"Its no good, Tony, the door's locked, but there's rope hanging over the side I thought we could climb down that."

"Are you fucking sure? How far is it?"

"It's not far, only about twenty feet or so."

"Only twenty feet, looks a bloody sight further to me."

"Keep ya voice down mate will ya, you wanna get us caught?"

"Nah, sorry John, it's just that I'm scared of heights and it's a long way down."

"Yeah it is to the bottom, but we ain't going that far. Seems there are two levels and if we can climb down to the first, we'll go from there."

Reluctantly I nodded, "Yeah okay, what we got to lose, I can only fall and break me fucking neck." Following him close behind, we made our way up the side of the hatch.

"I'll go first," John said, full of confidence, "just follow everything I do," and taking the rope in his hands, positioning himself over the side, "Here goes," then slowly he disappeared from sight down into the hold. Shortly after a voice rang out, "Come on Tony, its easy, nothing to it." My fear of heights was getting the better of me and I wished I was back in my bed in Sebastopol Street.

"Come on Tony, it's too late to chicken out now."

He was right, but it didn't make things any easier, then the sound of voices and approaching footsteps, also the thought of coming this far and getting caught gave me strength. Taking the rope in my hands dangled my legs over the side, gradually edging my way out of sight. Following John's every move, I wrapped my leg around the rope and started to descend, unfortunately for me the strength in my arms was not strong enough to take the weight of my body and I just slid down the rope, leaving friction burns on my hands, landing in a pile at John's feet.

"Shit, that fucking hurt."

"Nice one Tony, at least you're down and that's the main thing and by the sounds of it, not too soon hold up there's someone coming."

The sound of footsteps on the deck above made us duck back into the shadows. Fortunately, we'd not been heard and the footsteps passed by.

"That was close, come on, let's take a look around."

The fear of getting caught had instantly taken the pain from my hands, and following John into semi-darkness, our only objective now was to find somewhere to hide. Her cargo or so we thought, was mostly cars, and after a short look around knew that on a cargo check it would be easy to be spotted so we decided to delve deeper into the ships hull. This time it was easier and followed John down through an open hatch and a never ending ladder. The dim light shone down the straight and sheer drop to the bottom. Holding on for all my life was worth, I took every rung with great care until I finally reached the bottom and found myself standing on what seemed to be huge balls of string, in fact it was copra, the outside of coconuts. Hundreds of them, all stacked neatly on top of one another. At first, although it had a terrible smell, our noses soon got used to it. Movement up top was by now getting more obvious so we knew there was no turning back. This was to be our hiding place and home for the next week or so. The light was dim but fortunately our eyes soon adjusted to it and after a short study of the situation, decided on our plan.

"Right Tony come on let's get to work. Somehow we've got to find a place to hide down here so that we can't be seen if they come down and give the place the once over."

"Why don't we build a den" I suggested, remembering my days back home in the woods.

"Den what sort of den?"

"I don't know, how about if we move a few of these bales so to leave a hollow then stack the others neatly round the top."

"Sounds good Tony, let's give it a go." Making our way over to the bulkhead wall, which was obviously the one between us and the engine room as you could hear the humming coming from the other side, we started to build our nest and after a lot of manoeuvring and hard work we'd achieved my plan, climbing inside and pulling the last one over the top of us. By now all hot after our hard and dusty work, we decided to break into the first of our supplies by way of opening a can of coke.

"Cheers Tony, well mate, I didn't think we'd make it, but here we are."

"Yeah, but it had me worried for a little while there, cheers."

That drink was like the nectar of the Gods and it was good to clear the dust and copra from our throats which by now was in our clothes and hair and everywhere else you could mention.

"Steady on, that's go to last us you know, the supplies are short and who knows how much longer we're going to be stuck down here." John was right, we'd have to last a week at least, but for the moment there was not much left for us to do – just wait.

It was late and both feeling a bit tired, we decided to lay back and make ourselves as comfortable as possible so to grab a few hours sleep. The next thing I remember was waking up in the pitch black and the sound of the engines throbbing away from behind the wall.

"What the fucks happening? Where are we?"

"We're only off, that's what's happening, and we're moving. You've had a good kip, missed out on all the fun."

"What do ya mean what fun?"

"Ah nothing much, just a couple of blokes came down with their torches, shone them all around at one time straight on us, I thought we were goners for sure, then they just went back up top, closing the hatch behind them."

"Why didn't you fucking wake me, you bastard?"

"No point had to hold you're nose a couple of times to stop you fucking snoring, apart from that, thought I'd leave you. Looks like we're going to be doing a lot of sleeping during the next few days, there's fuck all else to do." He was right again, but then he always was, this was going to be the hard bit, the waiting and to make it worse in the dark, neither of us knowing what time or what day it was.

"Fancy a drink Tony?"John broke into my thoughts

"Yeah thanks, just the one swig I'm hungrier than thirsty mate."

"Well then, how about we have something to eat?"

"Yeah maybe later, that grub's gotta last us, I wish we'd bought more."

After our drink, we laid back and talked of our plans and what we were going to do when we arrived back in England. John lit up a cigarette, neither of us realising that copra was highly flammable and on our every puff, risked setting the whole ship alight and at the same time causing our own private cremation, no one knowing where we were. Just to disappear off the face of the earth, not to mention the rest of the crews' lives we were putting at risk. We finished our can of coke which made an instant ashtray. Soon after, we settled down once more to get some sleep. Laying back there in the dark you could hear the creaks and groans and feel the sway of the ship as she moved through the waters. Thinking we'd actually done it, what seemed only hours ago, an impossible idea, was now reality and although it didn't seem possible, here we were. Was it day or night? I thought to myself, without a watch it was impossible to keep track. Not at any time, thinking of the danger we'd put ourselves in, my only thought was that I was going home and in my day-dreaming fell asleep. Next thing I remember was waking and finding myself all alone.

"John, John" I called thinking he'd gone "where the fuck, are ya?"

"Shh keep ya voice down will ya, I'm over here." Thinking to myself who the fuck is going to hear us down hear. My eyes had not yet got used to the dark and couldn't see a thing as gradually they adjusted; John struck a match and filled the hold with a glow, making our shadows ten feet tall on the walls.

"There ya go; I'm over here having a piss, alright."

The lump left my throat as the thought of ever being here alone was just too much to handle. Scrambling out from our hide out, I started to make my way across.

"Mind ya step Tony, there's bloody great big holes"

"Ah! Shit" it was too late

"Told you to mind ya step those gaps between the bales there fucking deadly."

As I'd just found out they were small, but still there was room enough to lose a leg down.

"You okay Tony?"

"Yeah no harm done mate."

The match suddenly went out, "Stand still, Tony, don't move. I'll light another."

It was like being caught in the middle of a mine field. One wrong move and you were a goner. Again the hold lit up and John walked towards me.

"I think we'd better go back to the hide out, it's safer there." Following John close behind we returned to our nest.

"I thought you'd left me."

"Don't be stupid; where the fuck would I go?"

A good point, there was only up and it was early days yet or was it?

"I wonder what the time is." asked not that it made any difference

"Don't know mate, but I do know I'm hungry, let's grab a bite to eat," agreeing I opened up our one pack of bread rolls, taking one each.

"Um, bit dry, fancy a drink?"

"Yeah why not" I opened our second and last can of coke, passing it first to John.

"Ere Tony, imagine this roll is full of your favourite filling, maybe it'll taste a bit better."

"You wish," I said, laughing at his suggestion.

"Nah, go on try it, you never know."

I thought for a second and then came back, "Mine's cheese

and tomato topped with fresh salad, how about yours?"

"I think today I'll have chicken and coleslaw with maybe a few pickles."

"Sounds good, let's get stuck in." but no matter how we tried they still tasted like plain old bread rolls.

"Watch it Tony, you've dropped tomato all down your shirt," instantly I looked, although not being able to see, realised what he had said and burst into laughter. At least we still had our sense of humour. Settling back after our feast decided to have a smoke. John lit up and suddenly all hell let lose with the bale directly above catching alight.

"Oh shit, quick Tony give us that coke," and with John's quick thinking and the fact that the copra was slow burning, he shook the can furiously aiming it at the fire, extinguishing it almost immediately at the same time getting soaked in the process.

"Shit that was lucky could have turned into our own personal barbecue."John said laughing

With all the commotion not only were we now out of drink, but our food supply had disappeared down a gap in the bales, and couldn't see the funny side

"That's done it John, we've lost the grub."

"What do ya mean lost it? Lost it where?"

"It's slipped down the back here," our first thought was to somehow try and retrieve it spending what seemed hours trying to reach it, but each time we moved a bale it only slid further down and apart from reloading the whole cargo our chances of retrieving it were slim.

"Now what we going to do?"

"Well, look on the bright side Tony, at least we're still here and our stomachs are full."

"Don't be a smart arse John, I'm starving."

"Nah, its all in ya mind. Come on, let's rebuild our nest and get some shut eye."

By now our eyes were well adjusted to the dark and looking around in what seemed a half empty hold, could see the ladder which would eventually take us out of here. With only the echoes of our voices and the sound of the engines to keep us company, or so we thought, we started to rebuild our little nest, putting the bales back one by one, into place, when I heard a strange squeaking sound, turning sharply, looking across the hold I said, "What was that noise?"

"What noise? I didn't hear anything probably your imagination."

"No, that squeaking sound, hear it?"

"You're fucking hearing things mate the dark's got you spooked."

"No I ain't, there it goes again."

"Oh yeah, hang on, let's light a match." Although we could see in a very limited fashion it was still as if a big dark shadow had fallen upon us. John lit up, holding out the match in the direction of the sound.

"There .... See, what the fuck are they?"

"Rats, mate they won't hurt ya." And there wasn't just one, but two. The whites of their eyes made me feel uneasy as they ran around the tops of the bales and after a short scratch around they disappeared down between the gaps.

"Where the hell did they come from?"

"How should I know, probably loads of 'em. Anyway they won't hurt you. Come on Tony, let's finish off and get some sleep." But for me this great adventure was turning sour, first the fire, then the food and now rats. If they went down the gaps they could just as easily come up them and the thought of them crawling over me while I was asleep made my flesh crawl.

"Why don't we go back up on to the next level with all those cars, John, we might find something to eat or drink, besides I don't fancy staying down here with just those rats for company, being with you is bad enough."

"Fucking cheek" John laughed, "Okay then, why not?" Deep down I think he was glad I'd made the suggestion.

"Come on then, let's take a look," he said, leading the way, we headed for the ladder, a climb I wasn't looking forward to, but one I would have to make eventually, besides anything was better than sharing accommodation with rats. Soon at the ladder John started the climb.

"You stay down here I'll go ahead and see if we can get through first, OK."

Slowly I watched him ascend the ladder which from my angle seemed higher than ever. I waited patiently then edged my way up one rung at a time, clearing myself from our evil little visitors, then a slight noise and John was out of sight.

"John, you okay? Where are you?" There was no answer, I started to panic. "John, John?"

"Its all clear you can come up now."The sound of his voice was music to my ears

I didn't need to be told twice, still trembling, I started to climb every rung taking me higher and higher, my fear of heights was not a new one so took each step slowly and with care, holding on like I was part of it, gradually as I neared the top, I could see a light shining, eventually peering my head through the top of the trap door.

"Alright mate, come on, give us ya hand."

Terrified to let go, I continued climbing until once again I could step on to solid ground. During my short absence John had made good use of the time.

Fortunately, the cargo being cars, still complete with batteries and even better not being locked, we had light for the first time for what had seemed like days and could see properly, although at first a bit bright and took some getting used to, but it made for a pleasant change. Now I know how a mole felt when he came out in the day time. After a short and unsuccessful nose around, we returned to the car which John had so courageously lit up.

"You take the back seat Tony, and I'll have the front. Fancy a smoke?"

"Yeah thanks." By now I was tired and just wanted to relax after our ordeal, so after sharing our last smoke I turned off the light, then both laid back and made ourselves comfortable, as after what we'd been lying on, this was heaven and was soon to fall asleep. It was hard to tell for how long, five minutes or five hours, it was the sound of tapping that first woke me then in turn John.

"What's all that fucking noise?"

"Don't know mate, it woke me up, been going on for ages." Our first thought was to investigate; leaving the car to follow the sound, shortly after realising it must have been someone working up deck.

"Well at least we know its day time", John surmised "but which day?"

"Yeah, it seems like we've been down here for days. Don't know about you John, but I'm starving."

By now the hunger pains had set in and our throats were sore from the dry air. Things were looking bleak. It was then John came up with one of his bright ideas.

"Of course, what's the matter with me – windscreen washers. The bottles are full of water, here quick Tony, I'll show you," and pulling the catch on the bonnet lifted up the hood and after a short search, spotted it, "There you go, what did I tell ya?" Luckily, his age and experience of cars had given us a break, all we needed now was some food, but unfortunately, the one thing a car can do without is food. Working the bottle loose he removed it, "Just what the doctor ordered fresh water. Here ya go mate, take a swig of that."

Only thinking to quench my thirst, I took the bottle and drank a large gulp, "Err, shit what the?" spitting it all out.

"It's soapy, it's fucking soapy water, you bastard," John started laughing, seeing the funny side, after all, being the other way around so would I, but it didn't help me much. I felt sick and couldn't stop coughing.

"Keep it down Tony, someone will hear you." That was the least of my problems by now I didn't care. John raced off to check out the other cars, finally to return with another bottle.

"Ere, drink this quick," with tears in my eyes from my coughing, I just looked at him suspiciously, "its okay, I've tried it," a little apprehensively I put the bottle to my lips, first taking a small sip, realising it was clean I began to drink furiously.

"Steady on, that's all there is and that's got to last," although the taste of soap was still in my mouth, it wasn't nearly as bad so passed the bottle over

"Here ya go, thanks mate you're a life saver."

"Yeah, so what else is new?"

All this time the persistent tapping could still be heard setting us both thinking of what day it was. Then suddenly it stopped.

"Must be night time and they've knocked off for the day," I said, trying to convince myself. Then set ourselves the game of trying to work out what the rest of the crew would be doing and could both only come to the one thought, my favourite pastime eating,. The pains got worse until finally after hours of trying to decide, it was time to hand ourselves in. Now somehow we would have to attract their attention. First we agreed on our story and to give them as little information as possible so making it near impossible to trace us. Now time to find a way out, we were no sooner on our feet than the tapping sound returned which put shot to our night time theory. Well at least we would be heard straight away or so we thought. John climbed the final ladder which led to a water tight door. The very one he'd tried on our attempt to get down here. I waited patiently at the bottom.

"It's locked."

"Give it a bang," I suggested, "someone's bound to hear you." Then came the long and tedious wait. He banged and rattled the handle for what seemed ages, without success.

"It's no good mate, seems they can't hear a thing, looks like we're stuck down here for good."

"Come down; let me give it a go."

We changed places, this time me being up the top of the ladder, as I banged and rattled until my hands were sore, occasionally the tapping outside would stop, presuming someone had heard only to hear it start up again shortly after. By now John had also joined me, both of us making a frantic joint effort. It was still no good, we were doomed. Locked down here for ever or at least until she reached England, which by then we would have both starved to death, leaving nothing but our withered carcasses. The thought terrified me. I continued to rattle the handle then suddenly heard the sound of voices. We both banged furiously as the footsteps could be heard coming towards getting louder as they come closer, then stopped just for a few short seconds then started up again, eventually disappearing out of ear shot.

"It's no good John this door must be bloody sound proof."

"Just keep rattling mate, what else can we do?"

By now my arms were sore, enough was enough and I needed a rest.

"It's no good John, they ain't gon'na hear us down here so we may as well call it a day, I'm going down below."

"Yeah alright mate, you go ahead, I'll stay here and keep trying. Someone's gotta hear us."

Shortly after, the footsteps returned once again getting louder and louder as they got closer then stopped at what seemed right above us, then came the sound of a key being put in a lock, at last, someone had heard us, we were saved and not before time as we were both getting worried, what with no food or water, our chances down there of survival were negative.

"Quick Tony, there's someone coming."

I raced up the ladder to get there just as the door started to open, with the gap in the door widening, the sun burst in making our vision almost a blur and slowly as it regained, we could see, standing in the doorway our rescuer.

"Hello boys and what do ya think you're doing down there?"

Gradually our eyes adjusted fully to see there in front of us a short but stocky man with cropped hair and apart from his little doleful eyes, a face that was covered in hair. A regular black beard, "Up you come," he said, in his accent which was broad scouse. First with me, followed closely by John, we made our way up and out on to the deck, then he carefully locked the door behind us.

"You're lucky I saw the door handle move otherwise my lads it could've been canvas bags for you two."

"What day is it mate" I asked curiously.

"Oh you can talk then. It's Sunday, Sunday afternoon." I looked at John and could see that he was thinking the same, as we hadn't even been down there two days.

"This way lad's the Captain will want to see you two and he's not going to be at all happy, I can tell you now." Following the stranger, we took in our surroundings, fresh air at last and the calm blue seas. A life I'd yearned so long to be part of and was now here, although under different circumstances than I'd planned. All this time John never uttered a word, the pair of us just followed the man, first up to the accommodation area then up another ladder until finally we were on the bridge wing, "Wait there lads, I'll just see if the Captain's ready for you."

Where else could we go, disappearing out of sight returned almost immediately with a grim face and a very angry Captain in tow, with a broad Scots accent?

"Why did ya pick my ship, you little sods, you do ya know what you've done is a crime and I'll going to have notify to the authorities, not to mention the unnecessary paperwork you've caused me."

There wasn't much you could say about this man apart from being angry, he was arrogant shit, but then I suppose he had reason as we were the ones causing him all the grief.

"Well, I suppose we'd better have some details. Stand over there, neither of you smell the best. Take a couple of men and check out the hold for damage and whatever else they might have done."

"Yes Sir," our rescuer gave us a sly wink and went about his business.

"So when did you come aboard and with whom?" He asked looking at John and awaiting his reply, "Speak up lad, have you lost your voice?"

Butting in, I answered his question, "Friday, we just walked on."

"That's a likely story, and what's your name lad?" I hesitated for a moment, giving him a false one, "Richard Elms."

"Where are you from and how old are you boy?"

"17 Sir, I'm originally from England."

"You're a bloody long way from home then aren't you, how'd you come to be in Australia?"

That was as much as I was prepared to say which only made him angrier so turning to John he asked him the same questions.

"Barnes – John Barnes age 19 from Australia."

"And which part may I ask?"

"Central Australia."

Everything we said was taken down and then read back to us, then signed by the Captain and his First Mate then finally on his return Ralph the Boson.

"Right Boson, before they go anywhere, we'll let the sea air take the smell out of their clothes also find a stiff brush so they can clean themselves up a little. I think the Monkey Island is as good a place as any don't you."

"Yes Sir, right you boys this way."

Then we followed him up another stairway bringing us out onto the top of the bridge.

"I'm sorry to have to do this to you boys, but orders are orders."

"No worries mate, the fresh air will do me and Tony the world of good, but thanks for the concern anyway."

For the next two hours we were made to stand up there in the breeze, although at first, warm, as the afternoon drew on, it gradually got cooler and by now had our fair share of fresh air. The monotony was broken by the arrival of the First Mate on the scene.

"This way boys Captain wants to see you two back on the bridge."

Following him we went through into a small office where the Boson and the Captain were both waiting.

"Ah, here you are, Elms, if that is your name, why have you signed the name Bates down here? Which one is it?"

I'd been caught out. Trust me to make a stupid mistake like that.

"Well speak up boy, which of the two is your real name, Bates or Elms and are these your Christian names?"

"No Sir it's Anthony Roy Bates." The mate started to write it down in the log.

"How about you Barnes is that's your real name?"

"No sir it's Burns, John Burns, you've just misspelt it."

"Complete these changes and get it off to Auckland Police and see what they come up with Chief" the Captain then handed it over to the First Officer.

"Yes Sir, right away Sir."

"Well boys, you can consider yourselves very lucky, you could have very easily perished down there if the Boson here hadn't spotted you. Now read your statements through and sign them."

"All clear right then sign here. Boson put them under lock and key for the time being, and they can eat in their cells until further notice is that clear?"

"Aye Sir"

"Now get them out of my sight. I don't want to see you two again until we reach Auckland, now take them away."

Well at least that was over. We followed the Ralph down into the crew's accommodation, down past the cabin where once I had sat, not a few years since and on to the hospital to our cell and new home – for the time being. Inside were two single beds and a shower room, all the comforts of home.

"Excuse me mate," I said looking more or less straight into his eyes, "Do you think we'll turn back to Australia now?"

"There's no need lad, you'll be turned over to the Police in Auckland then it's up to them what they do with you."

"Auckland? Where's that? I thought this ship was going to England."

"Aye, it is son, but not yet. New Zealand's our first port of call on our way home."

"So how long does it take to get there then?"I asked

"Should be there come Wednesday evening at the latest." Looking across at John, we realised it had all gone wrong and we'd just be sent back to Sydney to face the consequences, once we'd arrived in New Zealand.

It quite took the wind from our sails after all the trouble

we'd gone through to get here, not realising the ship had a number of other ports to stop at during her voyage home. John by now was in better spirits and on jumping up on the nice soft bunk, commented "Never mind Tony, look on the bright side, we've got a three day cruise to look forward to."

Our jailer smiled, "You two must be hungry, see what I can rustle up for you."

"Thanks mate, I could eat a horse, come to that, two of 'em."

"Well, I don't know about that lad, but I'll see what's on the menu. You'd better get yourselves cleaned up and I'll be back later," then closing the door behind him, we heard the key turn in the lock. Well there was no choice but to make the most of it, now we'd been caught or should I say handed ourselves in, now we had to pay the consequences.

"I'm gon'na grab a shower Tony."

"Yeah right, no worries, after you." Stripping off, just wrapped a towel around my waist and laid on my bunk, digesting all that had happened in the last couple of days.

"Here John, maybe we'll be able to make a run for it, once the ship docks in Auckland."

"Yeah maybe, let's play it by ear for now," suddenly the key in the lock turned and the door opened.

"Couple of the lads' sorted out these clothes for ya, here's a couple of pairs of shorts and some shirts."

"Thanks mate, hear that John, got some new togs to wear."

"Yea tell em thanks mate."

"Oh and here's a couple of cold beers to clear the dust from your throats, but keep 'em, down, you're not meant to have alcohol in here, Ow and grubs up in about ten minutes."

"Thanks mate, you're a real sport."

"The name's Ralph, the lads call me bos" and closed the door behind him.

"This is the life a John," I said, cracking open a beer and taking a swig, "Ah that's good," and began to sort through the clothes, picking out a shirt which was black and white with short sleeves and fitted perfectly along with a pair of old denim shorts.

"All finished in the shower," John opened his beer, "I suppose you left me with all the rubbish to wear ya bastard."

"Na it's all the same. Anyway what do ya want for nothing, tailor made?" It was now my turn for the shower and was glad to get all the dust and shit out of my hair amongst other places.

"That's better, I feel human again," I said, looking at John, who was now dressed.

"Oh don't we look smart in our new outfit"

"Don't look to bad, do it?" He said, looking in the mirror on the wall and admiring himself. After I dried off and changed into my new clothes, we both sat back on bunks to finish off our beers, when a sharp tapping noise came on the window. Looking out to see a face I recognised, "Open up quick open up."

Unscrewing the bolts, I lifted the port, "Hello mate, remember me?" .

"Yea, you're the fellow on the gangway."

"That's right, name's Jim. You didn't tell the old man that it was me I let you on board did ya"

"No we didn't say a word" reassuring him his secret was safe with us

"Thank Christ for that, he'd have my balls if he found out

"Thanks fellas, anything you want? You name it, fags perhaps a few beers? It's yours."

"Sounds good tell ya what, I'm dying for a fag, you got any?"

Putting his hand in his shirt picket, he pulled out a packed of smokes, "There ya go, I'll bring ya some more later," just then John heard footsteps outside the door, "quick Tony, someone's coming."

"I'll see you later lads, I'd better scarper," and with that he disappeared, giving me just enough time to shut the port before our visitor entered.

It was Ralph and another lad returning with tucker, "Here you go boys, get stuck into this," he said, directing his young companion to set it down on the table.

"Just stick it on the table over there Gerry."

"Have a look John, a feast fit for stowaways, thanks mate, you're a gent."

"I'm Tony and this is my mate John" But there was no time for chit-chat as Ralph was under orders.

"Right come on Gerry, back to the Galley with ya," then turned to us "Okay boys, enjoy your meal, I'll be back later for the plates."

We needed no encouragement, without another word they both left and we tucked into vegetable soup, roast lamb and all the trimmings, finally jam rolly poly and custard and it was all consumed in no time at all.

"Oh that's me well fucked for the rest of the day, I can't move."

I gasped before crashing out on my bed, by now it was well past six and the night was drawing in.

"Ah shit, we can't have a smoke Tony we've got no light, that's fucking typical, ask that Ralph geezer, when he comes back, he's bound to have one."

Shortly after, he returned and in his hands he had a pile of books, obviously so we could improve our minds, "Here you are lads there'll keep you busy for a day or two, but I'm afraid there's nothing about escape amongst them." he said, laughing to himself.

"You ain't got a light have ya Ralph? I'm dying for a smoke."

"Well you're not supposed to, but what harm can it do, make sure you open the port so as to let the smell out."

"Yeah sure, thanks mate, you're a pal," and John opened it almost straight away.

"Now you've got everything, It's lock up now so I won't be back until morning, so sleep tight, well you should do after being down in that hole for two days."

"Yeah right," I said, as once again he closed and locked the door behind him. Sitting back on my bunk, I sipped the rest of my beer and smoked a long deserved cigarette and was just about to slip off into a deep coma when a voice came from the open port, "Here ya go lads," John was up like a shot.

"Alright Jim, what ya got?"

"Ere, take these," and passed six cans of beer through the bars.

"Got any empties, give them here I'll put 'em over the side. Can't stop, due to go on watch, see ya in the morning," and as he came, he vanished just as quickly.

"Here you go Tony we can have our own private party. If this is bloody jail, give me six months." John was right, for criminals, we were getting the A.1 treatment.

"Still, we might as well make the most of it while it lasts, I reckon we could have bad days ahead old mate," John was right, and while he settled down with a book, I just lay there thinking of the past events. I wondered how Pat was and knew by now he would have gone to the authorities having reported me missing.

Also the thought of when I got back and what would become of me? Little did I know we had already made the news after being reported missing my brother Pat. Somehow I would have to escape, I'd come this far and no way was I going to turn back. The excitement, also the beer, had got the better of me, as I dozed off into a sound sleep. It was late when I woke. The room was in darkness apart from the shadows from the clear night on the bulk head. John was snoring like a pig and as I got up from my bunk to undress, I glanced out the open port. The ship hardly stirred as we glided through the waters. It was night, yet it wasn't. The moon shone brightly as if just for us, the heavens filled with a million stars like sequins thrown up in the air, only the wash from the ship could be heard, as waves crashed onto her bow. I undressed and returned to my bunk, just listening to the night as if like a lullaby singing me off to a deep sleep.

"Wake up Tony, up and at 'em mate," peering through the tiny slits in my eyes, could see John all dressed and ready for the day.

Outside I could hear men talking, also the sound of running water.

"What time is it for fucks sake?" I asked trying to pull the covers over my head

"6:30," he said with a large grin on his face.

"Do what? It's still the middle of the fucking night, you shit."

Without another word, John whipped away my covers, giving me no choice but to get out of my bunk.

"What's up with you, can't you sleep?" Moving over to the port glanced outside to see the men on the deck, washing down.

"Good day fellas how ya going"? I shouted

"Hello, hello, it's our little stowaways" One shouted to the others

"Sleep alright did ya? Not making too much noise are we?"

"Yes thanks." They seemed a good bunch apart from the smart arse with the big mouth, then came the familiar sound of the key turning in the lock and the entrance of Ralph.

"Morning lads, sleep well?"

"Good'day Ralph, so what's new" John said, making himself comfortable on his bunk.

"Well, I've got some good news for you; the Skipper says you can eat with the rest of the crew. No more lock up until we reach the New Zealand coast."

"Oh great, do ya hear that Tony we're free?"

"Yea right"

"You've also got the freedom of the ship apart from the bridge and engine room, so when you're ready breakfast is in the Mess, okay?"

No sooner said than done I was showered; dressed and was ready for the day. Ralph had already gone ahead leaving the door wide open. "Come on Tony move your arse I'm starving." Following John out of the cell we made our way to the Mess room where the rest of the crew were just about to sit down.

"Morning lads help yourselves. Cereals up there and your breakfasts' are in the hot press."

Luckily I remembered my last visit, so knew my way around a little. Then the welcome sight of Jim came in.

"Alright Come over and sit over here, meet some of the guys," and we followed him over to his table, "Fellas, meet Tony and John, our distinguished visitors." They all laughed.

"This is Pete, Mick, Derek, and Gerry who you've already met. He's the Galley boy."

We were all much about the same age, with Mick being probably the oldest. This was his third trip and was now J.O.S. (Junior Ordinary Seaman). All the rest were deck boys, first and second trippers. As we ate they naturally asked of our ordeal making us out to be some sort of heroes being careful not to mention Jim, as we told our story. By now the other members of the crew had joined in on the conversation. The older hands had been at sea for years, and most classed the ship as their home. It was soon eight o'clock and time for work or turn to, as they called it.

"Right lads, let's have you."

Ralph had arrived on the scene. Gradually they all made move as Ralph gave them their work orders for the day.

"You two, as soon as you're done in here, I want you on deck." He was talking to Pete and Jim. Their job was Messmen; wash and clean up, clean alley ways, toilets sort of general dog bodies to the crew. So John and I stayed behind to give them a hand.

"If we take our time," Pete explained, "we'll be done just in time for smoko (tea break) then clear up again, by the time we get out on deck, it's eleven o'clock. No sooner out and it's time to come in for lunch."

They had it all worked out to the hour, so I watched and I learned, as one day this could be me and would be easier if I knew the ropes. While Jim and I did the Mess Room, John and Pete went off to do the showers and shit houses. The four of us cut the time in half so now all they had to do was keep out of the way until smoko so all ending up, going to their cabin,

"So how long you been at sea Jim" I asked.

"Just over two months now, but it's been great. Beats shore life any day." The clock ticked away and was nearly time for smoko.

"Come on we'd better get back better and make a move times getting on,

Mick you go and get the tab nabs I'll make up a brew"

"Tab nabs, what's that Jim?"I asked curiously

"Oh that's cake or biscuits, whatever snack the cook decides to give us." Pete had no sooner returned than was followed close behind by the rest of the crew John and I grabbed a cupper and off course some tab nabs which was bread pudding. Somehow it was like you never stopped eating. It was a miracle they could move at all with the amount they ate. Then at 10,15 it was back to work, and the long wait for lunch at 12 noon. As soon as they turned to, John and I went out on deck. Once outside the heat of the day hit us hard, but soon felt the cool sea breeze as we walked down the starboard side where earlier that day they were washing down. A couple of men were painting the bulk heads (walls) there too was Ralph, making sure everything was running smoothly.

"Hello boys and what can I do for you?"

"Any chance of a job mate" I asked

"Don't see why not, can you paint?"

"No worries got a D in Art."

"Right, there you go, start on those rails over there and mind you don't spill it on the deck or your get me shot what about you John?"

"Na thanks mate, I'd rather sun bathe." So off John went, leaving me with my paint and brush. Soon after Ralph was called to the bridge by the First Officer and only minutes later he returned.

"Sorry Kid, Skipper's orders, you're not to do work of any kind."

He was obviously put out by telling me, also at the same time had got into trouble for letting me do so.

"Sorry if I got you in the shit, mate."

"That's alright Son, personally I couldn't see any harm in it, in fact ships regulations state that stowaways' should work their passage. Still, he's the Captain not me."

Putting down my brush, I returned to the Mess. It would soon be lunch time and the lads would be back. The tables were laid ready so I made myself a brew and sat down just as Jim and Pete returned to get ready for the onslaught.

"Give us a hand will ya Tony."

"Yea sure, doing what?"I asked

"Fill the hot press," and followed them to the Galley

Loading ourselves up with dinners which were already made up, we returned to the Mess. No sooner done than in they came. Made you wonder how they made the room for it but they did. After lunch we all sat back and enjoyed a fag then one of the blokes asked me if I wanted to earn a few bob.

"Watch it Tony, he's after your arse." Laughter filled the Mess.

"Leave it out, no seriously, you do my dobbing (washing) and I'll give ya a quid."

"Yeah no worries, sounds good to me,"

"He'll want more than a fucking quid if he's gon'na wash your skids Jock."

"See you, ya little bastard, I'll hammer ya wee fucking head in." Luckily, they were only joking.

So I went into the laundry business, earning myself a nice few quid, That afternoon, I spent washing for not one, but half a dozen of the lads, drying it was easy, just take it down into the engine room and hang it over the rail's. A familiar sight once I got down there. After tea, which was another three course meal, we all sat around the Mess playing cards or listening to stories of the many events that had happened over the years to different men. It had been a full day and was in bed well before midnight. Sea life did' n appeal to John so he kept his nose buried behind a book most of the time. He was a country boy, born and bred, and felt uneasy without solid ground under his feet. Tuesday came and went with the day being much the same as the one before. I worked in the Mess with the lads and by now had accumulated a nice few quid doing washing. We were all on first name terms and I was beginning to feel as if I were one of them.

That night we all sat out on deck and slowly got drunk. I got so bad they had to carry me to my bunk. It was like a farewell party for us as tomorrow we docked in Auckland and the end of the road for us. Wednesday started much the same as any other. The only difference was that we could see the coast of New Zealand. After breakfast, I collected up all my washing, putting it all in the appropriate cabins then returned to my cell. John was already there by the port looking across, studying the coastline with care.

"Well Tony, we're here, so what'll we do now?"

"Escape what else? There's no way I'm going back to Australia." Our plan was ready, once in port, to slip over the side and swim for it.

"We're agreed then we'll head inland and look for work."

"Well, I've got £10 to come for all me washing so that's a start, how much Aussie we got left?"

"About £15, that's enough to give us a fair start."

We were all set for lunch. I collected all monies owed to me and soon after, Ralph approached us in the Mess.

"Alright lads, the old man wants to see you."

We followed him to a familiar spot on the bridge and were greeted by the charming person himself.

"Right you two, you've caused me a lot of trouble, not mention the expense to the authorities. You'll be met in Auckland by the Wharf Police from then on you'll be their problem , so until then you will be confined to your quarters is that understood, now get out of my sight."

All I could think of was the plans John and I had made and could also see the same in his eyes.

"Okay Boson, you take them back to their cell now."

Why he called it that, I don't know, it was only a hospital, with bars on the windows. After all we weren't criminals we were soldiers of misfortune, not to mention bad luck. Without saying a word we followed Ralph.

"Sorry Lad's but I've got to do this, you know how it is."

"Yea sure that's alright mate, it's not your fault thanks anyway."

"What for, wish I could have done more?"

"Just for being human, mate, which is more than I can say for that miserable pig you call a Captain." John was right and once we were inside he shut the door and turned the key and there was no way out. All we could do now was sit it out all the time the land getting closer and closer. Then later that afternoon we dropped anchor outside Auckland Harbour, the north Island of

New Zealand, and waited for the pilot to come aboard to guide the ship up the channel and into the Harbour.

			OFFICIAL LOG of the	

OFFICIAL LOG of the AFRIC 29-7-65 to 4-12-65
from SYDNEY towards AUCKLAND
1965

Date and Hour of the Occurrence	Place of the Occurrence, or situation by Latitude and Longitude at Sea	Date of Entry	Entries required by Act of Parliament	Amount of Fine or Forfeiture inflicted
1400 October 3rd	33°58'S 169°59'E	Oct 3rd	Two Stowaways were found in N° 3 hatch by R. Grist, O.S. N° 7, Bosun. They were brought in front of the Master and stated that they were RICHARD NEIL ENNS, aged 17 years of English origin and JOHN BARNS, aged 19 years of Australian origin. They say they boarded the vessel in Sydney between 0001 and 0400 hours on Friday October 1st. They proceeded to N° 3 hatch and hid there until discovered. They have no identification papers in their possession. R.F. Grist [signatures] Bosun.	
1600 October 3rd	34°00'S 165°44'E	Oct 3rd	A copy of the above entry was shown to the stowaways. After Enns had admitted giving the wrong name and that his name was ANTHONY ROY BATES he signed the copy. After Burns had pointed out that his name was BURNS not BARNS (the Master's error) he signed the copy. [signatures]	

N.B.—Every entry in this Log-Book required by the Act must be signed by the Master and by the Mate or some other member of the Crew, and every entry of illness, injury or death must also be signed by the Surgeon or Medical Practitioner on board (if any); and every entry of wages due to, or of the sale of the effects of, any Seaman or Apprentice who has died must be signed by the Master and by the Mate and some other member of the Crew; and every entry of wages due to any Seaman who enters Her Majesty's Service must be signed by the Master and by the Seaman or by the Officer authorised to receive the Seaman into such Service.

NOTE.—Reading over Entries of Offences.—The Master's especial attention is called to Section 228 (b), (c) and (d) of the Merchant Shipping Act, 1894, which is printed on page 2 of the cover on this Official Log-Book.

The Effic

CHAPTER 10

The Afric was soon along side and made fast against the quay, and the moment we'd been waiting for. At that time are only interested was on hearing the sound of the key being turned in the lock, as both John and I had decided to jump the first body that came through the door, so to make our escape. It was shortly after six, when finally Ralph and Gerry came, bringing our tea – or last supper as he put it, and on seeing them both, but thought twice about it. As apart from liking them – especially Ralph, as without him we'd have probably starved to death in the hold, besides, although he was short, he was wider than the two of us put together which made our chance of escape pretty slim. After a short discussion they left us to eat our tea in peace, once again bolting the door behind them.

"We should have jumped them Tony, we might not get another chance."

"Yea we will, sooner or later they've got to take us ashore, that's when we'll make a break for it."

"Yea right, but it's every man for himself, I'm not waiting around to see if you make it."

"Okay John, I'll tell you what, we'll both head for the nearest Post Office in the town, which is probably in the main street, it usually is."

We then, divided out the money in case we got split up. With the crucial moment coming just after seven, the key turned in the lock and the door opened and in walked Ralph followed by the First Mate and two Police Officers, one in plain cloths who did all the talking.

"Good day boys, welcome to Auckland, my name is Constable Bird, and while your here my job is to make your stay as comfortable as possible, I'm also the lucky one who's been put in charge of your sight seeing tour."

Me, I took it all in, hook, line and sinker, seemed like a decent bloke. This wasn't going to be as bad as I thought. John, on the other hand, just stood there and said nothing, just taking it all in his stride, and was obvious he knew something I didn't.

"Sorry about this lads, regulations." taking out two pairs of handcuffs and placing them first around my wrists, then on John's.

Not knowing where or what to do next, I followed along once again like a lamb to the slaughter, with our plans in tatters;

we made our way out on to the gangway. Where stood along the ships rails, some of the crew had turned out to see us off. Slowly we made our way down the gangway, first Bird, then John, with me followed closely by another Guardian angel.

"Good luck Tony, good luck John," they called out, as slowly we made our way down onto the quay. I looked up at some of the familiar faces, Gerry the galley boy, and Jim who had so kindly let us on board in the first place, then there was Pete, Mick, Derek and Jock and last but not least, Ralph the Boson.

Nearing the bottom, Jim was the last to call out, "see ya next trip Tony."

Raising my arms, with my hands clasped together I shouted, "No worries, you ain't seen the last of me yet."

Soon arriving on the quay, they all cheered which only made things worse for us.

"My, we are popular, right little smart arse aren't we," the Sergeant said in a sarcastic tone of voice.

"Well, you know how it is mate, some of us have got it, and some don't."

"Oh, is that right? Well I only hope you're just as popular in your new accommodation. This way lads, your chauffeur limousine is waiting for you sir."

The doors opened, John and I sat on either side of the Constable and Bird got in up front along with the driver then gave the order to move off.

"Well, I hope you like it here, we've booked you into the Plaza Hotel, you'll like it there, naturally it comes complete with room service."

"Great," It still hadn't sunk in yet and I believed his every word, but was soon to come down to earth with an almighty crash. As we pulled away from the ship and down the quay there was for me, a feeling of excitement. No one else except me said another word during our journey to town, which was short as our accommodation was very close to the docks. No sooner out of the dock gates and we were in the Main Street, and our destination.

"Here ya go boys, reservations have been made, step this way."

There was no sign of a hotel, just a bright blue light surrounding the word 'Police.' My excitement turned to horror as we stepped from the car, making our way inside the dingy looking building. Once inside we followed Bird down a flight of stairs and along a short corridor, until finally we came into a small room with a counter, from which behind stood a rather large man in a Police uniform.

"Hello Dicky, and what do we have here? Two likely looking criminals if ever I did see."

"Yea here ya go Sarge, these are the two stowaways from Australia, I trust an advanced booking has been made for them?"

No longer did I think him pleasant, more a smart arse, getting his kicks out of winding us up.

"Oh yes gentlemen, your suite has been reserved, although I'm afraid you'll have to share. If you'd just like to sign here Dicky, I'll take over."

Bird signed us over and before leaving took off our cuffs saying, "Sleep tight boys, see you in the morning."

Although a little shocked at my new surroundings, I was still unaware of what was to come.

For the next hour or so we were questioned separately, finally our statements were read out to us and were asked to sign. My story was the same as on the ship, giving no details and still giving my age as 17. Finally, it was time to be locked up for the night, still nothing I thought could be worse than being stuck in that hold or could it? By now all our belongings had been taken, including our belts and shoe laces.

"Okay boys, this way. Take some blankets from the pile and then follow me."

Well how was I to know it gas going to be cold, this was the southern hemisphere and we were living in a warm climate. So while I took only one, John took three as he'd obviously been this way before. Following our jailer down a long corridor then down a flight of steps, we came to a door. The Sarge tapped on the door and the shutter opened, from behind we could see two eyes peering through at us, then to disappear behind the shutter. The key in the lock turned and the door opened.

"Two more for you, Jim, identikits still to be done."

"Right Sarge, I'll see to it. In you come, you two."

The door shut behind us as we were led to our new accommodation. A little different to what I'd expected with the distinct noise of the protesting inmates. Clutching tightly to my blanket and closing my eyes, hoped this was some terrible nightmare. Then taking the keys from his belt, our jailer first peered through the spy hole, then turning the key, opened the door. Then came the realisation, this was no nightmare, this was for real, for behind that door was a large cell with neither beds or chairs, just four walls and a cold concrete floor and in the far corner, the toilet for all the world to see and to make things worse, we weren't alone. Inside lay eight or so bodies, instead of being given our own cell we were being put in the Drunk Tank. Heads raised as we walked in, a few just murmured at being disturbed.

"Okay boys, find a nice spot and make yourselves comfortable."

I still couldn't' believe this was happening and looked up at the officer to see if this was some sort of terrible joke. The fear must have shown in my eyes as his stern look broke into a smile, "You'll be okay Son, stay close to your mate, he'll look after you."

Following John inside, we made our way to the far side where a clear spot was visible, it was like walking through a mine field as we stepped one foot at a time over the bodies.

"Be careful will ya, that was my fucking hand."

"S-s-sorry mate,"

"You fucking will be, now Piss off."

"Shut up will ya, I'm trying to sleep," came a voice about two bodies away. The smell of booze was distinct, like a room that had a party the night before, leaving that horrible morning after smell, and none of these blokes looked the type you'd want to pass the time of day with let alone socialise with at a party, more like they'd knife you if you just happened to look sideways. I was terrified. Once at our spot, John laid out a blanket, "Here you go, Tony, you'd better share with me."

"That'll be right", one of them shouted "They've only gone and stuck a couple of fucking queers in here with us."

John was not at all amused and getting to his feet, he moved towards the one with the big mouth, "Listen here, shit for brains, one more word from you and I'll stick my boot so far up your arse, you'll need a toothbrush to clean my toe caps."

The shutter of the door suddenly opened.

"Settle down in there or I'll come in and sort you all out."

All went quiet, as John came back and sat down on the blanket, wrapping the other around me.

"Nice one, John, you put him in his place alright."

"Yeah, right, now let's try and get some sleep."

The cold hard floor made it impossible to get comfortable

and instead of one blanket, I wished I'd picked up ten. As I sat
there huddled up against the wall alongside John, Trying not to
get too close because of the remarks, I started to feel the cold,
the obvious answer would have been to share the blankets and to
keep each other warm, but this was not to be the case. Trying to
get some sleep I tossed and turned into a thousand positions but
without any success. Cold and frightened, I lay there looking up
at the dim light in the centre of the room, and fought back the
tears as slowly they trickled down my face. What was to become
of me I thought to myself hiding my head under my blanket, I
dried my eyes as here feelings didn't matter. Once again I was
just a number so would have to grin and bear it. The night was to
be a long one for me, possibly the longest of my life, unlike down
in the hold where it was in total darkness and easy to sleep. The
noises of the moans and groans, the snoring and the ever shining
light made it near impossible and when finally I did start to doze
off, the door would open and someone's name was called out for
some reason or other. Then later, he'd return. It must have been
well into the early hours when the door opened for us.

"Burns, Bates."

At last it was time to go. Picking up my blanket, and
starting for the door.

"You can leave those there, you'll be coming back."

The door slammed behind us, "this way boy" and we
followed the officer along a corridor.

"Where we going mate," I asked full of curiosity.

"For your identikit,"

"Identikit, So what's that mean?"

"It means Bates, that we want your finger prints and
photographs for our files. You're a criminal now you know."

Following him into a small room where a camera was
placed almost carelessly in the centre, "Right Burns, you first, I
want you standing up against that wall holding this board up to
your chest."

"Yes Sir," John said without any argument, he took the
board with him, which contained a series of numbers.

"Now look straight ahead, don't smile. Good, now your
left side, and once again to your right, now it's your turn Bates."

Taking my position, I went through the same routine only
first to have the numbers changed.

"Right, now for your fingerprints, Bates you first." Writing my name on my record sheet then taking hold of my hand, "Now just relax, and let me do the work." First taking my thumb, he pressed it into the ink pad then onto my sheet, then my fingers. "Now your left hand," and repeated the performance. "Now wash your hands over there." This for me was a good chance not only to clean my hands, but also my face to freshen myself up a little and finally a drink of cold water, just to clear the throat. John had finished and walked over to the sink.

"What's your date of birth again Bates?"

"2.9.49 Sir,"

He thought for a moment as though working something out in his head.

"That can't be right, says here you're 17."

"Err, yeah, sorry about that, I meant 48 – 1948."

"Are you sure?"

"Positive, I should know my own date of birth."

"Well, it still only makes you just turned 17. Don't know what the hell you're doing here." Taking his pen, he made a note on my papers.

"Right then, if you're ready, let's get back to your cell." and we followed him back down the corridor. "Not long now," he said trying to build our spirits up, "you'll get a cuppa at six, there's only three hours to go." Only three hours, I thought, he might just as well have said 24 hours. The doors opened and then closed behind us and we returned to our spot and wrapped the blanket round me as I settled down once more. This time after a while, I dozed off, waking every now and then with cramp or from the cold, finally to be woken by, "Morning boys, teas' up," by our friendly jailer who had arrived with our early morning cuppa.

By now our other inmates had deserted us and I'd neither seen nor herd the going of any of them.

"Thanks mate, where's all the rest gone?"

"They were thrown out at first light. Only the trial cases such as yourselves get to stay, it was unfortunate for you that we had a busy night or you'd have got a cell to yourselves, instead of putting you here in the Drunk Tank. Still, drink up it's just past seven and you'll be going upstairs soon to wash up also to have some breakfast before your hearing at nine o'clock. I'll leave the door ajar. You don't look like hardened criminals to me."

"Thanks." and on doing so, he went about his business. His gesture was a welcome one as any amount of fresh air was a blessing. Settling back down, we drank our tea and talked over our situation, not knowing what they were to do with us. Soon after, our jailer returned.

"Come on lads, let's get you cleaned up ready for the Magistrate," and leaving that horrible place behind, we followed him first to the washroom, then upstairs to await our breakfast and trial.

Once again, to be locked up, but this time in more pleasant surroundings, at least it had furniture, a mere table and four chairs, but furniture just the same.

"Right, sit tight you two, while I see what I can rustle up for breakfast." He returned a short while after with two lots of porridge, ham and eggs, and a mug of tea to wash it down with.

"There you go, that's the best I can do."

We both tucked in, demolishing it in no time at all, now feeling fresh and with food in our stomaches things didn't seem so bad and definitely couldn't have got any worse. John still talked of how we could get away, but it was pointless. We weren't even sure where we were in the building, nevertheless we continued to plan. Breakfast was cleared away and for a while we were left to ponder over our situation.

Shortly after nine, came the arrival of our first visitor. Detective Constable Bird.

"Morning boys, sleep well I trust. I believe the room service is exceptionally good here."

His jokes were by now a little stale, also his persistent grin began to get on my nerves.

"Right now, perhaps now you've had time to think it over, you could tell us a little more about yourselves. Our communications with Sydney tells us nothing which means you either don't exist or there's something you're not telling me. So which is it? Burns, John, born Australia 1946 of no fixed abode also Bates, Anthony born England 1948, doesn't tell us much at all does it now boys? It'll go down better for you if you tell me now."

Looking at John, I awaited for his reply. There was none. So I could only follow suit.

"Well, it's your funeral boys I'll see you in court."

Confident we were going to spill our guts, the smile left his face, leaving us in not the same happy mood that he had come in with.

"What's the point John, why don't we tell them? They're gon'na find out sooner or later anyway."

"Listen, if we tell now all they'll do is send us back to Australia and let them deal with us. This way we might stand a chance of at least staying here."

"What for I don't want to stay here."

"Well you tell 'em if you want, but leave me out, you hear?"

"Na mate, we'll play it your way"

"Shh, someone's coming."

The door opened with two guards entering, "Right boys, it's time," one of them said as if to a condemned man on his way to the electric chair. Once again, the cuffs came out, but this time only on one wrist, and the other to the officer.

"Sorry about this, rules"

Well any plan John may have had was now put pay to. as now there was definitely no escape. Our short trip to the court brought us out under the dock, now we only had to wait for our names to be called out, which was a short wait.

"Calling John Burns, John Burns."

John looked around and winked at me then went up the stairs into the dock.

"What do you think will happen to him mate?" I asked my still handcuffed companion.

"Jail more than likely, pending further investigation"

My immediate thought of going back to that place was just too unbearable for words, "What about me then?"

"Probably the same,"

The fear inside me came right up to my throat almost at once as I spilt my guts like a frightened kid, "but they can't, I'm only 16. I'm too young to go to prison."

The officer's face was a picture, first calling one of the other's over, then mumbling something in his ear, he led me off to an adjoining room where we both sat waiting, a short while after Bird walked in.

"You left it a bit late, didn't you right so what's it all about?"

It was then I told him the whole story.

"You could have saved yourself a lot of trouble if you'd have said this all last night."

In all the confusion I'd completely forgotten about John and wanting to know how he'd got on, "So what's happened to my mate then."

"He'll be sent to Mount Eden pending investigation. Talking about Burns, where is he from?"

"I'm sorry, but if he wants you to know I'm sure he'll tell you himself." I kept my promise although I knew we would probably never meet again, I respected his wishes as he'd been a good mate to me. We'd been through hell and back again together but were both survivors and each in our own way we knew what we had to do.

"Well please yourself, sooner or later he'll tell us, just as you have."

He made me feel guilty as he walked away smiling. Then my Guardian Angel took off my cuffs, leaving me to wait alone for what seemed like a long time and was later to find out that because of my circumstances, my case was kept until last and when finally I was called up, my stay in the dock was to be very short lived with the Sergeant doing most of the talking.

"You're Honour, due to new information we have just received and the defendant still being a minor, there is to be a special closed sitting of the Children's Court."

No more was said as the judge adjourned the case, then I was led away from the dock to wait in an adjoining room to wait until the presiding Magistrate was ready to hear my case. Shortly after, I was taken into a room, a much smaller version of a Court, where from behind a bench sat no less than five people with the Magistrate sat in the centre. Sergeant Bird accompanied me as I took my seat then once in session, Bird said his piece then sat down. I was then asked to stand.

"Right Anthony, or is it Tony?"

"Tony Sir."

"In your own words, tell us your story," and so I started going back to when I first left England. Luckily for me, there were three women on the panel and just the look in their eyes told me they were on my side. Finally I came to the end with the ordeal of my terrible night in the cells. I knew that would twang at the strings of their hearts.

"Thank you Tony, now would you mind waiting in the next room for a moment?"

Then, supported by a guard, we went off into the adjoining room. And waited for what seemed an age before we were finally called back in. Taking my seat, I awaited my outcome.

"Tony, we have just been in contact with the NSW police

and it appears that there are a lot of people concerned about you, seems your big news in Sydney. What would you say if I told you the recommendation is that we send you back?"

I thought for a second then said, "What can I say, it's your decision, but if you do as soon as I arrive back I'll just do it all over again."

"That's a very bad attitude Tony and one you shall have to get out of your head. Next time you might not be so lucky and you could get yourself killed, the Australian police were already looking along those lines"

With a sorry look on my face, I directed myself at the women on the bench "All I want to do is go home, is that so bad?" No sooner had I finished than the Magistrate gave sentence.

"Anthony Roy Bates, it has been agreed that you will be remanded in custody until the 14th October, so we can decide what's best for you , Until that time you will be taken to the Owairaka Boys Home at Mount Albert, and there to stay until further notice. Is that clear?"

"Yes Sir."

I was then ordered from the court and taken back to another room to await my transport.

"So how long we gotta sit here then"? I asked my guardian angle "I'm starting to get hungry."

"Arrangements have to be made but it won't be too long now, I don't suppose."

Just then, the door opened and we were joined by two Police Officers.

"Anthony Bates."

"Yeah, that's me," I said as though I was some sort of celebrity.

"You're to come with us." My companion exchanged a few words with the officers' then left the room.

"Now you're not going to give us any trouble are you Son? So I think we can dispense with the cuffs so long as you're not gon'na try and run."

"No Sir." The one chance John had hoped for and it had been given to me.

"I'll come quietly." What was the point, I had no money as it had all been taken from me, or anywhere to go come to that, so standing either side of me, made our way outside to an awaiting Police car, soon to be driving through the streets of Auckland and out into the suburbs. The view was not unlike Sydney with its rows of one storey houses old and new, its delicatessens and a pub on every corner. The drive was to last about 20 minutes, eventually we pulled off the road into a drive, coming to a halt at a pair of large gates. The driver pressed the horn and almost immediately they were opened, we drove in and parked, the gates shutting behind us, leaving the car, we entered the main building and were met by one of the House Masters.

"Afternoon Gentlemen, can I help you?"

"This is the new lad from Central. His name's Bates and this is his file along with his personal belongings."

"Oh yes, we've been expecting you Master Bates. Thankyou gentlemen, I'll take him from here."

"If you wouldn't mind signing here Sir, we'll be on our way."

"Certainly officer" no sooner done and they were off.

"Right lad, let's get you sorted. First you'll have to see the Superintendent, Mr Ricketts," and I followed him off to a nearby office.

Ryan, that was his name, was a sturdy looking bloke, medium build with short fair hair, reminded me a lot of my old school master, Harman especially when he called me Masturbates (A wanker) He too looked like a man not to mess with. There was a distinct smell of military about him and not the sort whose toes you'd tread on twice.

"Hello Tim, who's this then." asked a young woman as we entered

"Hi Pauline, the new boy Bates, is the Super in?"

"Hang on I'll give him a buzz."

Ricketts secretary was young, in her mid twenties, pretty with long blond hair, neither of us being able to keep my eyes off her noticing her low cut dress, showing evidence of her firm figure, just managing a little smile before turning towards the door.

"The new boy's here with Mr Ryan to see you Sir."Then came out almost straight away

"Okay, go straight in, he's expecting you."

Ryan knocked once and walked in.

"The new boy Sir" placing my file on his desk.

"Thankyou Ryan." taking a quick glance through, he then looked up, "Well, Bates, seems you've got yourself into a right old mess. Well, here we have rules and regulations. You stick to them or we come down hard. From what I hear, your visit to us will only be a short one. Nevertheless, our rules apply to everyone, understand?"

"Yes Sir."

I was beginning to wonder who was worse off, me here or John in Prison. Discipline was never one of my pet loves, and he obviously meant business.

"Okay then Mr Ryan, if you'd like to show Bates the ropes."

"Right Sir" Then we left neither saying another word

Our first stop was for me to see the visiting Doctor who checked me over from top to bottom, My first thought of Cummings was that he was a bit on the weird side wanting me to walk up and down with no cloths on, but then what did I know he was the doctor. Afterwards I was then taken to meet some of the other boys who were all congregated in a games hut at the back of the main building, with Ryan just leaving me there to go it alone.

"In you go boy, make yourself known they won't bite," doing no more, I turned the handle on the door, starting to open it, "Watch out will ya," I'd just stepped half way in, when a dart went sailing past my ear.

"Don't just stand there, come in and shut the fucking door" shouted a large Maori boy who was throwing the darts; I'd seen javelins thrown with less enthusiasm. Inside ten or so boys were gathered, some playing darts others on an old pool table, and in the corner a card school was going on, reminded me a lot of back on the farm.

"What's your name, mate?"

"Tony," I answered as he carried on throwing.

"So what you in for"

"Not really sure stowing away I think."

"Yeah where from"

"Australia."

"No kidding." Leaving his game, he came over" The names Sam"

Out of all in the room, he was the biggest and my experience in institutions told me he would make a good ally. As I told Sam my story, they all gathered round and by the time I'd finished I was more or less one of them. They were all here for some reason or another, but for that moment it was my story appealed to them.

"So how long did ya get?" Sam asked

"Don't know case comes up again on 14th October. They'll probably send me back to Australia. Anyway, what's it like here" I asked changing the subject

Sam pulled a face, "Oh, it's not too bad, I suppose. Staff ain't bad; Ryan's the bastard to watch out for."

"So what's his problem then?"

"Oh you'll see soon enough," He said with a glum look on his face, and so for the next hour we talked of their daily routine. Some went outside to school and the older ones were allocated jobs around the place. It was mostly self supporting with its vegetable gardens and poultry, not unlike the place at Scone the only difference being that discipline ruled here, plus it was surrounded by 10ft high fence. By now I was getting hungry as it had been a long day since breakfast and with all the fuss I'd missed out on lunch.

"Do you smoke?" Sam asked

"Yeah, but I haven't got any wish I had"

"What about money?"

"Yea a little if I ever get it back."

"Good, as in here money means fags and fags rule in here, so stick with me and you'll be right."

If it was going to cost me a few quid, I thought to myself, just to stay on the right side of Sam, I considered it worth it. In all our talking, we'd missed the bell for tea. The door flew open from which appeared a rather small boy with a hurried look on his face.

"Come on you lot, tea's up. Old Ryan's going fucking mad."

With that an almighty dash was made for the door.

"You stick with me Tony; I can use you as an excuse."

By the time we'd arrived in the Dining Room, all the others were seated. Mr Ryan met us at the door.

"You're late Sam, where the hell have you been?"

"Sorry Sir, I was just showing the new lad around. We must have been out in the grounds when the bell went of."

"Okay then, but don't let it happen again, you hear? Seeing as you're such good bum chums already, you can join Sam on Miss Waitford's table, Bates."

"Yes Sir," taking my place almost opposite Sam. Mr Ricketts said Grace and no sooner finished than all hell let loose. Hands came from everywhere, in amazement I waited for calm before helping myself. Unlike on the ship, here it was bread and lard a selection of jams tea and biscuits. The butter was only for the staff and on helping myself, could not understand why the rest gave me such a look, then a voice came from the end of the table by way of Miss Waitford."

"Leave it this time Tony, but the butter is for visitors and staff only."

I couldn't believe what I was hearing. How can you have bread and lard then put jam on top, but somehow they did, and they ate it. Miss Waitford or Alice as we called her could see my look of disapproval, but there was nothing she could do about it. Alice was the only Maori on the staff, still in her early thirties and very popular with the boys. After finishing my first slice of bread the constant thought of lard on my bread put me off my food, so I just settled for tea and biscuits and could only hope that breakfast would be more appetising. That evening, I was shown to the Dorm and my bed. I had no luggage, the only clothes I had were the ones on my back, so my need for a wardrobe was not necessary. After my initial tour I joined the others in the lounge to watch T.V. Later that night, I was called out and taken to supplies where I was given a pair of pyjamas, some new underwear, a couple of shirts and the baggiest pair of jeans you'd seen in your life then taking what cloths I had to washed. I felt and looked like an orphan, and was right back to wearing someone else's hand-me-downs. Returning to the dormitory, I put away my things, feeling low and some what tired after my long day, I lay on top of my bed to rest my eyes only to be disturbed by the sound of talking. At least I had company. It was 9.30, time for bed, for a while everyone messed about but at the stroke of ten the light went out.

"Right boys, lights out first one to murmur goes on report."

A deadly silence came over the dorm. Ryan's word was law and no one crossed him, but it didn't matter to me for I was too tired to care and must have gone out like a light, as the next thing I knew was the sound of bells ringing in my ears then the lights came on.

"Right lads, let's have you."

I woke up with a start, "what the fucks going on?"

"Come on Tony", Sam called over "its six o'clock, wake up call."

"You must be fucking joking; don't that man ever sleep?"

There was no time to talk, they were all up, dressed in shorts and sneakers and off out the door.

"Come on Bates, this is not a holiday camp, move yourself."

I was lost, what was going on?

"Don't just stand there Get dressed and follow the others."

"But Sir, I ain't got any shorts."

"See me later you'll have to make do today."

So dressed in just my underpants and shoes I followed Ryan out the door.

"Come on lad, I haven't got all bloody day."

After a short run we ended up on the playing fields at the back of the home.

"Right, twice round and no overtaking or you'll go round again, then in and shower. Well boy, off you go."

It was cold and wet and after a while I found it heavy going in my shoes, so took them off. So there I was running round a field in my underpants at six o'clock in the morning. It's just as well I'd gone to supplies the night before or I would have looked a pretty sight. At that time I was quite fit and soon caught up with the stragglers, the hardest part was not overtaking. Now I knew why it was best to get out first and I'd make sure to, to be quicker tomorrow. Soon the end was in sight and being last out was last in for a shower. Unfortunately, the last one in had to clean it out after him, which after I'd finished, made me feel like taking another one.

"Come on Bates, you not dressed yet."

Drying myself off, I rushed to the dorm, practically throwing my clothes on just in time for the next bell, this time for breakfast. There was no time to lose and was just in time again as they all got seated. It was like an army boot camp, you either did or you learnt the hard way. I'd never known anything like it and wondered what other surprises they had in store for me. Grace was said and the free for all started all over again. There was cereal, and as much toast as you could eat, provided you liked lard. It got to a stage where I was so hungry I decided to give it a go. It's hard to explain how it tastes until you've actually tried it. After one mouth full I pushed it away, getting up and walking away from the table in disgust. All heads turned my direction as if I'd broken some sacred vow.

"Sit down Tony or Ryan will have your balls."

Sam's concern was touching, but I'd had enough, "Well I'm not eating that shit," and with that I made my way to the door. You could have cut the air with a knife as Ryan came up right behind me.

"Bates"

I turned slowly, "Yes Sir"

His face was all red and filled with anger, like a raging bull as he came towards me, "My office, if you will."

He opened the door and followed me in, "Now what seems to be your problem? Is the food not quite to your liking?"

"No, the foods alright, it's just the lard on my toast that makes me feel sick."

"So why not wait until the proper time to talk over your grievance, instead of just getting up and walking out?"

"Why" I snapped back "because the six o'clock bit I can live with, but then to run round a field in my underpants, clean out the showers after barely leaving time to get dressed for breakfast, then you want me to eat lard on fucking toast. Well, I'd rather go back to jail; at least you know where you stand there."

I'd blown it, my big mouth had led me into who knows what sort of trouble now.

"Look Bates, you are not on holiday, this is a detention centre for boys who break the law and that includes you, and if I'm not mistaken you're only going to be here a few short days so why don't we make the most of it." His voice had lowered. Neither of us was getting anywhere shouting at each other.

"Right then, let's both go back in and finish our breakfasts."

"Na, it's alright, I'm not hungry."

"Well just sit there until we have until the rest have finished."

Thinking I'd pushed my luck to a point of no return, also to keep face for Ryan as his reputation with the other boys was at stake, we returned to our tables and sat down. No one said a word, but it was in their eyes, they couldn't wait to hear the outcome of our conversation. Looking down the table, Alice just smiled, pushing the butter towards me and smiling back I took advantage of her gesture, having myself a couple of slices of toast. Finally when everybody had finished, we all had to walk out in single file. Outside, Sam and a few of the others pounced on me.

"What happened, Tony?"

Considering myself lucky I toned it all down a bit.

"Oh, nothing really, the lard made me feel sick so I had to make a dash for the toilet."

"Na that's bollocks come on, what did Ryan say?"

"Nothing much, told him the same as I told you."

For the time being they accepted my story and would have to wait and see if there would be any further action taken.

We walked back to the dorm and made up our beds, then sat around talking. At 8 o'clock the bell went again, it was now time to carry out the daily duties.

"See ya later, Tony."

"Yeah, no worries Sam, I'll still be here when you get back." Wondering what they had in mind for me was short lived."

"Bates"

"Yes Sir," Ryan was back on my tail, "You will be confined to the main building today as you've got visitors coming from the welfare dept, so whatever you do don't wander off."

Left to plan my own day, I first returned to my bed to catch up on my loss of sleep, waking up round about eleven with a start, not realising how long I'd been there jumped up and ran out into the corridor. There was no sign of life apart from the singing coming from the Dining Room. Taking a quick look round the door, I noticed a woman singing away while she laid up the tables. She must have caught sight of me out of the corner of her eye as she turned.

"Hello, who are you?"

"Tony, Miss, I'm the new boy."

"Oh yes the English boy from Australia we've all heard about you."

"Yeah Miss."

She seemed to know all about me and I hadn't even met her before.

"I'm Rosita you are waiting for someone?"

"Yes Miss the Welfare people. I hope I haven't missed then, I've only just woken up."

"Don't worry they'll find you when they want you."

"Your father is an Italian yes?"she asked

"No miss why do you ask?"

"Because you have a good strong Italian name, I shall call you Antonio."

Rosita was like a breath of fresh air and totally out of place standing there about 5' 4" and in her mid thirties, very attractive. Her long red hair was resting on her shoulders and that cuddly figure of hers made you want to take her in your arms and give her a big hug.

"Do you wanna a hand with that miss Rosita" I asked "That would be nice." so I spent from then until lunch time helping her set out the tables. During that short time we became friends and she told me of her family and in return I told her of mine and how I'd come to be there in the first place.

"Bates, what are you doing here?" A voice called from the open doorway.

"He's helping me, Mr Ryan."

"Haven't your visitors come yet?"

"No Sir." He turned to walk away, "Oh by the way, it seems you're being classed as a visitor so you will be allowed to eat butter with your meals."

"Thankyou Sir."

"Don't thank me if I had my way you'd eat the same as the rest", apparently the decision had come from higher up, and one he was not happy with. Soon came, the bell went for lunch. Being already there just took my seat quickly while the room filled with the rest of the boys. Shortly after   lunch I met up with the others in the games room where Sam and a few of the others were playing cards so I went over to watch.

"Want to sit in Tony?"

"Dunno, what you playing?"

"3 card brag."

"Na, don't know that one."

"Come on, sit down and watch, you'll soon pick it up," and after watching a few hands, joined in, but without any success.

After lunch break was over it was time for Sam and the others to return to work, so I made my way back to the main entrance just in time to be greeted by my visitors from the welfare, accompanied by Rickett's secretary, Pauline.

"There you are Tony, I was just about to come looking for you. These ladies are from the Welfare Department and would like to have a word with you."

After the introductions, we went and sat in the Dining Room and I was asked a million and one questions, finally they asked me how I felt about returning to Australia. I explained it wasn't the country, or the way of life. It was the never having any money to spend on myself, the dead end jobs. Plus the feeling that I'd been dumped on a society that didn't really want me, as there was no room for a 16 year old misfit. Eventually they left, saying they would be in touch on Monday so with nothing else left for me to do, I went back to my bed for a lay down and there I stayed until tea. After that, it was the same thing, television or games then bed at 9-30, and lights out at 10. That night before going to sleep, I managed to borrow a pair of shorts. There was no way I'd be last out of the starting gate tomorrow.

Next morning being Saturday, early call wasn't until seven, by which most of them were up and ready for the off. The bell went and the race started, although not first, I was out in the first ten. It didn't matter if you were fast or not, once on the field no one could overtake you, but it did pay to be one of the first. The mornings were cold and you couldn't afford to get stuck behind one of the slower ones.

Quickly round and showered, I was well in time for breakfast which after, apart from a few small jobs, we had the rest of the day to ourselves, but even so there wasn't much to do, in fact the only thing that broke up the monotony was the meal times.

The best day of the week was considered to be Sunday. That was when the visitors came, bringing fresh supplies of cigarettes, sweets and money. Some boys even went to bed early so it would come sooner, during that evening, as usual, we watched T.V., only to be called for bed half way through a film. Saturdays it was 10 o'clock, they allowed you half an hours' grace, but it was still too early.

"Right boys, let's have you. Oh, Bates, Stevens, Davis and Edwards, tomorrow is you're lucky day, you'll be going out with the Doctor so you'd better run along and get your beauty sleep hadn't you."

"What's that all about Sam?"

"Now and again, if you're face fits, and Doc takes shine to you he takes a few boys down to the coast for the day."

"Oh well, it'll make a change, I suppose, give me a chance to see some sights."

"Do us a favour will ya mate, try and get me some fags "Yea no worries Remind me again in the morning or I'll forget."

No sooner in bed than the lights were out, "Who's that boy still talking? If I catch him he's on report." A deadly silence fell over the dorm as Ryan prowled around, "That's better, let's keep it that way."

That night I wore my shorts in bed as I was determined to be the first one out as soon as I heard the bell. Next morning the usual early call came, still slightly dazed I was up and off towards the door, only to hear everyone behind laughing at me, "Where you going Tony?" Sam called out.

"The track of course where else"

"Na, not today you berk it's Sunday a day of rest, even for us."

"You're kidding me." Still laughing at my expense I could also see the funny side.

"What's all the noise?" Ryan said, coming through the door with me almost knocking him over.

"Joke Sir."

"Well perhaps you'll let me in on it, Masturbates."

Ryan too, could see the funny side of it, "Well Bates, if you're that keen we don't mind if you do a couple of laps, do we boys?"

"No thanks Sir, I'll pass on that."

"Right you lot, showers, let's go now, move. You four boys going out with Dr. Cummings, meet me in the main entrance straight after breakfast."

After a quick shower I raced back to get changed. My selection of clothes was limited so there was no problem of choosing what to wear. Sam came rushing in after me.

"Glad I caught you on the quiet, here's the money for my smokes" and delving into his trouser pocket, pulled out a load of change, "there you go, should be a couple quid there just get as many as you can" Then waiting for him to get dressed before walking down to breakfast together.

"You never did tell me why you're in here, big secret is it?"

"Na its no secret got done for auto theft but with a difference."

"Yea what difference?"

"Well see, the cops were after me so I stopped the car to do a runner , but forgot to put the brakes on , leaving the car to roll down the hill crashing into another , then plant itself through a shop window nearly killing someone. That was six months ago, and I still got a year to do, but it's not bad here so long as you keep your nose clean. It was hard at first, the masters picked on me, but new blood is always arriving so it doesn't last long."

I don't think he really cared where he was as long as they fed and clothed him, but he was number one boy in there, (The Daddy) and that meant something.

Breakfast was the usual thing and couldn't wait to get outside and get a hamburger or two down me. Meeting up with the others, we waited for Ryan and the Doctor. The four of us were all due to go out in a while, but there was no talk of escape and I knew it was only a matter of time before my return to Australia. After this place even that sounded good.

"Morning boys," the Doctor arrived with Ryan, "Are we ready? Then I thought we' take a run down to Waiwera for the day, so I hope you've all got your swimming trunks, if not I suggest you go and get them quickly."

Waiwera must have been somewhere special as the mention of that place, lit up their faces, no sooner said than they were off back to their lockers.

"What's up Bates, don't you like water?"Asked the doctor

I waited for the old English joke about only having one bath a week, but it didn't follow through.

"Yes Sir, but I ain't got any trunks."

"Oh I see, well I'm sure Mr Ryan can sort you out a pair of trunks."

"Yes Doctor, I'm sure we can," not looking all that pleased with the request followed Ryan to the supply stores where from a box he took the first pair that came to hand, not bothering to check for any sort of size.

"Here, take these Bates."

"Thanks Sir."

Not even looking at them, I screwed them up and put them in my pocket, then returned to the others who were by now back and just waiting for me.

"Good we're all here, right let's go."

Soon in the car and out through the gates, we headed for the main highway and the coast. My three companions Alan, John and Steward were not in the same dorm as me so at first I felt a bit of a gooseberry, but not for long. We were all soon laughing and joking, determined to enjoy our day out together.

Waiwera was about 50 kilometres away, taking us about an hour or so to get there hugging the coast all the way, passing some of New Zealand's beautiful coastline. We arrived at about 10 a.m. parking almost outside Waiwera Hot spring's, opposite you could see the beach which looked almost as inviting as the thermal pools in which we were to spend the next half day. Once inside we made straight for the changing rooms, on pulling my trunks from my pocket realised they would not make me look my best, first finding they were much too big, then to make it worse there were no ties to keep them up and swimming trunks being what they are always seem to get larger in the water. Luckily Dr Cummings supplied me with a couple of safety pins which enabled me to take them in on either side, I was determined not to let anything spoil the day, so made the most of my embarrassing situation and followed the lads to the pool, where already it was crowded with people, so we dived in. Almost straight away my trunks left my hips and only the quick thinking of opening my legs kept them on, pulling them up I sneaked off to the side to tighten up my pins, just hoping that no one had noticed my predicament, then carried on as if nothing had happened. The thermal pools were something else, floating about in warm water was like being in a huge bath, the only difference being was that you were sharing it with others.

"Come on Tony, let's try the others."

"Yeah, alright you go ahead, I'll follow."

During that morning I was only to lose my trunks twice, the most embarrassing moment being going from one pool to the next, realising my dignity was hanging out for everyone to see, quickly I jumped into the nearest pool. Apart from that there were no more hiccups, although I must admit I was glad to take off those ridiculous trunks and get back into my own clothes.

After a short break and something to eat and drink, we cut across to the beach, a small inlet cove with a white sandy beach which in the centre, stood a huge rock which only time had left standing with the waves breaking softly on its walls. After a short stay we all piled backed into the car, our next stop was a few kilometres further up the coast in Red Beach and the holiday home of the Doctor, there to stop off before returning back to the home.

Arriving shortly after 3 p.m. we pulled into the drive of an old asbestos fronted beach house, and while Doc prepared a snack of hamburgers and salad we all messed about in the garden which after the winter months, had taken its toll and was thick with leaves and other debris scattered about. It was then, that someone came up with the bright idea to clean up the mess as a good day had been had by all and it was the least we could do, so we all agreed. Taking tools and a barrow from the garage, we started working. It took no time at all and the four of us soon had it licked, piling up all the rubbish in one heap in the corner. The Doctor was over the moon and kept thanking us all through tea which I might add, went down a treat after our burst of energy spent on his garden.

"You did a good job there boys; I only hope the wind doesn't pick up again putting it all back."

"That's easily solved Doc why don't we burn it" I suggested. At first he looked a little apprehensive, but then agreed.

"Okay, then while you're at it you may as well take all the old rubbish out from in here."

So taking the matches off the side I picked up a pile of newspaper, as it was my idea the least I could do was light it. Stewart took hold of the rest of the rubbish while the others stayed inside to help clear up. After a few tries of lighting up, I decided the fire needed a little help, as the leaves still being damp, only put the rest out.

"Excuse me Doc, got any paraffin about?" I asked.

"Yes, just inside the garage, but be careful."

Although paraffin was slow burning, it was sure to get the fire going. Unfortunately, for me, Doc thought I'd said Kerosene, which was coal oil, and highly inflammable and not realising tipped half a can over the top then kneeling down took the matches from my pocket to light up. The rest was a nightmare. The match was no sooner alight than Boom, with whole lot going up like a bomb badly burning my face and arms. With the sound of the explosion the Doc came running, followed closely by the others.

"What the hell's happened here? Oh my God, what have you done?"

Screaming with pain, he took me inside, wetting anything he could find to put on my burns so to ease the pain whilst the others put out the fire with the garden hose. All wrapped up with wet towels, I must have looked like a mummy, sitting there shaking while Doc tried to come to reason with the situation.

"Trust one of you to ruin the day for the rest, now we'll have to head back early."

At first thinking he would take me straight to hospital for treatment. As the pain was horrendous and no sooner had the pain eased of from the cold towels than it was time to change them. Understandably Doc wasn't happy. We'd been entrusted into his care and letting this happen didn't look good for him, but then no one was to blame. We'd both misunderstood after all; I'd lit hundreds of bonfires back home, always using paraffin so I knew its capabilities and nothing like this had ever happened before. My face and arms felt as though they were on fire, my eyebrows and lashes had disappeared, with it also a large clump of my hair. It was horrifying. At last it was time to leave and changing my towels for the last time, we got in the car, but instead of going to the hospital we were to drive back to the home without stopping once. Shortly after leaving, the cold towels were no longer working and the pain grew worse. Not knowing what to do with my arms or face, crying with pain, I begged the Doctor to stop at the next petrol station for cold water, but it was no use, he just carried on.

Finally as a last resort, I hung the top half of my body out of the window, leaving the cold evening breeze to cool my body. It worked, at last I'd found a comfortable relief although on arriving back at the home, I was now numb with the cold. The pain had eased off. For over an hour I stayed that way, the trip back taking longer because of the traffic and the day trippers returning to the city – a journey I wouldn't wish on a lame dog let alone a human being.

Once inside the home I was taken to the first aid room and treated for burns, smothering creams all over my face and arms which was like putting fat in a hot frying pan, melting straight away making me feel like a chicken on a spit. For me the only relief was simple, cold water as the Doc knew best. I was then sent to my bed, and given a bowel of cold water and some towels then left to lick my own wounds with the Doc returning every so often to check on me and to change my water. Soon it was time for the boys to come to bed and Sam and the others rushed in to see what happened.

"You alright Tony, how do ya feel?" It was a stupid question, so don't answer, "What a fucking mess have you seen your face yet mate, Here Carl, pass us that mirror will ya," and Sam showed me the damage.

My face was bright red and where I'd been bathing it mixed with the cream Doc put on, my skin was loose and hanging like I'd just popped a large blister.

"Come on lads, what's going on, break it up, ow yes selling tickets are we Bates?" Ryan was being his usual compassionate self "It's not a bloody sideshow so get to your beds now and be quick about it."

While Sam was changing, he asked to hear my side of the story, and then he told me what he had heard.

"Well according to Doc, you took it on your own back, putting kerosene all over a bonfire then without him knowing, lit it."

"Kerosene, I thought it was paraffin."

"You fucking wombat, you picked up the wrong can, apparently he reckons you tried to burn his garage down on purpose"

"The lying barstard, for a start, as if I'm going to do something like that and get myself hurt in the process."

"Well, I'm only telling you what I've heard."

"Right lads, lights out, cut out the talk." With Ryan's words, a deadly silence hit the room.

"Excuse me Sir is there any chance of some more cold"

"What am I your bloody wet nurse? You wait until the night staff come on"

"But Sir"

"No buts Bates you made your bed you lay in it, one more word from you my boy and you're on report." then he marched off into the night.

By now the water, being warm, was not helping me at all, making the pain only worse. During that long night, it was only to get changed twice and in the early hours of the morning I was put on report for disturbing the others with my cries of pain. Six o'clock came round and lights on, everyone rushing out to be first on the games field. Too weak and too tired to move, I just lay there. At one time, I thought Ryan was going to make me join them, but was reprieved at the last minute and allowed to stay in bed and there to spend most of the day. Later that morning the Doctor came around to see how I was progressing. On his first impressions he realised my burns were worse than he first thought and I should have gone straight to the hospital. Although the pain had nearly gone my face was in a hell of a state, the damaged skin was beyond repair and had started to dry out, forming a large scab all over my face. My arms weren't much better, but by now the doctor had treated and bound them up with special bandages. Luckily my instant reaction had made me raise my arms up to my face on the explosion taking most of the impact, probably saving me from losing the rest of my hair, also total blindness.

Later that day, I was allowed to get up, being confined to the main building only, most of the time I watched T.V. as there was nothing else to do. A couple of times the women staff asked how I was – apart from that all I did for the next day or so was sleep, eat and get square eyes. By Wednesday I was feeling much better and back to my old self. My face, by now, was like a hard crust, spreading all over and just leaving my eyes, nostrils and mouth, clear. It was uncomfortable to say the least. Eating was my biggest problem as I couldn't open my mouth too wide, when I did bits would fall of into my food so gave it up as a bad job as didn't wont to put the rest of the lads of there food. It also gave me a slight speech impediment and although I wasn't a pretty sight, at least I was up and about, and luckily still reprieved from those early morning runs. After breakfast, I just sat around doing the usual, watching T.V., when the Secretary came looking for me.

"Tony, Mr Ricketts' wants to see you."

"What for now, going to give me another ear bashing is he?"

"I don't know, he's got a visitor and I think she's here to take you away."

Pauline led the way back to the office, knocked on the door announcing me, "Tony Bates, Mr Ricketts."

"Ah yes, come in Bates, this is Miss Roach. She's from the Child Welfare Department."

"Hello Tony, what on earth have you done to your face and arms?" She asked with a horrified look on her face.

"Had a slight accident with some petrol, didn't I sir?"

Ricketts' attempt to cover it up was a little too obvious as he quickly tried to change the subject.

"Err yes, well Bates, Miss Roach has some good news for you, I think."

"Yes, well I hope it's what you want to hear Tony."

The suspense was killing me, and wished she'd hurry up and get on with it, so we could get the hell out of here.

"Well, I hear you have a love for the sea, well that's good because I've managed to get a job for you on a ship that is shortly returning to England."

Was I hearing right? Did she say England? This was too much to hope for.

"Did I hear right Miss, I'm going to England?"

"Yes that's right, in the end you've got your own way, you're going home after all."

I was speechless and just wanted to give her a big kiss but didn't dare.

"Don't just stand there Bates, go and get your things,"

Ricketts face looked as pleased as mine and somehow got the impression that my accident had caused more than a lot of embarrassment for him.

"Yes Sir, and thanks Miss, thanks for everything."

Running out of the office, I told everyone I bumped into, Pauline, Rosita, Alice and even stuffy guts Ryan, and then ran back to the dorm shouting at the top of my voice.

"I'm going home, I'm bloody going home."

My clothes were packed in an old box that I found and I was back at the office ready to go in no time.

"Well, it's been nice meeting you Mr Rickett and no doubt our paths will cross again."

"I'm sure they will, Miss Roach I'm sure they will"

"Well Bates before you go you'd better sign for your personal effects" at first not knowing what he was talking about handed me an envelope containing £14 taken which had taken from me on my arrival.

"Thankyou Sir."

Then leaving his office I said goodbye to Alice and Pauline then finally Rosita, my favourite.

"Goodbye my little Antonio, God bless, and don't forget to send me a card or I'll come looking for you."

"No worries." and I gave her a peck on the cheek.

"Come on Tony, time's getting on."

"Right Miss, ready when you are." and without having a chance to say bye to the boys, drove off through the main gates and away from the home.

"Well I'm not sorry to see the back of that place," I said, looking behind me.

"Yes well you do seem to get yourself into some spots don't you? I've been checking up on your case history. You're more slippery than an eel. It reads more like a script from T.V. soap; not knowing where or what you're going to get up to next and this is just another episode."

I felt quite a celebrity and tried to smile, but each time I did, tiny bits would flake off my face like dandruff and land on my lap.

"Tell me more about your burns and how it happened."

So once again, I told the story. She'd have probably heard Ricketts' version already with him making me out to be the baddy, still Miss Roach wasn't so bad, a bit like Ma Stevenson only a lot younger and much prettier. She listened carefully to my every word, taking it all in.

"I see that explains it, does it still hurt?" she asked

"Na, not any more thank Christ, I couldn't go through that pain again."

Dying to know what was in store for me, I quickly changed the subject.

"Tell me more about the ship I'm to work on Miss."

"Well, there's not much to tell, all I know is she's called the Suvic and she berthed at – hang on, I've got it written here somewhere...ah yes, Marsden Wharf. It's owned by the Shaw Saville Shipping Company and they've kindly offered to take you on as Deck Boy for the duration of the trip."

Still I couldn't believe my luck, all that trouble in Australia without success. I'd broken the law, stowing away on one ship, then to be offered a job on another. Who was I to argue? In the end I'd come up trumps. Soon to be on the outskirts of the city I recognised a few familiar landmarks from my previous trip on the way out to the boys' home, then making our way through the city to finally come out on Quay Street and the Harbour, turning left through the dock gates, then to be stopped at the Gate House.

"Can I help you Miss?"

"I hope so, we're looking for the S.S. Suvic, I believe she's on Marsden Wharf."

"Yes Miss, follow the road down to the right nearly to the end, it's not far, Marsden's the last on the left, you can't miss it."

"Thanks, you've been a great help," and we pulled away.

To think that only a week ago I'd gone through these very same gates, handcuffed going to God knows where, now I was back and wondered whether or not the Afric was still in port. Afric – Suvic, but of course, I said to myself, they must both belong to the same shipping company.

"How far did he say Tony?"

"Just keep going I think Miss." passing Captain Cook Wharf, the next being Marsden, taking a sharp left, and there she was the largest ship I'd ever seen in my life.

CASE REPORT

12 October 1965

Anthony Roy BATES — Age: 16 Years 1 Month

N.A.

2.9.49
Sussex   Sex   M   Legitimacy: L   Race: E   Religion and Attendance: Church of England / Nominal

England

whom living and relationship: No fixed abode.   Locality: N.A.

dress: N.A.

SCHOOL   Attending: N.A.   Attended: N.A.   Class: N.A.   Progress: N.A.

Attendance: N.A.   Intelligence and Test used: N.A.

WORK   Kind of work and Name of employer: Driver's Asst, Eta Foods Ltd, Sydney.
(Including after-school, etc., jobs)

ime in jobs: 2 weeks   Weekly Wage: £9   Money Handled: N.K.   Hours: N.K.

Changes in circumstances since commission of offence or initiation of proceedings: Arrested stowing away and placed in Owairaka Boys' Home, 56 Owairaka Avenue, Mt Albert.

PREVIOUSLY UNDER NOTICE No

FAMILY:

Reason for any break in family unit: N.A.

FATHER: Frederick John BATES   Age: 37
Stepfather, etc.:
   Country of origin: England
Address: 36 Billingham Crescent, Hove 4, Sussexx, England.   Anything known against character of parent.

Occupation and Employer: Seaman, British Railways   Hours: N.K.

MOTHER: Mavis Annette BATES   Age: 37
Stepmother, etc.:
   Country of origin: England
Address: 36 Billingham Crescent, Hove 4, Sussex, England.

Occupation and Employer: Housewife   Hours: N.A.   If working are children supervised? N.A.

BROTHERS AND SISTERS:

	Age	Sex	Occupation	Living at home	Previously under notice
Six brothers					
One sister					

OTHERS IN HOUSEHOLD: N.K.   Family Benefit No. N.K.

NAMES AND ADDRESSES of GRANDPARENTS: Paternal: N.K.   Maternal: N.K.

COURT ACTION:

Section: ____ Act: ____

LEGAL CHARGE/COMPLAINT: STOWED AWAY

Actual offence: Stowed away at Sydney on the s.s. "Afric".

Number, age, and sex of companions: One male aged 17 years   Initiated by Police/C.W.O./Traffic Officer.

RECOMMENDATION:

DECISION: ① adj to 21/10/65. ② Declared c' ...
17.

Made under Section __ C.W. (Amend.) Act 19 25   Date(s) dealt with @ 6.10.65
Magistrate: ____   14.10.65

DISTRICT OFFICE	HEAD OFFICE
AUCKLAND	No.:
Court AUCKLAND	Statistics:
Serial Numbers:	C.W.O.:

Mr _Pycroft_

Mrs _____

Miss _____

<u>SPECIAL SITTING</u>

<u>CHILDREN'S COURT, AUCKLAND</u>   D/B 2/9/49

Name of Defendant: _Anthony Roy BATE_ (since
Immigrant to Australia from England (May '65

Address: _Sponsored by Dr Barnardos Homes._

Offence: _Staying away from ship named 'Africa_
from Sydney the

Date and time of Sitting: _6/10/65 at 10" am_
Mag. Court.

Information received from _Const Byrd_ at _8.55_ on _6/1_
of Wharf Police.

"   "   by _JRPayne_

Referred to:.

Mr ` _____

Mrs _____

Miss _____

        Please attend this sitting.

                Senior Officer's initials _____

                        Date: _____

CHAPTER 11

As we got closer I could read her name, high on her bow, S.S. Suvic, looking twice the size of her sister ship. "Well here we are Tony what do you think?" She smiled knowing I was stuck for words. "It's.....great!" Stopping the car almost at the bottom of the gangway, got out and collected my cardboard box off the back seat then walked over to the gangway, followed by my companion.

"You go first Miss, hold tight and mind your step, it can get a bit slippery," she hesitated, "don't worry miss I'm right behind you, you'll be right."

Leaving the ground behind, I climbed the gangway. This one was to be higher and much steeper than the Afric, finally reaching the top to be met by the watchman, a giant six footer of a man who towered over both of us.

"Yes Ma'am? Can I help you?"

"You certainly can. My name's Miss Roach, I'm from the Child Welfare Department and this is the new Deck Boy, we're here to see the Captain."

"Right you are, if you'd like to follow me Miss"

And followed him up to the Officers quarters, "If you wouldn't mind waiting here," then he knocked on one of the doors. It opened and after exchanging a few words, an Officer came out and dismissed the member of crew, "Thankyou Smith, that'll be all."

"Yes Chief" and he went back to his duties.

"Good morning madam, my name's Clark, I'm the First Officer, can I help?"

"I do hope so, I'm Miss Roach, from the Children's' Welfare office and this is Anthony Bates, I believe you're expecting us."

"Ah yes, the new Deck Boy, won't you come this way," following him into an office. "Take a seat, I'll just see if the Captain's available, will you excuse me?" He shortly returned, followed by another distinguished looking gentleman.

"Miss Roach, I'd like you to meet Captain Cheldon."

"Good morning Sir."

"Good morning Miss Roach, and you must be the new lad Bates."He said looking me up and down

"Yes Sir."

"We've been expecting you," and after what was to be a few words, I was then asked to sign the ships articles which was filled in by the mate.

"Right, your duties will be Deck Boy, the pay is £23 a month all found, OK?"

"Yes Sir."

"Sign here, now what about these burns Miss Roach. Is he under treatment with the hospital?"

"Not that I know of, but it might be an idea to get them looked at."

"How does it feel Bates?"

"Fine, Sir, it only hurts when I look in a mirror." My sense of humour was not appreciated and the Captain carried on, disregarding my remark.

"I think it might be better to keep him on light duties for a week, Chief."

"Yes Sir."

"Apart from that Miss Roach, it appears the doctor's cleared him A1?"

"Right Bates, if you'd like to wait outside a moment." Still hanging onto my box with all my worldly goods in it, I left them to discuss my case, only to be met by a large fat man in the alley way.

"Hello kid, you the new replacement?" He was sloppily dressed with a large piece of string tied around his waist holding his trousers up and what looked like the remains of his breakfast all down his shirt.

"Yes Sir Deck Boy." I said putting my box down to shake his hand

"So what'd ya do to ya face then kid?"

"Ah, got burnt in a petrol explosion."

"Ugly little sod ain't ya?" He laughed as my thoughts on him were the exact same. The door opened with the return of Miss Roach, followed by the First Mate.

"Ah, Boson, just the man I wont, see you've already meet the new Deck Boy, Bates, put him in with Prichard and light duties for the rest of the week, oh and no shore leave until further notice." I looked on with surprise, as Miss said her farewells and walked down to the lower deck while the Boson carried on talking to the Chief.

"What's this about no shore leave Miss?"

"Well officially you're still on remand that is until your case comes up which is tomorrow so I'll meet you here at nine o'clock sharp on the Quay. We'll also see if we can dig you up some more clothes from somewhere."

The Boson finished his chat, coming right up behind us, "You'd better see the young lady down on to the quay, Bates. Meet me back in the Mess."

"Yes Sir."

"Bos or Boson not Sir"

"Yes Boson."

I knew where I was, even where we were going, but it hadn't quite sunk in yet, everything had happened so fast. Retracing our footsteps returned to the gangway, this time with me going first, finally to reach her car.

"Well Tony, nine o'clock sharp and don't be late."

"No Miss, Oh and Miss" she leaned from her car window, "thanks for everything."

"You're welcome," then watched as she drove off down the quay. Returning back on board I stopped to talk to the watchman. "Excuse me mate, where's the Mess?"

"You are by the looks of it, what happened to you?" A question I was to get asked a hundred times during the next few days."

"Ah, nothing much, a slight explosion I got caught up in."

"Looks painful does it hurt?"

"Na not so much now, it did at first."

"Dave Smith the name," he said, holding out his huge great hand.

"Tony Bates, good to meet ya Dave."

"So what ship you off then?"

"Me? None, this is me first."

"So how come you're joining us now then?"

"Well I suppose you could say I'm being deported."

"Deported what the fuck for?" He looked on in total amazement.

"Oh, me and my mate stowed away from Australia, we thought the ship was going straight to England, we got that wrong that's for sure."

"Oh, so you're the ones, are ya?" Stopping me in my tracks, "the Afric won't it?"

"Yeah, that's right how do you know."

"Ow heard about it from one of the lads on there. Fancy that, she's still here ya know, she sails on the early tide tomorrow, you going over to see em?"

"Like to, but I've been confined to the ship for the time being."

"Blimey, you're a one ain't ya so how old are ya?"

"Sixteen," then, trying to change the subject, I said, "So what you making there?" Looking down at his box of tricks on the deck.

"Oh that I'm making ships in bottles, it's a hobby of mine. You'll have to come along to me cabin sometime and see some of me work, then you can tell me more of what you've been up to."

"Yeah, right, I'll do that sometime."

"Now where was it you wanted, oh yeah, the Mess, through that door then first left, and first right?"

"Thanks Dave, see ya later."

"Yea, alright," following his directions, I came upon the crews' Mess Room where the Boson was enjoying a mug of tea and what looked like the rest of Tab Nabs.

"Where you been, I've been waiting here fucking ages," at the same time another lad was busy laying up the tables.

"Prichard come here a minute, meet the new Peggy he'll bunking in with you

And as soon as you've got this lot sorted, you can show him around."

"Yeah, right Bos, So where's your gear Pegs?"

"Oh shit, I left it up top."

"Well you'd better go and get it now before someone throws it over the side." the boson shouted

Thinking they would – the condition of it and all, I hastily made a return towards the Officers Quarters, where still tucked in the corner were my sole possessions, then quickly returned to the Mess?

"Take no notice of that fat pig, no one likes him, anyway the names John" "Tony, Tony Bates" and we shook hands, Yea it's his first trip as Boson and it's gone to his head." John was the same rating as me, but nearly two years my senior and a big lad for his age.

"So what the fuck happened to your face?" Once again out came the explanations. He showed me to our cabin which was the first cabin one as you left the Mess. It was small but compact, with two bunks, a double locker, dresser, and a couple of chairs.

"Top bunks yours and later I'll clear this locker out for ya," he said opening it up. Inside there was still some old clothing.

"Who's that lot belong to?"

"Ow that's the last bloke's that was here, he jumped ship in Littleton with four others that's how come you're here."

I didn't even know my predecessor, but I was grateful to him for giving me his berth.

"The cabin next door is also empty all five who jumped ship were from the deck side."

"Yea" I said, showing little interest. Putting my cardboard box on the seat, I broke the string and looked in on my miserable wardrobe.

"Leave all that, we'll do it later. First we'll get your linen then I'll show you around the ship" Leaving the cabin, followed John along the accommodation alley, as he pointed out the showers and toilet on one side, on the other cabins of all the rest of the deck crew, then at the end a games room which inside, consisted of table tennis, darts and a couple of card tables, Further on was the surgery and hospital where you'd have to queue up daily with your ailments, such as hangovers, etc and most common of all, the clap.

"Normally with a ship this size we have a doctor on board, but he left a couple of days ago so, the first mate stepped in for him."

"Yeah so how many crew are there on board" I asked

"Hard to say really, about seventy probably more"

It was hard to believe at first, but later could see why, so many. Then continuing my tour on the starboard side, "All down here's the engine room staff, stewards, cooks and Fatso's cabin is up the end there." Finally we'd come full circle bringing us back to the Mess.

"Oh shit, look at the time, give us a hand to get the dinners' down will ya, it's ten to bloody twelve." Both rushing off to the galley without a moment to lose and only just making 12 o'clock rush with the crew all coming off day work for their lunch. During the next hour I kept away from the Mess as apart from numerous explanations I would have to make about my face, it was also not a pretty sight over the meal table, so I decided to go on my own tour. First back to my cabin to stow my gear then making my way out on deck on the port side, which overlooked the harbour and there on the other side just as Dave had said was the Afric, lying low in the water all loaded and ready for the morning tide.

I promised myself that somehow I would sneak ashore so to take one last look and also to say bye to her crew. Miles away in my thoughts, I didn't hear John come up behind me, "Come on Tony, what you doing out here? Come and meet the rest of the boys."

"You sure what about my face"

"Na, don't worry about it, there's some that would like to be that good looking. Come on, you've got to eat as well." That was a good point.

"Yea, right let's go." No sooner back in the Mess and getting something to eat from the hot press, than John called me over. At first I felt a little strange, my face being more of an attraction than me. On taking my seat, I recognised Dave the watchman giving a nod to acknowledge himself, "Alright Tony, settled in yet?"

"Sort of"

"This here's my brother, Tel," and then continued by going around the table, "That's Jock, Ron, Alan, Danny, McLuskey, and Griff." And that was only one table. My memory for names was poor so I knew sooner or later I would be asking again.

"Lads, meet the new Peggy?" And that's how it was for the rest of the day. Meeting new faces and trying hard to memorise their names. During that afternoon, three more recruits joined the ship, escorted to the gangway by the local constabulary, two of whom were put in the adjoining cabin to ours, also like me, were confined to the ship until sailing. I was on my bunk when a head popped through the open door. "Hello mate, name's Bob, so what's the grub like on here?" Jumping down, I introduced myself, "Good mate, name's Tony, this is my first day."

"Ere Mac, seems' half the crew must have jumped in Littleton, even the Peggy's new." That's when I met Bob's cabin mate, "Alright mate, Name's Tom McCarthy, friends call me Mac. What happened to you then? Your face is in a right old mess ain't it?"

Once again, out came an explanation, after which, we spent the next hour or so exchanging stories.

Bob was about 19 years old, 5'8" and from Glasgow. Mac was also from Scotland, was only 18, tall, well over six feet and built to match, having hands the size of baseball gloves. They'd both jumped ship nine months previous. Since then they'd lived and worked in Auckland. Bob was due to marry when he was picked up and Mac was taken shortly after and both said that on arriving back in England would both return at the first chance they got. During the next few weeks I was to spend most of shore leave tagging along with the two of them. During supper they met the rest of the crew and another new member, Mick Daniels. On his arrival he already knew Bob and Mac so had a lot to catch up on, but never left me out of the conversation. After supper, while the rest of the crew got ready to go ashore, we all sat around Mac's cabin. By now we managed to get a few beers so we decided to have our own party. One by one, as the crew went off they dropped in whatever alcohol they had left in their cabins. Even though we were stuck on board, we were determined to have a good time. After a few hours of singing and drinking, I flaked out. Next thing I knew was John giving me an early morning shake, "Come on Tony, it's seven o'clock." My head felt like it had been shut in a vice. And my mouth, well words alone can't explain as I crawled from my bunk and staggered over to the port for fresh air. First thing I noticed was the Afric had gone as my promise to visit was way layed by a drinking spree.

"Come on Tony, ain't you dressed yet." Quickly dressing, I made my way to the Mess, which by now John had already laid up, all that was left to do was fetch the breakfast and make the tea which we managed to do by the skin of our teeth. Then I remembered at nine I was to meet Miss Roach for my court case, so I had to get myself cleaned up. Quickly washed and changed, I returned for breakfast to find, sitting in the corner, a woman, half naked, with her tits resting on the table while she tucked into her breakfast.

"Who the fuck's she John"

"Who her, Ow that's Wilson's the second cook. She's only here for bed and breakfast."

"What do ya mean?"

"Well, he fucks the arse off her and she gets to eat his breakfast goes on all the time."

She was a native of New Zealand and not a pretty one at that, but then George was no oil painting either, nevertheless, there was enough of her showing to stand my pecker on end.

After they all finished, I cleared away, giving John as much help as possible before leaving. Shortly before nine I made my excuses to the Boson before going ashore where already Miss Roach was waiting to greet me.

"Hello Tony, how are you? Settled in alright? Sleep well?" Not wanting to tell the Child Welfare Officer I was drunk as a skunk and there were women aboard walking around half naked, I went for the easy answers, "Yes Miss, they're a good crowd."

"That's good, shall we go then." Climbing into the car, we took the short journey to the Court House where after a short hearing, it was again adjourned until the 21st October, pending further information, strange, even though it had been mentioned that I'd already signed on the Suvic, so asked "Ow it's nothing to worry about it's just a formality once you leave Auckland all charges will be dropped."

"Oh right." It made no sense to me if they were going to drop the charges anyway why keep dragging it on.

"Right then Tony, shall we go for a coffee?"

"Yea can't see why not"

"I've also been authorised to get you a few new items of clothing, anything in particular you'd like?"

"Yeah, I'd like a new pair of jeans and a jacket." I'd seen the guys on board wearing them when they went ashore, all faded from the wash, and seemed to be a standard uniform and I didn't want to be out of place, "Oh and maybe a pair of shoes."

"Okay, but let's have our coffee first." We were to go to a large departmental store first to the coffee lounge then down to the men's' department where the Welfare had an account.

"Yes, Madam, can I help you?" Showing her I.D. and a letter, the man began to look me up and down, "and what size trousers are we?", taking out a tape measure and throwing it around my waist, then messing about with my inside leg, "the boy would prefer denims and a jacket to match" "Whatever Sir wishes," he said, walking straight over to a rack, he pulled down a pair of Levis.

"Here you go, Sir, 28 inch waist, try those for size." Although too long in the leg, the rest fitted a treat, "How are they, Tony?"

"Fine, Miss, they fit just fine."

"How about this one sir" The assistant said, passing me a jacket to match, slipping it on I admired myself in the mirror. Now I looked the part. All I needed was a new face and everything would be back to normal. Changing back, Miss Roach gave the shop assistant the OK then signed her name away. "They'll kill me, when the office gets the invoice, still, I'll say they were necessary for work now how about shoes?"

Soon at the shoe department, I picked out a pair of black working boots to complete my new image. After mentioning my peculiar taste, she again signed her name away. "Well, I'd better get you back to the ship now before they send out a search party." We were soon back at the car and making the return journey to the ship. After saying goodbye, I gave a wave as she drove off down the quay.

Arriving back on board just before lunch, I went straight to the Mess where John had already filled the hot press and was making his final trip.

"Alright Tony, how did ya go?"

"Ah, it's been adjourned again until 21st October."

"Don't worry about it, probably won't be here anyway. Give us a hand will ya?"

"Yeah, no worries, I'll just sling this in the cabin." Soon to be finished, and twelve o'clock, we left the crew to gorge themselves while we returned to the cabin for a quiet beer.

"See you've got some new gear then, Tony."

"Yeah, just some jeans and a jacket needs a wash though, they're all new and stiff.

"Best thing is to leave 'em in a bucket of soapy water for a few days, helps take the dye out, then once we're at sea throw them over the side on the end of a heavy line and drag 'em through the sea for a few hours, that'll lighten 'em up."

Everything was going great, new mates, new clothes, but still all this Court House rubbish was getting to me a bit, deep down inside, I was still thinking that any day they'd change their minds and send me back to Australia. During the next few days, including the weekend, I met the rest of the crew. During the day I had my work, washing alley ways, cleaning toilets and showers and helping John at meal times. No longer was I Tony, just "Pegs do this, do that." like an apprentice on the job and had to earn promotion. Night times would be spent in the Mess or on deck depending on the weather or Mac's cabin, but always it was a piss up, each time the crowd getting bigger and bigger, seemed to me we were having more fun on board than those ashore. One thing I can say is that all those men lived as though it were their last day, getting full enjoyment out of every moment. Gradually my face began to peel, leaving patches of bright red skin. My arms were almost clear and now I began to wonder how I would eventually look. Sunday in port was normally a day of rest, but now the unloading had finished it was time to reload for the journey home. It was like any other day only as our stay in port got longer, the amount of women on board got larger, walking around the accommodation like it was their home. One morning during an early morning shower, we found we were even sharing those, but you learnt to accept it – and at the same time wash away those dirty thoughts, and if you were inclined you could have your body washed down and more by some strange woman just for the price of a couple of beers.

During the day our cabin doors were left open so any time, if you wanted, you could stop for a chat, a regular home from home, a floating town. You needed for nothing. We even had culture. There was Martin the Professor. He was one of your educated seamen and some day planned to be skipper, but wanted to do it the hard way, up through the ranks. His cabin was so full of books there was hardly a place to sit. Our artist was without a doubt, Dave, his ships in bottles were a masterpiece, the envy of all who watched and he promised to make me one during the voyage home. As for comedy, well she was full of comedians from the deck to catering department, right down to the engine room. There was always something new happening – never a dull moment.

Monday, then Tuesday came and went while the loading continued and on the Wednesday afternoon all was completed, so tonight would be a last chance to go ashore. Mac and I not forgetting the others had now been confined to the ship for over a week and were beginning to get cabin fever. Somehow we just had to get ashore and already there was talk of a party at the 'Shererlee Club' which was above the great northern hotel and were all making plans to sneak ashore. The only problem for me was my face still being as it was; I'd stick out like a red light. Determined not to let it beat me, I spent the rest of the day picking off all the dry skin, the one thing doctors warned me not to do because of scarring, but with John's help and a lot of baby oil, it was soon all clear, leaving me with a bright red face.

"Fucking hell John, I look like a fucking traffic beacon."

"So what, who's going to see you in the fucking dark" John laughed

"What about in the club?"

"It's fucking darker in there than outside – you'll be

alright." My new look gave everyone a good laugh but it still looked better than before, Tea that night was over like a flash, no sooner had they finished than we stowed away their plates, "That'll do Tony, whatever's left now we'll just dump over the side in the morning, come on let's get showered and changed."

My denim suit had by now been washed a dozen times and although had not faded how I would've liked, it still looked good. The boots were on and I was ready for the off. The plan was to all meet in the Schooner, just outside the dock gates. It was dark, so if we went off a few at a time, no one would notice. Mac, John, and I were the last to go. Martin the professor was on the gangway, but he wasn't the problem. It was bumping into Officers or the Boson on board or even ashore, so we had to watch out. Making our way to the gangway, we had to pass our first obstacle, the Boson's cabin.

"Watch out, his door's open," ducking back into the Mess bumping a couple of the guys

"Hello fellas, what's going on, having a party? Where's the booze?"

Saved by the drunks, it was Wilson, the second cook and Ricky, one of the firemen, so quietly explained our problem. "No problem boys, you go round the other way, we'll keep him busy. John, you come with us."

Wilson and Rick, two better guys you couldn't meet, always in trouble, Wilson with his women and Ricky always drunk on watch went off to keep Fatso busy. We no sooner heard the talking, than we were off as they were doing a good job so making our way to the gangway were Martin was sitting reading his books.

"Alright Martin how's it going"

"Good Mac, I think I'll just go and grab myself a mug of cocoa so to miss you when you go ashore."

"Yea, sure, see ya later mate"

Soon down the gangway, we ran along the quay like convicts escaping from Devil's Island, we waited for the others who soon after, with John's help all three staggered along the quay, laughing and falling about all over the place. First stop was the Schooner to meet up with the others, this was to be my first of many nights out with the boys and by now after a week of getting paralytic every night, I was able to hold my liquor fairly well, along with the others. That night, I stood in the background while the others went to the bar as I didn't look my age and was lucky to get served a soda let alone a beer. After an hour or so in the Schooner we all headed up Queen Street and the 'Shererlee Club', which was entered through a side door of a pub and upstairs. The music could be heard from outside and once in the club; the flashing lights took away the red glow from my face.

"What ya drinking Pegs?"

"Beer please, Mac."

By now we'd all broken up into small groups although if anyone needed help you didn't need to look far. Wilson and Rick found themselves a couple of old birds tucked away in the corner and set to trying to chat them up. No doubt I'd find one of them in the shower come morning and to make sure, I'd get up especially early. Dave and Bob steamed in on the dance floor. It was like an 'excuse me'. Dave would go over to a couple, if he wasn't one of ours, knock him flying saying "Excuse me mate, I think this dance is mine." Bob wasn't much better. Most of the girls were regulars only coming the short distance from the Nurses Home and knew what to expect. Soon the drink had done the trick and I was out there along with John chatting up a couple of second year students, who I might add, were not the best lookers, but the more we drank the better they got later staggering back to the Nurses Home for a night cap. That night was one I was to remember for a long time, and was also the night I loss my cherry turning me from the boy to a man, and it was clear to see why men liked women in uniforms, only to be slung out at five in the morning. Then came the funniest sight you ever did see, as John and I staggered down Queen Street we met up with two more guys from the same ship, then another two. Thank Christ there wasn't an emergency on at the hospital that night as half the crew off the Suvic had stopped over, slowly we all staggered back to the ship, none the worse for wear.

We first passed Shelly, one of the deck hands of Irish decent, lying flat out on a stack of pallets. Shelly's biggest distinguishing mark were his boils all over his back and every so often you'd find his cabin mate Danny squeezing the puss out of them in the shower not a pretty sight. Each time Shelly yelled with pain, the rest of the crew would sing along. Picking him up, we started to drag him back only to find one more. Rick – his long session of boozing had got the better of him. There he lay, fast asleep in his own vomit. Waking him up, he eventually stood up looking down at himself, not saying a word took off his dirty clothes and slung them in the harbour and staggered towards the ship wearing nothing but his boots, just the picture you want to send home to Mum saying 'Glad you're not here'.

What a night. The Child Welfare had certainly made the right decision, well for me anyway. We were soon all back on board and there was no time to sleep, just a shower and change ready for a days work and of course the Mess Room looked like a bomb had hit it. Having less than an hour to clean up, lay and be ready for 7 o'clock and breakfast. We thought we had our problems. Rick was the Firemen's Peggy and could still just about stand up, so leaving me, John went to give him a hand but then that was the way it was. One day it would be our turn. Wilson, the second cook on the other hand, was in the Galley reaching in the sink, while not one, but two girls from the night before waited for their breakfast. They must have lost Rick on the journey back. It beats me where he got all his stamina from.

After breakfast I made myself ready for Miss Roach and my Court Case and waited on board for her to arrive. As I did, the second mate arrived on the scene with the one thing the whole crew had been waiting for, the sailing time and watched as he chalked it up on the board at the top of the gangway. All those going ashore had to be back by twelve midnight, all shore leave cancelled as we sailed on the morning tide.

The arrival of Miss Roach took me, I hoped, for the last time ashore and we were no sooner in the car than away.

"Hello Tony, My, your face looks a lot better, so how have you been?"

"Fine Miss, never felt better, how about yourself?"

"I'm good, thanks, but I'll be better still after we get you sorted out."

"Did you know we sail tomorrow, Miss?"

"Yes, but don't worry you'll be back."

It was easy for her to say, but I felt like the carrot in front of the donkey, just dangling not knowing how my case was to go. I needn't have bothered worrying as it was all over in no time at all with the Magistrate's summing up, "It is my opinion and that of my colleagues that it would be in everyone's interest, especially yours Anthony that you return to the United Kingdom. You have caused considerable concern not to mention expense to the New Zealand and Australian Government, also Dr Barnardo's

Home Australia. Therefore, it is agreed that you will be taken from here directly back to the ship known as the Suvic Shaw Saville and there to work as a Deck Boy until reaching England where the appropriate authorities will take over. All charges will be dropped under Section 17 of the Child Welfare Act 1925, when finally your ship sails. Have you anything to say?"

"No Sir, thankyou Sir."

"That will be all, you may go." As I turned to take me leave, the Magistrate called out, "Oh Anthony."

"Yes sir."

"Good luck!" And a smile beamed across his face. I actually think deep down, he meant it. Then quickly, I left the court room, before they had a chance to change their minds.

"See Tony, I told you everything would be alright didn't I. Now have you time for a quick coffee?"

"Yes Miss." Over coffee, she asked me all about the ship, her crew and so on. Not wanting to go into detail, I just skimmed over the surface.

"Sounds a good life, you've fought hard enough to get it. I hope you're suited."

Shortly after, we made the drive back to the ship, and for the last time stopping at the Gate House. No sooner had we pulled away when I recognised a face.

"Stop Miss, that's my mate John," pulling the car over to the side, I took a second look. I was right there large as life was my old partner in crime, John Burns. "Won't be a minute Miss, got to see me old mate John, I thought he was still inside."

"John – cloth ears – it's me," at first not recognising me, but then he came running over, "Hello John, what the hell are you doing here?"

"I work here; let me out a couple of days ago found me a job and new digs things couldn't be better how about you"

"Me, I'm off to England tomorrow on the early tide. They got me signed on a ship tied up on Marsden, the Suvic, as a Deck Boy."

"Oh great, looks like we both come smelling of roses."

"Yea, I just come back from Court, they're dropping all charges as soon as we sail, Say look what you doing tonight?"

"Nothing why"

"Fancy coming aboard, we'll sink a few beers for old times sake?"

"Yeah, no worry sounds great. What time?"

"Please yourself, straight after work if you like."

"No worries, until tonight then. I'd better go, Tony, better keep this job now I got it."

"Sure, see ya later, Oh and John it's great to see ya mate."

"Yea you too later"

Somehow he didn't seem as sure of his prospects as he made out. Still I'd find out later. I'd made a lot of friends, but at last to meet a familiar face. I couldn't wait for the day to end so we could get drunk and talk over the past couple of weeks. Running back, I climbed back into the car.

"Thanks Miss, you're an angel. Thought I'd never see him again and here we both ended up where we started, the day we arrived."

Pulling away, we were soon at the ship and after a short chat she gave me her home address in Auckland. "Now you write and tell me how you get on."

"Yes Miss and thanks for everything."

"You're very welcome Tony. I only hope you find whatever your looking for back in England," she turned round and gave me a little wave as she drove off down the quay for the last time, with me watching until she was out of sight. I was now a free man once again. Nothing and no one could stop me now. I quickly climbed the gangway to safety and British soil, returning back to my duties as Peggy and laid up for dinner.

Most of that day was for the rest of the men spent doing last minute stowing, lowering the derricks and finally making all hatches ready for sea. Thursday was a long day for all concerned, just waiting for the last minute orders to cast off. During the evening we all sat around the Mess exchanging stories while I waited patiently for John, my mate to arrive, but he never showed. The evening dragged on so went out on deck for some fresh air, it was late but there was still hope that John might turn up. The Boson was on watch sat in his chair at the top of the gangway reading, also to stop last minute stragglers going ashore. On hearing my footsteps he looked up.

"Oh Peg's, got a message for you. Some bloke named John came to see you earlier, said to tell you 'Good luck and he'll see you around one day'."

"Do what? So why didn't you let him come on board?"

"Not allowed Captain's orders. Got to have permission to

have civilians on board once the sailing time's up, because of stowaways, but then you'd know all about that," laughing loudly, he went back to his book.

The bastard, I thought, he didn't even come and tell me. From that day on I took an instant dislike to him and somehow would get my own back. That was the last I ever saw of John. Even after years of my trying to track him down but without any success. Returning to my cabin, I climbed into my bunk and just laid there, thinking of the past few weeks. How Pat was doing back in Australia, my days on the Afric my night in jail and of course the boy's home. I'd come a long way in a short time and we were soon to set sail for England. The final orders came in the early hours of Friday 22nd October and the order was given to turn too.

"Wake up Tony its stations," said John, pulling my covers from me.

"Stations what you talking about?"

"We're sailing stupid now get up and out on deck."

Once outside, I was sent aft with Mac, Dave and a couple of others.

"Right Pegs, just do as I tell you, don't get in the way and whatever you do keep your feet clear of them ropes and wires."

The orders came from the Bridge to single up, and down on the wharf the men let the ropes go, sending them crashing into the water below while our end was quickly put around the drum and winched safely aboard and at the same time, being neatly coiled out from harms way. Now down to two ropes and the back spring, we were told to hold fast. As the adrenalin pumped through my body I felt useless as I watched my shipmate's work, but I felt ten feet tall as I looked down onto the quay. The mate then ordered us to let go our head ropes as slowly she slipped away from the quay, sailing up the channel under her own steam. Once outside the harbour entrance, we anchored off and waited for the pilot's boat to come alongside, shortly after he'd left the ship we were under way slowly leaving New Zealand behind. Finally after seven months of wandering, I was on my way home to England just in time for Christmas with my family and old friends.

Barnardo's Homes
NATIONAL INCORPORATED ASSOCIATION

Patron: HER MAJESTY QUEEN ELIZABETH THE QUEEN MOTHER.
President: HER ROYAL HIGHNESS THE PRINCESS MARGARET, COUNTESS OF SNOWDON.
Chairman of Council: SIR ALFRED OWEN, C.B.E.
Honorary Treasurer: M. M. TEXLEY, ESQ., C.B.E.
Chairman of Committee of Management: LT.-GEN. SIR ARTHUR E. SMITH,
K.C.B., K.B.E., D.S.O., M.C.
Chairman, Finance Committee: NORMAN K. HILL, ESQ., B.SC.(ECON.), PH.D., C.A.
General Secretary: FREDERICK J. POTTER, F.C.A.
General Superintendent: THEODORE F. TUCKER, O.B.E.

Our Ref: Mgtn/WA/LD   Your Ref:

Head Office   MIGRATION DEPARTMENT,
STEPNEY CAUSEWAY,
LONDON, E.1

15th November, 1965.

Dear Mr. Price,

re Anthony Bates - N.S.W. 54/65

A copy of my last letter to you of 27th October was sent to Mrs. Jones in New Zealand and she has now replied and I quote from her letter as follows:-

"Anthony Roy Bates appeared in the Auckland Childrens' Court on 14th October 1965 charged with stowing away on board the "AFRIC". The matter was then adjourned until 21st October 1965 for a final decision.

In the meantime arrangements were made by the Child Welfare Department for Anthony to be signed on a Shaw Savill ship, s.s. "CUEVIC" as a deckboy. The s.s. "CUEVIC" left from Auckland via South Africa on 22nd October. It is understood that Anthony will be able to sign off the ship when it arrives in England.

In respect of the charge of stowing away, he was discharged under Section 17 of the Child Welfare Act 1925 when he appeared in the Auckland Childrens' Court on 21st October."

It is felt that Mrs. Jones quickly and successfully did all she was asked to do but we have been asked to obtain from you rather more clarification of the situation which in some aspects we still find somewhat puzzling:-

Mrs. Bates is appalled at the prospect of Anthony coming home, and being at home out of work. In fact, she is determined that he should not stay, because she believes he will be in trouble in a matter of weeks! His father has taken the most absurd attitude, and is impossible man, and will not help the lad at all, as he is even more irresponsible himself. If he works his way home, and gets a good discharge possibly he could stay on, but I suppose there are regulations. Mrs. Bates feels that they have let us down over the whole affair, and wonders what the Australian authorities will say. If the lad is genuine in his desire to be at Sea, this should prove whether he is tough enough to take the life. Mother hopes that somehow he may be settled in a sea berth, otherwise she fears that he will get in with the wrong people at home.

(SIGNED) Mr. Wright.

NEW ZEALAND POLICE

PROSECUTION SECTION,
P.O. BOX 40,
AUCKLAND C.1.

22 October 1965.

The New Zealand Secretary,
Dr. Barnardo's Homes,
P.O. Box 899,
WELLINGTON C.1.

Dear Sir,

ANTHONY ROY BATES

Anthony Roy BATES, as you are aware, appeared in the Auckland Children's Court on 14 October 1965 charged with stowing away on board the "AFRIC". The matter was then adjourned until 21 October 1965 for a final decision.

In the meantime arrangements were made by the Child Welfare Department for BATES to be signed on the Shaw Savill ship, s.s. CUEVIC as a deckboy. The s.s. CUEVIC departs from New Zealand for England via South Africa on 22 October 1965. It is understood that BATES will be able to sign off this ship when it arrives in England.

In respect of the charge of stowing away he was discharged under Section 17 of the Child Welfare Act 1925 when he appeared in the Auckland Children's Court on 21 October 1965.

Yours faithfully,

Signed
I.V. EDWARDS
Sergeant for Inspector.

"Suevic" not touching
Aust. Las Palmas & Canary Islands
Miller & Co SA Apartado 12

CHAPTER 12

As I watched from the ships stern, slowly the City lights became smaller, and took a good look as it would be the last we would see of land for the next 18 days. Our first port of call was to be Durban on the south coast of Africa, thousands of miles away across the Indian Ocean.

A certain silence came over the crew as we left. It was as though part of you stayed behind. For me I suppose it was the memories, some good, some bad, from both Australia and New Zealand, but somehow it all seemed so distant and long ago. Funny when you think about it, we all travel along life's highway one way or another, during which you meet and make so many friends, some for just a day, others for perhaps longer and how, in some tiny way, you may by chance, change the course of their lives just a little and they in turn with yours and could only hope for me it would be for the better.

As the twin propellers thrust away beneath, I watched the trail of white surf follow behind. On the horizon I could see the sun just coming up, meeting the early morning sky, still filled with a million stars – a sight which no words can describe.

"Come on Pegs, let's get some shut eye. You'll be shattered in the morning."

John was right a couple of hours wouldn't go a miss. Soon back in our cabin and on our bunks, my head only had time to hit the pillow and I was out. Next thing I knew was the early call.

"Wake up Pegs, 6 o'clock."

"Err yeah alright mate" as I woke with a start, at first wondering where the hell I was, then realised. My eyes were sore from only a couple of hours sleep. As I climbed down from my bunk it seemed only a moment ago I'd got up there. Quickly dressing, I gave John another shake. "Come on John, it's ten past."

"Yeah, you go on, I'll be with you in a minute."

After a quick wash I made for the Mess where the day workers were walking around in limbo with their cups of tea before heading out on deck. The crew were split into four shifts the day workers and the three watches first 8-12, then 12-4, and finally 4-8, each working an eight hour day, after if they wanted, they could do overtime on day work which at sea, could be anything from painting, washing down, even rope splicing for the more experienced deck hand. During a watch, each man would take his turn on the wheel and at night alternately, one would go on look out. Sometimes up on the bow or on the monkey island which was above the bridge depending on the weather. Their job was to spot the lights of the oncoming shipping, then report back down to the bridge on compass points, so many to Port or Starboard, a job which eventually I would have to take my turn at, but for now it was back to being Peggy. First to clean up and lay up the Mess Room, then think about breakfast. John had carried me for the last week or more so I left him there to doze for awhile, also to find out if I could cope on my own. By five to seven, all was done tea was made, hot press full, the lot ready and in record time. It was time to give John a shake. "Come on John, its five to seven."

"What! Why the fucking hell didn't you call me."

"Don't panic, it's all done," jumping from his pit, he quickly put on his jeans and rushed into the Mess checking it out to see if I'd missed anything which gave me quite a satisfying feeling to know that all was well.

"You've done a good job we'll make a Peggy out of you yet."

"My turn to lie in tomorrow OK"

"Err, yeah sure, why not, suits me." And that's how it was for the next 18 days. Breakfast over at eight, cleared up, washed down the Mess and accommodation in time for smoke, tea and tab nabs cleared away and laid up for lunch then out on deck until 11.20. Back in to get lunch clear up out on out on deck until 4, apart from me or John making tea at 3, for afternoon smoke. That's how it was from day to day and we had it off to a tee.

"You'd better go out on deck and give 'em a shout, sometimes the Bos forgets the time."

While John finished dressing, I went out to tell the others. The early morning breeze was cool and the start of another fine day. Looking around, could just see the outline of land. During those few short hours we'd left it miles behind. Now it was just us and the Tasman Sea. The lads were washing down the usual early morning routine.

"Breakfast up lads"

Like the rest of us, not at their best until after a good feed of cereal, eggs, bacon, sausage and tomatoes, toast and tea they slowly came to life.

"Yeah, right, thanks Pegs."

For the first couple of days, it was all fairly quiet.

Everybody settled down into a more relaxed routine, mostly catching up on lost sleep after a hectic month on the New Zealand Coast. During the evenings we'd hang around the Mess telling stories, playing cards and drinking before turning in for an early night, after a supper of cold meat, salad and fresh bread – that was one thing, you never went hungry. After about a week at sea and my afternoons working out on deck, my tan had turned to a golden brown and the constant application of baby oil to my face and the sun had taken away the red, giving me a nice tan and apart from my eyebrows I was good as new. At least I was thankful for that, a week later on the Friday a notice went up in the Mess, there was to be a film show on the after deck on Saturday night, which raised everybody's spirits. At last the official mourning period was over and everyone was back to normal. That night we decided to have a bit of a party on deck although we had to go aft because of disturbing the watches. Earlier that day they'd opened the bond for the second time since sailing so after queuing up with the rest of the ships company bought a case of beer and 200 cigarettes, so instead of drinking everyone else's I could repay their hospitality. Bob took along his guitar which made for entertainment. It was then I learnt some of the baldy sea shanties, drinking and singing well into the early hours. As the different watches came off duty, whether it is deck, engine room or catering staff, they all joined us until finally it was time to call it a night. Tomorrow or should I say today was film night, no doubt another night on the beer so I needed to conserve my energy and get some sleep. The party slowly broke up and I went off to my bed about 3 a.m.

A week had already passed and not a glimpse of land or any sign of another ship, made me think of a film I'd seen (On the beach)where germ warfare had killed the whole of the worlds population and we out here, were the only survivors.

Saturday came round, just like any other day, usual thing, three meals a day plus afternoon on deck with a paint brush in my hand and at the same time, laying back and soaking up the sun, moving the brush just enough to make it look like I was doing something constructive, while the cadets and a few officers put up the screen for the night's great event. Evening came around and now, just waiting for the sun to set, everyone took their places, on the hatches, and up on the derricks some even climbed the jumbo to get a better view.

Everything was ready right down to fire buckets filled with ice water to keep the beer cool. The sun had slowly gone down and it was nearly time for the entertainment. The Officers sat up front along side the Captain, as finally the main event started. The film was Billy Bud with Terence Stamp in a spaghetti western and just like the local cinema back home, deemed to have its share of hiccups. What with the voices slowing down to a groan, then speeding up, then to lose both picture and sound it was more of a comedy than anything. Empty beer cans flew at the screen in protest, much to the dislike of the Senior Officers on board, but they knew the need to let off steam was necessary or you'd go mad with the routine.

After that night, they were a bit reluctant to show any more films, but we did get to see a couple more during the voyage home. Next day we were in for another surprise. Due to the ever raising temperature, the Captain sent orders for the Chippy to erect a make shift swimming pool on the fore deck, small but enough to cool us down during our time off and made good for a party piece. Some days the heat got so unbearable that you could only work in the shade, usually washing down the paint work.

During those long days, Dave Smith A.B. taught me how to tie certain knots and in my spare time, also how to splice rope, giving me one of his old sheath knives along with a small spike to wear on my belt. Gradually I learnt my way around the ship and it was finally suggested that if I wanted to get promotion fast, first thing I needed to do was get my steering ticket which consisted of 10 hours on the wheel and after approaching the chief, he agreed, allowing me on the bridge in two hour sessions. My first stint was early evening, taking over from Mac on the wheel, "Right Pegs, it's all yours. The course is 360 degree's so don't let her slip away too far, OK?"

"Yeah, right," I said full of confidence.

Now all I had to do was watch the giro compass not letting it go more than two degree's either side of course, adjusting the helm accordingly, soon to get a grasp. Mac left me to gain my confidence, not going too far in case I got into trouble.

So there I was, 16 years old, at the helm of a 13,000 ton vessel, sailing the high seas. Not that I could do much damage, surrounded by water as far as the eye could see, but I did get a bit carried away at one time, she started to go off course, just a little at first 355, 350 then no matter how I tried I couldn't bring her back. By now the change of course had been noticed with Mac rushing back to take over, "Fuck me Pegs where do ya think you're going, back to Auckland?" he laughed. By now it was 343 – 18 degree's offcourse. The mate called me out on the bridge wing pointing to the large curve in the ship's wash; it was obvious if I'd have carried on any longer we would have gone full circle. Mac soon corrected it, letting me take over and giving me another chance.

"As soon as it goes, ease your helm back slowly and as it starts to move bring it back to amidships. Remember Pegs, nice and easy."

Taking more note this time, concentrating and not taking my eyes off the giro for a second. Luckily the sea was like a mill pond, giving me hardly anything to do. Once I'd got the knack, my first two hours went fast and returning to the Mess feeling really pleased with myself. Four more days and I'd have my ticket. Everything was going great, better than I'd ever thought possible. During the next four days each night after work, I spent two hours on the wheel, each time the Officer on watch made a note and on completion of 10 hours was informed that on arrival in England I would get my steering certificate along with my seaman's discharge. We had now been at sea over two weeks and spirits were getting low, just longing for the hour when land was sighted – nothing for 15 days now, coming through the Tasman Sea and across the Indian Ocean.

It was finally on the Monday afternoon of the 8th November, when the coast of Africa was first sighted and bringing everybody out on deck to take a look. Almost straight away their spirits rose. Tomorrow night we'd be off the south coast of Africa and Durban our next port of call. This called for a celebration, so that night we had another party on deck. Not that we needed an excuse, any reason was good enough. In the early hours, we drew closer to land, finally hugging the coast until Tuesday afternoon when we dropped anchor and waited for the pilot and the three tugs to come along side and take us in. We eventually finished tying up at 6.30 p.m. in between a number of other British Merchant ships, making it look as though the fleet was in. By now we were ready for some shore leave after our long stint at sea, which by the look of it wouldn't be tonight, as derricks had to be made ready, hatches unbattened, ready for the cargo handlers the next day and after all that, there was still the Mess to be done.

It was past 9.30 by the time we'd got done, still we were here for 3 days, Plenty of time for shore leave, I thought to myself, as a head popped around my door, "Come on Pegs, get ready if you're coming ashore." Even though I was tired, I couldn't say no.

"Yeah, alright Mac, give us ten minutes and I'll be with you, but I'm a bit short of the readies."

"That's alright sub list is up in the Mess. Pay me back tomorrow. We'll wait here for ya."

I showered and changed and was ready for the off, I made for the Mess where John was putting his name up on the sub's list.

"Err, Tony, how much do you want £5 be enough?"

"Yeah plenty" With that Mac slipped it into my hand.

"Thanks, I'll pay you back to you tomorrow."

"No worries. Now let's get going I don't know about you lot, but my prick needs servicing." We all followed Mac, laughing at his comment.

The town was further away this time and luckily we all managed to get into a couple of taxis at the dock gate, which, to my surprise, had women drivers. Bob sat up front, giving the driver her instructions, "Take us to the flesh pots of Durban." Not saying a word, she just smiled then pulled away, driving us into the city stopping at the local night spot area. We ended up going into a bar called the 'Smugglers' of all things. From there we went from one bar to another. Unfortunately, being the time of week, women were scarce, that was unless you wanted to pay for it, so John and I had an early night rolling back on board around 2 am. Just time enough to shut and open our eyes before the arrival of the Dockers to unload. That was when everything had to be nailed down. Ports bolted, cabin doors locked, because anything that moved, the blacks would nick it. We even found them in the Mess helping them selves to our food. That was when I realised what real poverty was, but if you gave in to one, the next time he came back, he'd bring more friends, it was terrible.

During our short spell in Durban I was to take my turn as watchman, along with the others. First a few hours in the afternoon then an all nighter still the rest was a welcome change, as the rest of the lads went ashore I made my way to the gangway, "Right, Pegs, sit there and what ever happens no ladies aboard, unless they're accompanied by and Officer. You got that?"

"Yes, Bos" Not being one for reading books, the night

dragged on and I couldn't wait to be relieved at 6 a.m. The only bit of excitement came when Ricky and Wilson rolled up in a taxi escorting a rather plump young lady. Rick was the first on board, followed closely by his lady friend, clutching on tightly to Wilson with rick giving me a sloppy salute

"Permission to come aboard Sir,"

"Hello Rick. See you've got the family with ya."

"Yes sir this 'ere is me long lost brother, but he's got a big problem."

"Oh yeah and what's that?" I asked

"Can't ya see stupid, he's wearing ladies clothes so we've brought him back here to get 'em off her, I mean him."

"Sounds good to me Rick, let me know if you need any help."

"Thank you Sir, you're a gentleman." And arm in arm, the three of them staggered towards Rick's cabin. Luckily in all the commotion nobody else heard and I'd just deny any knowledge of her come the morning.

During the next couple of days we loaded cargo, also took on fresh stores. Friday was my last chance to go ashore as we sailed on the early tide next day. Shore leave was to cease at 0200 Saturday morning. That night was the usual thing. Bars, discos, we even went down to the amusement ground down by the beach and tried our hand at go karts. It was more like dodgem cars and it wasn't long before we were thrown out for causing havoc. Time was getting on so we made our way back to the ship, having left a mark on Durban. With a few of the lads leaving with just a little more than they bargained for, spending the next ten days under the doctor. Tomorrow we'd have an early start plus nine more days at sea, before reaching Tema on the west coast of Africa and the notorious gold coast. Turn to was at 4.30am.and after singling up and everyone ashore we swung the gangway on board, lashing her down fast. All that was left to do was await the tugs which were coming up the channel, once along side throwing them a line and making fast.

"Let go aft, let go fored," came a voice from the bridge and slowly we left the quay, making headway down the channel and into the open sea. Soon we were out of the channel, tugs were gone and where just waiting for the pilot boat came along side and he was no sooner off and we were on our way once again.

Quickly things went back to normal. John and I got

breakfast while the day workers stowed the ropes. The watches changed around, giving the others a turn on the wheel. Apart from the few stories of events in Durban, it was like it had never happened.

For the next few days we hugged the African coastline and on the Monday, were due to cross the Tropic of Cancer, commonly known as the Line where King Neptune himself resides. I had heard stories of initiation ceremonies so kept myself out of the way hoping nobody would remember. Unfortunately, I wasn't that lucky. Stripped down to nothing but my boots, they first put the fire hose on me then my bollocks were painted bright red, which took me ages to get off and were sore for days. Finally, I was crowned with a slop bucket containing the lunch time leftovers. Apart from that incident, not much else happened. Another film night, which turned into an all out disaster with the Captain being hit on the head by and empty can, bringing the night to an erupt end, there were also a couple of boat drills which were good for a laugh, to check the life rafts still worked, where as always, something went wrong. God help us if we needed them in a hurry.

It had been a couple of days now since we'd lost sight of land. Still, four days to go. The breeze off the Atlantic Ocean made the night seem cooler, which made for a nice change also making it easier to sleep at nights. By now we were over half way through our journey so I decided to write home telling them I was coming, not giving them any date though, as I wanted to surprise them. The Captain in his wisdom wanted the ship looking like a brand new pin before hitting rough weather which meant as much overtime for those who wanted it. So far, with my bond and subs, I'd been just a little reckless and didn't want to arrive home completely penniless, I had to have something to show for my months of wandering so I grabbed as much overtime as I could, often working all day Saturday and Sunday, whenever I could fit it in. Land was once again spotted on the morning of Sunday 21st and was getting closer by the hour and at 10 o'clock that night we dropped anchor and waited for the pilot. Gradually everyone hit the sack as you never knew how long you could be waiting, eventually arriving just after 3am.was immediately put on call.

"Come on Pegs, move your butt," still wearing my work clothes I jumped down from my pit, I followed the rest out on deck. The order was given to weigh anchor and with engines at full steam, we went straight in bringing us almost against the quay, we hadn't even tied up when a voice shouted up, "Hey, sailor man, you English boy?" Looking down, I could see a strange little black man in his white suit. "You want woman, I sell you my sister."

"There ya go Pegs, there's an offer you can't refuse."

"Yeah, bet she's a right old dog." Messing about, Danny put his arm around me then threw him a kiss, putting ideas into the man's head that we were a couple of poofs, "You want smally boy? I get you one very cheap," he said, shouting up many other alternatives. I bet the old bastard would sell his fucking daughter for a packet of fags.

"Go on Tony," called out Shelley, "ask him if he has a daughter, I've still got carton of 200 we could all have a go," we all laughed, knowing Shelley wasn't joking.

"Hurry up Pegs, do your stuff," throwing down a line for the awaiting Docker to catch and attaching it to the eye of the rope.

"You missed Pegs," shouted Mac.

"What you talking about, he's got it."

"You're supposed to wrap it round his fucking black neck, you only hit his leg." As I looked down, I watched him limp along the quay. Leading the rope out so he could attach it firmly to the quay, "Put our end on the winch Pegs, and pull in the slack. That'll do."

Then by first putting on the chain stopper, made the rope fast. "Well done, Pegs," Mac called out, "We'll make seaman of you yet." Then we put out the back spring, two more stern ropes and finally the rat guards. Some places were worse than others for rats. Running straight up the ropes of the quay, this place was no exception and we had to take extra precautions or next thing we'd find the ship infested with them. By the time we'd finished tying up the sun was well up and on taking our first glimpse of Tema and hoped our stay was a short lived. It was definitely not your palm trees and sandy beaches port. More a desert trading post, still only one hatch had to be made ready here, so at least that told us something. The gangway was down and a storm of black officials clambered up the gangway, all seeing who could get to the top first, along with them came our friend in the white suit followed by an entourage of wogs selling everything from dirty postcards, watches, jewellery, authentic African spears. And for the woman who had everything, there was a large collection of vibrators in all different colours and some up to a foot long with a special reduction for married men.

"Mind your arse, Pegs, they're partial to a bit of white and if they see yours there'll be no stopping them."

"Piss off, Shelley, go play with yourself."

"You wait and see." I did and he was right, they were all queer as coots.

The order came around that no one was to venture ashore alone, only in groups of three or more, also all cabins to be locked and ports secured at all times so made straight to the cabin. No sooner in, than the wogs pounced on me, "Nice gold watch, you like dirty pictures?"

"Na, no thanks mate, trying to give 'em up" but no matter what you said they still followed, opening my cabin door I was shocked to see an ugly face looking through our port. On seeing me, he smiled, bearing the one good tooth he had in his head. Shutting the door behind my followers I slammed the port down making it fast when John came bursting in.

"Alright mate, watch these bastards, they'll rob you blind if you let them."

"Yeah, I know, just caught one admiring our stuff, soon put paid to him"

It was nearly time for breakfast so locking the door behind us, we went about our work. Gradually the locals left the ship with probably more than they came on board with. The unloading had already started under strict supervision of the officers, making sure we only discharged the required amount. I thought the Dockers in Durban were bad, but this was poverty at its lowest and they'd eat anything they could lay their hands on. At one time, after putting the slop bucket on deck, I came back to find a couple of locals sitting round it, picking out eating the good bits. It made me feel quite sick. So John and I thought we'd try something. After lunch all slops being in one bucker we added washing up liquid and disinfectant then put the bucket outside our port then went to the cabin to watch. Sure enough, not a few minutes hadn't gone by when our first gourmet expert stopped by, although at first, pulling a face at its peculiar flavour, he decided that if it was good enough for us ....he dug straight in, shortly after he was joined by two others. I just couldn't control myself any longer, falling about in hysterics. I often wonder how they felt later on.

Our stay there was to be a short one, leaving the following night on the same tide we'd come in on, giving us shore leave for just the one night. We decided it was best to go ashore mob handed, especially being the only ship in port thought it would be safer. So the Smith brothers, Alan, Mac, Bon, Shelley, Danny, Limerick and me, a mixture of English, Irish and Scottish, all met up in the mess ready for our night of sin and debauchery. Griff was stuck on gangway and on seeing us wasn't happy at the idea of being left behind on board alone.

"See you later Griff, don't work too hard will ya."

"Ow fuck this, I'm coming with ya," so leaving his post he mingled in amongst us. Our first stop was the Seaman's Mission, just out of the so called dock gate, which had fallen down years since. This, for us, was supposed to be the safest and by far the best place to spend the evening, but due to the lack of beverages, in particular beer, our stay was short lived. After trying a number of places we ended up at a Reggie Club, taking control of about half a dozen tables which didn't seem to please the locals too much. Apart from that, the evening went well that was until a couple of the natives got a bit restless so Bob did no more than put them out of their misery, leaving their bodies stretched out on the dance floor.

"Yeah, well boys I think it's time to make a move," looking around at about 100 sets of angry white teeth, the odds being at least 10 −1 against, Dave was right. Watching our backs we slowly made for the door, knowing we'd stirred up a bit of a hornet's nest. No sooner outside than Terry started to climb into a taxi, but Dave promptly pulled him out, "Don't be daft, he's not going to fucking help you."

Backing down the road they started to follow us, "Right fellas, last one back to the ship gets his throat cut," Mac grabbed me by the scruff of the neck, almost taking my feet off the ground.

"Come on Pegs, get your arse into gear, we don't want them bastards to use it as a target practise." Keeping hold all the time, my legs were going nineteen to the dozen. From behind, I could hear the shouting and the sound of bottles smashing, not stopping to look round, soon to come across a few of the others strolling down the road.

"Run, for fucks sake run!"Shouted Mac

Once nearing the dock gates the shouting stopped. We'd made it. My heart was pounding and my legs were like jelly.

"Well, that was good for a laugh." We all looked at Bob, not believing what he'd just said, but then all started to laugh as we saw the funny side of it. It was still early so we continued our party out on deck, not getting to bed until the early hours. Thinking about it, we were lucky to get back alive. The next day the unloading continued, finishing around mid-day. It was hot – well into the nineties, and with the cabins being locked it was like walking into a furnace. After lunch all hands turned to making the ship ready once again for sea, while I was put on gangway sitting in the shade with my feet up. All signs of my burns had now gone. My eye lashes and eye brows had grown back and the scars disappeared, covered only by a dark tan. John relived for Smoko, by which time all on deck was done. After break, word came from above we could knock off early that was all except me. I had to stay on gangway until 4.30. The boys decided to cool themselves off by swimming in the crystal clear waters of the harbour. Diving off the lower boat decks, it sounded like great fun, swimming up round the bow then climbing on to the quay and back up round for another turn.

"Come on Pegs, its great once you get in."

"Yeah, it's alright for you, I'm stuck here. What time you got, Tel?"

"Must be half past four by now; come on, no one's about."

The temptation was too great so leaving my post; I followed the others up on to the boat deck. Although it was a long drop, a good 30 foot or more, one by one they each jumped or dived in until it came around to my turn. The natural made harbour came straight in from the ocean with its clear blue waters, making it possible to see the bottom. Taking up my position, I dived in, hitting the water like a bomb. Eventually coming to the surface and starting to swim in the warm waters as suddenly my worst nightmare came as someone shouted,

"Sharks, look out, there's fucking sharks in the water."

Me I was swimming like crazy but getting nowhere fast, when suddenly felt something coming up beside me. My heart came up into my mouth and sank again with relief to hear a voice, "Come on Pegs swim." It was Danny, swimming like a mad man and being every man for himself, so he left me standing. Terrified, I carried on making for the nearest thing in sight, which was the anchor cable, with my every stroke taking me that much closer thinking only of the deadly predator on my tail reached the anchor, I climbed up and out of the water.

Apart from me everyone was safely ashore so putting a large distance between me and the water, I climbed frantically to safety, then just hung on, frozen to the chain as three grey fins glided by me below. Their bodies, maybe six or seven feet long, big enough to make a feast of me. Looking up, I noticed the outlet for the anchor cable, but on trying for it found the gap was too small. It was no use, the only way was to get back into the water and swim up and around her bow. A thought that didn't appeal to me one little bit, as it was one thing to be told about them, but to actually see them. Well, that made all the difference, so I decided to stay where I was.

By now all hands were watching the water, "Come on, Pegs, the water's all clear, there's no sign of them now." Dave's low pitched voice was not enough to convince me as my trembling voice called out,

"You've got to be fucking joking I'm not going back in there, ya bastard."

My voice echoed all round the dock yard, but deep down I knew they were right, that is unless they would put a boat out for me and I knew there wasn't much chance of that, so letting go, I threw myself into the water, coming up almost straight away and began to swim for my life being cheered on by the crew, knowing any moment that one could pounce, pulling me under, putting an end to Tony Bates. Legs kicking, arms swinging, I swam like a madman, eventually making it to the quay, but still not completely happy until my feet were clear of the water.

All the lads still cheering as the Boson took my hand pulling me ashore. Looking down at me with a big grin on his face he said, "It might have been better if the sharks had got ya as you're in for it my lad, you left your post early so I had to report you, didn't I."

At first, not completely taking in what he'd said as my only concern was my safety I started to walk away from him. He called me back. "Did you hear what I said, you're in trouble."

"Yeah, I heard, you said half past four so that's what time I left the post, so get off my back."

"'Now listen, you little smart arse, I said five o'clock, not half past four."

By now the ship's rails were lined with some of the crew including a few officers so I was not about to loose face in front of them, and turned back calling out, "You lying fat bastard. No wonder you've got no fucking mates," Then left him there to chew on my words.

"By the way Pegs" He called out "the Captain would like to see you."

That's fine by me, I thought, perhaps he would listen. He was right on my tail as I headed for the skipper's cabin, still dripping wet. His door was already open and he was sat behind his desk.

"You sent for me Sir?"

"Ah yes, Bates. Boson tells me you left your post before time is that right."

By then, Fatso was right behind me.

"No Sir, He told me 4.30 not 5 o'clock."

"Well, I'm sorry Bates, the boson tells me the story differently."

The fat pigs face lit up. There was no more point in arguing, I'd been tried and sentenced as the skipper handed it out.

"You will therefore forfeit one day's pay for the offence. Have you anything to say?"

"No Sir," I knew it was no use arguing, and I could feel the steam coming from my ears and nostrils as I thought of my hard earned overtime, gone just like that.

"Yes Sir," I said with a change of heart, "I suggest you take the day's pay, split it in two and along with the job, shove it right up your fucking arses," then left them there with a total look of surprise on their faces and knew after, I'd done it again letting my mouth rule my head. A bad habit I would have to curb. It wasn't the first time it had got me in trouble and definitely wasn't going to be the last.

Making straight for my cabin, I changed into some dry clothes then made for the Mess. It was gone 5 o'clock and my anger had given me an appetite, so helping myself to an extra portion as I heard Dave call out, "Pegs, sit here. So what did the old man have to say?" They all looked up, patiently awaiting my answer.

"Oh you know how it is, that fat pig cost me a day's pay, reckons I left my post before knocking off time, the lying git. So I told them both to shove the money and the job up their arses"

"You did what?" cried Dave, with a big grin on his face.

"Well they made me mad and I don't have to put up with

that sort of shit from any one."

My opinion of the Boson was much the same as theirs and although we had to live with him, didn't mean we had to like him. He'd already bullied Maltese Joe, the ship's lamp trimmer, until he was half out of his mind having to be taken of the ship in straight jacket earlier during the voyage. Now it was my turn. That was until Mac went and threatened to hang him over the side by his balls if he didn't leave me alone, and from then on, things were fairly quiet for me.

After tea a few of us sat on deck taking full advantage of the evening breeze, when someone noticed, coming down the wharf, one of the stewards dressed in nothing but his skids. Slowly word got around and by the time he reached the gangway, half the crew were cheering him on, much to his embarrassment and was far from being amused, as after going ashore on his own earlier that day disregarding any advice from above, had been robbed of his clothes and money and apparently lucky to get away with his life.

We never did get to the bottom of it but there were rumours that he had also been raped, but they soon died out. After a few beers most of the guy's settled for on early night as we'd be leaving in the early hours and needed our sleep. And was well pleased to get away from that place as it was not what you'd call a spot for any tourist guide book.

We were now off to our last port of call, Los Palmas, in the Canary Islands, 3- 4 days sailing on the North African coast. Soon slipping back into routine, the next few days went swiftly, The Captain getting just a little over anxious because there was still a lot to do before reaching London. It was all hands too, painting anything that didn't move. Finally reaching Los Palmas early on the morning of the 29th just stopping for supplies and fresh water, leaving early the next morning, which meant all deck hands were put to the brush painting over the ships side as the old man(Captain) was determined to have her looking her best.

At afternoon smoko we were called to collect our subs, being the last night ashore in a foreign port, I drew £5. As this was going to be a night to remember, being a more civilised place there were no restrictions, so we could go ashore in our own time. John and I were probably two of the last staying to first clear up the Mess, going ashore around seven.

Our first stop was the British Bar, frequented mostly by seamen of all nationalities. From there we decided to head for the flesh pots of the town, taking us into the back streets of Los Palmas, it was a real eye opener for John and myself. Women hanging out of their windows wearing as little as possible to make them look more appealing.

"Hello sailor boy, you want to have good time?"

I couldn't believe what we were doing; we must have walked up and down that street a dozen time's just trying to pluck up the courage to ask how much.

"You ask John."

"Na, you ask. Look at the tits on that."

By now we felt like a couple of perverts so it was either ask or leave, one of the two. Neither of us had the bottle so we left, dragging our erect tails between our legs.

"Come on John let's go back to the British bar." although he was somewhat reluctant, agreed.

"Yeah, alright, but it seems such a bloody waste."

"Oh well, think of the money we've saved, probably been over in a flash anyway, we might just as well gone and had a wank at least that don't cost you nothing."

"Yeah, you're right, let's go for a pint." Soon nearing the bar, we could hear the familiar voices singing.

"That sounds like big mouth Shelly, I'd know that voice anywhere," I said looking at John. Still laughing, we entered the bar.

"Hey Pegs, get em in" the back bar was taken over by a crowd of drunken seamen, namely ours, starting off with Shelley, Danny, Mac, Bob, Alan, Rick and a couple of his mates from the engine room.

"Eight beers Pegs, oh and have one yourself" This was more like it, at least here we were guaranteed a good laugh. After getting in the round, took a set in with the rest.

"So where you been lads?" Shelly asked who was by this time slowly sliding half way under the table.

"Ah nowhere special just been walking about." John laughed at my comment with Shelly straight away sussed us out, "You've been looking for dirty women haven't you Pegs you know they're bad for you. You'll end up like me if you ain't careful, with a throbbing dick and two penicillin jabs up your arse." Laughing it off, I just carried on drinking, then we all joined in singing:

"The mate as a bastard, he wears a white hat,

He says go to smoko and then hurry back,
When we get to London, we'll all get the sack,
'Cos we're going smoko and we ain't coming back,
Heave away, heave away from Kiwi to London's a
fucking long way"

After an hour or so John returned to the ship as time was getting on and he wanted an early night. Like a good Peggy I fetched and carried the beer until finally it was time for all of us to think about returning to the ship.

"Let's get a carry out Pegs. Here, go and get a couple of bottles of whisky," said Mac, handing over some money. By now our friendly Spanish barman was glad we'd decided to move on, as after driving half his customers away he'd be glad to see the back of us.

"Give us a couple of bottles of whisky senior por favor," I asked in my best Spanish accent. As he put them down on the counter, I handed over the money, with him almost instantly telling me that I didn't have enough, "Uno memento," I said and called over, "Err, Mac, Jose here reckons we ain't got enough cash."

All digging deep, we came up with what was the last of our money, "Here, that should cover it, Pegs," returning to the Bar I laid it on the counter to find he'd pocketed a couple of notes, still insisting I hadn't enough money. Knowing full well he was on the make, what started as a quiet transaction turned into a shouting match, all the time making out he didn't understand a word of what I was saying. It was then Bob staggered over to see what the problem was, so I explained.

"It's no good Bob, it's his word against mine and he's got the goods" So after a short time of reasoning, still saying he didn't understand, Bob lost his cool.

"Don't understand, ah you wog bastard, well you'll understand this," putting his hand over the bar, grabbed hold of him, lifting him clear off the ground until their faces nearly met then he nutted him, spreading his nose clear across his face, "Compendia Senior?"

The blood went everywhere as the barman slowly slid down the back of the counter. "Come on lads, I think its time we went." Bob had no sooner said those words, when the door burst open and in walked half a dozen coppers carrying long coshes. By which time Shelley and the others were half way to the door, with all the commotion Mac grabbed hold of me and pushed me under the table.

"Don't move and just stay under there Pegs." Then it started. At first, trying to talk their way out, decided it was useless then one of the Policemen took a prod at Bob with his cosh which was his first mistake and in return got more than he bargained for, with Bob laying him clear out cold on the floor, starting a riot for all concerned. Shelley got coshed at the same time hitting his opponent over the head with a full bottle of whisky, both of them hitting the floor at about the same time. Danny was down and Alan was being held by two cops, it was then the guns came out.

It was useless to carry on ,more reinforcements burst in, pinning them up against the wall, first cuffing and then dragging all four away, leaving us two behind to sort out the problem. Rick and the others had already disappeared out the back way, leaving Mac and me to talk our way out. Luckily the barman who was still dazed wasn't making too much sense, so eventually we were allowed to go. As we left, we looked around the place, it didn't look the same any more with chairs and tables smashed and broken glass strewn all over the place and a bar and barman that looked like they'd both been hit by a truck.

"Can you find your way back to the ship Pegs? I'd better go see what's become of the others."

"Yeah, no worries see ya later Mac," On the way back I met up with Rick and a few of the other lads, none of us believing what we'd just seen.

"Oh well, they'll probably only keep 'em over night, give 'em a good kicking', then let 'em out come morning," said Rick, convincingly.

"I doubt it mate" did you see those coppers' faces? They won't be entering any beauty contests for a while that's for sure, anyway they'd better get back soon we sail first thing."

"Anyway so what happened then Pegs, how did it start?" asked Rick.

Feeling it was partly my fault, I trod carefully, "Bob had a slight disagreement with the barman, so nutted him."

"Trust him, that's the second time he's nearly got us all killed. Remember that little episode in Tema that was his doing too."

Soon back on the ship, we joined the others in the Mess, The only topic of conversation being the fight in the bar. Shore leave ended at 2 a.m. and still there was no sign of Mac. Had they arrested him too trying to rescue his cabin mate Bob.

We sat drinking well into the early hours as this would be our last session altogether this trip. Around 4 a.m. I grabbed a couple of hours sleep, but there was still no sign of Mac. By now it was inevitable the police must have picked him up. John gave me a shake at 6.30.as we were having early breakfast as we sailed at nine, after which I stepped out on deck for a fag.

"Any sign of Mac yet Dave?"

"Na, not yet Pegs, but the police and British Consulate are on board. Came on half an hour ago and they're still up there with the old man."

Then from a distance, I could see someone staggering towards us and as he got closer I realised it was Mac.

"Mac, you old bastard," I shouted out. All that time thinking he'd been nicked, he'd been out on the piss. Dave stood up and looked down the quay at Mac strolling along like he had all the time in the world.

"Quick Pegs, get down there and hurry him up, with a bit of luck he might not be seen. Go on move your arse." So hurrying down the gangway, I headed along the quay. Most of the officers would be at breakfast so there was every chance we might get away with it I thought as I raced up towards him.

"Hello Pegs, me old darling, fancy a drink," he said pulling out a bottle of wine from his pocket.

"Where the fuck have you been?" I shouted like a concerned father.

Smiling all the time he said, "The bastards wouldn't let me in to see 'em so I went for a drink, Then I realised I had no money, luckily some old broad shouted me a few, who was I to argue? Then we went back to her place for a knobbing, it wasn't until then I found out it was a fucking transvestite and ended up with a pair of bollocks in me hand. Still what the fuck, the booze was free and I know she was grateful."

I couldn't believe my ears, just started laughing, "Come on you dirty old bastard, you ain't been missed yet, so chance's are you won't be." We hurried along the quay then up the gangway – all clear.

Hello Dave me old mate, where's our old buddy Fatso? I wanna have a word with him, don't we Pegs?"

"Keep it down Mac you'll get us all in the fucking shit."

Mac just laughed saying, "Well it won't be the first time tonight will it Pegs?"

Dave quickly grabbed hold of Mac and said to me, "Pegs you stay here and if anyone asks, I've gone for a shit, right?"

And escorted Mac to his cabin, leaving him there to sleep it off, soon after, returning to his post, "Did anyone come by, Pegs?"

"Na not a soul mate"

"Now listen, anyone asks, Mac's sick in bed and he's been there all night OK?"

"Yeah, sure, anything you say Dave."

So with breakfast over, I returned to the Mess, also telling John that Mac was safely tucked up in his cabin, "Where's he been?"

"Fuck knows John, it's a long story and he'll probably tell you about it later."

The order came to turn to and there was still no sign of Bob and the others, luckily Mac was aft with us so could at least cover for him, still being two short we were given a couple of the officer cadets. By now I knew my Job blind –folded, first singling up and with the pilot on board, just waited for the gangway to be hoisted. "Let go aft, let go fored," and slowly we edged away from the quay, leaving Los Palmas and four of our crew behind. We later heard all four had been sentenced to eighty days hard labour for disturbing the peace. Apparently Spanish jails not being the best in the world, knew they were in for a hard time. Soon clear of the harbour, dispensed with the pilot's services continuing on the last leg of our voyage, still hugging the north coast of Africa on the final leg of our voyage passing Spain, France then finally our destination Avon mouth, Bristol a Journey which would take five days.

Mac woke later that day feeling none the worse for wear and surprised to see his cabin mate Bob had been left behind. Things went quiet for the next day or so and apart from meals and work, each kept to themselves. A sort of limbo feeling, I suppose, after being with the same crew for months or more you were at a loss. Come Sunday, we'd all be paid off and then go our separate ways. Still, that was the sea, no sooner home than you'd be off on a new ship, new faces, and off to God knows where or how long. The ship came back to life on Thursday evening after receiving a mayday from a Panama freighter.

Answering her call, we rushed full steam to her aid off the Spanish coast. It must have been near midnight when we were called out on deck, seeing in the distance her orange glow on the horizon and ordered to get the nets over the side and life lines ready. We were going in full speed ahead to her aid, as we drew closer there was a whole fleet of smaller ships surrounding her and could see she was listing badly to port. Her cargo of timber was by now, well ablaze so going straight in amongst the others, we came in as closely as possible, the engines stopped and like a huge cork, just bobbed up and down in the water, waiting for survivors.

All the safety nets and lines went over the side and the life boats were put on standby. Anything that would support life was made ready. It made me feel quite sick as you could hear the men aboard screaming with pain as some jumped into the water with their clothes on fire while trying to get there life boats down. There was a strong westerly wind that night, spreading the fire even faster, also making it cold on deck for us.

Ironic isn't it. We were cold and they were burning up from the heat of their decks.

"Pegs, go and make a bucket of cocoa and be quick."

"Yes, Chief," running straight to the Mess as quick as I could, as I didn't want to miss any of the excitement. A bucket, I thought to myself, how the hell do I judge that? Doing as I was told, I just put a whole tin of cocoa powder in and added water, plus a bag of sugar. Well it looked alright and didn't taste too bad either. By the time I'd got back on deck, our life boats were down ready to pick up survivors and somehow the distressed ship managed to cut hers free, sending them crashing into the water, blowing her last whistle, the ship was abandoned. The anti-climax came when a Spanish fishing vessel came in between us going in much closer than we could because of our size, taking over the whole rescue. Still it didn't matter who got there first as long as lives were saved. We hung around her until daylight. The ship was still afloat and the fires had died right down and it was no longer necessary for us to standby so setting our course, we were off once again.

It wasn't until later that day we heard from a radio message that she sunk with little loss of life. As we got closer to home and crossed the infamous Bay of Biscay the weather got colder and colder until finally we were all dressed like Eskimos and on the

Sunday morning we sighted land, being the Isles of Scilly, off the coast of Lands End. We'd made it, soon after to enter the Bristol Channel, Avon mouth arriving home on 5th December.

We finally finished tying up just after six that night, having to stay aboard until Monday to sign off. Once the gangway was down I was first ashore kissing the ground that lay beneath me. During that evening we all packed, John giving me an old kit bag of his to pack away what gear I had. It was then Dave poked his head around the door, "Alright to come in lads?"

"Yeah sure, Dave, come on in."

Being very mysterious with one hand behind his back, I offered him a beer, "No thanks, Pegs, 'ere you are, a souvenir of the journey," and handed me one of his precious masterpieces, a Whaling ship, complete with long boat, crew and harpooned whale with the word Suvic written on the ship's stern.

"Thanks mate, 'ere John have a look at this will ya, its brilliant Dave thanks a lot."

"Yeah sure," and with that he left as quietly as he'd came, back to his own cabin.

After we'd packed we all met in the Mess for a last drink together, with nearly everybody going off to bed early. Next morning it was breakfast as after which there was nothing left for me to do but clear up and wait around with the others for my pay. Finally at 12 o'clock we queued outside the Chief's office to receive our wages and discharge. Eventually when it came to my turn, he handed me £38 and 18d and my discharge papers which read "For ability V.G." which meant very good "For Conduct D.R. which meant declining to report. At first not worried only counted my money then showed it Dave

"What's this D.R. mean Dave?"

"Where, let me see that" Then telling me that in seaman's terms that I'd been sacked. "Telling the old man to shove his job up his arse probably didn't help"

"We'll see about that," first arguing with the Chief Steward then the mate, but unfortunately the final decision stood with the Captain who'd already gone ashore.

"Don't worry pegs just take it to the shipping pool in Prescott Street London they'll sort it out for ya."

"Sure Dave, I'll get it sorted."

I wasn't too bothered, I was home that was my only concern. Collecting our bags, we all left the ship together meeting up on the quay, and the short walk to the main gate and the customs officials, who by now had gone over the ship with a fine toothcomb leaving nothing unturned. As we got closed we could see them waiting for us in their crisp navel uniforms just dying for one of us to do something suspicious, but we were lucky, although I was only carrying 200 fags and a bottle over the top. We just strolled past without as much as a blink. Outside the gate waited the taxis we'd ordered earlier to take us to the station and from there on to London. As I got in the last cab with Mac, Dave and Terry, I could just see the Suvic's funnel in the distance as we drove away and I remembered these few words I'd read somewhere and somehow thought they seemed fitting:

"They'd passed our way as a breed of men
The world would not see, the likes again"

The Suevic

OFFICIAL LOG of the SUEVIC

from LONDON 16-7-65   **towards** AVONMOUTH 5-12-65

Date and Hour of the Occurrence	Place of the Occurrence, or situation by Latitude and Longitude at Sea	Date of Entry	Entries required by Act of Parliament	Amount of Fine or Forfeiture inflicted
10.30 13.10.65	AUCKLAND	13.10.65	ANTHONY BATES, DECK BOY, ART. N. 29	
			Signed on Articles at Auckland	
			Mercantile Marine office as from and	
			including today 13th October at wages	
			of £28.00.00 per month	
			signature _G. Welden_	
			Ch. Steward Master	
11.15 13.10.65	AUCKLAND	14.10.65	ROBERT WARDLAW, S.O.S. ART. N° 30	
			THOMAS McCARTHY, J.C.S. ART. N° 31	
			MICHAEL DANIELS, J.O.S. ART. N° 32	
			all signed on Articles as from 13th October	
			at Auckland Mercantile Marine Office	
			Having been deserters and serving prison	
			sentences. They are not allowed ashore here	
			signature _G. Welden_	
			Ch. Steward Master	
14.10.65	AUCKLAND	14.10.65	GEORGE WILSON 2nd Cook, Art N° 8	FINE
			for having an unauthorised female	
2.00			on board all night up to 09.30 today	
			is fined one days pay for the offence.	
9 DEC 1965			_signature_ _G. Welden_	
AVONMOUTH			Ch. Steward Master	

N.B.—Every entry in this Log-Book required by the Act must be signed by the Master and by the Mate or some other member of the Crew, and every entry of illness, injury or death must also be signed by the Surgeon or Medical Practitioner on board (if any) ;

51

OFFICIAL LOG of the

from LONDON 16-7-65 towards AVONMOUTH 5-12-65

Date and hour of the Occurrence	Place of the Occurrence, or situation by Latitude and Longitude at Sea	Date of Entry	Entries required by Act of Parliament	Amount of Fine or Forfeiture inflicted
1700 11·65	DURBAN	12·11·65	MICHAEL DANIELS, J.O.S. Art. Nº 32 He was A.W.O.L from his place of duty from 1300 to 1700 hours yesterday, 11ᵗ He is fined one day's pay for the offence and ½ a day's pay will not accrue for the time absent. myaclark mate master	FINE:- £1·03 FORFEI £0·11
1·3·5 Fine enforced, cancelled Forfeiture retained by Master. *M.M. OFFICE* *9 DEC 1965* *AVONMOUTH*				
1000 ·11·65	DURBAN	12·11·65	THOMAS McCARTHY, J.O.S. Art. Nº 31 was sent to the Doctor at 9 am yesterday 11ᵗ Transport there and back was arranged. He failed to return to duty until 10 am today 12ᵗ He is fined one day's pay for the offence and ½ a days pay will not accrue for time absent. myaclark mate master	FINE:- £1·03 FORFEI £0·11
1·3·5 Fine enforced, cancelled Forfeiture retained by Master. *M.M. OFFICE* *9 DEC 1965*				
0410 ·11·65	DURBAN	13·11·65	THOMAS McCARTHY, J.O.S. Art. Nº 31 and DANIEL McGLUSKY, J.O.S. Art. Nº 21 returned to the vessel at 0410 today 13 prior to sailing from Durban. Leave expiry time posted on the board was 0200, 13ᵗ They are each fined a day's pay for the offence. myaclark mate master	FINE:- £1·03 FINE:- £1·03
1·3·5 Fine enforced, cancelled Forfeiture retained by Master. *M.M. OFFICE* *9 DEC 1965*				

N.B.—Every entry in this Log-Book required by the Act must be signed by the Master and by the Mate or some other member of the Crew, and every entry of illness, injury or death must also be signed by the Surgeon or Medical Practitioner on board (if any);

Date and Hour of the Occurrence	Place of the Occurrence, or situation by Latitude and Longitude at Sea	Date of Entry	Entries required by Act of Parliament	Amount of Fine or Forfeiture inflicted
0700 15·10·65	AUCKLAND	16·10·65	MAURICE GRIFFIN, E.D.H., Art. Nº 15, was AWOL from the gangway as nightwatchman from 2200 to 0700 on the night of the 14/15ᵗʰ October. He is fined one day's pay for the offence. *MJ Clark* Mate *G. Welch* Master	FINE :- 1·12·8 Cancelled (page 54)
	Fine inflicted, cancelled last...			
1530 19·10·65	AUCKLAND.	19·10·65	THOMAS LANDERS, ASST. STWD, Art. Nº 92 was AWOL from his place of duty from 1500 to 1530 during which time he should have been serving teas. He is fined one day's pay for the offence. *...* Ch. Stwd *G. Welch* Master	FINE :- 2·14·2 Cancelled (p.54)
	Fine inflicted, cancelled by Master			
1000 18·10·65	AUCKLAND.	19·10·65	GEORGE MATTHEWS, 3ʳᵈ Officer, P.R. Nº 4 is hereby promoted to the rank of temporary 2nd officer as from and including 13ᵗʰ October at wages of £85·0·0 p. month *...* Ch. Stwd. *G. Welch* Master	

N.B.—Every entry in this Log-Book required by the Act must be signed by the Master and by the Mate or some other member of the Crew, and every entry of illness, injury or death must also be signed by the Surgeon or Medical Practitioner on board (if any) ;

OFFICIAL LOG of the

from   towards

Date and hour of the occurrence	Place of the Occurrence, or situation by Latitude and Longitude at Sea	Date of Entry	Entries required by Act of Parliament	Amount of Fine or Forfeiture Inflicted
1100 .11.65	TEMA	23.11.65	J. BRANNAN, asst Stwd. Art. 83 sent to a further Company's Doctor at ACCRA. Treated and prescribed, but only a verbal report saying he would not be fit for some time available. *J.H.Muld...* mate *mast.*	
0740 .11.65	LAS PALMAS	30.12.65	The following members of the Crew missed the ship this morning and were signed off on an ENG. 2A Form which was voided: *Bed and bedding remain on board. Lists of gear attached to Official Log* Balance of wages £94.15.1 G.B.S G. CANTRELL, S.O.S. ART. 18, A. WISEMAN, J.O.S. Balance of wages £43.8.11 G.B.S Balance of wages £70.11.8 Art 20, D. McCLUSKEY, J.O.S., ART. 21 and Balance of wages £50.5.2 G.B.S R. WARDLOW, S.O.S. at 30 *master.* *...agreement mate* *mast.*	
NOON .12.65	AT SEA	1.12.65	I hereby cancel the fines only imposed on M. GRIFFIN, EDH. art 15 (page 50), on R. HART., EDH. art 17 (page 33), on R. DRAY, AB. art 28 (page 28), on R. RICHARDSON, Fireman, art 72 (page 38) and the second fine imposed on T. LANDERS asst Stwd, Art 92 (on page 51). *...master*	

N.B.—Every entry in this Log-Book required by the Act must be signed by the Master and by the Mate or some other member of the Crew, and every entry of illness, injury or death must also be signed by the Surgeon or Medical Practitioner on board (if any) and every entry of wages due to, or of the sale of the effects of, any Seaman or Apprentice who has died must be signed by the Master and by the Mate and some other member of the Crew ; and every entry of wages due to any Seaman who enters Her Majesty's Service must be signed by the Master and by the Seaman or by the Officer authorised to receive the Seaman into such Service.

NOTE.—Reading over Entries of Offences.—The Master's especial attention is called to Section 228 (b), (e) and of the Merchant Shipping Act, 1894, which is printed on page 2 of the cover on this Official Log-Book.

I certify that I have carefully examined this Official Log and find that no entries have been made on the pages subsequent to this certificate.

CHAPTER 13

Arriving at Templemead Station, we just managed to get the next Pullman train to London, which meant at least we could have a good feed. With what seemed like half the ship's crew taking over one of the carriage's the stewards didn't know what had hit them, with us ordering champagne by the gallon, popping corks, no end of food, and enough beer to drown in. After a couple of hours we were on the outskirts of London and soon to pull into Paddington Station. By now full of drink we merrily disembarked, leaving our carriage in what can only be called a disaster area, and it was here we were all to go our different ways. For the last six weeks these men had been my friends yet strangely no one exchanged names and addresses, although I think some of the older lads kept in touch.

"Well this is it Pegs, you never know your luck, one day we might ship out together," Mac said, taking my hand in friendship.

"You can bet on that, Mac."

"Now don't forget, take your discharge to Prescott Street and put your case to them. You'll be back at sea before you know it, see ya" With that Mac walked away. He'd been a good pal, in fact they all had.

"See ya Pegs." Shouted Dave to me and John

"Yea mate Oh and thanks for the ship."I called out

"My pleasure kid"

"Keep your peckers up boys" cried Terry, as he followed his big brother close behind.

"You bet yea, see you around some day."

One by one they all went their different ways, leaving John and me to make our way down South, "Come on Tony, we'll get a tube to Victoria." John led the way as this part of London was all new to me.

Our underground journey was short and soon to arrive at Victoria and the main line to all stations South. "Well, this is where we part Tony, Good luck mate, see you around some day."

"I hope so, and John, thanks for everything mate."

"Yeah sure" After shaking hands, he turned and walked off into the distance, as I stood there watching until he was out of sight, knew I was going to miss my good friend and cabin mate as along with the others we'd shared are fair share of laughs together. But now once again I was on my own but instead of being afraid this, I walked tall. For here I was just 16yrs old and

268

a man at last. I'd seen the wonders of the world and had my ups and downs, but now I had money in my pocket and was going home.

Purchasing my ticket I boarded the train and was soon after to be on my way. It was icy cold outside and the night was closing in bringing that blanket of doom over England during the winter months. Sitting there I happened to noticed a few of the passengers staring at me, it felt good sitting there posing with my golden tan and near-blond hair which had been lightened by the sun. All signs of my facial burn had gone, which had been more luck than judgement. And it wasn't long before curiosity got the better of one

"So where you been, Son?" Came a voice said from the opposite seat. I looked up to this gent in his city clothes.

"You name it mister, I've been there," I was a cocky little sod and reeled off the places I'd been to, just as Fred had done all those years ago when I was just a kid.

"Sounds exciting, May I ask what you do?"

"Yeah sure I'm a deckhand in the merchant navy, just got back from Australia. It's a good life - the best" Then went into detail on some of my adventures, his eyes stayed glued to mine the whole journey, not knowing whether to believe me or not. After all, what I'd done in eight months some people don't do in a life time and then letting him get a word in, he asked,

"How old are you, Son?"

"Sixteen," I said proudly, he just smiled.

The time ran away and we were soon pulling into Brighton Station. My journey's end after 26,000 miles, I was here at last. I said goodbye to my interested, but I'm sure, disbelieving companion, "See ya mate, keep ya pecker up." He looked back at me as if to say, 'you cheeky little sod' and with that I left the train.

I felt the eyes boring into me as I slowly strolled down the Platform heading towards the barrier, handing over my ticket to the collector, "Here you go my son." Now, how to get home – taxi – let's do it in style, I thought. I'll ring up old Stan Lock. I promptly made for the telephone kiosk, looked up Streamline Taxis and dialled the number, "Hello, that you Stan? It's Tony Bates here."

"Tony who" he asked.

"You know the Bates' Boys' of Bellingham Crescent."

"Oh yeah Mavis's boys I thought you were in Australia with your brother."

"Yeah, I was, but I'm back now and need a cab."

"Alright son, so where are ya?"

"Brighton Station, but as it's a special occasion Stan I'd thought I'd do it in style any chance of the Rolla"

He laughed, "You boys, you never change. It'll cost ya."

"No problem, I'm loaded."

"Are you sure? It'll be about four quid ya know."

"Yeah, I'm sure. I want every body to know I'm back in town."

He laughed again, "You don't need a Roll's for that, they'll know soon enough."

After all I'd been through I was going to make an entrance. It would give the folks something to be proud of. It wasn't long before the black Rolls Royce, complete with Stan wearing his chauffeur's hat, pulled into the station, coming to a halt almost at my feet.

"Hello Son you're looking well. Does your mother know your coming?"

"Na, I thought I'd surprise her."

Stan climbed from the car, giving a broad smile in his round chubby face, "You'll certainly do that. So where are your cases?"

"There's just this one, I'm travelling light."

Opening the door for me, in I got. Stan settled back into the driver's seat and looking at me through his rear view mirror he said, "Where to Sir?"

"Leave it out Stan, you know where I live."

"Right you are Sir."

Night was well upon us, as slowly we pulled off into the streets of Brighton, a journey I had done many times before but somehow this time it seamed different. I was bursting with excitement. Nobody knew when I was due to arrive and I just knew things would be different this time round. No longer was I the child that left nearly a year since, perhaps now we were all adults, we could live together accordingly. I had money on my hip and could pay my way, perhaps I'd even return to sea at a later date, but for the time being I only thought of the moment we'd pull up outside No36 for all the world to see, just as Fred did all those years ago.

The car passed by the cemetery which meant we were

almost there, then a quick right and on to the Knoll Estate and home.

"Well, there you go, Sir, Bellingham Crescent, home at last."

It felt good as after all those months of dreaming about this moment I was finally here. But for me the streets were empty, there was not a soul in sight as we pulled up outside of No36, from where only 9mths ago I had left to start my incredible journey. Stan honked the horn to let them know I was here. They were bound to look out, it had never failed yet, normally the slightest sound would send the neighbours to peer from behind their curtains, I thought as I paid off Stan then taking my bag from the back seat, got out, but still no one stirred. Stan wished me well and got back in the car and honked once again, "I'll see ya boy, good luck – Oh and say hello to your mum for me." Then he just drove off down the road. I couldn't believe it, all that commotion and no one looked out to see who or what it was.

I knocked at the front door, thinking to myself maybe no one heard so it would still be a surprise. The hall light went on and the front door slowly opened. Like a kid I was boiling over with excitement. It was mum. I had thought of this moment for months. How would she react? Hugs, a kiss, maybe even a few tears, who knows. "Hello mum, it's me I'm back." Her face was not one of surprise, as she said, with a sorry tone in her voice, "We heard you were coming back, but didn't quite know when. I suppose you'd better come in then. Fred, it's Tony, he's back."

. On entering the lounge, I looked around, nothing had changed, same old place, same old mess with Fred sat in his usual fire-side chair, trying to roast himself alive.

"Hello Son, have a good trip did ya," Then went back to watching the T.V. I couldn't believe it. Was this really happening? What had done to deserve such a crap home coming, you'd have thought I just been out for a packet of fags instead of coming from the other side of the world even Fred got a better home coming than me, and he'd been gone 11yrs, it just don't make sense, the reality brought me back down to earth very quickly,?

"So where is everybody?"I asked trying to make light of the whole situation.

"Tom and Ian are in bed and Terry's out somewhere or other, probably with that slut down the road," was the abrupt answer I got back while Fred just sat there saying nothing.

Was this it? After all that fuss trying to get back here, this was the big homecoming. I was disappointed to say the least. Judith ran over and gave me a hug tugging on my jacket trying to get my attention. She seemed to have shot up a lot since I'd last seen her.

"Are you going to stay with us, Tony?" She asked, clinging tightly to my hand.

"Well, I hope so."

Mum looked at me crossly, "Well, I don't know where you're going to sleep we've got rid of your bed. You'll have to top and tail with your brother for the time being/"

Me-I was lost for words. The lump in my throat was getting larger and larger. This was home alright, nothing had changed, neither people nor places. I knew by now I'd made a terrible mistake as it was like I'd never been away. My dreams of home had turned into a nightmare. Judith tugged my hand, bringing me back to reality.

"Come on Tony let's take your bag upstairs."

Only to be shouted down, once again, by mum, "Don't you two make a noise you'll wake those boys up, I've only just got them down."

Judith led the way, almost dragging me upstairs and into my old bedroom and there in the corner were my two kid brothers top and tailed in a single bed. Walking quietly over, I looked down at them. Ian was still a baby, 18 months old and had grown no end and down the other end of the bed was Tommy, he was now 4 years old, but hadn't changed a bit, he was still as small and thin as the day I left. I lent forward and kissed them both, knowing that it they were awake at least they'd be pleased to see me. Just then mum's head popped around the door, "Come on you two, I'll sort you're bed out later. Now do as you're told before you wake these two up." So with out another word we went downstairs, closely followed by mum, funny that Id only been home ten minuets and it was like Id stepped back in time, and I was twelve years old again.

"I suppose you'll be wanting something to eat?" she asked

"I wouldn't mind."

"Well, there's only egg and chips, that'll have to see you through."

"That'll be great, thanks mum. Alright if I pop over and see Ricky first?"

"Okay, but don't be too long – I'm not cooking at this time of night for my health."

"Yes mum, I'll make it short."

"Well be sure you do. Your tea's in fifteen minutes."

Hurrying out the back door, I headed for Ricky's house, across the road and round to his back door, knocking furiously until finally his mum answered.

"Hello Mrs Elms, it's me, is Ricky about?"

"Hello Tony, your mother did say something about you coming back, but she never said when."

"Well here I am. Where's Rick? Is he in?"

"Well he's having his tea at the moment, if you come back in half an hour he should be finished by then," she then shut the door in my face.

Call me paranoid but I was beginning to think that I had done something terribly wrong and everyone but me knew about it. Even my best mate would rather finish his tea first and leave me standing out in the cold. That just about did it for me, it was like I didn't exist any more and all memory of my existence had been wiped away, I desperately wanted to find someone and tell of my adventures, but no one was interested. They probably wouldn't believe me anyway, I told myself as I returned home and took my place by the fire, feeling well choked at the whole situation.

"Come on Son, your tea's ready." Mum's voice had changed instead of being harsh, it became soft and gentle. She smiled down on me as she put down a large plate of egg and chips on the table saying, "You'll feel better when you've got something inside you." Me I thought, feel better, I'm alright, it's all you lot that are covered in doom. Saying nothing, with head down I tucked into my tea. Mum and Fred slowly came round and started asking me questions.

"So what didn't you like about Australia then?" Fred said abruptly, breaking the ice, "Too good for you were they?"

"Na, it wasn't that at all. Just didn't like it."

"So what went wrong then son? what didn't you like about it?" Mum harped up.

"Nothing, you decided not to come so I came back, it's as simple as that."

"So what of your poor brother then, he's out there all on his own now." Fred snapped

So that was it, I'd left big brother on his own to fend for himself. It was all coming out now.

"Its alright for him he's eighteen, old enough to look after himself anyway I didn't see him much, always out with his mates, didn't give a damn about me." It didn't matter what I said I was obviously that I was the one in the wrong. Mum intervened, "That's not what his letters said, more the reverse. You were always in trouble and out of work leaving him to support you." Not wanting to disillusion them to the truth, I just shrugged it off. Anyway not a year since they couldn't have cared less about him so why the big change now?

"And what, may I ask, do you think you'll do for work, we're not going to keep you." Mum blurted out.

"I've got money – just been paid off." That was my first mistake.

"That's good. You can start by giving me two weeks money for your board, £10 please, and you can get yourself out tomorrow and find yourself a job."

Without any hesitation like that twelve year old I did as I was told, pulling my money from my pocket and paid her out, then had myself a quick count up. Smiling as I thought to myself, that's not bad, still got £20 left. It was more like an interrogation than a family conversation. Reprieve came by way of Terry, my older brother, making an entrance.

Hello brov, it's good to see ya." Taking a seat along side me at the table we talked for ages. With me telling him all of what had happened during the last eight months. He listened carefully to my every word with interest. At last I'd told someone of my adventures, as it all came out like a fairy story and must have been hard to believe for anyone not being there.

"So what are you going to do now you're home?" He asked, just managing to get a word in as I going in for my second breathe.

"I don't know yet. I might try and get back to sea, could be a problem though, I got a bad discharge first trip."

"Na, your joking, that's almost impossible."

"I know, but somehow I managed it."

Fred butted in "So where's your discharge book then?"

"I didn't get a book, just a written paper, been told to take it up with the shipping office in London."

"That's rubbish who told you that, if you didn't get

discharge book, then you didn't get a discharge."

I pulled the slip from my pocket and produced it to Terry if just to shut the old man up.

"He's right ya know Dad, 'Ability V.G. Conduct D.R"

"Rubbish, let me see that" and he handed it to Fred.

"Excuse me! This must be new, so how the hell did you manage that?" I think that was his Idea of an apology.

I could only put it down to Tema on the West Coast of Africa when we all went swimming over the side and I'd left my post.

"That's typical, never could do as you were told."

Terry reassured me, "Never mind kid, if there's a way round it, we'll find it."

"Well you'd better hurry up and make your mind up quick as we're not going to keep you." mum's few words were comforting, only being three weeks to Christmas, work would be hard to find. I hadn't been back five minutes and already she had taken a third of my money and at the same time was threatening to throw me out. Fred's attitude was much the same, but instead of saying anything, he just sat watching the T.V.

"Well I'm off now mum," leaving me sitting at the table. Terry made for the door. "See ya later Brov, good to have you back" then closed it behind him.

"You'll have to have a word with that boy, Fred, that girl he's hanging around with is no good, common as muck."

Now I knew nothing had changed. She was her same old righteous self not a good word for anyone, and I just had to get out of there. "Well, I'm off out, I'll see you later."

"And where do you think your going?" Fred turned sharply, giving one of his stern looks.

"Down Bev's, to let her know I'm back, why is that a problem" I asked why should he care were I was going or what I got back, I was not a kid anymore

"Aye, well don't be late or you'll have me to deal with."

"Oh, leave him, Fred, the boy hasn't seen the girl for months, let him go."

Yes, nothing had changed they were still playing one against the other. Saying no more, I left them to argue. The night air was cold as I started to walk the short distance to Bev's house, breaking into a slow jog to keep myself warm, as a coat was something I didn't possess, but I would have to get one soon or freeze to death.

Arriving at Bev's, I rang the bell and waited for the familiar sound of her footsteps coming down the stairs. The hall light went on, then the sound of footsteps, but they weren't Bev's and a shadow appeared behind the glass panel. It was Rene, her mum. "Who is it?" She shouted through the door, afraid to open it after dark.

"It's Tony, Mrs Saunders, Tony Bates." The door opened slowly, leaving the chain on and peering through the gap, "Hello Tony, hang on I'll take the chain off. Your back early we weren't expecting you back until after Christmas well that's what your mum told us, I'm afraid Bev's not in, but I don't think she'll be long. Come in and wait." Once inside, I closed the door and followed her up the stairs to the flat. It was only small with two bedrooms, but enough for them – there was no Mr. Saunders, he'd walked out on her years ago.

"Here sit down by the fire, your shivering."

"Well this is a little different to what I'm used to. Do you know where Bev's gone?"

Watching her words as if she had something to hide, "Err she said something about going to see a friend, but she said she won't be late so you might as well wait – Coffee?"

"Yes please." Her manner was a bit on edge, maybe just the shock of seeing me after all these months.

Rene was in her mid-forties, attractive for her age with rather a gravelly voice which after a while got to you.

"Here you are, drink that, it'll help keep out the cold. Well come on tell me what you've been up to? I've heard your mother's version now let's hear your story." We must have been talking for a good hour or more when the front door went.

"Here she is," and rushed across the room to the door at the top of the stairs, "That you Beverly?"

"Course it is, who else would it be?" Her voice was like music to my ears.

"There's a visitor come to see you/"

"Bit late, who is it?"

"You come and see for yourself," Rene backed into the room leaving the way clear for Bev. Slowly she came into view.

"Hello Bev did you miss me then?"

"Tony," the look of shock on her face was a picture, but a face I'd dreamt of night after night, "When did you get back?

Wasn't expecting you for another week or so," but the romantic scene that I'd longed and hoped for didn't happen. Maybe I watched too many corny movies. She just perched herself along side me and started asking all sorts of dumb questions.

"How are your mum and dad? Haven't seen them in ages, I've seen Terry a couple of times though." They were not the sort of things I wanted to hear, even Rene was getting embarrassed and got up to leave the room, "Well I'll leave you two love birds alone. I'm sure you've got a lot to talk about."

"Yeah, goodnight Rene, thanks for the coffee."

"Night Tony, It's nice to see you again. Not too late now Bev, you've got work in the morning."

"Yes mum, I know."

As soon as she'd gone, put my arms round Bev pulling her close to me. Hesitantly, she accepted my advances, but I knew something was wrong. It was then she told me, "Look Tony, I didn't write and tell you because .... Well, I thought you'd think it was because of your accident and the scars on your face."

"What scars?"

"I can see that, but I wasn't to know. You said in your letters you'd probably be scarred for life."

"So what, I'm back now." She was trying to tell me something, and by now I had a good idea what. The large red marks on her neck told it all.

"There's someone else. I'm sorry tony, but that's how it is."

I heard it, but I didn't want to. After everything that had happened, I just couldn't believe Id just been dumped still what did I expect, after all it had been nearly a year. Beverly was an attractive young woman just waiting to be snapped up, then there was the fact that Id been no angel.

"Do I know him?" I asked more out of curiosity

"No, I don't think so. Anyway he's much older than you"

"It's serious then?" I said, looking half away as I couldn't bring myself to look at her straight in the face.

"Very, he's going to leave his wife and two children so we can be together."

"His wife, for fuck sake, how old is he?"

"24, he's my boss."

Coming from a sixteen year old that I'd known for a couple of years, it came as a bit of a shock and I was stuck for words. I

277

knew I'd been no angel, but this was going over board a bit. Did she really believe he'd leave his wife? She did! The conversation went a bit stale after that and just couldn't find the right words to say to each other.

"Well, it's been a long day so I'll be off now. Don't worry about seeing me out Bev, I know the way,"

"I'm sorry Tony, I didn't think." I stopped her in mid stream

"Na, don't worry about it. I'll be off again in a few days; it's probably for the best anyway." Then kissing her on the cheek, and made my way downstairs, at the bottom I turned, "Keep smiling kid, and good luck."

"Yeah, bye Tony and keep in touch."

"Yea, course," and closed the door behind me.

The slow walk home gave me time to think, particularly of what I was to do now. I'd lost my girl; my welcome at home had been a total disaster to say the least. Australia, at that very moment, didn't seem half so bad. Still tomorrow was another day and things couldn't get worse or could they?

After a good night's sleep, I was up, washed, dressed and out showing off my sun tan, letting all the neighbours know I was back and on telling my stories of adventure, they all looked at me as if I were daft. Even Richard, my mate, had other friends and hung around with a gang of mods on scooters. Slowly my world started to fall apart. Money was running out and had no alternative but to get a job or be on the streets. Having no skills, my choice was limited to finally getting a job as a labourer with a local building contractor, who were at that time, building the Sussex University. The wages were £16 per week and I started on Friday 10th December, having not been home a week. Although the work wasn't hard, I suffered badly from the cold weather. Each night I'd go home, eat my tea then sit in front of the fire. Mum was alright while Fred wasn't there and vice versa, but together it was hell. There was no more drinking sprees, no more hell raising. My taste of the good life made me hunger for more and knew it would only be a matter of time. Christmas was coming, which I believed, was a time for families, so I'd thought I'd wait until the New Year to make my move.

The final crunch came on 21st December. After a hard day at work, no sooner in the door than the atmosphere could have been cut with a knife. Mum, Fred and Gran were sat by the fire taking great interest in an article in the local paper.

"Evening all, what a bloody day, it's freezing out there."

Fred looked up, "So you've ad a hard day have you" He said sarcastically "Where Brighton Magistrate Courts."

"Where" I said, looking totally bewildered at what they were on about.

"You know what I'm fucking talking about you little barstard." Then it was mum's turn. "I told you Fred, he's nothing but trouble. He's not staying here to bring the Police and shame on to my door step."

"What they going on about Gran? Do you know?"

"Don't play the innocent with us Tony, its all down here in black and white/"

"What is, for Christ sake?" Sill not knowing what the hell they were on about

"Here you read it" Fred said almost pushing the paper in my face pointing a small item at the bottom of the front page,

"That's not me," I said, totally confused, "someone must

have used my name."

"Course it's you!" Gran wound mum up, and she in turn, Fred.

"I suppose you stole the car as well, is that what they teach you in Australia?"

My pleading did not convince them – even the address was different.

"It's a mistake, they've got it wrong."

"No you've got it wrong my lad, if you think you're staying in this house a moment longer your mistaken," with that Fred lost his temper, grabbed hold of me by the arm and punching me in the head several times, with my mouth and nose starting to pour with blood. But instead of taking it, I fought back, making it much worse for myself. After continuously kicking and punching me, mum eventually managed to drag him off.

"Leave him, Fred, that's enough."

"See you, ya little bastard. You've been a knife in my back since the day you were born, you're defiantly no son of mine, so get your stuff and get out before I murder you."

Lifting myself from the floor, with a final say, I pleaded my innocence, "but I didn't do it." Covered with bruises from head to foot, I staggered upstairs to pack my kit bag, not knowing where I'd go to once outside the front door. Ironically, mum helped me pack. She also wanted to see the back of me, bringing my clean clothes up from the airing cupboard to my room, "Here Son, you'll need these." By now the pain and heartache had got too much, as the tears ran slowly down my face.

"Yeah, thanks for nothing."

"You've only got your self to blame, Son," she said, leaving me to pack, shortly after going straight downstairs and out the front door leaving my family and No. 36 behind me. My total wealth was about £9, but luckily I was not inexperienced at the art of finding accommodation.

Drying my eyes, I headed off out into the world once again. My first stop was the newsagents to purchase a local paper, the very same that had published the unknown story which had bought me here in the first place, as by some fluke of nature, given me the very same name as my criminal name sake who'd been caught stealing, at the very same place that I worked, must have been a ten million to one shot.

Soon after I went and sat in a café ringing around all the possible's, for my next port of call and finally ended up in a small furnished room just off Brighton seafront at £4 a week. It was small but comfortable with two slot meters in the corner, one for the light, the other for the gas, which ate money like it was going out of fashion.

My evenings were spent mostly with Richard, taking the long bus journey home at the end of the night, but at no time ever taking that short walk across the road to No. 36. On Friday 24th December, we broke up for Christmas and were given the next week off for the holidays, returning back on Monday 3rd January, which for me was to be a hard and lonely week, one which I would never like to relive.

Christmas Day was spent with Richard and his family. Although they felt sorry for me, they made me feel welcome at all times, but it wasn't the same as spending Christmas with your own, I missed my brothers and sisters.

Boxing Day was strictly for families so I spent all day on my own, only going out for food and was glad when it was all over. Funny isn't it, how, no matter where you are, if things go wrong, they always seem their worst at Christmas. Monday came round and the start of my week off, but apart from walking the streets and sitting in my room there was nothing to do and nowhere to go. Only the occasional arrival of Ricky on the scene, kept me sane. I think the worst time of all was New Year's Eve.

My money was nearly all gone, and couldn't afford to go out. Walking about all day just to keep warm, staying in half the night, just going into the town to bring in the New Year.

As I strolled along the seafront, the Clock Tower struck twelve and the sound of ships horns could be heard coming from the local Harbour. People were singing and shouting in the streets. The old year had gone and with it in came the new – January, 1966.

"Happy New Year, Mate." A passing stranger called out to me, wearing his party hat and streamer's around his neck.

"Yeah, thanks Mate, the same to you/"

It was then I turned my back on the world with his words bringing tears to my eyes, I walked over to the railings that lined the promenade wall and just stared out to sea.

It was a cold, but moonlit night and as it bounced its beams on the water, I could see the reflection of a large ship upon the horizon, and as the waves crashed upon the shore, they moved the pebbles gently back and forth, but really taking them nowhere.

That was just how I felt – like a pebble on the beach – going back and forth, but really going nowhere.

Use the Mayo Laundry for Quality and Service

Evening Argus
Incorporating the
SUSSEX DAILY NEWS

Tuesday December 21, 1965

LATE NIGHT EXTRA

Fourpence

GIFT IDEA!

"SOCIETY ISN'T AGAINST YOU

Fining Anthony Roy Bates a total of £30 at Brighton today, the chairman, Mr Herbert Cushnie told him"
You have got to get out of your head that society is against you. If you continue to live a life like this
nobody will want to give any consideration to you" Bates of Colbourne Avenue pleaded guilty to stealing
screwdrivers, pliers and other tools worth a total of £15 belonging to Alan Everson. He also admitted
stealing a lamp and pen worth 15s belonging to Susan Hill and asked for five similar offences to be
considered Insp William Tapsell said because of the large number of thefts from vehicles parked in the
grounds of the of the Sussex University the area received special attention from police officers An officer
who saw the accused sitting in his car in the area in the early hours approached him and found the
stolen property on the passenger seat and in the boot of his vehicle. After the arrest Bates made a
statement admitting stealing property from cars in the university grounds over a period Insp Tapsell said
Bates had a number of previous convictions

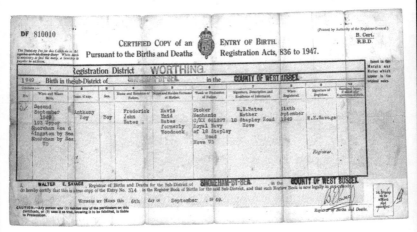

DF 810010

B. Cert.
R.B.D.

(Printed by Authority of the Registrar-General.)

CERTIFIED COPY of an ENTRY OF BIRTH.
Pursuant to the Births and Deaths Registration Acts, 836 to 1947.

Registration District WORTHING

1949 Birth in the Sub-District of ~~Shoreham by Sea~~ in the COUNTY OF WEST SUSSEX.

No.	When and Where Born.	Name, if any.	Sex.	Name and Surname of Father.	Name and Maiden Surname of Mother.	Rank or Profession of Father.	Signature, Description and Residence of Informant.	When Registered.	Signature of Registrar.	Baptismal Name, if added after Registration of Birth.
314	Second September 1949 193 Upper Shoreham Road Kingston by Sea Shoreham by Sea UD	Anthony Roy	Boy	Frederick John Bates	Mavis Enid Bates formerly Woodcock	Stoker Mechanic O/EX 601897 Royal Navy of 18 Stapley Road Hove UD	M.E.Bates Mother 18 Stapley Road Hove	Sixth September 1949	W.E.Savage Registrar.	

I, WALTER E. SAVAGE, Registrar of Births and Deaths for the Sub-District of SHOREHAM-BY-SEA, in the COUNTY OF WEST SUSSEX, do hereby certify that this is a true copy of the Entry No. 314 in the Register Book of Births for the said Sub-District, and that such Register Book is now legally in my custody.

WITNESS MY HAND this 6th day of September, 1949.

CAUTION—Any person who (1) falsifies any of the particulars on this Certificate, or (2) uses it as true, knowing it to be falsified, is liable to Prosecution.

Registrar of Births and Deaths.

CL 757063

CERTIFIED COPY of an ENTRY OF BIRTH
Pursuant to the Births and Deaths Registration Act 1953

Registration District Brighton

1948. Birth in the Sub-district of Brighton Central in the County Borough of Brighton

No.	When and where born	Name, if any	Sex	Name and surname of father	Name, surname and maiden surname of mother	Occupation of father	Signature, description and residence of informant	When registered	Signature of registrar	Name entered after registration
293	Twenty first May 1948 Brighton General Hospital U.D	Anthony Roy	Boy		Joan Elizabeth Bates Factory Canteen Assistant of 30 Michell Street Brighton U.D.		J.E. Bates Mother 30 Michell Street Brighton	Fourth June 1948	W.F. Savard Registrar	

Certified to be a true copy of an entry in a register in my custody.

R.J.Gallagher Deputy Superintendent Registrar

19-6-2000

CAUTION: THERE ARE OFFENCES RELATING TO FALSIFYING OR ALTERING A CERTIFICATE AND USING OR POSSESSING A FALSE CERTIFICATE. ©CROWN COPYRIGHT
WARNING: A CERTIFICATE IS NOT EVIDENCE OF IDENTITY.

CHAPTER 14

After what was for me the Christmas and new year from hell, 1966 started with me still working locally as a builder's labourer on the Sussex University, I stayed there up until the end of January, by then the cold weather was eating into my bones, so went in search of anything as long as it was working inside.

I was eventually invited to back in the family home, as after finding out I was innocent of all charges open the door to me. But there were no apologies, no retractions of things said in the heat of the moment, it was all about money, but still was better than nothing also cheaper than digs and not half as lonely as living on my own.

During the next couple of months I did numerous jobs but none of them lasted long. As just like in Australia I was always chasing the bigger picture.

Then in April, my brother Terry got me a job working with him on the British Rail cross channel ferries much to the displeasure of Fred. The job entailed working a rotor, 24 hours on 24 hours off, fortunately Fred and terry were on the opposite shift to me, which meant I didn't get to see Terry much, but it was a relief to be out of Fred's hair which suited us both. The ship I signed as a deck boy was strangely enough called The Brighton.

My plan was to stay there for one season, until mid-September, which worked out well for me as I had only taken the job as a stop gap, just to get my seaman's book and my passport to the rest of the world. I could then go back to the deep sea, to all the places I had already been and many more besides.

In my mind everything was on track and my life was all mapped out. During which time I was travelling back and forth to Newhaven to join the ship, then it was the short 4hr trip across to Dieppe, France, learning my trade. I had a number of girlfriends, but nothing too serious. As I had to work most weekends, which got in the way of my social life, but it didn't matter as the job came first and nothing was going to come between me and my new career - not even a woman.

I'd been there a couple of months and already it was July with its long summer days and warm evenings. It was during that month, I came home one day to find there were two new girls on the block, hanging around outside Ricky's house.

His house being just across the road gave me the perfect opportunity to stroll over asking, "Is Ricky in?" The taller one just nodded and opened the gate, but as I passed the other one, she looked me straight in the eyes and smiled. It totally bowled me over. On reaching the back door we almost crashed into one another as he said, "Have you met the girls yet?"

Their names were Ann and Linda and they'd come down from London on holiday for two weeks. At first they both seemed a little up themselves, so put it down to there big city girl act, with me just the small town boy.

"Hi Ann, this is Tony. Ann's my cousin and this is her friend Linda."

My face must have dropped as now I knew for definite that I had no chance as it had always been a long standing thing between me and rick that he always got first choice. If a girl was taller than him, which Ann was, plus the fact she was his cousin, meant I was out of the running for her friend. Linda was shorter than me with cropped blonde hair; her face was all made up and, although it looked good, she had gone a bit over the top with the foundation cream. Nevertheless she looked good, dressed to kill in a two piece green mohair suit that was all the rage back in the 1960s. I fell instantly in love.

Deep down I thought that nothing would come of it but that was until the chance arrival of one of Rick girlfriends. Her name was Eileen and she was not amused to find female competition hanging around her feller. She made her feelings very obvious, trying to drive the girls away, but they just laughed at her and you could see Eileen was no match for those two. They looked her up and down as if to say 'who the fuck are you' Then, they just walked past her, strutting off down the road with their noses held high in the air, still laughing. Leaving Eileen with steam coming from her nostrils, so turned on Ricky giving him a real ear bashing. And knew it was time for me to make my exit, so with a quick, "See ya later mate" and left them to continue their domestic. But at least Linda knew that Rick was taken and that left me in with a chance. So that evening I asked her out and to my surprise she said yes.

Unfortunately it was to be a mob handed affair, all four of us, but I had to get in quick as tomorrow it was back to work for the next 24 hours and a lot can happen in that short time.

I had to make my move and there was no time like the present, we all arranged to meet outside Rick's later that evening. My next thought was where to go, finally deciding on the local pub, The May Tree at the bottom of our road, as there's nothing like a spot of alcohol to make you feel more at ease. Also it was one of only two pubs in the area that, so long as I was with Rick, would serve me. I was still only sixteen, well under age, but I'd been going to pub since my return from Australia and was by now considered part of the furniture.

That evening we all met up. The girls were both dolled up to the nines, with Linda looking much older than me, which wasn't hard. On the short stroll to the pub, Ann took Rick's arm while I walked alongside Linda doing all the talking. She didn't say a word, I began to think she had agreed to come more out of boredom than my irresistible charm.

On entering the pub, there were the usual looks; most time's they'd have something sarcastic to say, but today not a word. It was total silence as they just stared at the two beauties on our arms. Taking no notice, we made our way to the bar ordering two pints of bitter and couple of gin and orange for the girls, I could see then, that this wasn't going to be a cheap date – as these weren't your half of bitter girls!

After about an hour the girls were on to their third drink and it was almost impossible to stop them talking. They told us about London where they lived, the nightlife and their jobs. Linda worked for a printing company as a wages clerk. Ann did much the same. Slowly, I edged Linda down the bar away from the others and it was then she said she felt a little tipsy and asked if I would take her outside as she needed some fresh air. My immediate thought was that all my birthdays had come at once.

Outside the pub she leaned up against the wall, and thought 'it's now or never mate' so I made my move. But as I did she went all pale and then just threw up all over my shirt. I'd kissed a fair share of girls in my time but this was the first one I'd made sick.

After getting Ricky and Ann out of the pub, we more or less had to carry Linda home, and that was the end of our first date. I went home that night smelling like shit with my tail between my legs, believing that any relationship between Linda and me was not to be.

The following day I went to work as usual putting the events of the previous night behind me and looking forward to my next 24 hours at work. For me, this was odd. Usually, I was bored with a job after the first few days, but this one was different. I got to meet all sorts of people some good some bad, and to spend some time in France. Then, there was the cheap cigarettes and booze to consider, which was a bonus

My biggest problem was that I didn't like any form of authority or being told what to do, which probably stemmed from being in and out of care homes as a boy.

Having discipline thrust upon me was a bugbear that was to follow me right through my working life. But during my time in the merchant navy there was only one boss, the skipper, who you would hardly ever see, as his home was up on the bridge. If you did get an audience you were probably on report - something which I had experience of during my voyage home from Australia.

The following day I arrived home about midday and on nearing the house I saw Linda walking towards me. She had gone to the trouble of finding out what time I came home by sending Rick over to my mine to ask when I was due home. On reaching me she apologized about our previous get together.

"I'm so sorry about the other night," she said and handed me a small parcel. "I hope it's the right size."

I opened it up to find a shirt.

"Hope you like it." she said smiling

Well, for once in my life I was stuck for words. "Yes, great thanks but you didn't have to."

I'd never had a near complete stranger, let alone a girl I fancied; buy me anything before, so for me this was a new experience. My good looks and charm must have won her over in the end after all. The sight of her and the present put a real spring in my step as we made her way back to Ricks. On reaching the gate she smiled then kissed me on the cheek "See you tonight, say seven okay, you can show me the sights."

This was just too much to take in all at once, "Yea, right, see you later." I was dumfounded. Was this the same girl that two nights ago I had had to ply with drinks just to get her to talk to me? That afternoon was for me probably the longest of my life as I watched the clock and even checked it a couple of times to see if it was still working. Before getting ready I ironed my jeans and my new shirt. I even cleaned my boots, anything to kill time until finally it was 6.30 - just 30 minutes to go. But I could wait no longer and went over to call for her.

"Hi Mrs Elms is Ricky there?"

She smiled: "He's having dinner at the moment but you can come in and wait if you like."

From the back door I could see through the kitchen and into the bathroom where he was sitting on the end of the bath eating. Rick was a strange one - in all the years I'd known him, I'd never known him sit down and have a meal with anybody, even me.

Ann came to the door followed by Linda, "Hi Tony." On seeing them both I thought, here we go again another foursome, but Linda edged her way forward. She looked stunning, all dolled up to the nines and me dressed in just my jeans and, of course, my new shirt. Her next words were music to my ear, "See you later Ann, don't wait up for me will ya." Then she took hold of my arm and we strolled down the path all the time looking up at me, saying, "Nice shirt someone special buy it for you?" I knew there and then we were to be an item.

On our first date alone we caught a bus into town and took a short walk down to the seafront, talking all the time about nothing in particular:

our home lives; our jobs and our futures with neither of us knowing what was in store for either one of us. By the time we reached home that night it was as though I'd known her all my life.

As we shared our first kiss, just her touch sent the blood rushing though my veins, and didn't want to let go of her just in case it was all a dream and any minute I'd wake up standing there all alone.

That's how it was for the next week or so. We were inseparable, until finally the day came when her holiday was over and they had to return to London. As we said our goodbyes and I finally let her go, promising to ring and visit her in London as soon as I could. .Although I knew deep down inside that it would be difficult for me with the hours that I worked. It had been good while it lasted and I thought that for Linda it was just one of those holiday romances you read about 'where out of sight means out of mind, and didn't realise just how much I was going to miss her.

July was soon over and I was back in my old routine, but it was no longer the same as I just couldn't get Linda out of my head. I didn't want to go to work, and when I did, I was about as much good as a chocolate fire guard. So, I decided to give up the cross channel ferries and join a ship on route to far off places. The ferries had served their purpose and now that I had my British Seaman's book in my pocket, and could go anywhere in the world I wanted to.

I handed in my notice and left the job at the end of August, shortly before the close of the summer season, when I would have been out of work anyway. It had been a good few months and I had learnt a lot, but it was time to move on to bigger and better things. I was once again a free agent and could go and do as I pleased. I had money on my hip, which reminded me of the day I arrived back from Australia and was paid off from the Suevic,

My first thought was to keep my promise to Linda, and make a short trip to London to see her before I set off on my travels. So, on Saturday 3rd September, the day after my seventeenth birthday, caught the midday train from Brighton to London Victoria taking an overnight bag with me - just in case. Then I had to find my way across London to Finsbury Park, which was no easy task. I asked directions and was told the quickest way was by tube, changing at Kings Cross onto the Piccadilly line. Which was easier said than done. I got lost twice but eventually arrived at Finsbury Park emerging at the station entrance, where I asked a passer-by for directions. Unfortunately for me, got the only Irish man in town or so I thought. He mumbled his directions, pointing out the way: "Bah Jesus now, let me see, go along there, take the first right, then keep going till you can't go no more, that will bring you out onto Hanley Road." Well who was I to argue? I was the stranger in town

"Thanks mate, appreciate it."

So I followed his directions to the letter, starting walking for what seemed like ages until I came to a main road. I was beginning to think I'd been sent on a wild goose chase, but I carried on regardless until finally I could see houses at the top of the road and could go no further - just as Paddy had said. On nearing the top of the road I passed a block of flats on the corner and a sign that read Hanley Road, and was standing outside Shelly Court, and the end of my journey.

I entered the block of flats making my way to the first floor and Number 18. I rang the bell and stood back and waited for an answer.

As I stood there wondering what her response would be as a month had gone by without any contact, apart from a couple of phone calls, and for a minute I asked myself what the hell I was doing. Slowly the door opened. It was Linda with a look of surprise on her face.

"What are you doing here? You should have called to let me know you were coming."

I just laughed, "Thought I'd surprise you."

She looked a little embarrassed, "You've done that alright, look at me I've got no make-up on. You should have called."

My mind went back to the last time I surprised a girl and the consequences of that. Was it going to happen all over again? Then looking into her eyes I pulled out all my boyish charm to reassure her, "You're just as beautiful without it."

She smiled as a little blush came over her face and it was then that all my feelings for her came flooding back - not that they had really gone away.

"You'd better come in then."

It was obvious we both felt a little awkward as she shut the door behind me, luckily at that very moment her mother came out of the kitchen and she introduced me.

"Mum, this is Tony. He's just come up from Brighton to see me."

We both stood waiting for her seal of approval. She was quite an attractive woman in her early forties, short about 5ft 4in with tightly permed blonde hair which was all the rage back then.

"Hello Tony, so you're the one we've heard so much about, nice to meet you at last."

Linda looked all embarrassed, "Mum!"

She was polite to me but I could see by the way she looked me up and down with my shoulder length hair and the earring in my ear with a small anchor attached; that I resembled something the cat had just dragged in.

"Just up for the day are we Tony?" she asked, looking down at my bag.

"Maybe, I don't know yet. I'll probably book into some digs for a couple of nights. There's no real point going back to Brighton as come Monday I'm of to the shipping office in East London to ship out, that's my job, I'm a merchant seaman," I said proudly.

A slight grin appeared over her mum's face that said 'Thank God for that'. Her whole outlook towards me changed, probably because it didn't look like I was going to be a permanent fixture.

Compared to the home I'd just come from, Linda's was a palace: a large three-bedroom apartment with all mod cons, for Lin, her mum, dad and Brother. The family surname was Dobrozyski, of Russian descent as Linda's great grandparents had originally come to England in the 1890s with the influx of Jewish refugees and settled down in London making a new life for themselves after years of persecution in Russia.

"Come on Tony, let's go down and see Ann," Linda said, putting on her coat. Looking at her mum I asked, "Would it be alright to leave my bag here till I get back?"

"Yes of course."

With that we went on our way and were soon out of the flats.

"Sorry about that, she's like that with any boy I meet," Linda apologised, but I told her it wasn't a problem.

Over the next two hours we met up with Ann and her family. Ann had three younger sisters and her mum, Julie, was Ricky's mum's sister. Like Tupp, couldn't do enough for you. As time ticked by and the evening drew in, we made our way back to Linda's house just in time to be invited for tea. By now Linda's dad, Bert had come in from watching a football match. He was a staunch Arsenal supporter and never missed a game. Bert looked a little older than Flo. His dark hair was receding to the point where it covered very little and he wore thick-rimmed glasses. When he went out, he always wore a suit and had a military air about him. On meeting me, he gave me the quick once over and a look of disapproval, and then asked, "Who do you support, then?"

Back then everything was about football. I suppose England winning the World Cup 4-2 against Germany had a lot to do with it, but me, I was totally oblivious to anything to do with sport. I just came back with what I thought was the perfect answer.

"Me," I said, "Just me."

This was obviously not the answer he was expecting.

"No," he said, looking at me as if I was daft. "What team do you support?"

Still my answer was wrong, and it was about to fall on deaf ears.

"Oh no, I don't like football, never have, can't see any point in it - all them grown men running after a football in the pouring rain."

Well! You'd have thought I'd pulled a gun out on him, as it was definitely the wrong thing to say. He sort of lost interest in me after that and went back to watching the football results on the TV.

Over tea Flo, Linda's mum, mentioned to Bert where I was going on the Monday as she thought he might be able to help saying that because of his job as a collection agent for the L.E.B. (London Electricity Board) he knew the East End of London like the back of his hand. His posh title didn't fool me, I'd heard 'credentials' like his a hundred times before; it was just another name for a debt collector or bailiff. Well, I suppose someone has to do it.

It was then Flo asked, "Have you found somewhere to stay tonight yet?"

A look of shock came over Bert's face as I told them, "Na, not yet, but it's no problem. I'll just head down the docks and book into the Seaman's Mission for the night."

Bert followed Flo out into the kitchen and after a short discussion they insisted that I stay as the dockland was considered far too rough an area for someone of my age. Little did they know! They were probably more concerned about keeping an eye on me and their only daughter.

"If you're sure, it's no problem for me," I said, not wanting to dump myself on anyone.

"Thanks very much."

That evening, while Bert and Flo went out for their regular night at the pub, we were alone for the first time since I had arrived. We had just settled down to watch TV, when Linda's brother Alan came in. On hearing the front door, we both jumped up from the couch and sat in separate armchairs. It must have looked pretty obvious, but he just poked his head around the door, said his hellos, then after a very short introduction disappeared to wash and change. He returned about twenty minutes later to say goodbye, "Oh, Sis, tell mum I won't be home tonight will ya. Nice to meet you Tony, see you both later." Then he was gone again.

Alan was shorter than me with cropped hair and a very snappy dresser, as he stood wearing a dark blue shinny mohair suit and looked the real business.

Later that evening Bert and Flo returned from their night out. Both pissed, they came in full of it, which made Bert a lot braver than earlier that day. Telling me, "If you want to go out with my daughter you're going to have to get your hair cut and get that bloody thing out your ear." Shortly after he was ushered off to bed by flo as he could hardly string two sentences together. She then made me up a bed on the couch, telling Linda it was time to say goodnight.

The next morning Bert was back to his normal self and never said a word, just sat there behind his newspaper. So Lin and I decided to go back down Ann's, just as we leaving Flo shouted, "Dinner's at one."

Over dinner, I complemented her on her culinary skills and there was the usual chitchat around the table with Flo asking me about myself. So I started to relay a bit of my story, but you could tell by the look in their eyes that they found it hard to believe. It was then that Bert spoke out, "How old are you Tony"? "Seventeen, I was seventeen on Friday."

Linda looked up, "You never said anything about it being your birthday."

It was then, I think, that her mum took a shine to me. Either that or she felt sorry for me.

On Monday morning, apart from Linda, the house was empty when she brought me a cup of tea and leaned forward to give me a kiss, "Sleep alright?"

I sat up with the blanket wrapped around me. "Where is everyone?" I asked, not really caring as I now had her all to myself.

"They all went off ages ago, we'll have to get going soon or I'm going to be late."

She left the room and I got myself up and dressed while she got ready. After a quick wash and brush up, I walked her to work, stopping outside to kiss her goodbye. "I'll try and make it back for lunch," I said, then kissed her again before making my way across London to the shipping office.

I arrived at the seaman's office in Prescott Street, East London shortly after 10am. Once inside, I looked around to get my bearings. In front of me stood the staff behind a counter and at the far end of the room there was a board on the wall with all the names of the ships, their destination and the crew they required it also listed the duration of each voyage. Funny! Not a week ago I was all prepared to go away for six months or more, but having met up with Linda again suddenly I wasn't so sure. I ran my eyes down the list studying it carefully to see if there was anything I fancied. Finally, my eye stopped at a ship that was due to sail the following Thursday. It was only on a short run down the Mediterranean, due back mid-October. I looked around wondering what to do next, as I didn't want to appear green. So I watched the others as they wrote down the name of their chosen ship then went up to the desk. I followed their lead, getting in the queue with the rest of them. Soon it was my turn.

"Seaman's card, ship request," said an abrupt looking guy behind the counter. It was obvious that he, along with millions of others, had that Monday morning feeling, so I just handed over my papers. Looking down, he ran his finger across a list in front of him then wrote something down. Looking up, he said, "Report to the ship on the morning of the 15th at West India Dock."

Then he stamped a card, put it inside my book and handed it back. "Next."

It was as easy as that and I was on my way once again.

My next move was to travel back across London to meet up with Linda for lunch. Although at first she was not too happy to hear my news, she changed her mind a little when I told her it was only for a few weeks and that the time would fly past. Pointing out at least we would get to see each other for a few more days, but the more time we spent together and the closer we became, the more apprehensive I got about going away. But I really had no choice. As by now I was running out of money fast, plus I knew if I didn't do it now, it would always lie there at the back of my mind.

Linda promised she would be waiting for me when I came home, so on Thursday September 15th 1966, nearly a year since I had joined the Suevic in Auckland, New Zealand, I signed on to the African Prince as a deck boy at £23 a month.

The African Prince was a lot smaller than other ships I'd been on. In fact, it was a third of the size at only 3,500 tons, but she was a nice looking ship with a crew of 35 of which nine worked on deck.

After a day of getting the ship ready for sea, we finally set sail in the early hours of Friday morning, setting off down the Thames through the many locks to reach the Thames Estuary and the open sea. Then we travelled down the East Coast to meet the English Channel and from there it was plain sailing in to the infamous Bay of Biscay. A stretch of the North Atlantic Ocean dreaded by seamen the world over and lay between France and Northern Spain, but as luck would have it, the crossing was calm that day. We continued down the coast, through the Gibraltar Straits entering the Mediterranean Sea on our way to our first port of call, Valletta in Malta. Over the next two days, we discharged part of our cargo and I spent a night of shore leave with the rest of the crew down the Gut, Malta's red light district. Famous the world over, and frequented by all seamen which basically meant anything go's - you name it! So the only sightseeing I did was staggering from one bar to another spending the hard cash I'd earned so far from overtime.

Our final bar before heading back to the ship was the Blue Peter, and no sooner had we walked in than a couple of local girl pounced on us, and sat down encouraging us to buy them drinks naturally we all thought we were on to a good thing. Being younger and still a bit on the green side we were easily conned, but after buying the girls a couple rounds, one of the lads lent over the table to taste what it was they were drinking. The girls were seriously displeased because we had discovered it was just coloured water and also that they were working for the owner, so we refused to pay for them. So he was none too happy with us either. He made a quick phone call and with in a couple of minutes these two Hench men arrived and came straight over to our table, followed by our angry friend. But there were four of us; apart from us the bar was empty so we weren't too bothered when the row started. Then a couple of our shipmates arrived wanting to know what all the shouting was about. We told them, and being a lot older and wiser than us, they took the situation in hand by decking the two men and grabbing the manager by his throat and asking for our money back. We didn't have the balls to say we hadn't paid him yet! They wouldn't take no for an answer and, after near wrecking the place, we legged it back to the ship before the police arrived. We learnt a valuable lesson that day - you don't get anything for nothing in this world, and you get less for coloured water.

Then it was on to Cyprus, first to Famagusta, which lies on the border between the far North and South of the island, then it was on to Limassol. Cyprus is split into two sections, the Turkish and Greek Cypriot, and it was there to spend the next few days on the coast. Then it was on to Iskenderun in Turkey, then down to Haifa in Israel and finally back to Cyprus to load, before heading for home.

During the voyage that lasted four weeks and three days, we visited a total of seven ports; all with quick turn arounds lasting less than 48 hours. I didn't get to see much, only the local haunts frequented by seamen. I'd sent a couple of letters to Linda but that was the only contact we'd had, so as we headed home, I counted the days and hours until I could see her once again. We finally arrived in the early hours of Friday 18th October and after making the ship fast and ready for unloading and were finally paid off around midday. I received £42.52 pence and was loaded once again. And after saying my goodbyes to my work mates and set a course to see Linda. I'd thought about ringing her at work but decided it would be nice to surprise her. After a short tube ride across London I arrived in front of her office. Linda was sat at her desk, which was right in the window, so I just stood there looking in on her, watching her at work. She must have felt my eyes burning down on her because she turned and spotted me, gave me a look of surprise, then rose from her desk knocking the chair flying as she rushed out of the door. Then literally jumped into my arms, I swore there and then that I would never leave her alone again. Her boss kindly gave her the afternoon off and we went back to her place to make up for lost time.

By now Linda and I were couple so decided that my career as a merchant seaman was over. It was time to stay on dry land, but first I had to get myself a job. And after moving back home to no 36 started work a week later at a Sack Factory. It was close to my home and the hours suited starting at 8am, finishing at 4.30 which made it easy for me to travel to London to see Linda a couple of evenings a week and at weekends. The job itself was up to now, the most boring I'd ever had and I'd had a few. My job was to stand at the end of a conveyor stacking paper sacks onto pallets ready for distribution. They gave us two 10 minute breaks, one in the morning and again in the afternoon, plus a 30-minute lunch break.

During those first couple of weeks I'd got myself into a routine and would travel up to London on Tuesdays and Thursdays after work taking a change of clothes with me. I'd catch the 5.30 from Brighton, wash and change on the train, arrive in London just before 6.30 and be with Linda just after seven. Then after just a few hours together, I'd catch the last train home and be indoors for 1am. Then again on Saturdays and stay over to Sunday. During those first weeks home my appearance was transformed. My hair was cut short, my earring came out. I also bought some new clothes, much to the pleasure of Linda's mum and dad, who were by now getting used to the idea that I was here to stay. Flo even had a meal waiting on the table for me when I walked through the door on those cold winter nights.

Those visits were for me a lifeline and the only thing that made the job bearable. During the nights we didn't see each other, Linda would ring the phone box at the bottom of my road, as she knew the fine art of how to tap the phones making all our calls free, so we'd talk for ages neither one of us wanting to put the phone down first. Also, after a couple of trips to London, I realised that on the fast trains there was no ticket inspector and if you could get through the barrier without getting your ticket clipped you could use it over and over again. If you were unlucky enough to get it taken, you'd only have to buy a platform ticket, then saying you were seeing someone off to the ticket inspector.

It worked a treat, many a time I'd be talking to a complete stranger just to get through the barrier, then at the very last minute jump aboard.

This carried on right up until Christmas of 1966, which I spent with Linda and her family in London.

R 821742   3   SEAMAN'S RE

INCOME TAX CODE NUMBER AND DATE

5.

24.4.4.

PENSION FUND AND REGISTERED No.

NATIONAL INSURANCE

UNION OR SOCIETY

Name. NU.S -

No. 346 558

GRADE NUMBER
AND DATE OF ISSUE OF CERTIFICATES OF COMPETENCY HELD

PHOTOGRAPH OF HOLDER

R 821742

M.M.O. EMBOSSING STAMP

DECLARATION.

I DECLARE (i) that the person to
whom this Discharge Book relates is
satisfied me that he is a seaman
and (ii) that the photograph affixed
bearing my official stamp is a true
likeness of that person, that the
signature within is his (own) true
signature, that he (also) possesses the
physical characteristics entered within
and has stated to me the date and
place of his (own) birth as entered
within.

SIGNATURE OF SUPT. MARINE OFFICE
Mercantile MARINE OFFICE

R. S. MAYNARD M.M.O.

NEWHAVEN, SUSSEX

DATE

CORD BOOK   4

NAME OF SEAMAN.

*SURNAME (in Block Letters)   *CHRISTIAN NAMES (in full)

BATES   ANTHONY ROY.

*Delete for Asiatics.

DATE AND PLACE OF BIRTH   NATIONALITY

2.9.1949 WORTHING   BRITISH.

Height	Eyes	Colour of Hair	Complexion
5'6"	GREY	BROWN FAIR.	FAIR.

Tattoo or other Distinguishing Marks

TATTOO ON RIGHT FOREARM.

Name, Relationship and Address of next-of-kin or nearest friend.

NAME FREDERICK JOHN BATES

RELATIONSHIP FATHER,

ADDRESS 36 BELLINGHAM CRESCENT,
HOVE. 4. SUSSEX.

CHANGE IN
ABOVE ADDRESS

ADDRESS OF SEAMAN
(if different from above)

CHANGE IN
SEAMAN'S ADDRESS

B.S.C. Serial No. 171998A.

SIGNATURE
OF SEAMAN   A R Bates

R. 931742

7 CERTIFICATES OF DISCHARGE 8

Compiled from Lists of Crew and Official and Copy of Report of Character

Log Books or from other Official Records, if desired by the Seaman.

No.	*Name of ship and official number, and tonnage.†	Date and place of		*Rating	Description of voyage	Copy of Report of Character		Signature of (1) Master; and of (2) officer and official stamp
		Engagement*	Discharge			For ability For general conduct		
1	BRITISH RAILWAYS BOARD SOUTHERN REGION VESSELS NEWHAVEN	first NEWHAVEN 19 APR 66	NEWHAVEN 16 MAY 66	Deck Boy	Mercantile H.T.	VERY GOOD 271	VERY GOOD 271	(1) G. Bally (2) MERCANTILE MARINE OFFICE CUSTOM HOUSE NEWHAVEN SUSSEX
2	BRITISH RailWAYS BOARD SOUTHERN REGION VESSELS	NEWHAVEN NEWHAVEN 2 JUL 66	NEWHAVEN 4 AUG 66		H.T.	VERY GOOD 271	VERY GOOD 271	(1) (2) MERCANTILE MARINE OFFICE
3	NEWHAVEN AFRICAN PRINCE. LIVERPOOL 187102 GT 3596.74 NT 1706.56 NHP 539		15.9.16 London SHIP E.2	DECK BOY	F.G.	VERY GOOD 263	VERY GOOD 263	(1) (2)
4	ANATOLIAN. LIVERPOOL O.N. 142017 G.T. 8220.47 N.R.T. 1615.94 N.H.P. 477			Job	784.	VERY GOOD 1	VERY GOOD 1	(1) (2) E.R. Bassler
5								(1) (2)
6								(1) (2)

*These Columns are to be filled in at time of engagement.

† In Engineers' Books insert Horse Power.

African Prince

CHAPTER 15

In the New Year I decided to up sticks and moved to London to be closer to Linda and did so in early January, moving into a bedsit which was just a short walk across the road from Linda. It was owned by a Russian couple Mr and Mrs Brinski along with there young daughter Rula and Mrs Brinski's elderly mother, whose room was on the floor below mine at the top of the house. Most nights by the time I got home the house would be in total darkness which gave me the willies. It had one of those push button lights that give me about 30 seconds to get to the top floor. But somehow it always seemed to beat me, leaving me in total darkness fumbling around trying to find the switch. I always dreaded passing the old lady's room as she had already frightened the shit out of me a couple of times. The first time was a few nights after I moved in. I was getting close to the top of the house when the lights went out and I looked up to see this ghostly figure all shrivelled up and dressed in white standing in the dark at the top of the stairs. I nearly shit myself, screamed and fell back down the stairs, waking the whole house up. As the lights went back on I looked up to see the Rula ushering her granny back into her room. Apart from this incident my stay was problem free; they didn't even mind me having visitors which for Linda and me meant we could get to know each other in private.

My first job was in a factory called Brady Waters, which specialised in making paper napkins were once again I was at the end of a conveyor belt. When I wasn't at work I was with Linda, which suited us both fine. We were like an old married couple and talked about setting up home together and getting a small flat. But this was way out of our reach and would take money we didn't have. By the time I'd paid my rent and bought food there was barely enough for us to go out at weekends. If it hadn't been for Linda's wages we'd probably have never gone out at all. This was starting to come between us and slowly the rot set in and we began to argue. So I decided to go back to sea one more time to get some money together. I gave up my job at the end of May but asked my landlords if I could keep my room on as I would need somewhere to come back to. They agreed to only charge me half rent during my absence, which I thought was good of them.

Once again I made my way across London to the Shipping Office and signed on to the Anatolian as an ordinary seaman at £36 a month all found. By the 1st June I was on my way back down the Mediterranean but for six weeks this time. The ship was a little smaller than the African Prince and a lot older. And looked to me as if she was ready for the scrapyard and, as I found out later, I wasn't far wrong as this was to be her last voyage. While in the shipping office I put Linda down as my next of kin so I could have an allotment made out to her. Which meant all my wages apart from any overtime would be sent to her to put in the bank to give us a lump sum on my return. When I first saw the ship, my thoughts were that it was just as well I had, as she didn't look like she'd make it down the Thames, let alone the Mediterranean. Deep down I didn't really want to go. I'd thought it was a bad idea from the very start but I'd gone past the point of no return. Saying goodbye to Linda was a lot harder this time around, but I kept reminding myself of the reason why I was going and telling myself it wouldn't be for long, but it didn't make the separation any easier.

We set sail on the evening of 2nd June and as we made our way down the Thames and through the different locks I thought how easy it would be just to jump over the side and go home. In hindsight, I wish I had, as I was about to embark on the trip from hell. From the moment we left the quay the ship seemed jinxed and the fact that she was painted red didn't help. The first thing to go wrong was the back spring, a large cable that held the ship fast to the quay snapped nearly taking off the legs of a couple of the men, including me, as it flew around the foredeck like a blind snake snapping at everything in its path. That was the closest I'd come to being legless for a long time. Little did I know that this was just the beginning and bad luck was to hover over us for the next six weeks? As Jonah had left his mark and we were truly cursed.

But we were soon through the locks, down the Thames and out into the open sea. It was early morning and we all got our heads down for a few hours. On waking, we were well on our way - sailing down the English Channel and onto our next challenge, the infamous Bay of Biscay. I had already sailed through this bay a number of times without too much fuss, but my luck was about to run out. The Bay was known to all seafarers as the Biscay Belly, an unpredictable 450-mile stretch of water, which was feared by most sailors. She was like a woman, soft and calm until you crossed her, but then like a woman scorned, she could flare up and attack when you least expected it. We all prayed for a smooth passage, but luck was not with us that day. We were about to sail into a Force 10+ storm with high seas and 80mph winds that made us bob about like a cork in a bath. When we entered the bay, it was just your average storm, but just in case, we were ordered up on deck to put out lifelines. For me this was all new as my job had always been as a mess man inside in the warm looking after the rest of the crew. But with my new promotion to ordinary seaman, I was out on deck with the rest of the men and you could see the look of fear on the older men's faces as we put on our wet weather gear. It made it easy to see why, as soon as they hit dry land, they lived each day as if it was their last. Me, I was frightened shitless and the storm had only just started; as the waves came crashing over the bow I held on for dear life and was glad to get back inside.

As we continued the ship weathered the storm creaking and groaning like an old man, but then I was told the time to worry was when the groaning stopped as that meant she was about to snap in two, it didn't make much sense to me but was nonetheless true. As we rolled and dipped nothing was safe. Everything was thrown all over the show and there was no getting away from it. Then came the moment we were all dreading: a call came from up on the bridge to stand to, as one of the derricks had come loose from its cradle and had to be made fast. So it was back on with the wet weather gear and out on deck again, clipping our harnesses onto the lifeline. You really had to be out there to appreciate just what I saw. The ship was about 360ft long and the waves - well – they must have been 60ft high and that's no exaggeration. You couldn't see over the top as it was just one sheer wall of water. As each wave reached us we sailed up and over it, with the sea hitting us from all sides and the wind howling across the decks. As we reached the top you could hear the propellers screaming as they came out of the water. Then we were hurtling back down the other side of the wave until the ships bow was half submerged, then out she'd pop up and around we went again. It took us nearly an hour to make the derrick fast, during which time we were being thrown about like we were driftwood.

At one time, pulling a couple of the other guys with me, I got swept away and ended up with my legs under the ship's rails. Luckily for one of the stanchions stopped me from going over the side. I was only small and without it to catch me I could easily have gone under the rail. The two other men grabbed hold of me and hauled me back. I remember thinking: 'fuck if it hadn't been for those life lines it would have been the Davey (Jones Locker) for me' as the sea takes no prisoners. It was probably the worst 24 hours of my life; I was terrified for every moment of it. I'd had a few near misses before but this was the worst. As we left the Bay of Biscay behind, I was glad to be out of it and sailing down the Spanish coast in calm waters. And I can tell you I was not the only one to breathe a sigh of relief.

It was plain sailing after that. We then spent the next day or so clearing up after the storm as the Bay had left its mark on the ship as well as us. We were then to make an unexpected stopover for maintenance in La Linea on the Spanish side of Gibraltar.

The crew were glad of some shore leave and the opportunity to get our feet back on solid ground. After a couple of days we were given a clean bill of health and were on our way once again first through the Gibraltar Straits, then hugging the coast line of North Africa, until we entered our first port of call, La Goulette in Tunis. And like many North African ports a real dump. We were all warned that if we did go ashore, we should not go alone, especially us young ones, as the locals were fascinated by our white skin and would take great pleasure in raping us then cutting our throats.

It was probably a little over bit exaggerated, but the older men took great pleasure in putting the shit up us by telling us stories about lads who never came back. Another thing about La Goulette was that during unloading we had to batten down our portholes and lock everything away. Poverty was rife and they'd steal anything. It reminded me a lot of a previous trip to the Ivory Coast, so I stayed on board. We were there for two nights and I was glad to leave there.

Our next port was Haifa and with it our misfortune to get caught up in the Arab-Israeli conflict known as the Six Day War and although we'd only hit the tail end, as we sailed through the night you could hear bombs going off in the distance and watched as the night skies lit up.

But as we drew closer, the crew began to get very nervous and it became the only topic of conversation. We were less than a day out of port, when we spotted this boat coming towards us at great speed. It turned out to be an Egyptian gunboat warning us to get out of its waters or else.

Unfortunately our skipper was a stubborn Scotsman and he continued on, so the next thing we knew there was an almighty bang as a shot was fired across our bow. Still on the same course, we continued. So they fired again, but this time the shot was closer washing spray right over our bow. I think even the skipper must have shit himself as we sharply turned hard to port. For the next hour or so, our aggressors followed us. Then, as quickly as they came, they sped off in the opposite direction and a sigh of relief went round the whole ship, as these boys hadn't been messing about.

On a change of orders from London, we were rerouted to Famagusta in Cyprus, arriving on the evening of the 15th June after a week at sea. There to unload part of our cargo bound for Haifa before heading on to Larnaca also on the Island. We anchored just off shore, so we could discharged our cargo into barges, a dangerous manoeuvre even in the calmest of seas. The following day started off like any other and we were out on deck by 5am opening the hatches ready for unloading. The Anatolian was an old ship which meant she still had steam winches which were not the most reliable at the best of times - sometimes they would slip dropping there loads, so you had to watch yourself.

Just after 7am the shore gang came on board and got stuck straight in, so we left them to get on with it and went to breakfast, reporting back out on deck at 8am. The sea was calm that day and the unloading was going well, that was until the dogman, who was giving instructions to the winch man came a cropper. The winch slipped, dropping its load a few feet and causing it to swing towards him. There was nothing any of us could do, but just watched helplessly as a sling of steel struck him. As he held out his arms to protect himself the steel sliced him open, like you'd gut a fish. We could see the muscles in his arms pop out as he held them out to protect himself as the load ripped into his stomach forcing him backwards putting a large dent on the ship's railings. Then it swung away again and watched as his insides were hanging out for all to see - not a pretty sight.

A deathly silence came over the ship but the man was still conscious and as he looked down at himself, started to scream. I will never forget that sound or the look on his face. It was then all hell let loose, as he was put on a stretcher and carried down the gangway with his stretcher-bearers almost dropping him into the sea. We were told shortly after that he was dead on arrival at hospital but we hadn't expected anything less. The unloading ceased and was followed by a day of mourning by the shore workers. Sataris J Kavayis was just 37 years old and apparently he had a wife and four children. It was sad for his family, but none of us knew him personally and we reckoned he knew like us the risks of the job.

For us it meant we would be anchored offshore for longer than planned without any leave. So, me along with a few others, decided that as it didn't look that far, well not from were we were standing anyway, it was well worth the loss of a day's pay to get a night ashore, then just hitch a lift back with the shore workers come morning . So we came up with bright idea of making a couple of rafts. After all we were seamen, how hard could it be? So along with deck boy David Farley, EDH Jimmy Clarke, EDH Bob Martin we put together our plan. We lashed a couple of oil drums together then placed an old wooden pallet on top and lashed them down. Then, slowly we lowered both rafts over the side into the water. Finally with our clothes in watertight bags tied around our waists, we dived into the sea, we must mad or drunk one of the two.

Bob popped up alongside me so both clambering onto the same raft, and waited until Jim and Dave were safely on another, then taking our makeshift paddles we started to row, slowly putting a gap between the ship and us. But somehow, no matter how far we got, the shoreline didn't look any closer and after a while our great seamanship started to let us down as the rafts started to fall apart. Leaving us in the water holding onto what was left, kicking our feet blissfully unaware that my worst nightmare was about to happen. We were about half way to the shore when we spotted a power launch coming towards us at great speed with someone on board shouting out something or other that we couldn't make out. It wasn't until they got closer that we could hear them, 'Sharks, Sharks,' and pointing into the water. That instantly put the fear of God up me. As they stopped to pick up the other two, while our legs were still splashing about in the water attracting the sharks.

By the time we were picked up we could see their fins moving slowly toward us and were more than glad to be out the water and on board that small but safe boat. Ten tiger sharks, some over eight feet long, slowly glided past. I'd love to catch up with the fucking know-all' who told me there were no sharks in the Mediterranean. I've got news for him, there are 15 different species including the Great White. This was the second time I'd been in this situation - the first being on the Suevic off the West Coast of Africa.

After expressing our thanks to our rescuers, and were ferried back to our ship and climbed aboard. Where we were greeted by the mate at the top of the gangway who just smiled and told us the old man would like to see us on the bridge. I remembered the last time I had been pulled up in front of a captain so this time kept my mouth shut. The outcome was we all lost a day's pay for leaving the ship without permission. The official log said we were 'absent from duty without leave'. Making our way back to our cabins, we laughed about what had just happened, but since then I have never put a foot in the sea. I'm just not going to tempt fate - third time around I might not be so lucky.

The next morning the shore workers returned to work, and after 3days completed the unloading then it was back to Famagusta our final port of call, to reload for the journey home. We arrived in Famagusta on the 3rd July at 8.30 in the evening and, by the time we had made fast, it was well after midnight so I hit the sack. There was plenty of time for shore leave as we were to be there for two days. Most of our leave was spent in the Turkish quarter where you could get more for your money, as a lot of men found out after a night of pleasure that resulted in a dose of pox a few days later. Then they had to front up to the first mate who took take great pleasure in giving them a penicillin injection in the arse. Well what could they expect for five bob? I can only say we all, in one-way or another, took full advantage of our last shore leave before sailing.

On the night of 6th July we slipped our lines leaving Cyprus behind to begin the nine-day journey home. Our only obstacle was, of course, the Bay, but she was in a good mood and it was plain sailing all the way. We arrived alongside West India Docks, London on the afternoon of Saturday 15th July and was paid off with the sum of £24 2s 6d which was just my overtime and didn't include the wages that had already been sent to Linda.

After a trip from hell I swore once again that this was the last time. So put my seaman's cards away in a bottom drawer, as I wouldn't be needing them anymore. Then, with the few quid I'd received and the money Linda had saved up from my wages, it was time to go on a spending spree as the idea of us getting a place together received a definite 'No' from Linda's folks as she was too young, as it had only been a week since her seventeenth birthday.

Our first stop was to the shops to get her a present, so took her to one of those posh ladies outfitters in the West End of London.

"We can't go in there," she said looking in the window at the cloths and there high price tags as this was not your average run of the mill shop.

"Why not, it doesn't cost anything to look."

So we went in, and while I just stood there Linda walked up and down the racks, finally stopping at a brown two piece suit with fur on the cuffs and collar, a very classy number if I do say so myself.

"This one's nice," she said, taking it from the rail as the shop assistant approached her.

"Would madam like to try it on?"
Linda followed her to the changing rooms and returned a few minute later.

"Well, what do think? How do I look?"

Words failed me, she already had lots of beautiful clothes but this was the dog's bollocks.

"You look stunning, do you like it?" Her face said it all. "It's yours."

As she threw her arms around my neck, then whispered in my ear, "Have you seen the price, it's far too much."

I looked down at the tag tastefully tied around a button so as not to damage the material - £18. Two weeks wages at sea, I thought to myself.

"No problem. Nothing's too expensive for my girl."

I thought the shop assistant was going to burst into tears as she said, "How sweet, any more like him at home?"

Linda just smiled and went to change while I peeled of eighteen crisp one pound notes. By the time of Linda's return the shop assistant had bagged it all up before saying, "Thank you sir, madam, do come again" as we left the shop.

Our next stop was to get a pair of shoes and a bag to match afterwards making our way home so Lin could show of her presents.

The following day we both made the trip down to sunny Brighton, booking into a B&B under the name of Mr and Mrs Dee and spending the most fantastic week in the sun enjoying every moment of our first holiday together. Needless to say, we made full use of the double bed in our hotel room!

Over the next couple of months I had couple of jobs. The first involved trying my hand at selling. I had all the patter so thought I'd give it a go. So I applied to a company advertising in the city, for a job selling office products - carbon paper, pens, and paper clips and such like- over the phone. So putting on my posh voice got the job, starting on Monday morning with a weekly wage plus commission. Great - nothing to it - or so I thought. Well, to cut a long story short, I managed to keep up my posh accent for the two days of my training, after which they gave me a desk, a phone and a list or clients. Then, they just left me to get on with it. I made call after call without any success and was getting bored, so dropping the pretence let my good old Southern accent come back. Soon I was chatting away to all these strangers and having a good old laugh. But at the end of the third day, I was called into the office and told they didn't think I was 'suited to this kind of selling and perhaps I should try the market down the road' and handed me a week's wages for my check.

My next job was a slightly less ambitious career move. I applied to the Royal Mail for a position as a great British postman and was accepted on the next training course a few days later. This lasted for six weeks, as there was a lot to learn. Back then there were no automated systems or computers - letters, parcels, everything was all hand sorted and you near enough had to know every postcode in London. I would never have started if I had known what it involved.

When I embarked on the course it was summer and the days were long and the nights were light. By the time the course finished the winter was setting in. After weeks of study night after night with the help of Linda and constant exams, I passed with flying colours and became an assistant postman. For the rest of my training they sent me to my local sub post office in Finsbury Park for a further two weeks. There I learnt the walks until finally I was ready to go out on my own. I was given a uniform, a badge and - most important of all - my very own bag. Sounds exciting, doesn't it. Finally, I got my own round but it was not all sunshine and roses.

On my very first morning it started to rain and didn't give up for two weeks. I was getting soaked daily and after a few days I was full of cold. In the evenings I had to be in bed by nine to be up at four in the morning, which put pay to any social life. I was out there in all kinds of weather and the rain just wouldn't let up. I'd had enough, but the final straw came when a car drove past and, although he must have seen both me and the huge puddle in the road, he drove straight through, covering me from head to foot and leaving me soaked to the skin. I just returned to the office, handed my bag to the supervisor and said 'sorry mate it's not for me'. That was the end of that, as they say.

At the end of the week I returned my uniform also to make sure I'd get any wages that were due to me. They asked me to give it another go but my mind was made up. The funniest thing was that as soon as I gave it all up the rain stopped. Makes you wonder, doesn't it, fate or what? I now have the greatest respect for posties the world over. It might be a good job in the summer but it's a regular bastard in the winter. Remember that the next time you see a postman.

By now my options were becoming limited and I remembered an offer my old mate Ricky had put to me last time we'd met up in Brighton. He'd suggested I go in with him, in the painting and decorating business, working on the new towns that were springing up all over the south of England. I gave him a call, saying I was interested in taking him up on his offer, and returned to Brighton in October. I said farewell to London and my landlords whom I'd lodged with for the last ten months. They said they were sorry to see me go as I'd been a good tenant, but work was work and I had to do something. Mind you the only painting I'd done had been ships rails, but – I thought - how hard can it be? Our first job was in Crawley, Sussex. We were to get £40 a house for insides, which included emulsion on the walls and undercoat and gloss on all woodwork. Some weeks we'd knock out two houses and at first the money was good. But nothing lasts for ever.

I was back to travelling to and fro to see Linda, but this time only staying over at weekends. October came and went, as did November, and Christmas was once again around the corner. On 8th December Linda decided to come to Brighton for the weekend. She was to catch the six o'clock train from Victoria, which was due to arrive in Brighton one hour later. Unfortunately, out of the blue, we had one of the worst snow storms on the south coast for years, and only just made it to the station before the whole town came to a standstill. I was told that all the trains were running late, so I waited, unlike today, there was no way to get in touch with Linda, as there were no mobile phones and such like. So I waited and waited until the train finally arrived seven hours later. By the time she got off she was frozen stiff, telling me of a terrifying journey with the train stopping every ten minutes because of snow on the line. Outside the station the snow was nearly a foot deep and there was no transport to be had anywhere, so after sitting on a freezing cold train she now had to walk the three miles to my house.

We walked all the way in the middle of the road trying not to fall arse over tit. By the time we got to 36 Bellingham it was well after 2am, and the house was in darkness apart from the blazing fire in the hearth. Mum had also kindly left me a note on the mantle piece telling me that my brother Terry had come home unexpectedly and there was nowhere for Linda to sleep as she had put him in the spare room. That was typical of her - she would do anything to rock the boat - so while I made Linda a bed up on the couch, she got undressed in front of the fire and tried to get warm.

As she stood there, near naked with just the glow of the fire to light up the room, she look beautiful but just as I was helping her to remove her bra, Mum walked into the room. She never said a word, not even hello, just gave us a look of disapproval and stormed off back upstairs leaving Linda feeling cheap and dirty. But that was my Mum; I can't remember her liking any of my girlfriends, come to that my brothers.

She made it as uncomfortable as she could for both of us during that weekend, so after putting Linda on the train home on Sunday night, I decided enough was enough. I knew it was time for me to move on and for good this time. Christmas 1967 was just around the corner and I had to get my priorities right as I would need extra money behind me to move back to the city.

So, I continued to slap on the paint. We'd recently moved to another site not far away in Horsham and for the first couple of weeks the money had rolled in. But week the before Christmas the contractor laid us all off telling us there was no more money, so we'd worked a whole week for nothing. Apparently, this was not the first time he'd stitched up his work force, so Ricky and I came up with a plan to get our own back. That night, after a few too many drinks for Dutch courage, we drove to the site and waited for security to do their regular drive around. They weren't the best security firm going, with everyone and his brother knowing what time they would arrive and how long they would stay. Everything was going missing: kitchens, bathroom suites, and doors you name it, If it wasn't' nailed down someone would nick it.

We made our way to the compound only to be confronted by the biggest Alsatian dog you ever did see. Unfortunately for us the dog was new edition and total unexpected and it nearly put an end to our moment of revenge. But then Ricky came up with a plan. Leaning over onto the back seat he produced a club hammer and passed it to me.

"Fuck off, I ain't going in there, that thing will eat me before I get a chance to whack it on the head".

Ricky started to laugh, "Na. You break the padlock on the gate and when I shout 'go' you open the gate right up and get behind it. The dog will come pounding out and I'll put the headlights up full and I drive in. Then, you just shut the gate. Easy."

I looked at him, "You're fucking joking, suppose he don't head for you, and comes after me. If you're so fucking brave you do it."

But good old Ricky, still laughing, had an answer for everything.

"I would but you can't drive."

He had me there and we'd come this far so I guessed we might as well give it a go. The dog was still barking furiously as I got out of the car. It was pacing up and down waiting for me to come in and could see the saliva dripping from its mouth. It took me three large whacks before the padlock finally broke and fell to the ground, by which time Ricky was waiting in the dark with the engine ticking over. "Ready Go," he shouted out as he revved up the engine and then switched the lights to full beam.

I opened the gate and tried to hide behind it as the dog came pounding out and made a dive for the Mini. Almost straight away it crashed into the dog sending it flying over the top and leaving it a bit disorientated for a couple of seconds. That gave me just enough time to shut the gate behind Ricky and chain it back up. The noise was horrendous and if anybody had decided to come and investigate they would have been in for a surprise as we were now on the inside of the fence and the dog was on the outside.

"There you go, easy, told ya didn't I," said Ricky. Me, I couldn't believe what we had just done as we both just stood there laughing.

"Yer, great, but we've still got to get out," I reminded him.

We spent the next half hour or so helping ourselves from the paint store, which belonged to the same man who had short changed us earlier that day. First we loaded up the car until it was down on its axles. Then we opened the rest of the paint tins and tipped them all over the place at the same times as trying not to get paint on ourselves. For us revenge was sweet, but then it was time for our getaway. The dog had quietened down by now, probably because he was just a little bit confused as to where he was, but he was still pacing up and down and must have been thinking to himself 'what goes in must come out'. As soon I approached the gate to remove the chain he was off and I could see he wanted blood - mine in particular.

"Right, mate", said Ricky. "You take the chain off and get back in as quick as you can and I'll push the gates open with the car."

It sounded good in theory and sure enough his plan worked. I had no sooner removed the chain than the dog was there. I only just made it to the car, shutting the door in the dog's face as it growled at me through the window.

Nudging the gates wide open, Ricky pulled away and we made our getaway out of the site onto the main road. But the angry Alsatian was on our tail and wasn't going to give up. He followed us for ages until he finally dropped back out of sight. I often wonder what happened to that dog. Did he ever find his way back? I'd like to think so – wouldn't you?

That was the start of my criminal career. We arrived back home, unloaded 30 gallons of white paint and stashed our ill-gotten gains in Ricky's garage. Then we started to plan our next big heist. Our target was a café we used every day on our way to work. We were going after the cigarettes and cash that, so we had heard, were left on the premises overnight. To cut a long story short, it was a disaster from the word go. We didn't even manage to break in - some burglars we were - but alongside the building was storage shed breaking the lock on the door so we could steal its contents.

The shed contained cases and cases of Coca Cola. Reckoning that anything would be better than going home empty handed, we loaded the car up to the roof. Then it was back to Ricky's garage were we stacked this bounty alongside the paint, it was at that point that I decided this was not for me. There must be easier ways to make money. So far, we had not made anything, while the risk we'd just taken for a few cans of paint and fifteen dozen bottles of Coke didn't warrant thinking about.

Ricky and I seemed to drift apart after that. He was hooked and out with his new partner in crime. Meanwhile, I stayed out of harm's way waiting for the Christmas holidays, which was spend once again in London with Linda and her family. I often wonder what if we'd got into the café, would I have carried on. Who knows? What I do know is that ten months down the line Ricky was arrested, his house and garage were searched and you'll never guess what was still in his garage stacked up in the corner. At the court hearing Ricky asked for thirty other offences to be taken into consideration including the café and the paint job. He got three years in prison. How lucky was I.

Anatolian

OFFICIAL LOG of the

Convention) Act, 1949, are to be made in a special Supplementary Log-Book Form 0.10.

Date and Hour of the Occurrence	Place of the Occurrence, or situation by Latitude and Longitude at Sea	Date of Entry	Entries required by Act of Parliament	Amount of Fines or Forfeiture inflicted
08:30 26·6·67	Larnaca	27·6·67	Sotíris J. Kavazís a labourer Engaged in discharge of cargo from No.1 Hold was struck in the back by a sling of steel bundle & badly injured. He was given first aid & passed ashore to Hospital as quickly as possible. It was later reported that he had died on arrival. _____ mate. A. Martin master	
00:00 26·6·67	Larnaca	27·6·67	R. B. Martin EbA, J. W. Black EbA & Andrew Baker Fine £4·10·6 O. Foley Ab Boy were this day absent from their duties without leave. For this offence they Each forfeit two days & fined one days pay _____ mate. A. Martin master	Fine £4·10·6 Fine £4·10·6 Forfeit £4·10·6
10:00 27·6·69	Larnaca	27·6·67	The above entry was read over to those concerned who offered no reply _____ mate. A. Martin master	

Fine £4·10·6 and collected
Forfeiture enforced and retained by Master

MERCANTILE MARINE OFFICE
18 JUL 1967
POPLAR, E.14

NOTE.—Signing and Reading over of Entries of Offences.—The Master's especial attention is called to Sections 239(4), 239(5)(a) and (b) and 228 of the Merchant Shipping Act, 1894, which are printed on page 2 of the cover on the Official Log-Book.

Holiday in August 1967

Me with best mate Ricky

Morning of 9th December 1967

CHAPTER 16

I moved back to London, and into another bedsit, and started work almost straight away in the fruit and vegetable trade as a counter assistant at £12 a week. John, the manager, spent the next couple of months teaching me everything I needed to know. He was a good teacher and I picked up the trade quickly. The fact that I was good at mixing with Joe public also went down well plus I even had found myself liking it.

John's only vice was that he liked to gamble and the day soon came, when he left me on my own to run the shop. Before leaving he would always help himself to a handful of cash, but never did I see him once put a slip in the till or wrote down how much he had taken. This got me thinking that maybe there was enough for two. But I was never greedy, each time he left the shop I would help myself to a quid, then spend the rest of the day making it up just in case. I also learnt the fine art of short changing my customers and by the end of January I had doubled my wages. This extra cash was to come in handy with the news Linda was about to drop into my lap.

"Tony, I think I'm pregnant." she blurted out

I couldn't believe what she had just told me. "You can't be", I said shocked at her statement "How do you know?" silly question.

She explained to me she'd missed her friend (her period) for the last two months. 'Some friend' I thought, although I wasn't that surprised as we'd been at it like rabbits for months. A couple of times I even tried using condoms, but they weren't that easy to get hold of in those days. When I did go to the chemist to buy some, and stood there waiting for a bloke to serve you, a woman would come up and say 'Yes, sir, can I help you?' I had more packets of aspirins than the local hospital. Linda tried all the usual housewives remedies - hot baths, Gin etc., but nothing worked. It finally came to the crunch on Sunday 10th February.

I can picture it now. We were all sat around the fire. Flo brought in the tea - it was crumpets of all things - then Bert got up and did something I'd never seen him do before. He switched off the television and asked Alan to leave the room. I remember thinking 'this must be serious'.

Looking at the pair of us, Flo piped up, "So, what's going on?"

Linda and I just looked at each other then said, almost in the same breath, "What do you mean what's going on?"

Flo was not amused, "You both know what I'm talking about."

It must have been the morning sickness that had given her away, but I suppose we were glad it was now out in the open. Although I'd had a little experience we were both a bit naive on matters of sex, but we soon changed that. After all, what did they think we were doing night after night in my room - playing tiddly winks? Bert hadn't said a word until that moment. Then he rose from his chair, grabbed hold of my arm and said, "Get out of my house, you dirty little bastard."

Linda just burst out crying, saying, "But, dad, I love him."

As Bert escorted me to the door and before I was totally evicted, I shouted out, "Don't worry, I'll be at Ann's when you want me."

She was up at the window still crying as I passed so waved to let her know everything was going to be alright. Then turning the corner she was out of sight. Going straight to Ann, told her the whole story then hung around at her house while she visited Linda to find out how the land lay.

On the Monday morning Linda's Mum took her to the doctor to get the pregnancy confirmed, while her Dad left word that he wanted to see me. So called round after work and after what was a short discussion, it was agreed that it would be best for all concerned if we got married - I could feel the pressure of this shotgun at the back of my head. But it didn't make any difference we had already decided that we would tie the knot sooner or later. This just brought our plans forward, but it meant that for Linda there would be no romantic proposal, no candle lit dinner for two, no knight in shining armour on one knee begging for her hand in marriage. It was all done just to keep the family happy and it didn't seem to matter what either of us wanted. All the arrangements were made for us it was all so matter or fact. We were to get married on the first available date, 8th March 1968 at 2 pm at Finsbury registry office north London. All we had to do was to buy the rings which cost a total of £14, but they were gold.

We also had to find somewhere to live, but trying to find a room let alone a flat in London was like looking for a needle in a haystack. Unfortunately for us North London had a high black immigrant population. We would go after the few flats that were available but on reaching the door there would be a sign up saying 'No Whites'. It was a strange thing for us to read in the country where we were born, and they say we're racists! We became more and more disheartened at every rejection. Although Linda's family had room for us, but their attitude was 'you made your bed, now you lie in it'. They wouldn't budge an inch, even though it meant we would be homeless. This situation continued right up until two days before the wedding.

At nights Linda and I would walk the streets looking up at empty flats, reading notices in shop windows, until we finally spotted an advert and rang it straight away. The place was not too far away in Effingham Road, Haringey. This was handy for us as we could both walk to work in ten minutes. All excited at the prospect of our own little love nest; we went and viewed it there and then before it got snapped up. The house was large semi and after the initial introductions we were shown to a two-roomed bedsitter at the top of the house. The first room had a television, couch, wardrobes and a double bed in the corner. The second room was a kitchen with a fridge, cooker, table and chairs. The bathroom was down on the next landing and was shared with the rest of the house. For us it was heaven and we rushed home to Bert and Flo with our news. They tried to look pleased, but the word around the family was 'We'll give it six months if that'. They obviously anticipated the inevitable but they weren't going to steal our moment of happiness.

Early the next day we moved our belongings on an old bike I had borrowed from the shop - one of those with a basket on the front used for deliveries. Then after went shopping for essentials. It was dark by the time left our new home so instead of walking Linda sat up front in the basket and we peddled of into the night to take her home for the last time. We were ready, ready for what the world had to throw at us as tomorrow would be the first day of married life.

Tonight was to be my last of freedom but for me there would be no stripers, no yard of ale not even a hangover from my so-called stag night. There were only four of us, Linda's dad, her brother Alan (who was to be my best man and photographer), and last, but not least, Don, Ann's boyfriend. We went to their local watering hole The Hanley Arms and the three of them spent the whole evening talking about fucking football. I was bored shitless. But still, I suppose it was better than Linda's evening, which was spent helping out her Mum with the food for our so-called reception. Ha! Ha! Families, you can't live with them but you can't live without them.

On Friday morning I was up bright and early packing my last few things before moving out of my digs. I was all ready for the big day, but the wedding its self was to be a quiet affair and for the two of us there wasn't much to do except turn up. As I had done so many times before, I went round to call for Linda, but this time it would be for the last time. When she answered the door she looked stunning in the very same suit I had bought for her birthday. Me? I was all suited and booted. Between us we both looked the business as we got into taxi taking us to the registry office with Linda's parents and her brother Alan followed closely behind.

On arrival we were met by a few other friends and family and almost immediately our names were called out and we were ushered into a large room. Inside we were confronted by a thick plush red carpet down either side of the room there were chairs all set out for the guests. In all there were just twenty of us including family from both sides and four of our friends.

In front of us was the registrar, behind a large desk. Because we were both under twenty-one, we needed our parents' permission to marry, so I had posted the appropriate forms for them to fill in. Unfortunately Mavis, my mother, had been having one of her funny moments when the papers arrived and just threw them on the fire after reading them. Fortunately Fred doing the one good dead in his life for me, was quick to retrieve them before too much damage was done. They were a bit burnt around the edges, but never the less signed them before sending them back. You had to see the funny side of it when we saw them lying there on the desk all burnt.

The Registrar asked for complete silence. Then asking us a few questions, like were we sure about the commitment we were about to make to each other? We looked at each other, and then back to her, saying "yes" almost at the same time. She then proceeded to take us through the ceremony. All went quite in the registry office, you could have heard a pin drop as the Registrar finally said "And do you Linda June Dobrozyski take Anthony Roy Bates to be your lawful wedded husband?" Her words rang out for the entire world to hear "I do "she said proudly, finally the Registrar concluded, "By the power vested in me, I now pronounce you man and wife. Anthony you may kiss your bride."

As I did, I thought of how far I had come. After years of being passed from pillar to post, in and out of care institutions, I was now my own man. At just eighteen years old and my new wife, aged just seventeen, was on my arm. At last we were married and our baby was on its way. Nothing could stop us now.

Outside confetti was thrown and photos were taken. Then we made our way back to Bert and Flo's for a bit of a do. As we now needed every penny, there were no cars waiting for us, not even a taxi, so along with our friends we jumped on a number 41 bus. I for one was glad when it was all over, but I felt sad for Linda because, although for us it was the happiest day of our lives, it had all been done on a shoestring and she deserved better. We promised ourselves there and then that when our child was born, no matter whether it was a son or a daughter, there wedding day would be the best money could buy and would be talked about for years after.

That night it felt strange going back to our little bedsit. It was all legal now and we could do anything we wanted. While Linda got ready for bed I made a cup of tea and put the fire on. Then, drinking our tea, we snuggled up in bed and talked about the day. It had been a long one and I had to be up early as Saturday was our busiest in the shop. So we turned out the light and fell asleep in each other's arms.

During the next few weeks we made our little love nest into a home. We would leave the house together in the morning and by the time I got home in the evening Linda would have my dinner on the table. It was all so perfect and we were so in love that I didn't think it could get any better. But on Friday 5th April, four weeks to the day we got married, Linda and her granddad turned up at the shop. At first I thought there was something wrong. "Hello what are you two doing here?"Linda just shrugged her shoulders,

"Granddad met me from work, said he's got something to show us, but he won't tell me what."

He just looked at me and said, "Boy, go ask your boss if you can take an hour off. I've got something to show you."

John told me to take an early lunch and we set off, following old Fred past the station on the very same route I'd taken all those months ago on my very first visit. Fred was Linda's granddad on her mother's side. He stood about 5ft tall, was very wiry and, although he was in his early sixties, was fit as he walked everywhere. He could certainly strut a pace and we found it hard to keep up with him. "Come on you two we haven't got all day," he called out to us. Finally, we arrived at the flats where Linda's parents lived, but we didn't stop, we just turned left onto Hanley Road, crossed over, passed the maternity hospital, passed more flats, and then turned right into Ormond Road. We were nearly at the top when he stopped outside Number 7.

"Well what do you think?" he said, looking up at the building. We didn't have a clue what he was talking about until he knocked on the door and a short, plump lady answered.

"Hello again, that was quick," she said.

Fred introduced us, "This is the couple I was telling you about. This is my granddaughter, Linda and her husband, Tony."

She opened the door right up, "Hello, I'm Pam; you'd better all come in then." We walked in and she closed the door behind us. Looking straight at Linda, she said, "Very persistent your granddad, he wouldn't take no for an answer and gave you both glowing references."

We followed her up to the first landing. "Well, this is the kitchen," she said, walking into a large empty room with just a sink unit. "This is the toilet," she continued, opening a door on the landing, "but you have to share that with the people upstairs. They're a young couple like you with a little boy."

By now Fred was all smiles, while Linda and I were just gob

smacked. Pam continued the tour as we went up a few stairs to the next landing, "This is your bedroom." We took a quick look. "And finally this is your lounge." It was huge.

Linda threw her arms around Fred, "Thanks granddad it's fantastic".

"Nothing but the very best for my favourite granddaughter," he smiled and I could see the tears forming in the corner of Linda's eyes.

Pam's voice brought everything back into perspective, "Now the rent is £4 a week with one month in advance."

Once again Fred came to rescue. He took out his wallet and produced £20, which he handed over to Pam, at the same time saying to us, "Don't tell your father."

Me, I was stuck for words. As nobody had done anything much for us, and here was Fred giving us what seemed to be his seal of approval.

"Thanks Fred, you're a star."

"That's alright boy, you just look after my little girl."

We all followed Pam downstairs where she handed me a set of keys saying, "It's all yours now Tony. You and Linda can move in whenever you like."

We said our goodbyes and found ourselves back out on the street, still in shock. Fred turned to us and said, "Well, can't stand here all day, got things to do. See you at the weekend." With that, off he went on his merry way leaving Linda and I to take a slow walk back to work, making plans all the way. Later we found out that good old Fred had been walking the streets of London for weeks, knocking on doors every time he saw an empty window, until eventually he found the right door and came through for us. He knew what it was like as many years before he and his wife had found themselves in the very same situation, but then there was nobody to help them.

We were a bit sad to say goodbye to our first little love nest but a few days later, with the help of the firm's bike once again, we moved into our new three roomed unfurnished flat at 7 Ormond Road, North London, at £4 a week. Unfortunately, our new flat had no bathroom, just an old tin bath which was hanging up on the outside shed door. This took some getting used to, but we managed, and in the end bath night became quite a novelty, and will always remember the fun Linda and I had furnishing the place out.

First, Linda's mum and dad gave us their old bedroom suite, which I painted white. Then her brother and her dad wallpapered the lounge in a white and green bamboo style. After that we bought this piece of green square carpet that wasn't quite large enough to fit the room so we put black lino tiles around the edges. We had a gas fire fitted and purchased a three-piece suite in black PVC with green cushions for £29, it was the bollocks. The final touches were the Formica table and four chairs and our very own rented TV, which sat in the corner. For the kitchen we bought a new cooker and fridge and, to complete the mod cons, granddad Fred bought us a kitchen unit.

The flat was our pride and joy and we loved to show it off to anyone. Now all we had to do was just wait for the birth of our baby to make it all complete.

In May John caught with my hand in the till at the shop, but was told if I left quietly no charges would be pressed. So left without a scene as it was made clear to me that there wasn't enough for two of us, but he would give a good reference. It was then that I applied for a job with the Barny Greenhill packing company as a supervisor at £14 a week. There I learnt all about the pre-packing business, Specialising in fruit and vegetables, which back then was in its infancy. But unfortunately after two months it was time to move on again as Linda was getting so big she had to pack up work and I needed more money to support her and the coming baby. In July I started work at Home fair supermarkets as an assistant manager in its fruit and vegetable department at £20 a week. I was doing well for myself and was slowly working my way up the ladder.

On Tuesday 13th August, Linda was taken into hospital in the afternoon with labour pains. I rushed home from work, only to be told it was a false alarm but they were keeping her in overnight. I sat with her until they kicked me out later that night. When I got outside I looked up and there she was for the entire world to see in her baby doll nightie waving away furiously from the wide window ledge above her bed. All of a sudden she disappeared from view, so I carried on walking home. Unbeknown to me, her waters had broken and she had gone into labour while I was making my way back to our empty flat. If I had just stayed that little while longer I might have been there for the birth. Back then there was no ringing around for the next of kin, not that we had a phone, so Linda had to go through it all alone. She eventually gave birth at 2.45 am on Wednesday 14th August to a beautiful little girl who weighed in at 6lb 1oz. At first the baby was put in an incubator as they said she was slightly premature.

Early the following morning, totally unaware of what had happened I arrived at the hospital but Linda was nowhere to be found. They told me she was in the maternity ward and that mother and baby were both doing well. I was a little confused, as they had told me the night before it was just a false alarm. I arrived on the ward to find Linda sobbing her heart out as they wouldn't let her see her baby. All sorts of things went through my mind. Like had we done something to harm the baby when Linda first fell pregnant? I kicked up such a fuss that they took us there and then to see the tiniest little baby you ever saw. She was the spitting image of Linda and just as perfect in every way. At that moment I was the proudest man alive and this was the second happiest day of my life. We called her Pauline Jane and now everything was perfect.

Linda and Pauline were then to spend the next week or so in hospital, and I spent every moment I could with them - on the way to work, lunch time, and on the way home in the evening. It must have driven the staff round the bend and they were probably glad to see the back of us when we finally all went home to start our life together as a family. For me it was extra special because a proper family was something I had never had.

It was shortly after that my new boss found out that I had some previous experience of pre-packing produce, which was now up and coming in the retail world, and asked me to head up a new department. This involved ordering all the stock, training the staff and getting them organised and to everyone's surprise I was still there in December. Christmas was really special for us as it was our first as a real family; I was now a husband to my beautiful wife, Linda and father to my daughter Pauline. I had a nice home, and a good job with prospects. Life for us just couldn't get any better; little did the three of us know what the future had in store for us.

BUT NO LONGER WAS I THAT PEBBLE ON THE BEACH

March 8th 1968

Linda and her Bridesmaids - Barbara and Ann

The Proud Grandparents - Bert & Flo

Father & Daughter Pauline
It doesn't get any better!

EPILOGUE

Since the events recounted, Tony and his family have lived a very colourful life, and have lived all over the UK and Australia. During that time, Tony has started a number of businesses, some successful, some not, but that's another story. Despite being dyslexic, Tony took a year out to research and write his story.

Tony's extensive research into the events of his childhood led to him being reunited with his half sisters Janet and Valerie, and literally bumped into Derek Tanner (son of chunky and brother of half sister Judith whilst on holiday in Australia (what a small world) and have remained close friends ever since.

Finally after years of searching, he found his brother James Allen who he last saw 58 yrs ago, just before he was put up for adoption.

- It Doesn't Get Any Better Than That -

Reviews

Tony, you are a natural story teller, who has not allowed your struggle with dyslexia to prevent you from writing this book about your life – with all best wishes

Susan Hampshire - Actress & Former President of the Dyslexia Institute

My goodness Tony, you have been through the mill! Well done for turning into a very inspirational read – good luck you deserve every success

Fiona Phillips – Formally of GMTV

Thank you so much for your fascinating book, I've passed it on to our Forward Planning department.

Penny Smith – Formally of GMTV

After starting to read your book, found it hard to put down! It is beautifully written and tells a very touching story. I have now got a copy of your book on my bookshelf at all my offices as an inspiration to other people with dyslexia – I wish you every success for the future

Lyn Smith – Dyslexia Consultant and Davis Dyslexia Correction Facilitator

Reviews

What a life Tony! And what a story, it's compulsive reading and comes straight from the heart

Adam Trimingham – Career Reporter

Congratulations on "like a pebble on the beach" – a good read!
I wish you lots of success

Lorraine Kelly – TV Presenter

Thank you so much for a copy of your book, I read it with interest, and couldn't put it down, well done.

Sylvia Syms – Actress

For more reviews go to:
www.tonydiamond.co.uk